Foundations and Best Practices in Early Childhood Education

Foundations and Best Practices in Early Childhood Education

HISTORY, THEORIES, AND APPROACHES TO LEARNING

Third Edition

Lissanna Follari
University of Colorado, Colorado Springs

PEARSON

Boston   Columbus   Indianapolis   New York   San Francisco   Hoboken
Amsterdam   Cape Town   Dubai   London   Madrid   Milan   Munich   Paris   Montreal   Toronto
Delhi   Mexico City   São Paulo   Sydney   Hong Kong   Seoul   Singapore   Taipei   Tokyo

Vice President and Editorial Director: Jeffery W. Johnston
Senior Acquisitions Editor: Julie Peters
Editorial Assistant: Andrea Hall
Executive Field Marketing Manager: Krista Clark
Senior Product Marketing Manager: Christopher Barry
Project Manager: Jenny Gessner
Procurement Specialist: Michelle Klein
Senior Art Director: Jayne Conte

Cover Designer: John Christiana
Cover Art: Lissanna Follari, Jackie Baudry
Media Project Manager: Noelle Chun
Full-Service Project Management: Penny Walker, Aptara®, Inc.
Composition: Aptara®, Inc.
Printer/Binder: Courier/Kendallville
Cover Printer: Courier/Kendallville
Text Font: Bembo

Credits and acknowledgments for material borrowed from other sources and reproduced, with permission, in this textbook appear on the appropriate page within the text.

Every effort has been made to provide accurate and current Internet information in this book. However, the Internet and information posted on it are constantly changing, so it is inevitable that some of the Internet addresses listed in this textbook will change.

Photo Credits: Suzanne Clouzeau/Pearson: p. 1; Lissanna M. Follari: pp. 7, 12, 15, 23, 44, 54, 61, 64, 67, 69, 74, 80, 84, 88, 91, 96, 100, 104, 111, 116, 120, 126, 131, 133, 148, 157, 162, 166, 169, 173, 183, 191, 200, 204, 205, 209, 211, 213, 219, 222, 227, 234, 236, 240, 243, 249, 252, 263 (left), 267, 269, 272, 276, 279, 283, 292; Scott Cunningham/Merrill Education/Pearson Education: p. 20; Franklin D. Roosevelt Presidential Library & Museum: p. 31; North Wind Picture Archives/Alamy: p. 35; Scott Bultman/Froebel Foundation: p. 38; Brittany Campbell/Merrill Education/Pearson Education: pp. 53, 59, 143, 154, 187; Anne Vega/Merrill Education/Pearson Education: p. 145; Anthony Magnacca/Merrill Education/Pearson Education: p. 176; Suzanna Brown: p. 198; Karen Glas: pp. 256, 257, 263 (right), 266.

Library of Congress Cataloging-in-Publication Data is Available from the Publisher Upon Request.

10 9 8 7 6 5 4 3 2 1

ISBN 10:   0-13-356444-4
ISBN 13: 978-0-13-356444-0

Preface

The field of early care and education has been growing and evolving for centuries. There is much to be learned from our past as we create a vision for our future. Even more can be learned from exploring the unique approaches and beliefs that shape current practices around the world. This book is an invitation to embark on a broad exploration of the scope, roles, and practices of working with and for children and families.

This text is written for beginning educators as well as for those with experience teaching young children who are furthering their education. For the beginning educator, this is an invitation to consider your place in this dynamic field by tracing its history and current trends. For the more experienced educator, this text can provide more in-depth explorations of specific methods and approaches to guide the ongoing process of professionalizing your practice. The overarching goal of this text is for educators to make connections between beliefs and philosophies and practice. To do this, I have included stories or extended vignettes, which come from a variety of classrooms and highlight how teachers and programs are integrating guiding principles and beliefs into applied practice. It is my hope that you will use this text to begin or continue your reflective journey on the evolving path of defining and reshaping your own practice with children and families. Go forth and find your voice—the voice you will raise in advocacy on behalf of all children and families.

NEW TO THIS EDITION

This third edition reflects recent changes in early care and education practice based on legislative and policy changes as well as the latest research on effective practice. Throughout the text, content has been expanded to include even more emphasis on inclusive practices and family diversity. You will find important revisions and updates in the following areas:

- Chapter Learning Goals anchor chapter content, organize chapter sections, and are presented at the start and end of each chapter to provide a map for understanding key chapter concepts
- The Pearson eText contains embedded video links to illustrate key concepts and practices.
- Summaries are streamlined for greater accessibility
- More graphic features include charts and graphs to present content in reader-friendly formats
- Integrated evidence-based practice and Common Core State Standards definition, examples, and application activities in multiple chapters
- Chapter 1: New sections presenting developmental snapshots of young children and broadened definition of early care and education

- Chapter 2: Updated to include Race to the Top initiative
- Chapter 3: Updated throughout, more text converted to graphic features, integration of evidence-based practice
- Chapter 4: All new expanded content on the Bioecological model
- Chapter 5: Completely new chapter on family and child diversity and culturally competent practice
- Chapters 6-11: Content reorganized, streamlined, and updated
- Chapter 12: Additional coverage of professional dispositions, evidence-based practice application activities, and emphasis on criteria of high quality practice

FEATURES OF THE TEXT

The **Classroom View** cases from the field included in most chapters provide a snapshot of diverse early care and education settings and illustrate the key concepts presented in the chapters. I invite you also to reflect on your own observations in light of these stories, comparing your experiences with those included here.

The **In Your Own Words** boxed features encourage you to reflect on specific aspects of your own beliefs and practice. We also pause frequently along this journey to think about specific suggested applications, which are highlighted in the **Putting It Into Practice** boxed features. These highly applied elements are essential features to help make the theory to practice leap that is so important for high quality practices.

Several themes run like threads throughout the text: teachers' roles, views of children, inclusion, and diversity. These are key aspects of all practice that you, too, must integrate into your thinking and teaching. The reflection prompts, questions at the end of each chapter, and application activities are all designed to facilitate the development of your own beliefs and practices about these key themes. The appendixes contain tools that can be used in this process, including samples of graphic organizers to facilitate content understanding and a comprehensive professional portfolio plan.

GUIDING CONCEPTS

Several concepts that guide this text are used as a lens through which we will view the field. First, this text takes a *child-centered approach* to early childhood education. Childhood is a unique and valued period of life, and children are capable, competent, and active participants in their growth and learning.

Another guiding concept is the belief, flowing from *constructivist* learning theory, that children are busily and actively building knowledge from their earliest moments through meaningful experiences and relationships with people and environments. Children continue this lively inner process even when they are quiet. Their learning, thinking, and feeling are expressed in myriad "languages," or ways of communicating. Teachers must be receptive and respectful of them all.

I strongly believe that teaching is a personal as well as a professional endeavor. Adults and children form social bonds and relationships that are at the heart of learning.

Above all else, I believe that children deserve to be respected and loved by the adults in their lives who joyfully engage in this challenging, complex, and rewarding field. It is with this spirit of love and respect that I present this text to you and wish you a challenging, surprising, rewarding journey.

PROFESSIONAL PREPARATION: PORTFOLIO AND FOCUS ON CORE CONTENT

In addition to the overarching themes, two aspects to help you in your professional preparation are woven throughout this book. In each chapter you will be guided to activities that help shape your professional portfolio. Your portfolio is used to present a picture of who you are as a developing teacher and as a teacher education student. The other element woven throughout the text is an emphasis on core content aligning with teacher preparation exams, such as the Praxis™ Early Childhood test. The foundations, key theories, and examples of best practices presented here represent a major part of the content of such exams.

ANCILLARIES ACCOMPANYING THIS TEXT

All ancillaries are available online. To download and print ancillary files, go to **www.pearsonhighered.com** and then click on Educators.

Instructor Resource Manual   This manual contains a glossary handout, chapter overviews, additional Web resources, and additional application activities for in-class and out-of-class which are designed to enhance students' understanding of chapter concepts and build students' professional portfolios.

Online Test Bank   The Test Bank includes a variety of test items, including multiple choice and essay items, organized by chapter and ready for use.

TestGen   is a powerful test generator available exclusively from Pearson. You install TestGen on your personal computer (Windows or Macintosh) and create your own tests for classroom testing and for other specialized delivery options, such as over a local area network or on the web. It contains the same test items as the Online Test Bank. Using TestGen, assessments can be created for both print or testing online. The tests can be downloaded in the following formats:

TestGen Testbank file—PC

TestGen Testbank file—MAC

TestGen Testbank—Blackboard 9 TIF

TestGen Testbank—Blackboard CE/Vista (WebCT) TIF

Angel Test Bank (zip)

D2L Test Bank (zip)

Moodle Test Bank

Sakai Test Bank (zip)

Online PowerPoint® Slides   Colorful PowerPoint® slides prompt student engagement with reflective questions, highlight key concepts and strategies in each chapter.

ACKNOWLEDGMENTS

I wish to offer my heartfelt appreciation to all my students. It is for you that I undertook this project. I hope that the inspiration and collegiality we share in our classes continue to fuel your work as they do mine. It continues to be an honor to travel this road together. I wish you all a successful and nourishing journey.

I would like to thank Luci Coke for all her assistance in gathering the tremendous research that went into the first edition of this book and Julie Peters for her continued support and valuable feedback. This project is stronger for your caring involvement.

I would like to thank the following reviewers for their helpful comments: Stephanie Davidson, Jackson State University; Maureen Gerard, Arizona State University; Mary Larue, J. Sargeant Reynolds Community College; and Catherine Neimetz, Eastern University. A very special thank you also goes out to the dedicated teachers and families at the Northampton Community College Child Care Center, the East Stroudsburg University Child Care Center, the Sheridan, WY, YMCA Child Care Center, and the Colby-Sawyer College Windy Hill Lab School. The inspired, exemplary, joyful practice I have been fortunate enough to experience in each of these settings continues to fuel my passionate dedication to our field.

Finally, I lovingly dedicate this project to Greisan, the motivation behind it all.

Brief Contents

Contents

Welcome to the Field of Early Childhood Education

Chapter Learning Goals

- Identify key highlights of development and learning in children from birth to 8 years old.
- Explore the scope and features of early childhood education.
- Discuss the role and tasks of a teacher-education student.
- Describe the complex roles of early childhood teachers.
- Articulate important issues facing today's early childhood profession.
- Organize initial ideas about your professional identity.

B eing an early childhood educator is a constant journey. It is exciting, challenging, tiring, invigorating, and always changing. Above all else, it is rewarding. There is no more influential period of life than the first 8 years. Because of the tremendous leaps that occur in development during the early years, early childhood educators are positioned to have profound effect on children's lives. The role of the teacher of young children is, therefore, crucial to our future generations. As early childhood educators, we take on many different roles in the course of our days: teacher, researcher, lifelong learner, caregiver, family and child advocate, provocateur (provoking children's thinking), playmate, and many others. We are called upon daily to face many daunting challenges and tasks. This chapter provides a broad definition of early childhood education (ECE), highlights of who young children are developmentally and as learners, and presents important trends and issues in current practice today. You will begin to reflect on how you see yourself as a professional as you consider your role in the lives of children and families.

WHO IS THE "YOUNG CHILD"?

The ages from birth through 8 years old define the term *young children* or the *early child-hood years*. At no other phase of life do we undergo such radical, rapid, and significant changes. For the sheer developmental effect of this time, early childhood is considered the most significant and influential time of life. While there are always variations in the timing and sometimes sequence of young children's growth and development, copious research also demonstrates that there are predictable patterns, ranges, and trends, which are universal in typically developing children. Figures 1-2 through 1-4 provide an outline of typical development in infancy, toddlerhood, preschool, and early school ages along with examples of learning processes and experiences found in quality early care and education settings.

Infants

Figure 1-1 provides a snapshot overview of major trends in infant development along with responsive caregiver practices.

Toddlers

As older infants develop independent mobility, they move into toddlerhood, where sense of self, autonomy in self-care and activities, as well as choice-making blossom. Building on secure, trusted relationships with caregivers, toddlers' exploration of their world broadens along with expansions in language development. Figure 1-2 provides a snapshot of infant/toddler development and responsive caregiver practices.

Preschoolers

The preschool years are marked by an astounding burst of language development as well as marked growth in physical coordination and curiosity about the world and how things work. The autonomy and independence cultivated in the toddler years sets the stage for preschoolers to make choices about activities and interests and act on their decisions and plans. Figure 1-3 provides a snapshot overview of 3-5 year old's develop-ment along with key teacher practices.

Early Elementary

As children enter formal school settings in the early elementary years, social activities, peer relationships, and opportunities to create, imagine, and construct become especially

---

FIGURE 1-1

Infant Typical Development and Learning

	How Children Develop and Learn in Infancy	What Learning Looks Like in Quality ECE	Examples of Infants' Learning Experiences
Infants (birth– 2 years)	• Infants **learn primarily through their senses and interactions** with adults and other children. • **Infants need to touch, see, taste, hear, and smell objects** to explore and learn about the qualities of materials in their world. • **Social exchanges** strengthen infants' brain connections and build language skills. • **Warm and responsive face-to-face interactions,** rocking, holding, and gentle play develop relationships and stimulate infants' responsiveness. • Long before babies can speak fluently, they learn **social conversation conventions,** turn taking, sounds/words, tone of voice, eye contact, nonverbal expressions, etc., through interactions with caregivers. • **Physical coordination** is a key task of this age group. • Infants **explore and begin to control their motor skills,** such as reaching, grabbing, picking up, sitting, crawling, standing, and beginning of independent mobility.	• **Warm, loving, responsive interactions** are the key to early development and learning. Teachers talk, sing, read, and play with infants. • **Relationships** formed in infancy are the basis of lifelong healthful emotional development. • Caring adults focus on **sensitively responding to infants' needs.** • **Peer interactions** provide opportunities to learn about socialization, compromise, awareness of others, community, and sharing. • **Play, self-selected explorations, language interactions, and manipulating varied materials** are the primary ways infants learn. • **Physical activities,** including music, dance, outdoor and indoor large- and small-motor actions, encourage coordination, mobility, and strength. • **Playing with rhymes, songs, and lots of talking with adults and friends** support the all-important emphasis on language development. • **Strong family partnerships** are essential in all ECE.	• **Songs and stories during routines** such as changing, feeding, and play • **Outdoor experiences,** including buggy (stroller) rides, walks, and play in grassy areas • As infants become more mobile, **small climbing equipment** is exciting • Opportunities to **explore self and reflections in mirrors** (building self-awareness) • Infants love to **fill and dump items from bins, stack cups, and build with soft or lightweight blocks** • Safe, **sensory materials** are available for infants' choosing and exploration, such as sand, water, and paint

interesting. Children's curiosity and natural desire to explore, test, observe, and understand their world consumes their focus in these years. Competence and self-esteem are supported and strengthened through developmentally aligned learning and social experiences. Figure 1-4 provides an overview of development for 5-8 year olds along with effective teacher practices.

FIGURE 1-2

Toddler Typical Development and Learning

	How Children Develop and Learn in Toddlerhood	What Learning Looks Like in Quality ECE	Examples of Infants' Learning Experiences
Toddlers (2–3 years)	• Building on trusted **relationships and exerting autonomy** are key milestones. • **Toddlers begin to explore and master self-care skills** (feeding, potty training, hand washing), and these achievements build a lifelong sense of self-competence and self-esteem. • **Physical coordination** and expanding abilities are further refined as toddlers learn to walk, run, kick a ball, balance, hold utensils, etc. • Toddlers love to **explore their world** and their growing physical capabilities. A toddler's day should be filled with active play. • Toddlers need opportunities to explore and experiment with classmates and children of varying ages to learn the **foundations of social skills** necessary to be successful learners and members of a community.	• **Toddlers learn through self-chosen activities and inquiry projects** designed to explore aspects of their world. • Toddlers are still **sensory, hands-on learners** and need to be actively *doing* to learn. • **Curiosity about the world around them,** inside and outside, sparks keen observation. • Toddlers have opportunity for lots of **active play,** including climbing and large-motor games, **balanced with rest and quiet periods.** • Toddlers **strengthen self-care skills** through eating, dressing, and cleaning experiences. • Sharing **stories and books** helps build early language and literacy skills. • **Building with varied materials such as blocks** develops language, visual-spatial, math, social, and physical development. • **Small-group play in self-selected center areas** provides toddlers with the opportunities to practice social negotiation and build awareness of others. • **Teachers and children develop strong relationships** through sensitive caregiving and meaningful interactions. • **Strong family partnerships** are essential in all ECE.	• Projects **exploring how things work** through hands-on and sensory play • **Exploring perspective and reflection** with mirror, light, and shadow • **Noticing changes in their world** through outdoor observations and discovery • **Helping to care for materials, self, and environment** by putting items away, helping to clean up small messes, hand washing • **Family-style, relaxed, social meals** promote nutrition and social skills • **Dramatic play** in authentic, themed center areas such as kitchen, market, post office • **Ample opportunity for construction** of real and imagined worlds with blocks, scarves, sticks, sand, etc. • **Daily language experiences** such as stories, book sharing, poems, singing, puppets, listening to music • **Climbing or large-motor equipment** is part of the inside and outside environment • **Counting and sorting materials** based on color, size, and shape builds early math concepts • **Exploring materials for creative expression,** including art, music, and drama, to learn about aesthetics and expression

FIGURE 1-3

Preschooler Typical Development and Learning

	How Children Develop and Learn in Preschool	What Learning Looks Like in Quality ECE	Examples of Preschoolers' Learning Experiences
Preschool (3–5 years)	• Preschoolers continue to **actively construct their knowledge about their world** through meaningful, authentic experiences. • **Preschoolers learn and develop through play** in all domains and learning areas. • **Play is active, hands-on, and child centered** with some teacher support and facilitation. • Short, **teacher-guided activities** can support focused learning goals in developmentally appropriate ways. • **Preschoolers are curious** about how things work, move, change, and grow. • **Emerging coordination and increasing focus** allow preschoolers to engage more deeply in hands-on activities that explore meaningful aspects of their world. • Preschoolers' **rich imagination and exploding language development** encourage increasingly detailed story-making, dramatic play, and constructions. • **Social interactions and peer relationships** are important to preschoolers and are essential for developing negotiation, compromise, and awareness of others.	• Preschoolers' days are balanced among **active play (indoors and outdoors); hands-on, inquiry-based projects; guided activities; rest; and routines.** • **Dramatic play** centers, including restaurant, supermarket, kitchen, post office, doctor's office, etc., support socialization and opportunity to think about their world. • **Child-guided projects** encourage skills, knowledge, and attitudes necessary for success as lifelong learners, including problem-solving, academic skills, content knowledge, curiosity, initiation, choice-making, persistence. • **Preschoolers practice and play with language** and develop increasingly complex language knowledge and skills and emergent writing and reading skills. • **Daily routines are organized, predictable, flexible,** and responsive to children's dynamic interests and needs. • **Teachers interact sensitively and responsively** to children, promoting initiative and providing individually tailored challenge and support. • **Teachers systematically assess children's development and learning** and use assessments to plan for each child. • **Documentation of children's development and learning** is used as evidence and to prompt reflection and dialogue with children and families. • **Strong family partnerships** are essential in all ECE.	• **Play,** individually or in small social groups, with a variety of hands-on materials • **Plentiful language activities,** including stories, dramatic play, songs, rhyming • **Refinement of small-muscle coordination** and utensil grasp through art experiences, cutting, writing, eating • **Manipulating hands-on materials** exploring shape, color, weight, height, seriation, sequence, pattern, order • **Exploring the world as scientists:** wondering, guessing, testing, observing, reflecting • **Building with blocks** to test, think about, and represent ideas about their world • Exploring roles and social rules through **dramatic play** • **Language throughout the day** with story reading and telling, dictating own stories, acting out favorite stories, songs, dialogues, emergent writing and reading, illustrating

FIGURE 1-4

Early Elementary Typical Development and Learning

	How Children Develop and Learn in the Early School Years	What Learning Looks Like in Quality ECE	Examples of K–3rd Graders' Learning Experiences
Early Elementary (6–8 years)	• **They actively construct their knowledge of the world**, self, and others through direct experience and dialogues. • **Growing awareness needs and interests in self and others** prompt interest in social interaction and belonging. • **They have increasing focus and attention** when interested, confident, and motivated. • **Coordination of large and small muscles** promotes complex active play. • **They enjoy games** with rules and making up own rules as a form of problem-solving. • **Social interaction** strengthens self-regulation, sense of belonging, and friendships. • **Literacy (and numeracy)** skills strengthen toward conventional literacy.	• **Organized routines with flexibility** focus around children's interests and needs. • **Individual, small-group, and large-group experiences** balance child-guided activities with adult-guided activities. • Children take increasingly active roles in **initiating and carrying out plans.** • **Dramatic play** becomes increasingly complex and longer and includes more interactions among peers. • **Reading, writing, listening, and speaking are used frequently;** skills continue to refine and develop toward conventional literacy. • **Content area knowledge and skills** increase in competence and focus. • **Teachers systematically assess children's development and learning** and use assessments to plan for each child. • **Documentation of children's development and learning** is used as evidence and to prompt reflection and dialogue with children and families. • **Strong family partnerships** are essential in all ECE.	• **Problem-solving** using math, logic, and science knowledge and skills • **Group projects** designed to promote problem-solving, social negotiation, and self-regulation • **Story dramas** where children script and act out familiar stories and books • **Writing** activities, creating stories, journals, reports, illustrations, dialogue circles • **Reading** in groups and independently • **Constructing representations** of ideas, solutions, re-creations • **Games with rules,** including cards, board games, physical games

We base all of our work with young children on a foundation of knowledge of child development. This is the starting place for all the myriad of decisions we make for and about children. The previous section is but a brief primer highlighting some of the key milestones and processes in young children's development and experiences. Educator professional preparation also includes a far more comprehensive exploration and review of important theories, theorists, and milestones.

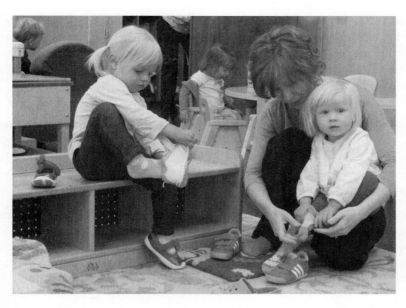

In toddlerhood, teachers support children's autonomy by giving just enough help without doing tasks for children.

WHAT IS EARLY CHILDHOOD EDUCATION?

Early childhood education (ECE) refers to systems of education and care for young children from birth through 8 years old by people other than family members in settings outside of the child's home. Early childhood settings are diverse, including large or small center-based programs, in-home or out-of-home family care, faith-based programs, intervention programs, in-school preschool programs, and public or private early elementary programs. Early childhood care and education professionals are described by a number of terms, including educators, teachers, assistant teachers, child care providers, aides, or caregivers. Professional titles may represent differences in program focus and roles, though some titles are used interchangeably. There is wide variety in the scope, structure, implementation, and programming among early childhood programs serving infants, preschoolers, and early-elementary-age children and their families. This **video** highlights some of these diverse programs for preschool-age children, including procedures, policies, and activities children engage in across different types of early care and education settings.

The children and adults in these settings also bring vast diversity to the programs in terms of ability, interests, culture, values, languages, professional preparation, and so on. Developing sensitivity to diversity and attitudes and skills to celebrate all members of a group is vitally important. In any setting, relationships are the heart of education. Teaching and learning occur in a social context, in which we continually negotiate a complex system of relationships (schools, families, colleagues, beliefs, practices, communities). Teachers are required to make a myriad of decisions in selecting the most appropriate tools and methods from an astounding array of choices (technologies, ideologies, theories, materials). Teachers also use those decisions to carefully create learning environments that plan for universal norms and also validate and support individual development and choices based on their particular setting. Within infant and toddler programs, focusing on nurturing relationships to strengthen socioemotional development is essential. In preschool-age programs, supporting children's increasing

Early childhood education

Early childhood education refers to systems of care and education for children from birth through eight years old.

activity and interactive exploration is an important focus. For early elementary settings, activities that deepen children's learning and support peer interactions are developmentally important. Increasingly teaching also involves assessment and accountability to internal and external audiences. To be successful requires that one has a strong foundation of knowledge and skills, as well as dedication and commitment.

Scenes From the Field

Snapshots of Diverse Practice

There is wide variety across the span of early childhood practice as we consider the differences in program scope and structure when serving infants, preschoolers, or early-school-age children. Even greater variations exist among diverse settings such as urban schools, rural programs, suburban centers, programs in religious institutions, and schools operated by Native American tribes or Alaskan Native villages. Just as with all early childhood practice, there are common threads along with vast and rich differences based on community setting and program scope.

Carlos oversees programs for infants and toddlers in 14 rural community centers with up to 100 miles between centers. "My programs are all funded with federal grant money designed to serve children from families living in poverty. Enriching care and education are our program goals, but meeting basic needs for food, shelter, clothing, and stable home environments have to be our first priority. Accessing services and focusing on family support and parent education are central to our workday. Nothing else can happen for our children without their basic needs being met."

Noa teaches preschool in a faith-based program in an affluent urban community. "My families are all highly involved. I'm lucky because some of my old college friends teaching in other places struggle to make connections to families. I'm lucky . . . but I also feel a lot of pressure too. My families have super high expectations of me and their children. Sometimes I worry about all the pressure on them. I just try to be true to my beliefs about children's development while also showing families just how much their kids are doing, and especially how this time is laying foundations for later learning. They especially want to see a lot of technology. It's a lot to manage, but I feel good about the positive impact I have on my kids. And because there is so much interaction with families and we do a lot of documentation, I know that we're working as partners and that they'll let me know if they have questions or problems."

Elise is a second-grade teacher in a suburban school. "Over the last five years or so, I've really seen a shift in our work. We really focus on competencies and evidence now. Yeah, it's about testing, but really our district pushes evidence-based practices and lots of kinds of assessments. My team [of second-grade teachers] meets weekly to plan and review the students' assessments and use that as a basis for planning instruction. We are constantly implementing and evaluating what we're doing with each student. Every new plan has to include a rationale stating what evidence we're basing the plan on. Then we also have to write out what evidence we'll collect to use for the next phase of planning. It sounds like a lot, but now that we're in the habit, we just use evidence for everything we do. At first it was harder, but now it actually makes sense."

YOUR ROLE AS A TEACHER-EDUCATION STUDENT: CONSIDERING YOUR PROFESSIONAL IDENTITY

Your task at this point in your professional development is to embrace a reflective perspective. You must learn about the history of this field to envision the future, and you must explore a variety of practices to be able to cultivate your own style. Through your studies and work, you will learn from the past and present, from sound research, from children, from families, from colleagues, and from yourself as you develop your professional identity. The topics in this text provide a foundation from which you can start to build your own teacher identity. Throughout this book and during your teacher-education studies in general, you will be called upon to create a body of work that represents your beliefs and abilities as an educator. Creating a **professional portfolio** is your first (and an ongoing) effort to define and redefine yourself as an educator.

A portfolio is a collection of work, or artifacts, which represent you: your beliefs, your abilities, your goals, and your accomplishments. It will change throughout your studies and practice. Many people choose a binder, an expanding folio, or some other material that will allow artifacts to be added or withdrawn. You must carefully and thoughtfully select items that reflect your progress, highlight your experiences, and demonstrate your abilities related to state and national teaching standards (Gelfer, Xu, & Perkins, 2004). Your portfolio may be used to assess your progress in your studies, to demonstrate your competencies in interviews, and to document your professional development throughout your career. Periodically reflecting on your portfolio in presentations or interviews will prompt you to summarize your work, learn from your experiences, and articulate who you are or will be as a teacher (Bullock & Hawk, 2001). Throughout this book, you will have opportunities to explore options and strategies for creating your portfolio.

Reflecting on a variety of learning theories and teaching methods and critically examining how they can inform your own practice are important tasks for an education professional. As you read on, continue thinking about general and specific elements presented in each chapter. Find elements that you can envision integrating into your own unique philosophy and practice. Critically examine your own beliefs and potential biases in light of your readings and discussions. Reflect, adapt, and allow yourself to change your beliefs and expectations of teaching, children, and families as you learn about historic and current educational theories and practices. This ongoing process of exploring research and practice while examining your own beliefs is an essential part of becoming a reflective practitioner.

Professional portfolio

An organized collection of work that reflects your beliefs, experiences, and competencies as a teacher.

ROLES OF THE EARLY CHILDHOOD PROFESSIONAL

As you travel through the history, theories, guiding frameworks, and approaches presented in this book, you will delve further into the many roles embodied by early childhood teachers. Think about how you fit into these roles in the evolving future of the field as you watch this **video** and read the following sections. While the video outlines the previous version of the National Association for the Education of Young Children (NAEYC's) professional standards, the descriptions of varied roles of the early childhood professional paint a rich picture of the many facets of this work.

Your Professional Portfolio

Consider aligning your portfolio around widely accepted standards such as those from the National Association for the Education of Young Children (NAEYC, 2011) or the Interstate New Teacher Assessment and Support Consortium, InTASC (CCSSO, 2011). The headings for each standard, including examples of possible artifacts to include, are as follows (artifacts are described throughout the text):

NAEYC Standards for Initial Early Childhood Professional Preparation

Standard	Possible Artifacts
Standard 1: Promoting Child Development and Learning	• analysis of metaphors describing children • statement of beliefs about teaching and learning • brochure highlighting development in each domain • theorist studies
Standard 2: Building Family and Community Relationships	• family workshop outline • family brochure or newsletter • family survey • community needs survey • community resource list/brochure
Standard 3: Observing, Documenting, and Assessing to Support Young Children and Families	• observation reports • program comparison report • assessment tools • rubrics and checklists created to evaluate classroom environments and children's progress • child study
Standard 4: Using Developmentally Effective Approaches	• technology-integrated lesson plans • review of journals or self-evaluations • learning center designs • planning webs and charts • photo documentation panels • multiple intelligence self-test and response • field supervisor evaluation reports • analysis of assistive technology resources
Standard 5: Using Content Knowledge to Build Meaningful Curriculum	• content-area lesson plans • planning webs and charts • content-focused games and materials
Standard 6: Becoming a Professional	• NAEYC membership • NAEYC position statements review • journal article reviews • conference attendance records • teacher interview report, including questions on law and policies affecting families and children • peer coaching report and self-reflection
Standard 7: Early Childhood Field Experiences	• comparative paper from observations in two different early childhood settings • selections from practicum or field experience journal • lesson plan reflections • field supervisor evaluation reports

InTASC Model Core Teaching Standards

Standard	Possible Artifacts
Standard 1: Learner Development	• analysis of metaphors describing children • statement of beliefs about teaching and learning • brochure highlighting development in each domain
Standard 2: Learning Differences	• statement on diversity in education • analysis of inclusive learning setting • individualized learning plan
Standard 3: Learning Environments	• classroom floor plan • learning center design plan • outdoor learning environment plan
Standard 4: Content Knowledge	• content-area lesson plans • content-focused games and materials
Standard 5: Application of Content	• integrated project planning webs and charts • team-teaching plans integrating multiple content areas • documentation panels illustrating student learning • field supervisor evaluation reports
Standard 6: Assessment	• observation reports • program comparison reports • assessment tools • rubrics and checklists created to evaluate classroom environments and children's progress • child study
Standard 7: Planning for Instruction	• integrated lesson plans • differentiated lesson plans • individualized plans
Standard 8: Instructional Strategies	• lesson plan reflections • video/photo of lesson plan implementation • artifacts of student work with reflection on instruction • teacher interview • field supervisor evaluations
Standard 9: Professional Learning and Ethical Practice	• reflections on own practice (journals, postlesson plan reflections) • peer coaching reports with self-reflection • family survey • teacher interview
Standard 10: Leadership and Collaboration	• professional association membership • conference attendance records • school community event participation

Using tabs or dividers of some kind, you can create separate sections for each standard, including a section for personal data such as a résumé, educational philosophy, reference letters, licensure test scores such as Praxis, and transcripts. In the standards sections, you can begin to include class assignments such as papers, teaching lessons or units, family newsletters, and any field experiences, including any observation reports or evaluations that fit within the standard topic. As an introduction to each section, consider writing a one-page self-reflection analysis in which you describe any of your experiences that helped prepare you for that standard. This summary and the reflection statement demonstrate not only your writing skills but also your knowledge of standards and your self-awareness.

Working directly with children on hands-on activities is a primary role of the early childhood professional.

Teacher

Your role as a teacher may seem the most clear, embodied in the following activities:

- Facilitating children's development
- Valuing children's play as important to their development as well as intrinsically enjoyable
- Creating beautiful and engaging learning environments that welcome every child
- Providing learning experiences that pique children's curiosity and spark their imaginations
- Asking questions to encourage children to think and sometimes to challenge their thinking
- Observing and documenting children's actions and words to assess their learning and development
- Building strong relationships with children and families
- Being a learner alongside children as coconstructors of curriculum, knowledge, and classroom community

The meaningful, interesting, challenging learning experiences you design should also integrate all areas of development and balance both child-initiated activities and more structured, teacher-guided activities. Every skillful teacher must find balance among developmental domains, structure of activity, context, and group or individual time. In each of the approaches we discuss in this book, you will see how teachers manage this important task.

Good teaching is built on a solid understanding of developmental theories, which include universal expectations and awareness of individual differences (Bredekamp & Copple, 2009). Teachers understand that learning environments are designed to facilitate growth in all developmental domains. **Developmental domains** include the following:

Developmental domains

The major areas of human development: physical, cognitive, socioemotional.

- Physical development: small-motor skills (picking up, pinching); large-motor skills (walking, skipping), balance, coordination, and general control of movement
- Socioemotional development: getting along with others; understanding, regulating, and expressing feelings; developing moral and ethical beliefs; becoming independent and able to work within a group; sense of self
- Cognitive development: thought process, language, intellectual skills, creativity

Teachers need to be aware of the paths that children's development generally take so learning experiences may be planned to enhance that development. For example, infants begin to refine their physical control by lifting their heads then sitting up and eventually progress, as toddlers and preschoolers, to walking and running. Development in all domains generally follows predictable sequences, though also with great individual variety and pace (Allen & Marotz, 2003). Educators in today's diverse and inclusive educational settings must use foundational knowledge of child development while always recognizing and valuing each child as an individual, each with strengths and unique areas of challenge. Each child has a unique repertoire of styles, skills, abilities, strengths, preferences, and needs, and it is every teacher's primary responsibility to ensure that care and learning experiences validate and support every child.

Although some skills may be categorized within one domain, development should always be viewed as integrated and interrelated. That means that competencies and abilities within each domain affect and are influenced by other domains. For example, learning to walk can be categorized within physical development but is also affected by the infant's social interactions through encouragement, models, and support. In fact, nearly any developmental milestone you can think of is probably related to the child's environment just as much as to the child's internal drive. Children should be viewed holistically and contextually as whole people living and growing among a range of influences in their unique family and community contexts (Noddings, 2005).

Although developmental theories remain an important foundation for teaching, teachers must also become careful observers of individual children and classroom dynamics. For example, teachers often overhear children in dramatic play remarking that two girls or two boys cannot participate in a dramatic play wedding sequence because only boys and girls can marry. Or teachers may notice some children excluding other children of different ethnic backgrounds. Teachers often see preferences in terms of sex as well; boys may gravitate toward certain materials that girls do not play with. On the surface these may seem like typical behaviors. When these scenes are viewed more critically, however, insights into gender biases, stereotypes, or dominant culture can be revealed. Reflective teachers must become aware of these more complex realities of the early childhood classroom (Ryan & Greishaber, 2004). Children's play is highly complex and a critically important window into their lives and development.

Something that may be a less obvious facet of the role of the teacher is that although teaching is highly complex, demanding, professional work, it is also deeply personal. You must love and enjoy what you do; children deserve to be loved just as they deserve to be respected and valued. Genuine enthusiasm and caring will make you a truly inspiring educator. Your personal commitment and the joy you bring to your teaching also ensure

---

Scenes From the Field

Valuing Extended Families

Soon after I started directing a medium-sized center in a diverse community, a Korean family enrolled their 2-year-old son, Jae, in our program. The parents spoke English, but Jae and his grandmother did not. In an effort to ease Jae's transition to a new country, culture, language, and school, his grandmother came to school each day. At first the teacher tolerated her presence, although she was not particularly pleased with the situation. Whereas her goals for the children included fostering increasing independence, Jae was held on his grandmother's lap and spoon-fed at meals, spoke in Korean to her and did not speak to other children, and played with her during choice time. The teacher worried that he would not achieve the same goals as the other children.

She made several failed efforts to encourage the grandmother to let Jae reach out and communicate with the teacher and other children. Finally she requested a meeting with the parents and asked them to not allow the grandmother to come to the school. They agreed and she stayed home, but we felt their hurt and reluctance. Jae remained withdrawn and appeared uncomfortable but slowly learned some familiar words in English.

One evening when Jae's mother came to pick him up, I asked her to talk to me about their family life. She shared with me that, in her family, a grandmother has a very important place as the child's care provider when the parents are working. She talked about how close bonds between them are highly valued in their culture and said that the caretaking of their young children is an important family goal. As she spoke, I began to realize just how much we had hurt the grandmother personally by denying her role as Jae's caretaker and also how disrespectful we had been to the family's culture. I shared my sincere appreciation with her for helping me learn this lesson and assured her that we would make efforts to support the family as a whole.

The teacher and I met several times and talked about how we could do things differently to value both the home culture and the shared goals of developing linguistic and social independence for Jae. We invited his grandmother in three times a week to share in social times, help all of us learn familiar words in Korean, and share stories. Immediately the other children took a new interest in her and Jae, and soon we had learned several new words. Both the teacher and I were amazed at how quickly both the grandmother and Jae learned more English, and we could see the sense of pride in how the class really wanted to learn more about their language and culture. Both Jae and his grandmother became valued, appreciated members of the class. And the teacher and I learned an important lesson about not making assumptions about goals and values.

---

that you will continue to find satisfaction and nourishment in your work. At any age, students need to feel that their teachers care about teaching, about their learning, and—most of all—about them as people (Noddings, 1995). With young children, a loving bond formed with teachers is important for healthful emotional development as well as healthful brain development, especially in infancy (Baker & Manfredi/Petitt, 2004). You may spend long hours with children, sometimes even more waking hours than children spend with their families. It is natural and healthful that close bonds be formed.

Keep in mind that children's attachments are not exclusive. They form personal bonds with any caring, responsive adults who spend long periods of time with them. This is a normal and healthy response, one that actually strengthens the parent-child bond (Baker & Manfredi/Petitt, 2004). Also keep in mind that your role as a teacher is to form close connections to families. Let families know that you both share the same goal: to provide the best environment possible for their children. Reassure them that your relationship with their children supports each child's development as well as the family as a whole. When families and teachers know they are working together, everyone's satisfaction improves. Amid all the work you do as a professional, never lose sight of the fact that teaching is personal. Remember that the heart of this work is about relationships. This includes relationships with both children and families (extended families too).

A meaningful way to form close bonds with children can be through their play. Play has been valued throughout our history and across international practice as the primary vehicle for children's learning and socialization (Fraser, 2007; Bredekamp & Copple, 2009). In particular, teachers need to preserve children's right to engage deeply in child-initiated play and recognize not only the intrinsic joy but also the power of play to support learning and development (Jenkinson, 2001). Children's play is often highly complex and varied; something that is sometimes underestimated when observing children's play. "Different types of play . . . help young children develop a wide array of social-emotional, linguistic, cognitive, and physical knowledge and skills. The more complex the play, the greater the opportunity for children to develop and express their growing understanding of the world" (Gainsely, 2008, p. 1). Although we may strive to make teacher-guided learning fun (a common theme among my students' professional philosophy statements), we must also hold fast to children's right to time and space for play in their lives. The spontaneous, imaginative self- and cocreated worlds that emerge in their play serve to nourish them in body, mind, and spirit and give them opportunities to create social bonds in a way that cannot be achieved as meaningfully through other adult-controlled activities. This nourishment is essential to children's development and a natural and valuable part of early childhood programs.

Communications with families happen in both formal and informal ways every day.

Researcher

Throughout this book, you will read about the various theorists' views of the teacher as a researcher. For as long as there have been teachers, educators have been advocating and practicing their role as researchers. And in our current moment, the call to implement strategies with clear evidence of effectiveness is at the forefront of our professional commitments (Bredekamp & Copple, 2009). In practice this means critically observing your children, your own teaching, and others' practice through a reflective lens to continually assess the effect and efficacy of your work in the lives of children and families.

- Explore innovations and seek evidence of effectiveness.
- Learn from others' work by observing and reading journals, joining informal discussions, and attending conferences.
- Stay current with what other professionals are doing.
- Approach your own work in your own classroom with an inquiry stance—question, try, watch, reflect, and try again.

In the spirit of our field's great pioneers, take every opportunity you can to observe children and reflect on what you see. Everything we know about children has come from the willingness of researchers to observe children and analyze what they do. Learn about your children from your analyses of their actions, behaviors, and conversations. If you experience tough days in the classroom, approach these as challenges to be investigated; there are vast resources for working through various classroom situations, including your colleagues, the faculty, books, and Web sites. Take suggestions from all the sources you can find, and try them out in your work. Not all the ideas you learn about will be the right fit for you, your children, or your families, but embrace the try-and-reflect process. There is no end to what you can learn through research, observation, and reflection throughout your career. As a researcher, you not only become a better educator, you also open yourself to being a lifelong learner. In this **video**, see how a preschool teacher describes and uses observation techniques to learn about children's development in authentic contexts.

Lifelong Learner

Although your tenure as a student may officially end when you receive your degree, certification, certificate, grade, or course completion, your role as a learner never ends. At times books, lectures, discussions, and projects may be your education. As you embark into the professional world, experience, collaboration, observation, and reflection become your education. Just as you hope to instill in your children an enthusiasm, curiosity, inquisitiveness, and desire to learn, so you, too, must cultivate these qualities. One of the most motivational aspects of teacher-education programs—and your work thereafter—is the chance to learn by seeing and doing. Cultivate a habit of seeing the potential for growth, learning, and development all around you. Look to your own hobbies and interests for inspiration in your teaching. Share your personal interests with your children. Engaging educators also seek to integrate children's personal interests into the classroom. Continue to expand your teaching by widening your own interests, skills, and knowledge. Try new things; visit new places. Remember that who you are as a person is how you teach. This truly makes all life's experiences adventures in personal and professional growth.

Child and Family Advocate

Overarching everything teachers do is the guiding principle that we are advocates for children and families. We respect them. We believe in them. We want to empower them to succeed. We strive to foster healthful growth as individuals and as a family unit with unique and shared culture, beliefs, and goals. The day-to-day practice of working with young children further demands a heightened sensitivity to the unique qualities of childhood. Recognizing that experiences in the early years can greatly affect later developmental outcomes reminds teachers of the care and forethought that must go into each decision we make on behalf of our children. Viewing infancy and childhood as periods of particular vulnerability reminds us that the nature of our behavior affects children and families in many ways. This realization, perhaps more than any other, endows teachers with a tremendous responsibility to hold themselves to the highest standards of professional demeanor and ethical behavior.

Our work and influence stretch far beyond the classroom walls and the end of the school day or school year. We teachers have an effect on children's lives, and they have an effect on ours. As a teacher, you have a voice in forums where children do not. It is your role to advocate on their behalf in larger public forums through participation in community groups, professional organizations, and other networks. Being an advocate for children means that you must understand public policies affecting children and families. It also means that you may be called upon to help shape those policies in ways that recognize the diversity of today's families and ensure a positive effect on all children and families (Jalongo et al., 2004).

The view of the "family" as strictly a nuclear unit consisting of a mother, a father, and child(ren) has expanded. Many children live with single parents, extended families, blended families, and nontraditional family members. These may include grandparents, aunts and uncles, other relatives, stepfamily members, partners, or other people who share the child's life. Some children also live with foster families or appointed guardians who become the child's family. Keep in mind that all the people in children's lives influence them and are valued members of their world. It is also important to consider that different generations, just like different cultures, may have different styles and roles in children's lives. The emphasis on teaching as relationship building encompasses all the influences that create a child's unique world. Appreciate the vast potential for learning and development provided by children's families. Working together will make your experience richer and provide great opportunities to enhance everyone's learning.

BIG IDEAS IN TODAY'S EARLY CHILDHOOD PRACTICE

The field of early childhood education is dynamic and evolving, as a review of our history will reveal. Many issues that early theorists wrestled with remain topical today. In addition, there are new and complex issues that face teachers and guide our practice. Changes abound all around us: social changes, political changes, technological changes, and demographic changes. As our world becomes increasingly more complex, diverse, and global, teachers' responsibility to educate children capable of navigating this complex world becomes all the more urgent. This **video** clip outlines some of the major trends in today's practice. The major themes at the forefront of present-day practice include

- programming and advocating for care and education of young children that is meaningfully aligned with children's development and unique family culture;
- recognizing, valuing, and responding to the increasing diversity within classrooms and communities;

Inclusive classrooms

Classrooms that meaningfully integrate all children, including those with disabilities.

- promoting **inclusive classrooms**, where diverse learners and abilities are equitably supported, challenged, and appreciated;
- integrating appropriate and comprehensive learning standards and providing evidence assessing and evaluating accountability for children's achievement of them; and
- systematically engaging in and using assessment evidence to guide decision-making.

Active Learners Need Interactive Teachers

Traditionally classrooms have been places for rows of desks with students quietly receiving instruction from a teacher. Students complete an abundance of prescribed activities at their seats. Teachers transmit information while students passively take it in (Stanford, 2003). Within this model, there is an unspoken expectation that "one size fits all" in terms of classroom instruction style (Burchfield, 1996; Eisner, 2004). There is very little challenge to higher level thinking (Pool, 1997). This picture may seem more appropriate for some elementary school levels, but there has been a trend toward pushing down this kind of instructive, academic-focused classroom style to kindergarten and preschool programs. The unfortunate result of this classroom style is that children are placed in a passive role that does not align with the way in which children learn best (Hirsh, 2004).

Young children are naturally active, social, exploratory beings and generally seek out opportunities to manipulate objects in their world. They are often so engrossed in their own explorations that they do not attend to classroom schedules, lengthy lectures, or even peers' feelings. When children have something to say or something they want to do, their natural inclination is to satisfy their desires. This sometimes boisterous, self-directed behavior does not mesh well with restrictive classroom environments in which teachers expect a schedule to be kept and focused attention to be maintained. It is a common goal of early childhood teachers to want to instill some sense of order and adherence to rules in a classroom. Also common is the desire to increase children's self-regulation, attention on learning, and focus on key skill-building tasks. Although these are worthy goals, they are not successfully achieved through a restrictive style of teaching.

Whole-group and teacher-directed instruction for extended periods of time most often results in teachers' having to resort to restrictive responses to children's fussiness. This perpetuates less child initiation, language, and active exploration (Cassidy & Buell, 1996; Girolametto, Weitzman, & Greenberg, 2003). Restrictive teacher practice in early childhood settings may control children's actions and preserve order in the room; however, the cost is children's initiation, deeper learning beyond memorization, and development in a meaningful, active learning process. Although some teacher-guided and whole-group activity is important in any classroom, these must be minimal to ensure ample opportunity for emergent, authentic, meaningful experiences that children can easily relate to their own lives.

Children's motivation to learn is one of the single most important contributors to success in school and as a learner throughout life. Supporting children's interests through active, hands-on experiences on topics that are relevant to children's everyday life is an important part of facilitating children's learning and development. Throughout instructional, free choice, self-care routine, and social times of children's day, the quality of interactions with adults serves as a strong predictor of children's positive learning and developmental outcomes. Interactions that are warm, responsive, focused on individual children's strengths and needs, and supportively challenging promote positive outcomes in children as well as engender strong bonds.

Changing Demographics

As a first-year second-grade teacher, Brendon felt ready to take on the challenges of being a teacher. His school used a mentoring system, and he was paired with Sally-Anne, a 21-year veteran of the public schools. In one of their meetings before the school year officially started, SallyAnne reminisced about the changes she'd seen over the years. "I remember when this community was a small farm town. The kids here didn't have much sense of the world outside the town. In some ways it was hard to get them to imagine what life could be like elsewhere. But slowly, over the years, more and more people moved here from the city. Small pockets of immigrant families began to shape the community. Back then, we didn't really have any plan for kids who didn't speak English or who couldn't keep up with the class. They were on their own." Brendon couldn't imagine such a time. With all the classes he'd taken that talked about the importance of making plans for each individual child's abilities and valuing home culture, he was glad to be reminded of how far education had come.

SallyAnne agreed. "At first it was hard for all of us. But we were lucky that our principals have been progressive enough to want to make change happen and that we were able to find resources to make it possible. So many schools still struggle today to make programs accessible for children with diverse needs. We all had workshops and formed collaborative teams to work on new ideas and plans. We started to rely on our parents and community to help us. Once they started to see they could have an impact on the advisory board, they really became involved. I learned a lot from them—even day-to-day things like new words in Spanish and Russian to communicate with several immigrant children. We became a team—real partners. Like I said, we were lucky. I know some schools that really resisted these demographic changes. In the end, it was hard not only on the kids but also on those teachers. They didn't have anyone to rely on, no partnerships like we did. Now we see almost one third of the class representing different cultures and languages. I love being able to rely on parents to bring a richness and liveliness to our culture studies. I see my kids getting excited about the differences out there. It makes them want to explore their world and understand each other."

Brendon was glad they had met that day. SallyAnne reminded him about the beauty of their diverse community. She also reminded him about the importance of coming together as a community to create a responsive, stimulating, collaborative learning environment.

Valuing Diversity

Early childhood environments of today reflect the rich diversity of our communities. The need for teachers to continue to develop ways to create environments that celebrate shared and individual cultures is at an all-time high. As educators, we must begin our work from a place of respect, sensitivity, and genuine interest in knowing and valuing our children and families. It is important for their development now, but it is also essential for their development later as they move out into the world beyond our classroom walls. The diversity around us holds many opportunities to bring meaningful, authentic experiences into the classroom. Partnerships with families and communities allow teachers to expand learning beyond the classroom and more realistically mirror children's lives. Sometimes

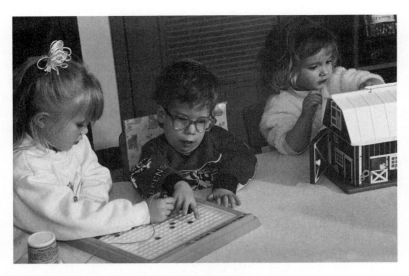

Inclusive classrooms support active participation for all children.

teachers avoid recognizing differences in an attempt to promote equality ("we're all the same and equally welcome here"; "we're color-blind in this room"); however, this does not actually value what makes each individual special. It is our rich diversity that makes life so interesting and colorful. Celebrate what makes each person unique while exploring the ways in which we share common experiences.

In addition to sometimes downplaying differences, teachers also occasionally avoid topics or situations with which they are inexperienced. Unfortunately this leaves teachers unprepared to handle situations when they arise. For example, many early childhood teachers are uncomfortable discussing issues of reproduction, gender identity, gender bias, or ethnic and racial biases in children's behavior. They may not seek to challenge children's assumptions about how children play, what kinds of roles they can play, or the materials with which they can play (for example, two boys getting married in dramatic play, an Asian child pretending to be a white cartoon character, or a child with a significant visual impairment playing the bus driver on the playground). Children are surprisingly astute at internalizing social rules and norms. As teachers, we need to be aware of certain biases in these norms, perhaps even in our own beliefs, and challenge them so all children become aware that they are empowered with choices and self-direction (Ryan & Grieshaber, 2004).

Equality and Equity: Everyone Has a Place at the Table

Individuals with Disabilities Education Act

The 1975 law that ensures access to equal learning environments for all children with disabilities.

Educators have been advocating for the inclusion of all children in programs and classrooms for more than a century. It has been only a little more than a quarter of a century, however, that inclusive classrooms have become mandatory in schools. Today educators rely on the **Individuals with Disabilities Education Act** (IDEA) as a foundation for inclusive practices, but they go beyond the laws to fully embrace the spirit of inclusion. That law, dating back to 1975, has been reauthorized over the years to make provisions for schools and programs to address the needs of children with limited English proficiency and children who are homeless as well as children with disabilities (Gargiulo, 2006). The law provides guidelines for schools to offer intervention services, specialized staff, and

Putting It Into Practice

The Potential in All Children

Creating a class book is one way to highlight each child's potential within the class as a whole. Children can create pages about themselves, what they like, and what they are good at through dictation, signing, drawing, writing, selecting pictures, and so on, which then can be combined into a larger class story. A similar classroom community project is to create a documentation panel on large cardboard sheets. The panel can include photos, children's work, stories, quotes, and family notes. Viewing the classroom community as a patchwork of individuals coming together to create a unified whole can also be represented in a class quilt, in which each child creates a square with his or her family and unites them with others in a quilt at school.

technologies to children who are in need of assistance to help them succeed in school (Bruder, 2010; Darragh, 2010). Of particular importance to early childhood professionals is the trend in the law and in models of high-quality practice that emphasizes the essential interrelationships between young children and their families. This translates into a call to provide essential structure and supports for families to be knowledgeable and meaningfully involved in all aspects of referrals, decision-making, service provision, and assessment.

In the same way that we believe in the value of diversity to enhance and enrich our lives, so too we value the unique contributions children at all developmental levels bring to the classroom. By viewing each child as an important member of the classroom with something special to share, we can begin to create authentic communities of learners who rely on and validate each other. When classrooms are viewed as a community, there is an opportunity for each child to feel valued. Communities are connected by the interrelationships of their systems, structures, and members. Within this framework, each individual contributes to the identity of the whole. Children can be unique and special at the same time that they are part of a shared culture. It is important for teachers to look for ways in which to encourage each child and family to have a role within the classroom community. A growing body of research reveals that children in inclusive classroom settings hold more positive attitudes about children with diverse abilities, especially when teachers take an active role in helping to facilitate acceptance and inclusion (Dyson, 2005; Nikolaraizi et al., 2005). This underscores the important role teachers play in promoting and modeling a culture that genuinely values diversity within the classroom.

An important element of valuing diversity is to view children as unique and on individual developmental paths. Not all children achieve the same milestones at the same time, just as not all children speak the same language or prefer the same activities or foods. Each child has capabilities to achieve meaningful goals. Our task as educators is to help identify what goals children are working on at the moment and to develop ways to facilitate their progress toward realizing their highest potential. Once again the partnerships with families and community support become important in this quest. When additional support and help are needed for individual children, teachers must be able to connect with the community resources that offer such help. At the heart of all we do, we must view all children as capable and always remain committed to finding ways to unlock each child's amazing potential.

Standards in Early Childhood Education

Quality early childhood programs are highly intentional about integrating developmental theories with important learning standards though active learning experiences. Standards, in the form of the Developmentally Appropriate Practice framework, Head Start Performance Outcomes, various state early learning standards, the Common Core State Standards (CCSS), and national content-area standards, seek to provide overarching goals for what young children should learn and be able to do. Many teachers struggle with feeling limited to teaching only to standards. This creates a limited view of children's lives. In a time when we are recognizing the importance of the context of children's lives and experiences—meaning that children learn and grow in a dynamic system of influences, including home, family, school, and community—teachers must understand how to use standards effectively as one of many tools for effective teaching.

Although it can feel limiting to use standards as a starting place for instruction, teachers can instead start with elements of good practice and fit standards into practice. Good practice means (Jalongo et al., 2004)

- understanding broad developmental trends while planning for individual development;
- balancing instruction to engage diverse learning styles and address all domains;
- creating environments that are safe, stimulating, and welcoming for children of all ability levels;
- meeting children's basic needs for sustenance, shelter, clothing, and health care;
- encouraging processing and representation in a variety of ways;
- helping children make personal connections and find meaning in their experiences; and
- supporting families with respect for family diversity.

Standard learning goals within each domain or content area, such as math, literacy, science, or arts, can be successfully addressed in a balanced approach to teaching encompassing children's play and interest-based projects. As noted previously, play is pure enjoyment for children but also a powerful vehicle for active, meaningful learning (Elkind, 2003; Fraser, 2007; Hirsh, 2004). It is through play that children are engaged in authentic activities stemming from their own internal interests, developing self-regulation skills within the context of a group, and building strengths in all areas of development. Here are some examples:

- Pretend play promotes social development through shared creation of dramatic play scenarios and role negotiation.
- Building with blocks helps children develop spatial abilities, counting, and shape recognition.
- Painting helps children learn colors, develops imagination and creativity, enhances spatial thinking, and develops pencil grip.
- Dictating, writing, and acting out stories promote language arts development (reading, writing, speaking, listening) and understanding of story structure, comprehension, as well as valuing personal experiences and perspectives.
- Moving water or sand in a sensory table develops children's knowledge of physics, how different materials behave and change form, and sense of touch.
- Climbing on a play structure promotes physical development, coordination, and balance.

Standards can be appropriately integrated into learning activities and assessment so that children's experience remains authentic and enjoyable.

Skillful teachers tune in to children's play and interests and prompt, question, provoke, and support the depth of children's activities. While investigating interesting topics, children are able to actually apply emerging academic skills and learn more richly through firsthand discovery. These kinds of instructional practices robustly enhance children's learning and development in individually meaningful, developmentally aligned ways. Furthermore, giving children space to choose activities and topics develops choice-making, curiosity, and initiative. All these goals are part of learning standards and, more important, are part of quality practice. When viewed as a part of the picture, standards do not have to be at odds with what teachers believe about the best ways to educate young children.

Tools of the Mind

Research on the benefits of play-based, constructivist approaches to early care and education is guiding current views of best practices. Based on the work of Russian-born psychologist Lev Vygotsky, the *Tools of the Mind* curriculum "is a novel approach emphasizing intentional development of specific academic skills and self-regulation of behavior and emotions with play featured in a leading role in the curriculum" (Barnett et al., 2008). Mental tools are strategies that children integrate into their thinking and processing that then allow them to become more capable to regulate themselves (thought, behavior) and their environment (Bodrova & Leong, 2007). Vygotsky valued language (a mental tool) as a pivotal tool in learning, memory, and self-regulation as well as a key component of how teachers can support, prompt, and challenge children's learning (scaffolding their learning and development as they reach higher and higher levels of independence). Through the mastery of language as an organizer of thought, children can learn to talk themselves through challenges, connect new ideas to existing mental frameworks, and elaborate on existing ideas to expand knowledge. Additional examples of mental tools include using symbols to represent something, creating rhymes to remember content, and aligning with rules and roles of sociodramatic play. When viewed through a constructivist lens, children's play is seen as a key means for children to organize and regulate their behavior. We see this in the following aspects of play:

- Roles are defined and guide behaviors (pretending to be a teacher, a horse, or a mommy) and dictate actions.
- Rules are implied and at times negotiated and are based on play roles (such as rules about how a teacher behaves).

Furthermore, research has revealed that in play, children's mental skills, such as attention, memory, recall, and imagination, are at a higher level than during any other activity (Bodrova & Leong, 2007). Connecting these important findings, the *Tools* curriculum guides teachers to facilitate children's acquisition of essential mental tools through play, carefully guided activities, and systematic observations. With the strong connection between self-regulation and school success, the *Tools* curriculum has important implications for early childhood practice. For more information about this curriculum, visit www.toolsofthemind.org.

With the widespread adoption of the CCSS for K–12 by all but a handful of states, many educators are seeing an increased focus on standards and content outcomes. The CCSS are currently made up of two documents, one for English Language Arts and one for Math, and were designed to be a list of the most essential academic outcomes students in kindergarten through 12th grade need to know to be successful in college and career (Doorey, 2013). Efforts are also under way to develop and publish additional content area standards. The standards themselves are not a prescriptive directive of how to teach, and their creators promote many approaches to instruction (including play) as viable ways for children to achieve competence in the outcomes (NGACBP, CCSSO, 2010). These standards are, however, higher than many previous state standards in terms of academic rigor and focus on key differences in content such as informational texts and approaches to early reading instruction (Shanahan, 2013). Some educators are finding that the CCSS provide a helpful framework for instructional benchmarking. Other educators are experiencing stress and pressure of curriculum narrowing, inappropriate use of products and materials lists marketed as CCSS specific, and high-stakes assessments (Grennon, Brooks, & Dietz, 2013). Implementation of the CCSS, although specifically written for K–12, has important implications for those working with children from birth to 5 years old. Of particular concern for early childhood professionals is the ongoing worry about the inappropriate pushing of academic expectations onto younger and younger children (NAEYC, 2012). It is essential that providers of early care and education to children prior to school age participate in the ongoing dialogues about best practices in ECE (through third grade), the important place standards can have in our work, and appropriate ways to effectively ensure all children are having robust, healthful early learning experiences. Early childhood professionals are called upon to recognize that early learning standards (NAEYC, 2012)

- must include all developmental areas (the CCSS content areas are but two parts);
- are only one of many components of quality ECE (including teacher preparation and support, adequate program funding, equitable access, overall program quality, appropriate curricula, etc.);
- must work in concert with flexible, developmentally appropriate, and responsive instruction; and
- are able to be assessed through a variety of appropriate means.

Through diligent effort to understand and recognize the role standards play in our practice, effective early childhood professionals can take a lead role in advocating for and "pushing up" best practices in ECE.

Evidence–Based Practice and Data–Driven Decisions

Intentionality is a first and foremost requisite of effective teaching. Teaching with intentionality means that professionals make careful, reflective, deliberate decisions about all aspects of children's care and learning experiences, including

- environmental design,
- material selection,
- organization of time,
- how children are grouped,
- activities and guided lessons,
- assessment tools and practices, and
- promoting family participation.

Many teachers are highly thoughtful in these decisions, but a true mark of intentionality is that teachers deliberately make evidence-based decisions in all aspects of their work. **Evidence-based practice** is defined as the process of making decisions for practice that carefully and intentionally factors in three essential elements (Buysse, Winton, Rous, Epstein, & Lim, 2012; Spencer, Detrich, & Slocum, 2012):

Evidence-based practice

A decision-making process that integrates research evidence, family perspectives, and professional wisdom.

1. The best available evidence: practices that have demonstrated effectiveness through a number of high-quality research studies as reported in relevant, current professional literature
2. Professional judgment: defining situations, needs, and problems and evaluating potential solutions or actions based on professional preparation and knowledge and appropriate personal experience
3. Children's family context: values, goals, and core beliefs of children's families as they relate to children's learning and development

Thus, evidence-based practice requires that professionals review current literature on effective instruction, consider knowledge of individual children and families, and use professional judgment and experience to appropriately respond to each child. Engaging in practice this way positions teachers as reflective researchers critically examining evidence;

assessing options; contextualizing actions within program, family, and community contexts; and making deliberate decisions with clear rationale.

Within the scope of effective evidence-based practice is the integration of systematically collected assessment data on each child. To make the most appropriate decisions for each child, professionals must consistently and regularly gather assessment evidence on children's developmental and learning progress. It is only by gathering data on a variety of appropriate assessment measures that professionals are able to tailor instructional decisions to effectively support each child's unique strengths and needs. Numerous tools and procedures are available to accomplish this:

- Developmental checklists
- Observation notes
- Work samples with notes on context
- Reports on completion of performance assessments
- Transcripts of dialogues and quotes
- Scores on appropriate tests or measures

The key principles in effective use of assessment data are to engage in a systematic process in which data on each child's progress is gathered regularly (at least bimonthly), through only developmentally appropriate activities and that the assessment tool or activity be relevant to context of children's experience. Through ongoing data collection and reflection, professionals are able to use relevant data to make individualized decisions tailored to each child. Figure 1-5 shows the cycle of planning, teaching, and assessment.

One example of a school system–wide practice that emphasizes both a strong evidence base as well as ongoing data-driven decision-making is the Response to Intervention (RtI) model. RtI is a multitiered system of support, meaning that programs are designed with several levels of instruction and individualizing is embedded in each level and based on an assessment-instruction-assessment structure (Bayat, Mindes, & Covitt, 2010). Instruction is based on a research-supported curriculum and delivered deliberately through high-quality practice. Assessment is implemented with all children at initial, formative (during), and summative (end point) stages, and resulting data are used to guide instructional and service decisions (Jackson, Pretti-Frontczack, Harjusola-Webb, Grisham-Brown, & Romani, 2009).

The most popular tier model is a three-tier structure, which increases in intensity and individualization as a child progresses "up" the hierarchy, representing an increase in need for individualized instruction and support. The application of tiers of instruction is also flexible across developmental or educational outcomes and will vary based on each child's functioning in each outcome (DEC, NAEYC, & NHSA, 2013). Figure 1-5 provides a diagram of a structure for RtI.

BEGINNING THE JOURNEY

As you move forward through this book, keep in mind your developing beliefs about teaching, your image of yourself as an educator, and the issues that affect the field of early childhood. Whereas some issues, such as use of technology, are uniquely modern issues, there are others that echo throughout our history. You are entrusted with the task of

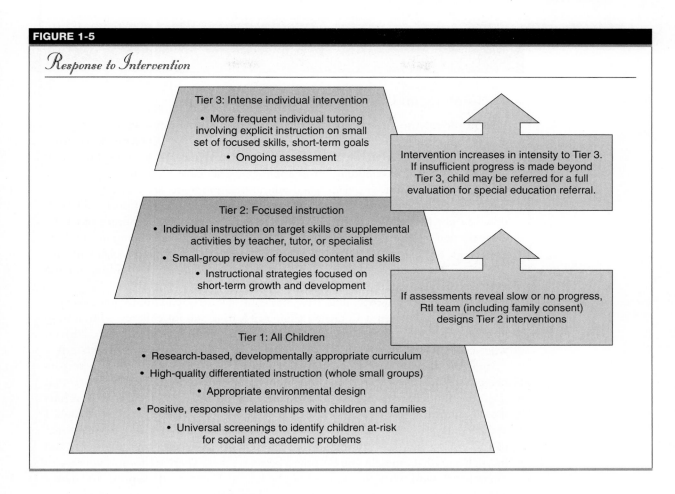

FIGURE 1-5

Response to Intervention

continuing the dedicated march toward reshaping practice, improving professionalism, embodying lofty ideals, and empowering children and families.

Assisting you in facing the challenge are volumes of writing from centuries of thinking about childhood, learning, teaching, and society as well as our own reflections and experiences. The challenge for teachers now is first to inform ourselves about the voices from history—their messages, meanings, and teachings. Equally important is the hand-in-hand effort to learn about ourselves, our assumptions, our own beliefs, and our own personal histories through continued self-reflection (Landerholm, Gehrie, & Hao, 2004). Through this outward and inward learning, you must find your unique way to bring together the sea of professional knowledge and recommendations with your personal passions and drives. The work of the educator is at once both highly professional and deeply personal. It is about thinking, feeling, and doing. In essence, this is work we do with our heads, our hearts, and our hands.

Through this work, we can realize our ultimate goal of ensuring that all children live successful, meaningful lives. Each chapter presented in this text is a story, a voice from the field that shares new ideas and experiences. Let these stories inspire you as you begin creating your own story. Welcome to the journey!

Putting It Into Practice

Technology and Teaching

You no doubt use any number of technological tools throughout your day and throughout your life as a student. You may not even really think twice about many of these tools. As an educator, however, you must make careful decisions about what tools are beneficial to children. For example, you may have access to computers for your classroom. Numerous games and educational programs are available for children's use on the computer. Many programs call themselves "educational," although this may not necessarily be true. It is your job to be a careful consumer of all the materials you select for your classroom. Many of the programs and computer applications work on skills that can be addressed in other, more active and socially interactive ways. Think carefully about why you select materials, always looking for the most active, meaningful, healthful choices.

Technological improvements have also come a long way in improving the experience of many children with diverse abilities. Hearing aids for children with hearing impairments, speaking devices for children who cannot speak, computer-driven wheelchairs for children with limited mobility, and digital picture boards are a few examples of the assistive technology tools that make it possible for children to participate in inclusive classrooms. Translation programs and bilingual materials that speak in multiple languages are also helpful for dual-language learners. Teachers should familiarize themselves with these tools to be able to better serve all families. I also encourage teachers to become skilled in using technology as a tool for their own use. There is a wealth of information (reliable and not so reliable) available online and through apps that can help you become a better teacher. There are forums where you can network with other educators across the world. There are ideas, plans, and strategies you can find to assist you in your work. For all of the valuable ways to use these technologies, you must maintain a critical eye and carefully select applications that best serve your children and families as well as being deliberate about when to unplug.

SUMMARY

- The ages from birth through 8 years old define the term *young children* or the *early childhood years*.
- At no other time of life do we see greater leaps and changes in human growth, making early childhood educators profoundly important in children's lives.
- **Early childhood education** refers to systems of education and care for young children by people other than family members in diverse settings outside of the child's home.
- A key task of the professional is to hone the skills, attitudes, and knowledge necessary to meet high standards of quality practice and to demonstrate these in a professional portfolio.

- Your portfolio is representative of your professional identity and capabilities and may be aligned with one of several national standards frameworks.
- Early childhood professionals take on several important roles in the lives of children and families, including the following:
  - Teacher
  - Researcher
  - Lifelong learner
  - Child and family advocate
- Children's play is a primary vehicle for their learning and development and is often highly complex and varied.
- High-quality teaching today must reflect the diverse context within which children are growing and learning and value diversity and inclusion of each child and family.
- Today's high-quality practice calls upon professionals to be highly intentional about effectively integrating knowledge of development, individual children, community contexts, and appropriate learning standards to meet each child's needs.

CHAPTER LEARNING GOALS SELF-ASSESSMENT

Use this chart to write down three to five key points for each learning goal that you gained from this chapter.

Identify key highlights of development and learning in children from birth to 8 years old.	
Explore the scope and features of early childhood education.	
Discuss the role and tasks of a teacher-education student.	
Describe the complex roles of early childhood teachers.	
Articulate important issues facing today's early childhood profession.	
Organize initial ideas about your professional identity.	

APPLICATION ACTIVITIES

Discussion Prompts

1. Which of the many complex roles of the early childhood teacher do you feel most ready to take on, and which do you feel most challenged by?
2. What prior experiences and internal qualities do you feel strengthen your skills and dispositions as a teacher?

In Class: Describe Your Favorite Teacher   Think back to when you were in school—any age or grade. Think about one of your favorite teachers. What do you recall? What was it about this teacher that made you respond? Write a few phrases, words, or sentences to describe your memories. Share them with your class or small group. What common threads emerge? How do your memories and points from the class discussion fit into your vision of the ideal teacher—the kind of teacher you hope to become?

When I do this exercise with my own students, it is always the personal qualities that come through as the most memorable: someone who cared, someone who went out of his or her way for you, someone you felt you could talk to about anything, someone who felt like a friend and teacher, someone who truly wanted to see you succeed as a person and a student. Did you find the same thing in your memories and in your class discussion? Keep in mind your memories of your favorite teacher and the effect he or she had on you as you develop your own teacher identity.

In the Field   Create a list of questions about learning standards, managing a classroom, guidance strategies, and promoting success in meeting standards for all children (children with diverse abilities included). Arrange to interview an early childhood teacher to find answers to your questions. Choose a teacher who has been teaching for at least four years.

For Your Portfolio   As you begin your journey into this introduction to early childhood education, you might already bring with you years of experience and prior coursework, or this might be the start of your professional path. In either case, a good starting point for your portfolio is to create a brief autobiography, including basic information about yourself as well as a section describing why you want to be in this field. Once you decide on a specific portfolio organization plan (perhaps based on standards, your teacher-education department's own framework, or the Child Development Associate content areas), your autobiography fits nicely into an introductory section along with a résumé and transcripts. Your autobiography is also a useful document to share with classroom teachers when you complete field hours or student teaching.

RELATED WEB LINKS

Association for Childhood Education International
www.acei.org

National Association for the Education of Young Children
www.naeyc.org

Council for Professional Recognition
www.cdacouncil.org

CHAPTER 2

Historical Overview: People and Beliefs That Shaped the Field

Chapter Learning Goals

- Identify overarching themes in the history of care and education for young children.
- Discuss key influences on early education in the 1600s and 1700s.
- Examine values about children and education in the 1800s.
- Compare beliefs and practices in the 1900s, and make connections to present-day practice.
- Explore early childhood best practices in the context of today's diverse world.

T he field of early childhood care and education has a long history involving divergent viewpoints, dedicated educators and theorists, and a pattern of pendulum swings in terms of popular practice. The study of how young children have been viewed, treated, and educated is rich and complex. It is entwined with the histories of social welfare, cultural movements, religion, and politics. This chapter provides you with an overarching historical backdrop to help you understand where we are today and why we believe what we do about best practices.

The backdrop of early childhood education's past and evolution will help you understand the more detailed approaches, frameworks, and theories that you will explore throughout the rest of this text. The history of education is a bit of a roller-coaster ride, so hang on! Use the charts in Appendices A, B, and C to help you keep names, dates, and important theories straight. Think about what values, beliefs, and practices stand out to you as elements that may guide your own eclectic practice.

HISTORICAL TRENDS IN EARLY CHILDHOOD BELIEFS AND PRACTICE

Several hotly debated issues run like threads through the patchwork of U.S. early childhood history. At some times more prominent than at others, these are the underlying trends that have influenced practice. As you travel along the historical time line of this chapter, the following issues will be your traveling companions:

- The prevailing views regarding children
- The role of families, particularly women, at home and in society
- International theories, research, and trends that influence educational programming in the United States
- The effects of **family income** on early care and education practice
- Early childhood settings as **custodial care** (focus on keeping children safe rather than educational programming) or education; the goals and purpose of the programming

Think about children's experiences throughout history as you think about what you want your own practice to be like and what experiences you hope to provide for children. The core beliefs about what to teach, how to teach, and who should be responsible for early care and education have shifted and changed throughout centuries of dynamic practice. Practice has been closely connected to how society perceives children and families in general and the role of societal systems in the care and education of children.

LIFE IN THE 1600S AND 1700S: HARSH TRADITIONS AND NEW IDEAS

In Colonial America, children were generally treated as small adults, and childhood was not necessarily valued as an important phase of life. Colonial American society generally agreed that children should be taught to read the Bible from an early age, initially at home with their fathers as teachers (Spodek, 1985). According to Colonial society, it was desirable to curb children's sinful nature early in life. In 1647 Massachusetts enacted a law requiring the establishment of local schools for young children. These schools were often called **dame schools** because they were run by the women of the community (Beatty, 1995). The schools were places to care for children while adults worked and to instill piety through readings of the Bible. School activities stemmed from a desire to teach children the value of hard work, strong moral character based on religious beliefs, and trade skills they would use as adults (Hacsi, 1995).

Influential People, Contexts, and Ideas of the 1600s

By the earliest decades of the 1600s, philosophers and educators were beginning to focus their attention on early childhood as a distinct stage of life. Several key theorists emerged with ideas that countered the harsh educational practices being used in Europe and America (Matthews, 2003). Eastern European religious leader **John Amos Comenius** (1592–1670) was one of the earliest authors to produce a text outlining a modern system

family income

The status within community and society based on income level, family economic stability, and social acceptance.

Custodial care

Type of program for young children that emphasized care and service to parents but did not have strong educational components.

Dame schools

Early local, public schools established in the mid-1600s to provide basic care for children of working mothers.

of education for all children (Beatty, 1995). He continued to advocate for universal education, which Martin Luther (1483–1546) had successfully promoted in some European countries (Sandsmark, 2002). Comenius's vision of education as a means to promote social harmony and end the war and political strife he had witnessed in his life reflected his deep religious convictions and commitment to working toward peace. He saw nature as a prime method of fostering children's growth and advocated letting children play and grow in natural, harmonious settings. He was among the first to propose that young children had a great potential for learning and ought to learn through active means (Schickedanz, 1995).

Comenius also promoted the role of mothers—not school—as the best educators of children under the age of 6, and he wrote a guidebook outlining all the concepts, skills, and activities he felt children should be taught. Although his guide was quite specific in its details, Comenius nevertheless insisted that mothers individualize instruction because children develop at different rates, and he warned against excessive academics too early. Does it surprise you that some of these modern beliefs (individualized instruction, parents as the child's first teacher, young children as capable learners) were being written in his book in the 1650s? Best practices in our field have come a long way, but as you can see, the historic roots run deep.

A scant 40 years later, doctor and philosopher **John Locke** (1632–1704) produced another guide to education that had a great effect on educational practices in America. Much of his work contradicted customary practices and promoted views of children that were more favorable, free, and playful. Locke strongly emphasized the importance of firsthand experiences as a means of learning. This viewpoint gave rise to the concept of experiential education, which is still in favor today. Locke emphasized the importance of education (less emphasis on innate drives) and proposed that children were like blank pages or wax that should be molded and shaped by experience (Henson, 2003). For Locke, experience was education.

Locke believed that the development and education of young children were best served by parents as educators. He advocated instructing children as young as 1 or 2 in literacy, but he cautioned that academic instruction should feel more like play to children (Beatty, 1995). He also encouraged parents to use children's internal need for approval and guilt to manipulate them into desired behaviors, preferring reasoning with children to physical punishment (Hulbert, 1999). He differed from previous theorists in that his beliefs were more centered on children and less centered on religion.

The beliefs of Comenius and Locke did much to counter the negative view of children that generally pervaded the 17th century. The pendulum had begun to swing toward more favorable beliefs about children's innate character. Fortunately for children, this trend toward a deeper awareness of the nature of young children and a respect for childhood as a unique stage of life formed the foundation for the vision of the next round of influential theorists.

Influential People, Contexts, and Ideas of the 1700s

For the romantics, or some of the enlightenment thinkers who permeated the 1700s and 1800s, education was a naturally unfolding process. However, it needed to involve careful teaching to come to fruition and to create balanced individuals who could operate in society (Kontio, 2003). Many people believed that children were best educated in rural settings through authentic experiences that were interesting to them. The following example illustrates the harmonious, respectful, natural education advocated by these philosophers.

CLASSROOM VIEW

A small child bursts forth from a little stone cottage on a sunny, green hillside dotted with grazing sheep. The child decides to fill the small trough from which the sheep drink. He knows the stream is through the trees behind the cottage, and he sets off. Once there, he scoops some water up in his hands and begins to make his way back to the trough. As you are probably already thinking, the water has seeped through his fingers by the time he gets back to the trough. His clothes and shoes are wet. He stops and looks at his hands for a while. His teacher watches from a distance, careful not to scold the child or direct him to the pail by the side door. The look on the child's face shows that he is processing his experience, trying to formulate some kind of plan that will successfully achieve his goal. His gaze turns from his hands to the trough. He reaches out and touches it, feeling the wooden sides. The teacher patiently waits and watches. The child looks at his hands again, spreading his fingers. Slowly, he looks around him, searching for something more like the trough than his hand—something that can carry the water.

The child sees his teacher and approaches him. He tells the teacher about his plan and about his experience with the water running through his hands. The teacher listens. The teacher asks the child if he can think of anything he has used before to hold water. The child pauses. "A cup at supper," he remembers. The teacher and child talk about the child's cup, how it works, and what it looks like. As they talk, the child decides to look for something with tall sides and a bottom, like his cup. With a start, his eyes alight on the pail, and he runs off to give it a try. The teacher continues to observe the child's self-initiated actions.

French philosopher **Jean-Jacques Rousseau** (1712–1778) authored influential books that spawned educational reforms in Europe and America (Beatty, 1995). His founding principles are seen as threads running through the beliefs of many prominent educators throughout history (Lascarides & Hinitz, 2000). In one of his books, *Emile,* he proposed the radical idea that children were innately perfect and optimal development would unfold naturally without the corrupting influence of some elements of society (Null, 2004). Rousseau did, however, validate the importance of each person's maintaining individual will while also promoting the will of society (Kontio, 2003). In his view, the individual learns to operate within and for the social group. Happiness is derived from individual freedom and the capability to develop attainable goals.

Although Rousseau's book was fictional, it did serve as something of a guide in which he encouraged manipulating and directing children's actions and thought indirectly (Procher, 1998). He took care to caution against exerting direct control and authority over the child, which would lead to anger and rebellion. The concept of individual freedom and aversion to dominance was of prime importance to Rousseau (Kontio, 2003). Rousseau validated children as pure, fundamentally different from adults, and in need of protection from corruption (Henson, 2003). He advocated that childhood be prolonged and reserved for activities of interest to children, not those imposed by direct adult instruction. Unlike earlier theorists, he believed that young children should not be pushed into academic instruction but rather be allowed to develop naturally and harmoniously (Null, 2004). Rousseau did not believe that mothers were capable of properly educating their children. Instead, he advocated that mothers turn over their children to male tutors for proper upbringing (Beatty, 1995). Here we see the first major pendulum swing relating to the parents' role in young children's education.

Johann Heinrich Pestalozzi, 1746–1827.

In another shift in perspective, Swiss educator **Johann Heinrich Pestalozzi** (1746–1827) focused on the welfare of poor children. His concerns grew out of the increasing industrialization of society and the dramatic rifts among upper, middle, and lower classes in urban areas. Unlike earlier theorists, he worked directly with children, experimenting with new methods (Schickedanz, 1995). Inspired by the romantic view of childhood, Pestalozzi followed some of Rousseau's ideas and designed schools and curricula based on a holistic approach to teaching the whole child physically, mentally, and emotionally (Henson, 2003).

Pestalozzi strove to instill a strong community-minded consciousness in students and valued active involvement with the environment. One of his enduring innovations was a system of teaching that fostered learning through reflection on experience (Adelman, 2000). Growing up with few resources himself, Pestalozzi designed an original method of teaching children living in poverty that centered on several key beliefs (Null, 2004):

- All children are capable of learning.
- Learning begins at birth with parents as the first teachers.
- Teacher-student discourse and activities should focus on hands-on manipulation of real objects.
- Natural experiences in the course of daily living are the source of learning.
- Arts and physical education are essential components of a comprehensive education.

Unlike Rousseau, Pestalozzi validated the mother and home as the most natural learning environment and held a low opinion of schools for young children. He envisioned all children learning through hands-on manipulation of objects with loving, affectionate mother figures, a view based on his own early experiences (Bowers & Gehring, 2004). His application of concrete objects remains visible today with the many manipulable materials lining preschool shelves (wooden and plastic blocks, puzzles, and unit cubes). Although his initial efforts were directed toward educating children and mothers in poverty, his method became popular with all classes of society abroad and in the United States. Many Pestalozzian schools were opened in U.S. cities in the early 1800s (Beatty, 1995).

EDUCATION IN THE 1800S: KINDERGARTEN IS BORN

Influential People, Contexts, and Ideas

British educator **Robert Owen** (1771–1858), who shared Pestalozzi's concern for impoverished children, became a pioneer and champion of educating children outside the home. He fueled the British infant school movement, in which he sought to create institutions where kindly teachers would encourage large groups of children to explore actively and amuse themselves. Owen also embraced beliefs about the importance of learning from nature and concrete objects. Owen's chief mission was to create moral adults through education promoting cooperation and social cohesion (Beatty, 1995). He firmly opposed the harsh, punitive practices common in his day (Owen, 1999).

In the 1820s Owen became increasingly interested in spreading the infant school movement in America. One of the earliest intervention programs (like the Head Start programs of today), infant schools targeted comprehensive services for children in poverty as a means of social reform (Spodek, 1985).

A parallel social movement, which was developing in the United States at about the same time, was to have a great effect on the decline of the infant school movement (though infant schools continued to flourish in England). As social life continued to change with industrialization, the role of men as the economic providers and the place of women in the home became increasingly promoted as the proper family dynamic (Spodek, 1985). This shift in domestic responsibilities led many experts, as well as mothers, to reject the practice of sending children to schools outside the home in place of in-home education (Dombrowski, 2002). This family dynamic was possible for only upper- and middle-class families; many working-class mothers simply could not stay at home to embody this ideal.

Divisions Emerge: Care or Education, Early or Elementary Education

Day nurseries

Group day-care programs providing basic care and designed as a service to working parents.

For working-class mothers who had to work to survive, **day nurseries** were the only option for keeping their children safe and off the streets while they were at work. Often organized by middle- or upper-class women, the day nurseries' mission was to provide welfare and care to children on the days when their mothers were working. A pervasive attitude of blame was placed on these working mothers, who were often made to feel deficient (O'Connor, 1995). Also, the programs had no real educational goals, and a stigma developed over the social welfare–oriented programs (providing custodial care) versus education-based programs. This stigma remains today to some degree; however, today there is ample evidence to support the importance of quality, comprehensive programming for all young children. The day nurseries managed to remain an institution primarily because they filled a pressing social need.

Romantic views of children and childhood as godlike and of womanhood as the domestic ideal led not only women but also policy makers to reject including infant schools with public schools for older children. With the ousting of early childhood programming from the public schools, the funding problems began (and still plague the field today). Once again the pendulum was swinging as previous beliefs about the importance of early academic instruction shifted to a fear that it would do harm to young children's development. It became customary by the 1840s to refrain from any reading or academic instruction until children were 6 years old (Beatty, 1995; Schickedanz, 1995). A familiar theme remained, however, which was the importance of good moral upbringing from infancy.

Amid this rocky period, one of the most famous and influential people in early childhood history began to make his mark. **Friedrich Froebel** (1782–1852) is best known as the father of the first kindergarten. Froebel's initial training in forestry and his rearing in a strict religious home gave him a closeness to God and nature that can be seen throughout his educational philosophy and methods, much like previous educators (Lascarides & Hinitz, 2000). Indeed, translated from his native German, the name he chose for his method—kindergarten—means "child's garden." Froebel sought to build on previous theories and create a formal system of education for young children that would uplift human society (Adelman, 2000).

Laying a foundation that remains in place today, Froebel advocated a play-based learning environment in which children would actively engage with special materials he created, called *gifts*. Teachers were to observe and guide children's activities, not to interfere in their naturally unfolding processes. The teacher's role was that of a careful gardener, nurturing children as tender seedlings growing naturally and harmoniously (Lindqvist, 1995). It was through directed play that Froebel sought to keep children's interest so they could become engrossed in learning activities with hands-on materials (Saracho & Spodek, 1995).

Froebel suggested 20 gifts and occupations and gave detailed instructions for their presentation and use with children (Saracho & Spodek, 1995), including the following:

- Solid, three-dimensional geometric shapes fashioned of wool and wood
- Flat shapes of wood, wire, and other natural materials
- Handwork activities such as weaving, sewing, paper folding, cutting, and modeling
- Gardening
- Finger plays, songs, and games

Theories About Knowledge

Froebel based his kindergarten on rationalism. In this view, knowledge is not derived from experience but is gained by logically thinking through concepts from a given premise. In practice, this is evident in Froebel's method of having children work through prescribed activities with his gifts and occupations as the starting place. By working and thinking through prescribed tasks, children would acquire the knowledge that was symbolized in the materials and activities.

Gift 1:
Six colored balls of soft yarn or wool

Gift 2:
Wooden sphere, cylinder, and cube

Gift 3:
Eight cubes, presented together as a cube

Gift 4:
Eight rectangular pieces,
presented as a cube

Gift 5:
Twenty-one cubes, six half-cubes, and
twelve quarter-cubes

Gift 6:
Twenty-four rectangular pieces, six
columns, and twelve caps

Gift 7:
Parquetry tablets derived from the
surfaces of the gifts, including
squares, equilateral triangles, right
triangles, and obtuse triangles

Gift 8:
Straight sticks of wood, plastic, or metal
in various lengths, plus rings and half-
rings of various diameters made from
wood, plastic, or metal

Gift 9:
Small points in various colors made of
plastic, paper, or wood

Gift 10:
Materials that utilize rods and
connectors, similar to Tinker Toys

Froebel's Gifts.

Influenced by Pestalozzi's view of the important role played by mothers in children's education, Froebel also advocated strong family involvement. However, he preferred educational settings outside the home that served as extensions of the home. Here, mothers held key positions and status and infused maternal love throughout the school setting (Read, 2003). His repositioning of women in valued roles outside the home struck a chord with many upper- and middle-class women, who took up the cause of promoting kindergartens with great passion. Kindergarten programs began to open across Europe and spread through other continents as well. Froebel did not necessarily trust modern women's abilities to raise their children properly, however, and so created a training program for mothers and teachers (Beatty, 1995). It was the close bond of mothers and children that opened the door for Froebel's kindergarten method to find favor in the United States, despite the concerns about out-of-home schooling that had caused infant schools to fall out of favor.

A German immigrant started the first U.S. kindergarten in 1856 in Wisconsin. In fact, German immigrants started most of the early kindergartens, thanks to Froebel's influence (Beatty, 1995). The early kindergarten programs and published guidebooks carefully outlined exact instructions for proper Froebelian methods, continuing the tradition of harmonious, natural learning instead of academic instruction. Although these programs earned some public attention, the onset of influential U.S. educators paved the way for more widespread acceptance as well as fierce rivalries between Froebelian purists and those who would change the kindergarten to fit American culture (Spodek, 1985).

One such American educator who became a champion of the kindergarten was **Elizabeth Palmer Peabody** (1804–1894). Inspired by the Wisconsin kindergarten, Peabody opened the first English-speaking kindergarten in Boston in 1859 (Swiniarski, 2005). She traveled to Germany, where she studied Froebelian methods, took her new knowledge back to America, and firmly opposed early academic instruction in favor of teaching through hands-on objects (Beatty, 1995; Peabody, 1999). Peabody adapted Froebel's ideal child's garden to include **individualized instruction**, in which she adapted activities to suit particular children's abilities. Based on her wealth of experience with children, she believed children needed careful direction to develop fully (Swiniarski, 2005).

Assisted by the efforts of **Susan Blow** (1843–1916) to remain true to Froebel's theory and practice, the kindergarten movement gained ground and implemented programs for children and quality training programs for teachers across the United States (O'Connor, 1995). Blow was particularly concerned about inferior teacher-training programs because she believed that qualified, quality teachers were essential for the continuation of the Froebelian kindergarten movement (Blow, 1999). Peabody created the American Froebel Society to regulate the quality and authenticity of kindergarten programs, and she advocated for inclusion of African American women in the new kindergarten training programs (Dombrowski, 2002). She worked tirelessly to provide educational opportunities for post–Civil War slave children in the South as well as Native American children (Lascarides & Hinitz, 2000).

MOVING EDUCATION FORWARD IN THE 1900s: PROGRESSIVE AND DEVELOPMENTAL

Over time, Froebel's method became increasingly rigid and formal, so children's activities were directed by teachers and by the self-correcting, **didactic materials**. Kindergarten practices still included play, but Froebel's own writing that undirected play was frivolous

Individualized instruction

The process of adapting learning experiences or material selection based on the unique needs and abilities of individual children.

Didactic materials

Materials that are specifically designed to be used in one way or focused to teach a particular concept. Opposite to *open-ended* materials, which are less defined to allow for many uses.

and wasteful contributed to more direction of children's activities, even their play (Lindqvist, 1995). This was the start of the "push-down curriculum" problems that are still debated today and that gave rise to the Developmentally Appropriate Practice statement and movement. The rigid practices that were taking over kindergartens led to criticism by new progressives and proponents of the child study movement, who were beginning to take their place as the leaders in the field in the 1900s.

CLASSROOM VIEW

On this crisp, autumn day, you are taking advantage of the new lab school on a nearby college campus to peek into the lives of children. The classroom is set up with a one-way window, which allows you to observe without the children's knowing you are there. This is a real opportunity to see them in a natural setting. You settle in at the window and start to notice the room and materials. The most prominent feature, which takes up a large portion of the room, looks like a house, but in miniature. There is a kitchen area with a small wooden stove and icebox, a table and chairs, and a hearth. There is also a social gathering place with sofas and chairs. Children are busy acting out scenes from typical daily life at home. Some are making food, some are at the table eagerly waiting for a meal, and two children are cleaning up with small brooms. The children are talking among themselves as they act out this little drama.

You notice that the teacher has been watching them, writing in a notebook. She acknowledges two other adults in the room who are also interviewing a child and taking notes. They are engrossed in this child study. The teacher leaves her notebook and begins to interact with the children. She elaborates on their dialogues and asks the children if they think the table should be set for supper. Two children jump up from the table and run to get table settings. The room hums with activity, but you're wondering about all this playing and whether the teacher is going to start directing the children on academic tasks soon. Later, when you have an opportunity to talk with the teacher, she describes her view on education as "progressive."

Influential People, Contexts, and Ideas: The Rise of Child Study

The 1900s mark a dynamic period of change in early childhood theories and practice. As the new millennium approached, discourses on education shifted from religious influences to more scientific approaches. Charles Darwin's pioneering work in developing his theory of evolution significantly influenced the new social scientists who were leading the field of childhood development and education.

G. Stanley Hall (1844–1924), the first American to receive a doctorate in psychology, integrated Darwin's ideas with those of the romantics and created the child study movement. His approach to education emphasized aligning the educational curriculum with the stages of development. He began the effort to elevate education into the ranks of respected science with his scientific approach to studying children (Null, 2004). Hall's systematic research yielded volumes on children's development and introduced classroom teachers to a new role as researchers. He also became an advocate for modifying the Froebelian kindergarten to align more with his developmental theories, for example, placing more emphasis on large motor development early as opposed to Froebel's emphasis on fine motor skills first (Beatty, 1995).

Hall supported an interdisciplinary approach to working with young children that integrated supports and services for health and education (Hall, 1999). Through his observations of children, he voiced concerns about children spending too much time in classrooms, at the expense of time outside playing freely in fresh air (Hulbert, 1999). His concerns that schools were making children nervous and pushing them ahead of their time remain concerns today.

Arnold Gesell (1880–1961), a student of Hall's, placed great emphasis on the developmental importance of the early childhood years and promoted the role of parents and teachers as researchers (Gesell, 1999). He emphasized the importance of careful, documented observations and made the university lab school a popular feature of the child study movement. The classroom visit at the start of this section illustrates the lab school in action:

- Observers making **naturalistic observations**
- Teachers chronicling their observations and using them to guide children's education
- Researchers interviewing children to gather data on developmental trends

Naturalistic observations

A research method of directly observing subjects in their natural environment.

Much information was gleaned in these settings about how children develop and respond to educational environments, although the children studied represented mostly the upper-middle class. Gesell wrote prolifically about his research findings, pioneering the use of photographic research. His work defining the stages of infant development as well as his support of connections between home and school remain influential today (Lascarides & Hinitz, 2000). The child study movement was challenged by behaviorists (promoting education as habit training), who dismissed the role of teachers and parents in the research process and questioned the scientific integrity of the child study movement. Behaviorists, such as Edward Thorndike, sought more quantifiable data and devised the earliest standardized subject achievement tests (Trotter, Keller, Zehr, Manzo, & Bradley, 1999). The tension between educational psychology schools of thought continues today (Takanishi, 1981).

The Progressive Era Dawns

At the turn of the 20th century, another movement was afoot—one that sought to synthesize old ideas with new discoveries in an effort to move education forward. **John Dewey** (1859–1952) cultivated his role as one of the most influential contemporary American education scholars and popularized the progressive movement in education (Henson, 2003). Dewey was influenced by the discourse on educational philosophies of his predecessors (including Hall) and by Darwin's theories of evolution. He valued the child's psychological and social dimensions and believed that education should emerge from the child's own unfolding development and interests rather than be rigidly imposed upon the child by the teacher (Matthews, 2003). He emphasized three key factors of education (Dewey, 1938; Powell, 2000):

1. Experience with authentic materials
2. Meaningful to the individual student
3. Based on problem-solving activities

Contrary to previous perspectives of early childhood programs as protective gardens, Dewey suggested that the classroom environment mirror society (Henson, 2003). In his writing on the role of democracy in education, Dewey presented the idea that social engagement was central to the development of responsible citizens (Archambault, 1964). Dewey firmly believed that the environment exerts great influence over the child, especially the social environment (Antler, 1987). Furthermore, the disposition of the learner began to emerge as an area of concern for modern educators.

In addition to focusing on the acquisition of skills, Dewey believed that the development of a love of learning and a desire to continue learning ought to be the primary aims of the educational environment (Dewey, 1999). He believed that the intellect and interest of students were best engaged through collaborative, critical inquiry in an environment that supported the learner as a shared authority with the teacher. In his progressive view, learning occurred through the direct interaction of students, teachers, and materials in experiential, problem-solving endeavors. A key role of the teacher was to uncover children's interests, thoughts, and feelings and to plan engaging educational experiences based on them (Hyun & Marshall, 2003). **Emergent curriculum** methods of today, such as the Project Approach, integrate Dewey's ideas. The results of this learning environment were expected to be the raising of independent thinkers, fully capable of making meaning out of their world through critical inquiry, collaboration, and judgment (Gregory, 2002). Observe a classroom example of an integrated, hands-on project in this **video**.

Emergent curriculum

Learning experiences and plans that emerge from children's interests and lives.

Amid fierce rivalries over conservative Froebelian methods and more Americanized kindergartens, Dewey sought a balance between too much teacher direction and leaving children to go forth unguided in their education (Beatty, 1995). He advocated more open, unstructured play and careful guidance in developmentally appropriate activities, such as the dramatic play in the classroom view (Saracho & Spodek, 1995). Kindergarten teachers such as **Patty Smith Hill** (1868–1946) designed new child-centered, interest-based methods that integrated ideas from Froebel, the child study movement, behaviorism, and progressive approaches to education. Hill also laid the foundation for today's National Association for the Education of Young Children through her efforts to professionalize the field in the 1920s (Bredekamp, 1997). One enduring belief promoted by Hill was the universality of early childhood education and the integration of all social classes together in the classroom. She lamented the loss of kindergarten's strong social welfare ties as public schools became more and more involved, although she was pleased with the improvements made to earlier, more rigid Froebelian methods (Hill, 1999).

Despite Dewey's view of education for social justice and Hill's dedication to improving conditions for impoverished children and Native American children, many programs fell short of these goals. In relation to Native American children, the goals of education were to assimilate children into mainstream American culture at the expense of their home language and culture, a practice that is strongly opposed today (Beatty, 1995; Lascarides & Hinitz, 2000).

As kindergarten methods progressed and changed, advocates of early childhood education continued to push for public acceptance and universal kindergartens. Many debates ensued as states slowly began to integrate kindergarten programs into the public school arena. Areas of debate included the following:

- Methods and scope—literacy instruction, play, and worksheets
- Mission—social reform, individual development, academic training, and first-grade preparation

- Salaries for teachers
- Half-day versus full-day, double sessions

As kindergarten programs aimed at 5-year-olds became more entrenched in public schools and universal in scope (and perhaps more narrowly focused on elementary education goals versus broader developmental goals), a new wave of early childhood programming began to rise: nursery schools for 2- to 4-year-olds.

Assimilation of Native American Children

As settlers moved westward across the United States, clashes with the indigenous people became frequent and violent. By the 1900s, Indian schools had been created by Protestant and Christian Anglos (European Americans) with the purpose of assimilating Native Americans and sometimes Hispanics into the new white American culture. The goal of **Americanizing**, which was regarded as a salvation for the so-called barbaric and savage natives, was to enable such students to step into the new society as fully functioning members. Children were removed from their homes and families to be raised in boarding schools or with surrogate white families. Their hair and dress were changed to match those of the dominant culture. They were forbidden to speak their native language or recognize any cultural traditions other than those practiced by the new settlers. This "systematic programme of cultural extinction," a common and accepted practice at the time, was funded by the government as a public service (Margolis & Rowe, 2004).

Natives, considered worthless, were dehumanized by how they were described and treated. The prevailing view felt it was necessary to erase all vestiges of the Native American to create a civilized human in his or her place. It was decided that it was less expensive to reprogram or reeducate the natives than to kill them (Margolis & Rowe, 2004). The school programs differed from state to state, but it typically included occupational training for boys (farming and woodworking), domestic tasks for girls (cooking and knitting), and heavy manual labor for all children. Activities, including recreational activities, were strictly regimented to ensure complete deference to authority.

By the 1920s, however, the goal of assimilation to integrate Native Americans into society had been lost. The expectation for the reeducated Native American was not to find an equal, or functional, place in society. The new goal of assimilation programs was to train Native Americans (along with many immigrants) to accept their lesser status in a racist system (Hoxie, 1984). The skills learned in the schools would provide jobs as servants working for white families (Margolis & Rowe, 2004).

Slowly, beginning in the late 1920s, the culture of assimilation in Indian schools began to change. Public schools were encouraged (with financial incentives) to include Native American children. These schools began to include studies of native culture and arts along with academic subjects. The practices that had previously stripped Native American tribes of their autonomy, financial self-governance, and landownership were starting to change. The practice of corporal punishment (physical abuse) in schools was outlawed in 1929, changing the previous system of abuse that had run rampant in Indian schools.

Americanizing

The practice of actively diminishing and erasing diverse backgrounds and influences in an effort to promote dominant U.S. beliefs and culture.

Nursery Schools Emerge

In the years following World War I (1914–1918), concerns over a child's overall welfare became a driving force for various organizations and agencies to come together to meet children's and families' needs. The nursery schools forming at this time, influenced by growing voices in the psychodynamic field, sought to provide caring and nurturing as well as educational programming. At that time, nursery schools, which served diverse populations, had roots firmly planted in social welfare for needy children. Once again integrating trends from international circles, the work of sisters **Margaret** (1860–1931) and **Rachel McMillan** (1859–1917) in London became influential in American nursery schools.

With backgrounds in social welfare and an interest in alleviating the challenges faced by children living in poverty, the McMillans created an open-air nursery school where hygiene; outdoor play; and active, hands-on learning were primary goals (Beatty, 1995). In addition to the emphasis on nurturing and welfare, Margaret McMillan envisioned nursery schools as fueling children's imagination and curiosity. The sisters felt these were attributes children would need as future leaders of society (Spodek, 1985). Margaret wanted her schools to be lab schools where professionals from a variety of disciplines could explore new methods to influence their own practice (Lascarides & Hinitz, 2000). Throughout the 1910s and 1920s, many nursery schools and teacher-training centers were opened based on McMillan's insights. In her writing, she emphasized the effect that nursery school teachers have on the brain development of young children during the brain's most plastic and formative period (McMillan, 1999). These words were truly insightful and prophetic in 1919, considering research on brain development and education have come to the fore just within the past few decades.

Amid the burgeoning Progressive movement and with more and more attention being afforded to the education of young children, two dynamic and highly influential women were poised to change the field. Firmly committed to validating children's play as the most powerful force in their learning, **Caroline Pratt** (1867–1954) opened the Play

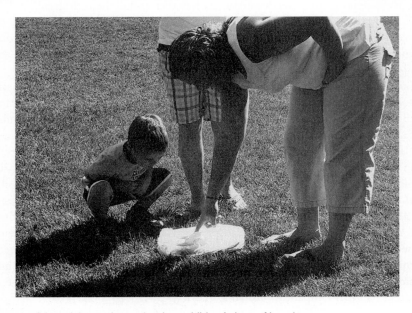

Active, meaningful, social experience develops children's love of learning.

School (later renamed the City and Country School) in New York City in 1913. Her primary goal was to create an education system that would teach children how to think—to generate knowledge that they would carry over from the classroom to the world (Antler, 1987). Her philosophy of **intrinsic motivation** and education for oneself ran like a current throughout the school. Absent formal, teacher-directed, passive activities, children at the Play School chose their own paths. In effect, the children directed their own learning through free choice with materials and activities. The ultimate vision of the Play School was to engender social reform through education. Above all else, Pratt valued not obtaining information, but rather the process of learning information. This belief was also emphasized by Jean Piaget (Lascarides & Hinitz, 2000).

Intrinsic motivation

The desire, interest, and motivation that are driven by internal forces, as opposed to external rewards.

Early in the life of Pratt's Play School, a long and fruitful collaboration with Lucy Sprague Mitchell began. After many years of working in academic environments at the university level, **Lucy Sprague Mitchell** (1878–1967) became an integral founding member of the Bureau of Educational Experiments. She remains one of the most influential people in contemporary early childhood history. Through Mitchell's tireless work, the bureau's early emphasis became the exploration of experimental educational methods and philosophies. The bureau served as a lab school for the study of child development (Antler, 1987).

The systematic study of children's growth was, in turn, used to inform practice and refine child-centered methods. Mitchell's own interests in social reconstruction, the influence of friend and teacher John Dewey, and a personal fascination in geography guided her belief that children's education in history and geography ought to stem first from their own life experiences. It should begin with the children's own neighborhoods, for example. Overriding everything, she felt, was that education was about each student's finding relationships—of concepts, people, events, or places (Antler, 1987).

Building on her lengthy work with and research involving children through the Play School, Mitchell embarked on an expansion bureau project at its new location on Bank Street in New York City. In the new location, a teacher-education facility was built with the lab school and research center. The goal was to develop teachers who would think—who would observe, reflect, and experiment actively in their own work and would value the social context of education (Grinberg, 2002). Today the importance of well-trained, educated teachers continues to be a key to the quality of education and children's success. In fact, the training and level of education of teachers remains the top predictor of program quality (Horn, Caruso, & Golas, 2003).

Mitchell practiced education as both a science and an art, and she strove to instill the same commitments in her student teachers (Lascarides & Hinitz, 2000). The influence of the Bank Street innovations had moved beyond experimental schools and into New York City public schools by the mid-1940s. The once radical ideas and experimental practice of progressive schools continued to become widely accepted, mainstream elements in education (Sullivan, 1996).

Education and Socioemotional Development

As has always been the case, early childhood education has been greatly affected by various sociopolitical events. During World War II (1939–1945), public interest in young children was renewed for several reasons:

- Habit training and behaviorism were giving way to more child-centered, affectionate, nurturing beliefs about how children needed to grow.

- Encouraging children to express their feelings became an educational goal.
- More women were entering the workforce, giving rise to an increased need for out-of-home care. (Public views that mothers ought to raise their children at home still reigned, contributing to many guilt-ridden working mothers.)
- As more out-of-home care opportunities opened for children, more women were able to find employment.

The increased need for early childhood programs translated into federal involvement in the form of legislation securing public funding for children's centers in the areas most affected by the war efforts. More than 130,000 children were served daily, on average, in publicly funded programs at the time (Lascarides & Hinitz, 2000); however, only a fraction of the eligible children were involved. After the war ended, much of the federal funding for early childhood programs did too. It wasn't until the national War on Poverty campaign of the 1960s that federal funding was once again on the increase. The Head Start program is one of the enduring initiatives of that campaign.

The unique considerations for children's emotional needs, especially during traumatic events such as war or family crises, influenced several researchers during the middle of the 1900s. **Erik Erikson's** (1902–1994) life-span theory of socioemotional development remains a foundation of current beliefs about children's personality advancement (Vander Zanden, 2003). Erikson's theory has been used to guide interactions with infants and children. The early stages of his lifespan development theory are presented in the text box along with implications for early childhood professionals and practice. Young children are highly susceptible to the influence of relationships with adults in their lives, including families and caregivers. Consider the importance of socioemotional development in the early years and strategies for supporting development as you watch this **video**. Early childhood professionals must strive to form close relationships with children and always remember the emotional nature of young children.

Erikson's Life-Span Theory of Socioemotional Development

Birth–1 year	Trust vs. mistrust	Early experiences with parents and caregivers foster feelings of trust and security or mistrust in self and others. Responsive caregiving is essential. Give appropriate stimulation; respond to infant's cues for nourishment, love, play, and sleep.
2–3 years	Autonomy vs. shame and doubt	Newly mobile, children seek to assert their will and control their actions. Supporting children's choice-making and encouraging self-direction are important. Think about the toddler who angrily grabs a shoe, crying, "I do it!" This child needs to build confidence in his or her abilities.
4–5 years	Initiative vs. guilt	Children become curious and want to explore their world. Children need to be encouraged to manipulate objects and direct their own activities.

Another influential psychologist of the time was **Susan Isaacs** (1885–1948). Isaacs used richly detailed qualitative reports, mostly objective observation reports, in an effort to illuminate children's development (Isaacs, 1999). She advocated the importance of

Bank Street College of Education:
The Developmental-Interaction Approach

Blending psychology and education (primarily Dewey's theories) in the creation of the curriculum for young children, development and interaction were at the forefront of the interdisciplinary approach to education at Bank Street. In this active, hands-on, child-centered learning approach, all forms of interactions served as the basis for learning, including children's interaction with

- peers,
- adults,
- materials,
- society/community, and
- ideas.

This led to renaming the program the Developmental-Interaction Approach.

Pervading all Bank Street's work was the mission to foster a new collective society that would nurture all members—young and old alike. This often meant that student teachers were engaging in observation and volunteer work in the community. This mission also guided the curriculum emphasis on social studies—that is, of the experiences of human life across all disciplines. The research on children, practices, theories, and society—as opposed to being a separate entity within the school— ran as a thread throughout both children's programs and student teacher programs. The research and innovations generated through Bank Street's efforts contributed significantly in terms of theory-to-practice applications (Grinberg, 2002).

Lab School

Starting with an interest in researching innovative and experimental practices, Bank Street integrated a nursery school program into the organization's structure. The lab school served as a place to study children, teachers, and learning environments as well as a place where student teachers gained valuable classroom experience. The nature of the curriculum was open ended, where children learned through play and work using a variety of materials.

Teacher Education

The teacher-education branch of Bank Street evolved during a time when discussions of politics and education were at their height. Although much effort was being exerted on the generation of theories and exploration of international approaches and influences, Bank Street became a leader in implementation and practice. Here teachers were inducted into a culture of learning through experience; student teachers were encouraged to approach their teaching as artists but also to employ a scientific approach to inquiry, action, and reflection. Above all else, the progressive approach used at Bank Street sought to open teachers' minds to explore the possibilities in the complex social context of children's lives. The faculty at Bank Street served as in-class models as well as teachers for the student teachers; students could learn through discussions with them and learn by watching them in action. Student teachers took a variety of classes in child development as well as arts and personal development courses.

applying the growing knowledge base in psychology to children's education (Goswami, 2001). She also founded the Department of Child Development at the University of London in 1930, where her work, building on the ideas of Dewey, Freud, and Piaget, influenced methods aimed at promoting social and cognitive development (Aldrich, 2002). She endorsed the belief that children's contact with the world around them formed the basis for their learning, de-emphasizing their internal constructive process (Hall, 2000). On this point, her ideas differed from Piaget's.

Although learner-centered education enjoyed much support from educators and began to garner research support as well, events from across the globe were about to change the educational landscape. In 1957 Russia made headlines when it launched the *Sputnik* satellite into space. At this point in history, this "space race" represented technological advancements, progress, and national pride. The shock of being behind in this leg of the race spurred Americans to look for answers. Their attention and blame turned to current progressive education practices, which some viewed as being permissive and chaotic (Henson, 2003). The pendulum of popularity was swinging again.

In response, more scientific, skills-based approaches to education were embraced. One such scientific method, which gained favor in the early decades of the 1900s and, after a brief fade, regained popularity after *Sputnik* and throughout the latter half of the 1900s, was **Maria Montessori's** (1870–1952) method. Montessori based her method on systematic observations of children's spontaneous activities (Montessori, 1966). She then designed materials through experimentation and reflection. She was highly influential in her homeland of Italy and later throughout the world, and her methods have been influencing early childhood practices since her first early childhood school opened in 1907. The academic, skill-and-drill training emphasis ruled many public school programs until the introduction and enduring effect of constructivism in the latter half of the 1900s.

Education and Intellectual Development

Constructivist theories influencing practice today are grounded in the highly influential work of 20th-century Swiss psychologist Jean Piaget and Russian psychologist Lev Vygotsky.

Jean Piaget (1896–1980) spent his long life studying children's cognitive development, primarily through observation and analysis of children's answers to problem-solving tasks. Piaget observed that children think in qualitatively different ways at different ages, giving rise to his stage theory (Piaget, 1999). Piaget wrote prolifically about cognition, language, intelligence, and children's development (Piaget, 1929, 1954, 1969, 1975). His work has become a foundation for programs such as High/Scope, and it has inspired countless educators and psychologists. He proposed that children seek **equilibrium**, or balance, in their beliefs and understandings of experiences. New information is processed through **assimilation** and **accommodation**, which involve either fitting it into a child's existing belief or by the child's changing his ideas to accept the new information (Piaget, 1969). Piaget regarded these as ongoing cognitive processes, such that a balance or equilibrium at one point would give way to disequilibrium with more new experiences that challenge the child's thinking.

You can see from this brief synopsis that Piaget valued the role of experience as well as the internal processes engaged in by the child on his or her quest to know the world. One important aspect of his work is that Piaget believed that both nature (biological

Equilibrium

Presented by Piaget, the cognitive state of balance, where the child feels comfortable with beliefs, ideas, and knowledge.

Assimilation

Integrating new experiences, ideas, or beliefs into existing knowledge structures (schemas).

Accommodation

Changing existing beliefs based on new information or experience that challenges current knowledge, so new knowledge or understanding is created.

growth) and nurture (people, experiences, events) influence development (Piaget, 1975). This both-and thinking, as opposed to either-or thinking, has become an important feature of current theory and practice.

Although Piaget's work remains foundational, his theories have been challenged in some areas. Many critics believe that changes in thinking occur more as trends, not as steplike stages. Some also believe that the cognitive processing of infants and children may be more advanced than Piaget thought (Sameroff & McDonough, 1994). Proponents of emergent curricula methods, such as interest-based projects, also disagree with Piaget's belief that young children are not capable of advanced thought sufficient to generate hypotheses and propositions (Hall, 2000). New research has shown that, with the help of adult guidance, children demonstrate higher levels of thinking at younger ages than Piaget proposed (Vander Zanden, 2003). Although they were contemporaries, the work of Lev Vygotsky has taken us beyond the theories of Piaget.

Piaget's Stages of Cognitive Development (adapted from Vander Zanden, 2003)

Birth–2 years	Sensorimotor	Infants realize the relationship between sensations and their motor actions. Infants reach and grab items they see; they put items in their mouths; they move their bodies to make objects move, such as a mobile. Around 9 months, infants also learn that objects exist even when they can't see them—called object permanence.
2–7 years	Preoperational	Children begin to think symbolically. They begin to use and master language—a symbol system. Symbolic dramatic play, in which children use an item to represent something else, such as a block for a car, emerges.
7–11 years	Concrete operations	Children begin to think rationally, and they begin to be able to understand conservation—that while an item's shape may change, the mass, weight, number, length, or volume does not. For example, a younger child will see a ball of clay flattened and think the flat one has more mass because it is longer. Children in this stage understand that the lump may be longer but that it remains the same amount. Piaget believed this happens because older children can reverse the flattening action in their heads and imagine the lump as a ball again.
11–older	Formal operations	Abstract thinking develops. Children can now think on the basis of hypotheses and propositions, not just on concrete objects. Children can master more complex scientific and mathematical operations using reversibility and reciprocity.

Lev Vygotsky (1896–1934) spent his relatively short life writing works that were not available to the public until long after his death. Political oppression in his native Soviet Union and late translations into English kept his work from the West for many years. Vygotsky's ideas differ from those of Piaget due to his emphasis on the importance of

Model Language

During the early childhood years, children's language arts development blossoms, including speaking, listening, reading, writing, and thinking. You can help facilitate this development by engaging children in conversations, by expanding their verbalizations, by repeating and extending their ideas, and by modeling your own use of language as a tool of communication and thinking. Talk about your thoughts. Talk yourself through tasks. Explain what you are doing. Show children how you use reading and writing in numerous ways in your own daily life. Keep the language environment rich.`

Private speech

Children's use of language to organize their thinking, first by talking aloud and later as silent, internal talk.

Zone of proximal development

Vygotsky's theory of learning, which posits that learning occurs when children are supported in working on challenging activities that are beyond what they can achieve on their own.

Scaffolding

A teaching technique that involves giving verbal cues, prompts, and suggestions on appropriately challenging activities.

language development as a tool for facilitating and organizing cognitive development. More than just the primary vehicle for communication among people, according to Vygotsky (1978), language is the primary means by which children begin to organize their thinking. With the onset of coherent receptive and expressive speech, children begin to notice how people use words to share ideas as well as talk themselves through problems or think out loud, which later becomes silent thought.

This self-talk, which Vygotsky termed **private speech**, is often intuitively modeled by adults and, in turn, used by children. As children are given verbal cues, directions, or strategies from adults, they often repeat these or similar verbalizations to themselves while they work through problems independently. In this way, they use language not as a means to communicate with others, but as a means to organize their thoughts. Vygotsky believed that private speech was a powerful organizer that became silent and internal as children aged but continued to influence thought (Berk & Winsler, 1995; Vygotsky, 1978).

Firmly opposed to teacher-directed, habit-training modes of education, Vygotsky saw great potential for education to lead development within appropriate limits. His **zone of proximal development** theory suggests that each child has a developmental range within which he or she can be assisted in operating at higher levels than are possible alone. Key features of this theory include an awareness of the child's independent ability, as well as what is beyond his or her ability, and the assistance of a teacher to guide, coach, and prompt the child's thinking. This assistance, called **scaffolding**, changes based on each child's need and current cognitive level. Scaffolding treads a fine line between offering too much help (too easy, doing it for the child) and not enough help (too challenging for the child) (Vygotsky, 1999).

Vygotsky's work also emphasized the role of society and culture in children's development, underscoring the social, group nature of education. This makes sense when you think about why a child raised in England learns to speak English, whereas a child raised in Italy learns to speak Italian. In many more subtle ways, children's family and community culture affect the way they grow, think, and develop. Some cultures value group interdependence, but other cultures emphasize personal independence and self-reliance. These norms and values greatly influence the course of children's development in all domains, particularly social and cognitive. This reflects an interdependent view of growth and development that has great implications for parents and teachers. Current constructivist theorists, including **Jerome Bruner** (b. 1915), continue to build on and refine ideas about how children think, process and store information, and learn (Bruner, 1991). Bruner valued self-discovery as the most important process for learning, emphasizing that children should be given freedom and autonomy to explore their interests (James, 2008).

Another influential theory that emphasizes the influences of a child's cultural context is **Urie Bronfenbrenner's** (1917–2005) bioecological systems theory. Bronfenbrenner has suggested that children live within a system of influences at many levels. The interrelationships among children, family members, neighborhoods, schools, and peers affect the children's growth most directly and profoundly. He also has suggested that larger systems, such as government, broader educational systems, media, and larger social and cultural beliefs, exert influences on children, although perhaps in less direct ways (Bronfenbrenner, 1986). Bronfenbrenner's view underscores that children's development is influenced by dynamic, complex factors that are more or less directly based on the child's home and community context. As you read in previous sections, families and children also influence society and policies, as in, for example, Head Start legislation (which Bronfenbrenner cofounded), school desegregation laws, and the Individuals with Disabilities Education Act.

Vygotsky's Zone of Proximal (or Potential) Development

The lower level of the zone of proximal development (ZPD) is where children operate independently; the upper level children can do only with help (it is beyond their current abilities); and the space in between is where children are engaged in challenging activities with the varying assistance of a more capable partner (Vygotsky, 1978). It is within this central area where learning and knowledge construction occur.

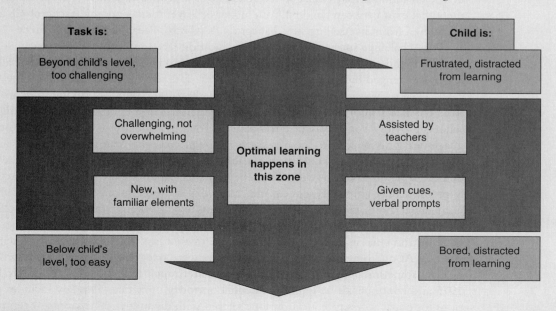

MODERN TRENDS IN EARLY CARE AND EDUCATION: FOCUS ON EQUITY AND DIVERSITY

The multiple influences of families, children, and society are apparent in some of the events of our recent past. The history of education is full of inequities such as separate classrooms and even separate schools for different social classes, ethnicities, races, and abilities. Current laws and beliefs, however, call for integrated, responsive programs that meet the needs of each child and respect all children and families. Some of the most influential legislation affecting schools has come from the sacrifice; tireless work; courage; and blood, sweat, and tears of parents and children.

Political, Legal, and Changes in Practice Over the Past 60 Years

Against the backdrop of the growing civil rights movement in the 1950s, African American families raised their voices and stood up for the rights of all children, regardless of race, to equal schools. The landmark 1954 Supreme Court decision in *Brown v. The Board of Education of Topeka, Kansas* paved the way for the desegregation of U.S. schools. Included in the overarching equality movement of the last part of the 20th century, public policy makers, families, and educators alike sought to even out the disparities affecting children living in poverty.

Throughout history, society has looked to early childhood education as a vehicle for social reform. The 1964 Head Start legislation was enacted to combat poverty and to meet children's diverse needs through comprehensive preschool programming and parent involvement. Other early intervention programs, such as the Chicago Parent Child Centers, which were launched in 1966 and run by the Chicago public schools, are enduring and successful examples of the tremendous positive effect high-quality programming can have on children and families (Reynolds, Miedel, & Mann, 2000). Providing access to quality early education has long been connected to efforts to reduce disparities in academic achievement that exist between children from higher or lower socioeconomic backgrounds as well as children from diverse linguistic backgrounds (Castro, Paez, Dickinson, & Frede, 2011).

The challenge in receiving an equal education faced by many dual-language learners (children whose home language is other than English) is an area that has been socially and legally challenged by families for many decades. The revolutionary 1974 Supreme Court case of *Lau v. Nichols* was filed on behalf of nearly 3,000 Chinese-speaking students in the San Francisco school system who were receiving instruction in only English. Although the schools provided some assistance to Spanish-speaking students, no assistance in other languages was provided. The case was based on the premise that, due to the students' linguistic diversity and lack of native language support from the schools, the students were being denied equal access to public education as protected under the Civil Rights Act. The Supreme Court ultimately agreed, indicating that an English-only curriculum could discriminate against non-English-speaking students, even if unintentionally (Moran, 2005).

Continuing the work of breaking barriers to equality in education, families once again were instrumental in changing established practices of institutionalizing children with disabilities. At one time, children with disabilities were relegated to unsatisfactory programs or even sometimes to prisonlike institutions. After much lobbying, IDEA became law in 1975 and continues to be highly influential on today's practice. This law includes provisions for equal access to education for children with disabilities. The law has been revised in recent years in an effort to continue the process of providing educational opportunities

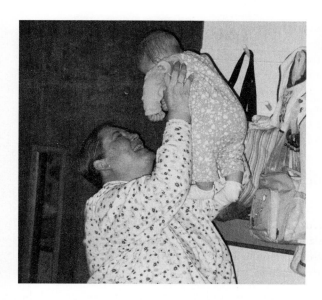

Families, as well as society, impact children's lives; children also impact families and communities.

and full participation in the **least restrictive environment** for children with special needs (Turnbull & Cilley, 1999). This means that children with disabilities should be included in regular classrooms with typically developing peers whenever possible to allow them to reach their fullest potential. They may be included in regular classrooms with assistance or at times may participate in special classes, as dictated by individual needs. Listen to the professionals reflect on the progression of inclusive practices in this short **video**.

Our current educational climate is influenced by politics, which place an increasing emphasis on holding schools and programs accountable for children's performance. The belief is that if schools and teachers are held to high standards and made responsible for whether children succeed, then the quality of instruction will improve. Accountability and standards have, at their core, the goal of ensuring that all our children have access to the very best educational experiences. While the underlying ideals may be worthy, the associated actions have not always translated into children's best interests.

The quality of education in America has been at the fore of the political agenda and public financial responsibility since the 1965 passing of the Elementary and Secondary Education Act (ESEA). In 2001 President George W. Bush included the **No Child Left Behind Act** (NCLB Act) in a reauthorization of the ESEA (passed in 2002). The NCLB Act sought to improve the quality of education and improve outcomes for all students, particularly lower-income students, by increasing the quality of teachers and the schools' accountability for student achievement. NCLB addressed teacher proficiency by requiring that all teachers be *highly qualified,* meaning that all teachers hold a bachelor's degree and state teaching license as well as demonstrate competency in the subject matter they teach (U.S. Department of Education, 2004a). NCLB sought to motivate education reform and improvement by linking school funding to student scores on achievement tests (U.S. Department of Education, 2004b). This kind of accountability has led to the term *high-stakes testing* where student test scores are used to determine school effectiveness.

The resulting pressures of unrealistic expectations and "all proficient or lose funding" high stakes led to increased time spent on narrow test preparation at the expense of meaningful instruction; increased anxiety; and reports of teachers and administrators cheating, misrepresenting data, or simply pressuring low-scoring students to drop out in an effort to increase overall school proficiency rates (Desimone, 2013; Verbruggen, 2012). However,

Least restrictive environment

Part of the IDEA, the goal that children with disabilities be provided with educational programming and services in classroom environments that reflect their highest functioning level, ideally in regular education classrooms with supports as needed.

test scores alone do not provide an accurate picture of a child's learning, and major conflicts arise from such practices with young children (Jones, 2004). As good educators know, fair and accurate student assessment, particularly assessment of young children, should include a variety of authentic assessment measures (such as observation) and be viewed as an ongoing process (Geist & Baum, 2005). Best practices in assessment of young children extend from best practices in early education: integrated, authentic, relevant, and aligned with developmental expectations (Bredekamp & Copple, 2009). As politics and practice shifted once again, a new take on the old theme of education improvement took shape.

Politics Today: Early Childhood in the Spotlight

In 2009 the Obama administration unveiled the Race to the Top (RTTT) Fund, which is administered by the U.S. Department of Education (USDOE, 2009). RTTT is a competitive grant program that emphasizes major school improvement and reform with special focus on improving student achievement in historically lower-performing students. Key provisions of the RTTT initiative include

- using standards and assessments that prepare students for success in college and the workplace;
- instituting data collection and tracking systems to assess and inform practice;
- recruiting, retaining, and supporting effective professionals, especially in higher-needs schools; and
- improving outcomes for currently low-achieving schools.

In 2011 a new focus in the RTTT initiative emerged as a spotlight focus on improving quality and access of early learning programs. The Race to the Top Early Learning Challenge (RTTT-ELC) grant program is a joint initiative between the U.S. Department of Education and the Department of Health and Human Services and provides $500 million in federal funds

In culturally responsive practice, teachers value children's diverse family backgrounds, unique abilities, and promote positive interactions among all children

for states to improve early care and education, particularly for children from lower socioeco-nomic backgrounds and dual-language learners (Kelleher, 2011). Once again, assessing and tracking children's progress are key features of the policy, though grantee states appear to be proposing more appropriate practices this time. The focus for many states is squarely on creat-ing cohesive systems and structures to support professionalizing and increasing quality. Devel-opment and implementation of quality rating systems for early learning programs is a prime focus for current early learning initiatives and includes important emphases on (Maxwell, 2012)

- family involvement policies and practices;
- connecting learning experiences across the early years (birth through third grade);
- addressing standards in all developmental and learning areas, including those for dual-language learners; and
- observation-based tools to determine school readiness in children and preparation effectiveness in their preschool program.

Culturally Responsive Teaching in Today's Diverse World

Early childhood practice today requires that we continually strive to create learning envi-ronments that align with changing laws and policies but also uphold high standards of qual-ity and developmentally appropriate practice as advocated by professional organizations and supported by our current research base. It is not an easy task, but it is of paramount impor-tance for our children. Our task as teachers and advocates is always to find a balance among

- accountability for children's outcomes in early learning standards as well as overall development;
- authentic assessments and standardized tests and measures;
- individual interests and needs;
- developmental needs and appropriateness;
- integrated social, emotional, cognitive, and physical learning and development;
- divergent theories and expert beliefs;
- expert advice and our own intuitive knowledge; and
- strength and needs of ourselves, our children, our families, and our society.

Few countries can boast of the richness of diversity that thrives in the United States. Although as a nation and society we have made great strides in realizing the centuries-old dream of social equity and equality, we still have work ahead of us. Understanding and respecting diversity is currently a top priority for all early childhood educators as we finally embrace more **culturally responsive practices**.

Culturally responsive practices involve acknowledging and respecting diversity and supporting all students' unique family cultures. Family cultural context may be shaped by many differences including language, ethnicity, race, ability, family economic status, reli-gion, family structure, and family values and traditions. Current guidelines for quality practice include the following research-based suggestions for culturally responsive teach-ing (Castro, Paez, Dickinson, & Frede, 2011; NAEYC, 1995):

- Maintain children's home language (which assists, not hinders, in learning English).
- Include a child's home language in your classroom whenever possible (label shelves, incorporate numbers and simple words into the class vocabulary).

Culturally responsive practices

An approach to programming that values, supports, and embraces diverse racial, ethnic, linguistic, and cultural influences and backgrounds.

- Use visual tools, gestures, and emphasis to encourage language learners' comprehension.
- Invite families to participate in class activities whenever possible.
- Foster home-school connections, using translation software or community services when needed.
- Seek out resources and information that will help you understand and value individual cultures.
- Design classroom experiences that are responsive to, and inclusive of, each child's unique family experience and context as well as each child's unique strengths and needs.
- Give all children opportunities to represent their knowledge and experiences in a variety of ways (verbal, visual, kinesthetic, etc.).
- Maintain predictable classroom routines while being flexible as needed.

CONCLUSION

Along the winding road of the history of early childhood education, many prominent people have contributed, influenced, and informed current beliefs about best practices, particularly in learner-centered approaches to educating young children. We've certainly come a long way, but the road is laid out before us too. It might be bumpy in places and not well traveled, but ours is a profession built on innovation and a willingness to take risks and change practices for the better. Although we stand on a foundation laid over centuries, we are still pioneers ever committed to the quest of improving practice and life for our children. At the heart of all early childhood practice is the enduring belief in the worth of all children, the value of play as a means of learning, and the potential for quality early education to improve children's and families' lives. Our task as educators is to continue reflecting on our beliefs, challenging ourselves to improve practices, and dedicating ourselves to ensuring success for each child.

SUMMARY

- Throughout the long and complex history of early childhood education in the United States, there have been overarching trends that have distinguished various periods.
- During the 1700s in Colonial America, schools were designed to instill moral and religious values through the reading of the Bible, and at home fathers were regarded as the guiding influence.
- In the 1800s the role of mothers as the primary providers of child care came into the spotlight.
- As more women entered the workplace, the need for early childhood education outside the home increased, and early childhood education emerged as an important profession.
- European and U.S. educators in the 1800s called for education as a key to social reform and as a means of ameliorating the negative effect of living in poverty. This goal still remains important today.

- In the 1900s new scientific views of the study of children and childhood took hold and expanded the knowledge base.

- Many enduring practices and beliefs formed during the progressive era of the 1900s, including learner-centered programming, interest-based project curricula, lab schools, and teachers as researchers.

- Amid the scientific revolution of the middle to later 1900s, education continued to grow as a science worthy of study and an important profession.

- Early childhood education became a public concern as federal legislation was enacted to meet the needs of children living in poverty or with disabilities.

- With the new century, accountability and standards took center stage and continue to be prominent aspects of early childhood practice.

- In today's increasingly diverse world, teachers must use culturally responsive practices to value each family's unique culture and background.

CHAPTER LEARNING GOALS SELF-ASSESSMENT

Use this chart to write down three to five key points for each learning goal that you learned from this chapter.

Identify overarching themes in the history of care and education for young children.	
Discuss key influences on early education in the 1600s and 1700s.	
Examine values about children and education in the 1800s.	
Compare beliefs and practices in the 1900s, and make connections to present-day practice.	
Explore early childhood best practices in the context of today's diverse world.	

APPLICATION ACTIVITIES

Discussion Prompts

1. What are your beliefs about the innate nature of children? How should children learn, and how should they be taught?

2. Do you think parents or schools are best equipped to care for and teach their infants, preschoolers, and school-age children?

3. What do you believe should be the primary goals and functions of early childhood programs?

In Class   In small groups, create a time line of events, beliefs, and people to represent the history of early childhood education. You can select highlights from the chapter—key people and theories that show change and trends throughout time. You do not have to include every name and date. Use whatever materials you have available. Here is your chance to make the sometimes dry reading of history more lively and colorful.

In the Field   Visit an area child care center or school, or visit the center or school's Web site. Arrange to interview the program director or school administrator. While exploring the site, find the program's mission. Ask the administrator to explain the school's philosophy, mission, and prevailing views of children and families. Make notes about your impressions of how the environment supports the responses. For example, a center that speaks of the importance of family involvement in children's education might have a parent bulletin board, family resource room, family welcome space, and the like. What visible signs do you see of the philosophy, mission, and view of children? Write a brief reflection paper that summarizes the interview responses, includes the school's mission, and presents your perspective and impressions, integrating your thoughts on the chapter opening and closing questions about early childhood programs. Include any brochures or other literature that are available to you on your visit or from the Web site.

For Your Portfolio   This activity could be used as an artifact in your portfolio under knowledge of the field or development. Throughout this journey through history, there were swings in beliefs and practice related to the following issues. For each issue, write a brief statement about your own beliefs, including what influenced them.

- The prevailing views of children and how children develop and learn
- The role of families, particularly women at home and in society
- International philosophers or educators and trends influencing American programming
- Effects of socioeconomic class divisions on programming
- Early childhood settings as custodial care or education
- The goals and purposes of the programming

RELATED WEB LINKS

History of American Education Web Project
www.ux1.eiu.edu/~cfrnb/index.html

The Gilder Lehrman Institute of American History
www.gilderlehrman.org/teachers/modules.html

Info USA
usinfo.org/enus/education/index.html

CHAPTER

Professionalism in Early Childhood Education: Framing Best Practices

Chapter Learning Goals

- Identify role and purpose of professional associations.

- Identify scope and key professional guidelines of the National Association for the Education of Young Children.

- Create connections between professional guidelines and best practices.

- Discuss key features of evidence-based practice in professional decision-making.

- Examine features and outcomes of professional quality rating scales.

The field of early childhood education has a long history of reflecting on evolving practice. Throughout the history of early childhood education, evidence has emerged highlighting the importance of appropriate learning experiences in the early years for healthful development. Because of the increasing numbers of children entering early childhood programs and the growing numbers of children from homes where English is not the primary language, the need for articulated professional standards emerges as an essential emphasis for providers. An array of professional associations exists to guide providers in the many facets of professional practice, which include curriculum planning, teacher education, learning standards, inclusion, assessment, ethical practice, and program quality rating systems.

One of these, the National Association for the Education of Young Children (NAEYC), offers a channel through which to generate and disseminate information and guiding frameworks about practices serving children from birth through age 8 and their families. NAEYC has worked closely with a variety of other professional associations to create many joint position statements in an effort to ensure an integrated, collaborative approach to working with and for children and families. Nearly 20 years ago, NAEYC addressed the need for standards of practice by writing their Developmentally Appropriate Practice (DAP) and Code of Ethical Conduct (also referred to as the Code) statements. The statements present standards of best practices and standards of professional behavior, respectively. In concert, the regularly revised statements provide a solid foundation for making sound decisions about practice and meeting professional responsibilities in teaching and caring for young children.

Today professional associations continue to provide support for early childhood professionals through research, publishing, conferences, accreditation of quality early childhood programs, and quality rating systems. This chapter presents information about the scope and work of professional early childhood associations as well as practical application of two key emphases in today's professional practice: evidence-based decision-making and quality rating systems.

CLASSROOM VIEW

Director Interview: Ethics in Action

It's a warm, clear morning in May as you prepare to visit a mid-sized infant, toddler, and preschool center in a small suburb. The center, a franchise, has a capacity of 125 children, and the owner/director, Lisa, is committed to child-centered practices. She finds resource and inspiration in constructivism and diverse learning styles as well as in her own experience as a teacher.

The center fully supports NAEYC's Developmentally Appropriate Practice (DAP) and program accreditation guidelines, which have more stringent facility and program standards than the center's state regulations. Lisa describes how she learned about DAP in college and how she conducted many observations of programs to understand what DAP really means in practice. As a new teacher, she worked in a center that relied on teacher-directed, whole-group activities. She became frustrated with having to redirect the children many times during the day to sit quietly and pay attention to the teachers.

After several years, she left her first center, knowing that she needed to do things differently. She found another position in a center that encouraged child-initiated activities almost exclusively. Teachers prepared the environment and materials and stepped back to observe how children interacted with their materials. At this center, Lisa learned a lot about how to design spaces that invite children to explore and how to use observations effectively to assess and plan.

Over the years, though, she came to realize that children need some guidance and active support to make the most of their explorations. She opened her own center and made a commitment to a balanced, holistic approach to educating and caring for young children. First and foremost, Lisa describes the importance of balancing the following key factors:

- *Teacher-directed activities and child-initiated explorations*
- *Whole-group, small-group, and individual experiences*
- *Skill-based lessons and interest-based projects*

- *Teachers and children sharing control over classroom activities and topics*
- *Integration of principles of child development*

To see these things in action, Lisa invites you to visit the toddler classroom across the foyer.

Toddler Classroom: DAP in Action

There are eight toddlers and three teachers in the room this morning. On some days, there are 12 toddlers with 3 teachers. Lauren, one of the teachers, explains that they use a primary caregiver system, in which each teacher is assigned four children. Although all the teachers work with all the children, the primary caregivers maintain responsibility for observation reports, assessments, parent communication, and generally overseeing the children's daily activities. They are sort of the keepers of official information about their four children and are the parents' main contact person.

The goal of their primary caregiver system is to promote strong bonds between one teacher and the child and family. "Being a primary caregiver lets me really focus on a smaller number of children in some ways, although the other teachers and I share information about all the children so we can answer any parents' questions. I like being able to do more in-depth observation reports and assessments too. By sharing these tasks, we are each able to do more for our children. I know my primaries so much more deeply than I did when we were all responsible for all the children. And sharing the responsibilities makes us [the teachers] all feel like equals. We really work as a team."

As you continue to observe the room, the last few children are just finishing up with a snack and are on their way to wash their hands. The toddlers enjoy splashing in the sink while a teacher cheerfully talks to them about the sensation of the bubbly soap and the warm water. Another teacher is encouraging a small group of toddlers to put their coats on by themselves. The children are intently focused on getting their arms through the sleeves while the teacher patiently watches, praising their efforts. You notice how responsive the teachers are with the children. Even during mundane tasks such as hand washing and coat dressing, the interactions feel warm and personal. The teachers do not talk above the children's heads or speak at them. They express a genuine interest in being there with them and exploring all the wonders of their world. They seem so present with the children. The children respond with curiosity, confidence, and delight at their discoveries and achievements. You feel a sense of love and joy in this room; it reminds you of why you want to be a teacher.

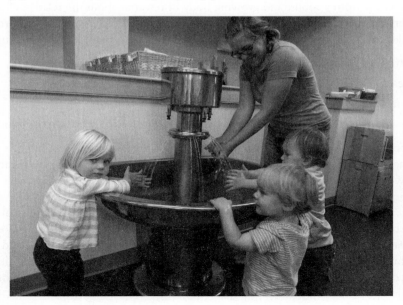

Most toddlers enjoy sensory experiences, even routines like handwashing.

The children and teachers prepare to go outside. They are excitedly talking about what they think they will see in the garden. Some of the children reach their hands over their heads and stretch out their fingers. One teacher translates the movement by saying, "Yes! I think we might see flowers blooming! Our bulbs are growing more and more each day, just like you!" The three teachers and most of the children sing a song about flowers growing as they make their way outside. Later on, Lauren explains their interest in the garden.

FRAMING PROFESSIONALISM: ASSOCIATIONS THAT GUIDE AND SUPPORT BEST PRACTICES

Lisa's memories of conflicts, resolutions, and becoming a professional underscore the heart of what professional associations strive to promote. It is about setting high standards of professionalism and practice, about meeting challenges as a community of partners, and about maintaining a high degree of personal integrity in handling any situation that arises as we ensure the very best in early care and education. Achieving these goals is an ongoing process that demands continued reflection, self-assessment, partnerships, and outreach. In this **video**, consider this teacher's perspective on being intentional about learning goals and environment. In addition, there are four common threads that serve to define essential components of professionalism in early care and education (Caulfield, 1997):

1. Specialized knowledge of children's development
2. Partnership with families
3. Observation and assessment
4. Code of ethics

Meaningfully integrating these common threads requires teachers to be well prepared, dedicated, motivated, and passionate about their profession (Moyles, 2001). Reflecting what we currently know from a robust and growing body of research about the relative effectiveness of teachers based on qualifications, essential policy considerations in support of a professional early childhood field include (Barnett, 2004; Martin, Meyer, Jones, Nelson, & Ting, 2010)

- strong teacher preparation (specialized college degree programs),
- teacher certification and assessment based on high standards,
- ongoing professional development, and
- wages and benefits comparable to other segments of the teaching profession.

In concert with quality teacher education and professional development training, becoming familiar with early childhood–related associations and organizations can support both new and experienced teachers. There are scores of associations and agencies working to enhance the practice and professionalism of early care and education, just a small sample of which will be highlighted in this chapter along with the work of NAEYC. For a sizable list of related associations, visit the Council for Professional Recognition's Web site at www.cdacouncil.org, click on the Resource Center at the top of the page, and click on Early Childhood Organizations on the left. The associations listed are specifically chosen for early childhood teachers and can help you prepare for your first days of teaching as well as provide options for enhancing your professional development.

The Association for Childhood Education International (ACEI) was founded in 1892 on a platform based on the work of Friedrich Froebel and sought to promote quality professional preparation of kindergarten teachers (ACEI, n.d.). Today ACEI has an expanded mission to enhance development of young children (infancy through middle childhood) all over the world and to support high standards of professional development for early childhood educators. With a uniquely global perspective, ACEI's recommendations for equitable practice are outlined in the Global Guidelines for Early Childhood Education and Care in the 21st Century (Sandell, Hardin, & Wortham, 2010), which guide early childhood practice in the following areas:

- Environment and physical space of settings for children
- Curriculum content and pedagogy
- Early childhood educators and caregivers
- Partnership with families and communities
- Services for young children with special needs
- Accountability, supervision, and management of programs for children

The guidelines provide clear, concrete indicators of quality ethical practice within a comprehensive approach that emphasizes the larger context of children's lives. In addition, they correspond to a program assessment tool that, like the guidelines, is freely available in several languages on the ACEI Web site. The program assessment tool offers teachers and administrators the opportunity to self-evaluate, rate practice, and reflect on how practice compares with these key indicators of quality. These tools support teachers in the ongoing process of self-reflection and assessment, but the association also publishes research-to-practice journals aimed at reviewing and informing policy and best practices.

Whereas groups such as ACEI and NAEYC take a comprehensive, global perspective on guiding practice, other organizations focus on supporting segments of the early childhood population such as infants and toddlers, family child care providers, or children with exceptionalities. The Division for Early Childhood (DEC) of the Council for Exceptional Children represents the largest association serving children with exceptionalities and their families. With a mission to promote policies and best practices, DEC publishes position statements, journals, tools, and tips for administrators, teachers, and parents and provides training opportunities across the country. The "tools you can use" section of the DEC Web site includes free checklists and workbooks to assist providers in integrating successful inclusion strategies and to help parents evaluate the inclusiveness of early childhood programs.

Just as inclusive practices and valuing the diversity among children and families have become hallmarks of quality early care and education, the past several decades have yielded scores of reports emphasizing the critical importance of the first 3 years of life. Since 1977 ZERO TO THREE has used a multidisciplinary approach to supporting and enhancing the health and development of infants and toddlers through research, advocacy, publications, and practical tools for families and professionals. The scope of work encompassed within the ZERO TO THREE organization demonstrates a truly comprehensive, multidisciplinary approach by integrating current research-based recommendations from relevant fields, which cover topics such as the following:

- Mental health
- Nutrition

- Disaster relief
- Child welfare
- Language and literacy
- Abuse and neglect
- Developmental screenings
- Early education, brain development, play
- Behavior and temperament

The multipronged approach of addressing professionals, parents, and public policy is a hallmark of professional associations and reflects the importance of a system-wide approach to optimizing developmental outcomes. You may have noticed that the emphasis on

Supporting caregivers' efforts to promote healthy development in infants and toddlers is also an important aspect encompassed within the scope of early childhood education.

policy advocacy and especially on including families in the early childhood professional effort is a common thread throughout these associations, and you will see it emphasized in the work of NAEYC.

FOUNDATION AND SCOPE OF **NAEYC**

Evolving out of the progressive era and the founding of the National Association for Nursery Education by Patty Smith Hill, NAEYC was officially established out of Hill's efforts in 1926 (Bredekamp, 1997; NAEYC, 2004). Even at this early stage of the organization, the goals included a desire to promote high-quality programs that met certain accepted standards and a desire to remain flexible and responsive to innovations in the field.

Since the 1960s there has been a growing focus on the lasting effects of early childhood experiences. Whether the effects are positive or negative depends on the quality and appropriateness of the program. As more and more children entered early childhood programs in the 1970s and 1980s, new research on the effects of such programming emerged. From this research arose a need for the crystallization of a guiding framework to help early childhood professionals align their teaching with sound theory-to-practice suggestions (Dunn & Kontos, 1997). In response to this long-standing concern about quality, NAEYC developed a system for evaluating and accrediting programs in 1985 and the first DAP framework in 1987. Both were based on high standards of evidence-based practice that emerged from developmental theories (and later sociocultural and ecosystems theories) of growth, learning, and teaching. The Code of Ethical Conduct was adopted in 1989 (Baptiste & Reyes, 2002).

At the heart of these statements is a set of *core values,* which are foundational to the DAP and the Code statements. The core values include a commitment to (Bredekamp & Copple, 1997)

- appreciate childhood as a unique stage to be valued in the present, not just as a time of preparation for the future;
- use knowledge of child development as the basis of all work with children;
- appreciate and promote the bonds between children and family;
- maintain a view of the child that encompasses the context of their family, culture, and community experience;
- interact with all individuals with respect; and
- make every effort to ensure that all children and adults reach their full potential.

The DAP and Code of Ethical Conduct frameworks have become cornerstones in defining ideals in the practice of early childhood care and education.

The DAP Framework: Background and Overarching Values

The original and revised versions of the DAP framework were undertaken in response to the trend toward a pushing down of inappropriately academic elementary education curricula into the early years and requests from practitioners for guidance on best practices in education and care of young children (Bredekamp & Copple, 1997; Bredekamp & Copple, 2009). In response to ever-evolving changes in cultural contexts of families as well as our research base, NAEYC convenes a diverse group of individuals to engage in a major

Accurate assessment is an area that is sometimes challenging for teachers but is increasingly emphasized in our standards-driven and evidence-based era. Best practices guide teachers to engage in systematic authentic assessments that are used to inform curriculum-planning decisions and evaluations of children's progress (Bredekamp & Copple, 2009). Appropriate assessment strategies include observations, work-sampling portfolios, and performance on authentic tasks, such as younger children's stacking blocks and pouring water into a cup or older children's orally presenting a group project. The assessment process is also an important time to foster reciprocal relationships with families. Families have a wealth of information to provide about their children in the broader context of their lives, which, when paired with information from the classroom context, presents a more accurate picture of the child (Moore, 2000). Validating the contributions families make to enhance children's learning and development is a key thread that runs throughout the DAP statement.

revision process to the DAP statement at roughly 10-year intervals, with the most recent revision completed in 2009.

With a theoretical basis relying on decades of research in developmental psychology, sociocultural constructivism, bioecological systems, and others, the DAP statement validates young children as active, motivated learners who are curious and capable of exploring their world. Within the DAP framework, excellent teachers design learning around child-centered play- and interest-based integrated activities, which include child- and teacher-guided experiences. Above all else, these experiences and settings reflect both age and individual appropriateness and unique family and community cultural contexts. Age appropriateness is defined as the awareness of universal progressions of typical development (developmental milestones) in each domain that are expected in all children. NAEYC also recognizes that not all children develop in precisely the same ways or reach milestones at the same times. Therefore, teachers are also called upon to incorporate knowledge of individual differences in children as they design environment and instruction to ensure appropriateness for each child (Bredekamp & Copple, 2009). Listen to the professionals in this **video** describe how general knowledge of children's development and specific knowledge of each individual child's needs are essential aspects of all high-quality early childhood programming.

Several overarching themes are essential aspects of DAP:

- *Excellence and Equity:* committing to creating opportunities for each and every child to have access to high-quality, stimulating, supportive, and challenging learning experiences

- *Intentionality and Effectiveness:* excellent teachers are deliberate and thoughtful in the decisions they make for children, relying on research evidence and individualized assessment data to inform decisions for children

- *Continuity and Change:* recognizing that the field of teaching is ever changing and evolving as our collective knowledge base grows and shifts, while also holding fast

All children learn best through sensory, hands-on experiences.

to core values such as the value of play, a holistic view of children (whole person or system), and a dedication to meaningful partnerships with families

- *Joy and Learning:* carefully attending to the balance of experiences for children that provide enjoyment and delight with appropriately challenging and complex problems and tasks that empower children as capable and competent in their world

Perhaps the biggest theme in the DAP statements is the emphasis on avoiding *either-or* thinking (such as in teacher-directed versus child-initiated curriculum) in favor of a *both-and* approach to working with children. For example, the original version's strong cautions against the use of direct instruction on academics have softened somewhat with the recognition than some adult-guided instruction can be developmentally appropriate and beneficial to children's learning. There remains an emphasis on the importance of social-emotional factors in predicting later school success, especially the development of self-regulation. In regard to instructional strategies, teachers are now encouraged to follow several basic goals, including the following (Dickinson, 2002; Bredekamp & Copple, 2009):

- Skillfully balancing child-initiated activities and teacher-guided instruction
- Recognizing universals and individuality in children's development
- Valuing each child's family cultural context
- Providing routines, boundaries, and limits and allowing children to make choices
- Supporting children's need to work in groups and alone on individual tasks
- Creating bridges between preschool-age programs and early elementary school experiences, to promote success in school and beyond (especially literacy and mathematics)

In the director interview with Lisa at the start of the chapter, we can see some of these changes taking place. Lisa first found herself teaching in a heavily teacher-directed program. She then switched schools and taught at a center with a strictly child-initiated program. When she balanced both approaches to more effectively meet the children's needs, she settled into a style that felt right.

Changing Demographics

Across the nation, schools are seeing increases in diversity in student populations with the percentages of Black/African American, Hispanic, Asian/Pacific Islander, and Alaskan/Native American students increasing, as reported by the National Center for Educational Statistics (USDOE, 2009a). In 2008 the distribution of national public school enrollment by race/ethnicity was

- 56% white,
- 21% Hispanic,
- 17% Black/African American,
- 5% Asian/Pacific Islander, and
- 1% Alaskan/Native American.

Hispanic student enrollment increased by the greatest percentage (5.5%) between 2000 and 2009 (USDOE, 2009b), while percentage of white students dropped from 61% to 56% (the only racial/ethnic category to see a decrease). Although changes in national averages may seem relatively minor, there is tremendous variation based on specific state and locale (city, rural, or urban fringe). By 2008, nearly half of all public school students of color were enrolled in schools in cities. State-by-state comparisons demonstrate the wide range of student race/ethnicity enrollment, with the District of Columbia reporting 95% enrollment of students of color in 2008 (Black/African American students made up 83% of the student population) and Maine and Vermont reporting 95% enrollment of white students. In the same year, New Mexico reported that Hispanic students (56%) made up the largest segment of their student population (USDOE, 2009a).

These changes, variety in student populations, and diversity from one area to another require teachers to be prepared to work sensitively and effectively with all unique family cultures and backgrounds.

Core Messages of the DAP Framework

All professionals working with and for young children must continually make decisions about how best to meet children's needs and enhance development. Several sources of information should guide professionals' decisions about effective teaching practices (Bredekamp & Copple, 2009):

- Knowledge of universal norms in child development and learning (typical timing, pace, and sequence of development and skills)
- Knowledge of each individual child
- Knowledge of each child's unique social and cultural background

Because each of these elements is continually changing, teachers must learn from research, from each other, and from children and families. The roles of the teacher as a knowledgeable reflective practitioner, thoughtful decision-maker, and learner define

TABLE 3-1 Foundations of Decision-Making in DAP

Knowledge of Children's Development	Knowledge of Individual Child's Development	Knowledge of the Child's Unique Social and Cultural Background
• Think about children's development from a holistic perspective to create learning environments and experiences that meaningfully foster all areas of development. • Understand typical expectations of milestones in distinct domains (cognitive, social, emotional, and physical). • Recognize interconnected relationships among domains. • Support development and learning across domains and content areas by creating learning experiences that integrate several development or content areas within one topic or lesson.	• Observe each child to attend to unique pace and path of individual development. • Individualize materials or experiences for each child to naturally support diverse abilities and styles within one classroom community. • Developmentally appropriate practices validate and support the many ways children think, explore, understand, communicate, and represent their ideas.	• Each child's specific family and cultural context has tremendous influence on their learning and development. • Invite meaningful participation with families to learn about and integrate each child's home life into the program or classroom. • Understand and value families' unique goals for their children, strengths, and needs for support. • Use play as an authentic framework for children's learning and to present experiences that challenge children within the upper limit of their current developmental level.

the teacher as a professional (Bredekamp & Copple, 2009). The unwavering emphasis on valuing diversity among children's families, community, and cultural context has become an overarching theme in culturally competent teaching today. Table 3–1 outlines key considerations in the essential components of professional decision-making in DAP.

Teachers use everyday experiences as opportunities to get to know children and strengthen relationships.

Putting It Into Practice

Integrated learning experiences

Activities that build skills and foster competency in more than one area.

Examples of Integrated Learning Experiences

As children develop the cognitive ability to combine sounds into words, their social development is affected by the ability to interact with the people around them.

As infants' physical development allows for more refined, purposeful grasping of objects, their cognitive development is enhanced by the opportunity to explore and learn about those new objects in their hands.

Toddlers in the garden project experienced the physical sensation of digging in the dirt and the texture of the cool water moistening the ground. They talked about how it felt, looked, and smelled. They delighted in singing songs with movements that represented the growing plants. They visited with the older children at the center to hear stories about the garden. Each day, the children looked for changes in the garden. Many of them enjoyed looking at pictures of plants and flowers in gardening books. Some of the children also painted flowers on the easel like the ones they saw in the books.

CLASSROOM VIEW: The Code of Ethical Conduct: Key Principles

Staff Meeting at the Center

Lisa, the director from the opening program visit, describes an example of applying the Code of Ethical Conduct in practice. "All the staff come together for bimonthly planning and sharing meetings. Building a feeling of mutual respect and open sharing of knowledge has really helped make this center a place where teachers want to work. So many centers have a difficult time with teacher turnover, which is hard on the children. Particularly our infants and toddlers, but all children in general need the stability of regular teachers in order to form close attachments. Without a strong, secure emotional foundation, their learning and development here at the center are jeopardized. I take every opportunity I can find to remind teachers just how important their influence is on our children and to validate the work they are doing." She goes on to talk about the early days of the center when teachers were used to doing their jobs and no more.

There was a pervasive feeling of disconnect among the teachers; each took care of his or her own room and did not network with others. Lisa knew this situation wouldn't change unless she directly addressed it, and she called a full staff meeting to air her concerns. The meeting quickly turned into a complaining session in which teachers shared similar issues with Lisa and each other. They turned to Lisa to fix their problems. Lisa saw an opportunity to use what she learned about resolving staff conflicts through the Code of Ethics guidelines, and she took it.

She focused on the kindergarten teaching team. Lisa facilitated a brief conflict-resolution session in which each teacher listened to the others as they openly shared their issues. The teachers each shared several things they thought were working well and a few things with which they were dissatisfied. Lisa then told them that it was their responsibility to work out their issues directly with one another in a respectful, supportive way and that she was there to facilitate that direct approach. She reminded them that this was their center as much as anyone else's and that the children depended on each of them working as a team. Lisa recalled how nervous she was when she said to them, "You are professionals. You are here because you chose to be a positive influence in the lives of your children. It is up to you to see that commitment through in all the big and little things we, as teachers, do. It may mean cleaning up or staying a few minutes late one day, and it certainly means respecting the need for families and teachers to work together. It is up to all of you to take pride in your work."

As she spoke, she saw their demeanor change. She saw them sit up straighter and nod their heads. In fact, all the staff seemed to become a bit more open. One teacher said, "I am so glad you said that." The kindergarten teachers agreed that they did not like their room to look dirty and made a schedule of tasks to complete during their shifts. They often felt disconnected from parents because drop-off and pickup times were often rushed. They agreed to keep a "back-and-forth" journal in which they could leave notes about things to share with parents when either of them was not there. Other teachers began to share ideas that they could use and some they themselves wanted to try. They decided to schedule a time for parents to come in for group activities. They rearranged morning and evening tasks so they would have more time to linger with parents.

"By the end of our first meeting, the teachers seemed energized and excited. After a long day's work, this was a new sight for me! They usually were tired and ready to bolt out the door. But here they were lingering, talking, and praising each other's ideas. As conversations wound down, I told them all how proud I was to be working with such a dedicated, enthusiastic team. The tone of the center has become one of teamwork and of personal and professional integrity and one in which we always remember why we are here: to provide the absolute best possible environment for our children. Remembering why we chose this work in the first place is humbling and makes us appreciate ourselves and each other for our shared commitment."

Lisa reflected on the process by saying, "It certainly has been hard work to get where we are today, but our staff, parents, and community have no doubt about the rewards. Seeing our children developing into capable, healthy, curious people who embrace challenges and work together to solve them reminds us every day that there is no more important work."

Putting It Into Practice

Individual Development

Although your studies will give you a background in developmental theories, the only way to really see individual diversity is by carefully observing individual children. Observing children and making notes must be a regular part of your day. You can create a rotating schedule, making observation notes on each child within a week or two. Then you can use your notes to tailor individual plans to maximize each child's development, notice emerging interests, and assess progress. Whenever you individualize instruction in this way, be sure to start your observations by noting what the child likes or is interested in, then what he or she is good at or can do well, and finally what the child is learning to do or what developmental goals he or she is working on at the moment. Use what you know about the child's likes and abilities to address the current project.

The process of reflecting on and rethinking your own beliefs while embracing and validating many different perspectives is a requisite for being a professional educator. This is why you may find yourself writing reflective statements, generating personal philosophies, and exploring so many different approaches and beliefs about teaching and learning throughout your studies. This reflective habit should continue as you move throughout your professional career. The commitment to high standards and making equitable decisions as you carry out the duties of the profession are the hallmarks of professional ethics.

With the growth of the field and reports of wide variations in practice, the need to professionalize early childhood education practices became clear. By the end of the 1970s, the conversations on professionalism and ethics had crystallized into published books on ethics in early childhood education. Lillian Katz and Evangeline Ward's *Ethical Behavior in Early Childhood Education* (1978) was one of the first. By 1988, an official Code of Ethical Conduct had been drafted by an NAEYC working group, which the NAEYC board then adopted in 1989 (Baptiste & Reyes, 2002). NAEYC retains an Ethics Panel, whose responsibility is to review and revise the Code every 5 years (Freeman, 2000), with the most recent update in 2011. The adoption and widespread dissemination of the NAEYC Code has given practitioners a research-based framework for making sound decisions in their work, especially when faced with ethical dilemmas.

Ethical dilemmas

Complex situations that are not solved by research or law and for which there is more than one possible course of action. For any course of action taken, there are potentially positive and negative implications.

Ethical dilemmas are complex situations that cannot be solved by research or law and for which there is more than one possible course of action. For any course of action taken, there are potentially positive and negative implications (NAEYC, 2011). The difference in power and authority between teachers and children presents an added need for standards of ethical practice. Teachers, by definition, are in positions of authority over children, and conflicting situations arise for which there are no clear-cut answers. These realities of teaching prompted NAEYC to respond to teachers' requests for guidance in handling ambiguous situations where they felt multiple responsibilities created conflict (Freeman, 2000).

An example of an ethical dilemma a teacher might face is being asked by parents to withhold snacks or naps from their 3-year-old, even if the child is tired or wants what other children are eating. The parents explain that they need the child to eat and sleep earlier in the evening for the mother to be able to get rest herself for her night job. Conflicts between the responsibility to respect parents' choices for their children, the family's needs, and the child's needs at school present a challenge in handling such ambiguous situations. In another example, a teacher witnesses a more senior colleague carrying out questionable practices that do not align with the goals of the center. The conflict between the responsibilities to promote the center's goals, maintain a respectful and supportive relationship with colleagues, and promote the best learning environment for the children can leave teachers unsure about the right thing to do.

IN YOUR OWN WORDS

If you have ever found yourself in a situation you would characterize as an ethical dilemma or ever been unsure about the right thing to do, how did you feel and how did you respond? In retrospect, would there be anything you would change about how you handled the situation? Can you think of other possible ethical dilemmas and how they could be handled?

Putting It Into Practice

Knowing When to Step In

In the staff meeting vignette, Lisa decided not to solve the teachers' problems, which is what they wanted her to do. She recognized how important it was to facilitate problem-solving among the teachers so they would ultimately be able to work together. This is also true for children. Too often teachers step in and implement their own solution to a conflict, such as taking away a toy, separating children, or removing a child to a cool-down area. Although these strategies probably solve the immediate problem, they alone won't teach children how to solve problems on their own. It is important for teachers to watch conflicts carefully to determine whether children will be able to work through them. If things escalate, teachers can facilitate mediation between the children, asking each one in turn to talk about the situation while the other child listens. Then ask the children to generate some ideas for how things could be resolved. Ask them to agree on one choice and implement it. When solutions come from their own ideas, children are more satisfied with the outcome and learn how to problem-solve for themselves. Through this deliberate process, we can help children develop social problem-solving and conflict negotiation skills.

Key Ideals and Principles   The NAEYC Code is a series of ideals and principles that outlines professionally responsible behavior in the care and education of young children. The Code is divided into sections addressing professionals' ethical responsibilities to

- children,
- families,
- colleagues,
- community, and
- society.

It is not designed to be an answer sheet that spells out exactly how to handle any situation a practitioner might face. NAEYC policy makers have always affirmed that there is tremendous variability in the situations teachers face that are based on the unique and complex contexts of children's lives (Feeney & Freeman, 1999; NAEYC, 2011). However, the Code does provide guidance on what constitutes ethical and unethical practices in the same way that the DAP framework outlines basic standards of appropriate and inappropriate practice. You can find the entire Code under the Position Statements link on the NAEYC Web page. Key foundations that inform decision-making and practice are summarized in Table 3-2. Think about ethical responsibilities for each child's health and safety as you watch this **video** in which professionals talk about their policies and practices in being responsible for safeguarding children's health regarding food allergies.

TABLE 3-2 Key Foundations of the Code of Ethical Conduct

Ethical Responsibilities to Children	Ethical Responsibilities to Families	Ethical Responsibilities to Colleagues and Community
• Recognize that adults have an advantage of size, strength, authority, and power of persuasion over children. • Above all else, do no harm. • Preserve each child's right to safe, healthful environments. • Respect and empower the potential of each individual child. • Use evidence-based practices to make sound decisions for each child's learning and development.	• Respect each child's family values and cultures. • Share knowledge of development and knowledge of their child in meaningful ways. • Help families build valuable support networks. • Create confidentiality policies and practices. • Involve families in program and classroom decisions.	• Create communities within centers and within schools that remain up to date on current research as it pertains to teachers' work. • Welcome the respectful and open sharing of divergent views. • Collaborate to solve problems through a stated conflict-resolution policy. • Create policies that promote the well-being of employees. • Cooperate openly with partner agencies. • Continually reaffirm a core commitment to provide the highest quality programs possible for all children and their families.

MEANINGFUL APPLICATIONS: PROFESSIONAL GUIDELINES IN PRACTICE

First and foremost, teachers seeking to align their teaching with NAEYC's benchmarks of quality practice must become familiar with the content and underlying goals of the statements. Teaching is becoming an increasingly complex profession. Teachers are daily faced with a variety of challenges demanding thoughtful, deliberate decisions. As a teacher of young children, you are a powerful force shaping their development and laying a foundation

Respecting parents as children's first teachers is a part of being a professional educator.

Putting It Into Practice

Knowing Your Resources

The principle that achieves the ideals of ethical practice, above all others, is that teachers "shall do no harm" to children. This seemingly simple statement includes the responsibility to recognize the signs of abuse, neglect, and family stress; know the procedures for documenting and reporting suspicions or concerns; and access the social welfare resources for assisting children and families who may need them. Take a moment and locate your own state's child services Web page. Make a note of the link. Go on the page and locate the toll-free number you can call if you want to talk to someone about or report suspicion of abuse or neglect or find resources for families needing food, clothing, or shelter.

During your visit to the toddler playground, Lauren discussed her experiences with ethics. "When Lisa gave us all a copy of the Code, it was my first experience with the statement," Lauren said. She shared her own story of a child who consistently took more snacks than the portioned amount and who had been caught trying to take food from other children's plates as they cleaned up or threw out their leftovers. "We reminded him that he could have two crackers or five pretzels each snack, and we scolded him for reaching in the trash. We started to become frustrated with the child and were pretty disgusted that he was eating from the trash. In one of our staff meetings, we asked for ideas to deal with him. Teachers asked about the contents of his packed lunch, his clothing, and what his mom or dad said about the situation. As we explained more about him, we realized that his clothes were sometimes quite dirty, that his packed lunches were usually a can of spaghetti or soup, and that we had few interactions with the teenage sister who picked him up and less contact with the parents. Some teachers wondered if there might be some issues of neglect. We realized that we needed to know more about the boy's home life to understand his behavior at school." Lauren looked down for a moment and said, "I was pretty ashamed to think I had been frustrated with this child, when in reality his family may not have enough to eat or proper clothes to dress him in!

"I stayed a little later the next day and talked to the sister. She explained that the child's mother had left them 6 months ago and that the father was struggling to provide for her and the toddler. I went to Lisa right away to talk about what resources we could find for this family. Together we were able to initiate contact with the father and put him in touch with an agency that provides clothing, in-home support, learning materials, and paperwork for food vouchers. We also were able to organize a coat drive in the winter, which helped this family and others in the community. As soon as this boy started having a balanced breakfast and lunch with us, he stopped reaching for scraps in the garbage. His whole outlook changed, really. He is doing well, and his dad has even been able to come to parent nights and participate in some class activities. I feel like we are a team now, working together to help support this child's development."

Lauren's story illustrates the importance of a teacher's position in families' lives. Scolding the boy for misbehaving served only to add to his problems. Experienced teachers immediately considered signs of a family in need of resources and recognized the importance of finding out more about the child's home life. When the teachers came together to understand the context of the child's life, they were able to start a course of action that supported the boy and his family.

Children's Choice-Making

The High/Scope system of plan-do-review is an excellent example of how some programs are integrating children's choices into the curriculum. During group discussion time, children in High/Scope classrooms are prompted to choose activities that they will work on during their choice/center time. This actively promotes initiative, responsibility, and self-direction. Children then disperse and work out their plans in centers. After their choice time, the children come together again and reflect on their work. This review phase instills a sense of accomplishment in the children while they reflect on the results of their work and choices, validating their ability to direct their own actions. Teachers facilitate children's self-direction and support their activity in the classroom, but they respect children's developing self-discipline and self-regulation. In this way, teachers foster relationships with children that reflect trust, respect, and a belief that children can take active roles in guiding their own learning. Self-regulation is promoted in the new DAP statement as a key foundation for later success in school.

for later school and life experiences. Given such an influential position, all teachers must acknowledge and adhere to high standards of practice and rely on evidence of effectiveness and assessment data in making instructional decisions.

Standards of professionalism require teachers to cultivate a solid foundation of key theories of development and learning and remain current on important research findings. Therefore, reading textbooks for class, reviewing current research evidence in journals, and catching up on current events affecting children and families will give you knowledge needed to make sound decisions on behalf of children. In addition to reviewing literature, teachers must develop their skills as researchers. Making regular observations and careful documentation that allow for interpretation are important activities for the reflective practitioner and one of the most important sources of information about the children in your care.

You will also undoubtedly be asked to complete many observations as part of your teacher-education program. Although this may seem repetitive, honing your observation and documentation skills is an essential part of becoming a good teacher. When teachers develop their skills of observation and analysis, they build an ability to gather pertinent information, which they can then use to guide their practice. An important part of implementing a program that is developmentally appropriate involves being keenly aware of the interests, abilities, habits, and routines of each individual child. This awareness is best developed through carefully observing and listening as children interact with each other and their world. The observation and analysis process is perhaps the best tool teachers have to guide their environment and curriculum planning as well as to assess children's progress. Keep this in mind as you undertake the many observation assignments you are given as part of your education classes.

Putting DAP and the Code Together in the Classroom

With a theoretical base informing expectations and an awareness of individual differences, teachers are equipped to make plans and decisions to prepare optimal environments, schedules, activities, and material selections. DAP guidelines suggest that optimal learning environments are those that challenge children within the upper limits of their individual developmental abilities. Engaging children in complex and meaningful classroom activities is achieved by presenting interesting materials to choose from and worthwhile projects that reflect their individual and group interests. When learning experiences align with the context of their lives and invite choice, children see the meaning and value in them and are more deeply engaged in the experience (Bredekamp & Copple, 2009). Your observations of children's play and conversations provide insights into their experiences.

The garden project of Lauren's toddler class provides an example of how teachers maximize children's interests through observations. Earlier that spring, as the children went out for their daily outdoor time, the small tulip shoots popping up from their playground garden had captured their attention. The preschoolers had planted bulbs the previous fall, and the tulips were just beginning to peek up out of the ground. The toddlers became interested in the phenomenon in the garden and made daily visits to assess the growth progress. They invited the preschoolers to visit their classroom and talk about the planting process. The toddlers kept a journal of their observations, which the teachers wrote down from their dictation. They took photos and drew sketches. They heard stories describing seeds growing into plants, their parents shared stories about gardening at home, and they planned how to plant their own gardens. The teachers planned movement activities where the children curled up like sleeping bulbs and slowly stretched their limbs as they grew into plants. (Remember the toddlers in line, ready to go outside, stretching their arms overhead? They were telling the teachers that they were thinking about those bulbs growing.) They explored seed packets and learned how to care for plants. The teachers scoured libraries for books on planting, plants, and gardens and shared them during story time.

The children's interest in gardening and plants, which lasted for 4 weeks, resulted in a chronicle of the growth of the tulips and a new, small garden on the edge of the toddler playground. The children's interests guided the classroom activities, and the teachers engaged them with directed, skill-building activities in literacy and science. "There were some challenges that arose during the project that sent me back to the Code," Lauren explains. "One child became visibly upset when we got out the potting soil and little shovels. She became upset because she wanted to plant too but had been forbidden by her parents to get dirty. We wanted to respect the parents' wishes but were sorry that the child could not engage in the activity. After a morning of tears, we decided to talk to the parents about the value of our messy activities." Lauren explained that it was hard at first because the parents felt criticized. The teachers shared their goals for the children and their knowledge of active learning experiences, taking care to validate the parents' concerns about the child's clothing. The parents explained that it was customary in their culture to send children to school in their finest clothing and that they had only a few such outfits. After discussing the matter for some time, the parents agreed that the teachers could change the child's clothes for messy activities. Lauren explained that the teachers embraced the project because they know that toddlers are naturally active and love sensory experiences such as playing in the garden dirt. But it was only when they understood some parents' concerns did they realize how important it is to be sure that they are both listening to parents and explaining their practices.

A MODEL OF PROFESSIONAL DECISION-MAKING

Today's professionals are expected to knowledgably use research evidence to inform decision-making while thoughtfully integrating professional wisdom and knowledge of family values and context. Together, these three parts of the decision-making process are

FIGURE 3-1

Cherice's Evidence-Based Practice Plan

THE SITUATION:
Owen is 4 years and 3 months old. Cherice has worked with him for almost 2 years. His development is in a typical range in all domains, though Cherice has noticed that he is not yet participating in rhyming activities. He enjoys story time and handles books well. He can recognize the first two letters of his name and is noticing *O* and *W* in print around the environment. Owen will not respond with simple rhyming words when asked, "Can you say a word that sounds like *cat?*" or other familiar word.

THE GOAL, PROBLEM, OR ISSUE:

Cherice wants to support Owen's literacy development. She is aware that rhyming is a typical milestone for this age and is an important part of the literacy development process.

EVIDENCE/RESEARCH:

1. See *Make Way for Literacy!* by Owocki for research on use of poetry and repetition (pp. 144–156).
2. Cherice knows rhyming is an early skill on the trajectory and a developmentally appropriate expectation for Owen.
3. Owen's family sees education as a way to improve life. They have limited resources and need support to access materials for home use.

INSTRUCTIONAL DECISIONS:

- Create take-home book packs with simple rhyming stories, animal poems, and Dr. Seuss books.
- Play two-piece picture card puzzles with rhyming pictures for a matching game (card with picture of a hat matches card with picture of a cat).
- Read rhyming poetry from the children's collection at transitions and circle time.
- Play rhyme-clapping games at line-up times

Evidence-based practice

A way of making decisions that seeks to synthesize quality research outcomes with family and professional judgment.

described as **evidence-based practice**. Figure 3-1 represents a practical example of how a preschool teacher might use a flow-chart approach to the evidence-based practice decision-making process. When preschool teacher Cherice wanted to individualize instruction for Owen to support his emerging literacy, she relied on professional resources in her center's teacher room, as well as family input and her own experience. In Gretchen Owocki's 2001 book, *Make Way for Litearcy!*, Cherice found compelling research on the importance of experiences with poetry to promote rhyme knowledge. Her teacher room also had blank flow charts for her to access and use to map out her planning as well as to provide evidence of her instructional rationale. Cherice will keep the chart in Owen's file to document his experience and her teaching.

ACCOUNTABILITY FOR HIGH-QUALITY EARLY CHILDHOOD EDUCATION

There is overwhelming evidence of the tremendous potential for positive outcomes in children's development and learning from participating in high-quality early care and education programs, particularly for children from families with limited resources and dual-language learners (Bredekamp & Copple, 2009; Downer, et al., 2012). Along with that good news comes an increased focus on assessment and accountability for program quality and evidence of success. In this **video**, listen to this team of professionals talk about how they can use assessment data to drive program improvement and help ensure success for each child. And as we experience increased professional and societal focus on evidence and accountability, more and more programs and schools are implementing classroom and teacher rating systems. These quality assessments are used to evaluate teachers and programs but even more so as a tool for continuous improvement. There are a variety of rating scale instruments with varying areas of focus, including

- global scales, which assess environment, materials, program policies and spaces, instructional processes, teacher-child interactions, and parent participation;
- focused instruments, which assess teacher-child linguistic tone, quality, and appropriateness;
- content-focused assessment scales (such as literacy);
- environmental scales, which assess safety and learning opportunities in outside spaces; and
- health and safety assessment checklists.

One of the increasingly popular and widely used rating systems is the Classroom Assessment Scoring System (CLASS). The CLASS was developed at the Center for Advanced Study of Teaching and Learning at the University of Virginia's well-known Curry School of Education and boasts a robust research base both in its development as well as in its implementation effectiveness. The CLASS is organized around three central areas that measure classroom interactional processes and how teachers use environment and materials (Hamre, Goffin, & Kraft-Sayre, 2009a, 2009b). The three overarching areas are

1. *emotional support:* climate, teacher sensitivity, regard for student perspectives;
2. *classroom organization:* guidance and management, productivity, learning formats; and
3. *instructional support:* concept development, quality of feedback, language use and modeling, and literacy focus.

There are six separate CLASS tools specifically designed for distinct programs serving children from infancy through secondary education settings. Within each of the three broad domains listed above, there are several dimensions, which vary based on CLASS target age. Each dimension is scored using a 7-point scale from low to high range of quality. In concert with other assessment efforts targeting specific areas, using the CLASS to focus on assessing teacher-child interactions (instructional support) has huge implications for improving the quality of children's early educational experiences. While the CLASS is used to measure instructional quality, it also serves as a key resource for mapping out professional development and target improvement goals. The process of implementing the tool provides an opportunity to structure feedback on strengths and areas for improvement and serves as a key documentation of teacher effectiveness.

Another widely used resource for assessing program quality is the age-leveled series of Environment Rating Scales developed by researchers at the University of North Carolina's Frank Porter Graham Child Development Institute. The series includes four separate instruments:

1. ECERS—Early Childhood Environment Rating Scale (updated 2005)
2. ITERS—Infant Toddler Environment Rating Scale (updated 2006)
3. FCCERS—Family Child Care Environment Rating Scale (updated 2007)
4. SACERS—School Age Care Environment Rating Scale (1995)

The scales are designed to assess quality of interactions between children and adults, among children, and with families; materials and usage; and program structures such as schedules,

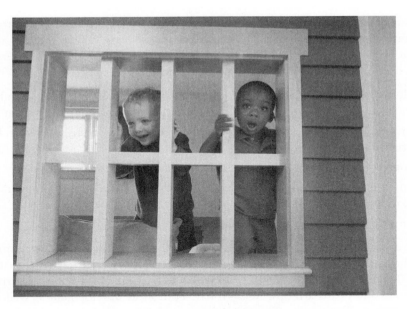

The focus on accountability for excellence in early care and education emerges out of the realization that the early years are foundational to positive learning and development outcomes.

policies, and routines. The scales consist of 38–49 indicators of quality, which are scored using a range from Inadequate to Excellent.

The scales, the ECERS in particular, have been used effectively in numerous research projects both to assess the value of the scales themselves as well as to estimate early childhood program quality. Program administrators are also widely using the rating scales as a means of quality improvement, with repeated implementation over time to track changes. Many states are mandating the use of the ECERS in program assessment and reporting requirements for public funding or state-level quality rating systems (Cassidy, Hestenes, Hegde, Hestenes, & Mims, 2005; Warash, Ward, & Rotilie, 2008). The most prolific and promising use of the rating scales, however, is by early childhood care and education providers themselves as a means of self-assessment, reflection, evidence, and improvement.

Professional practice in early childhood education today calls upon us all to focus on evidence of effectiveness to inform decisions as well as document accountability for children's development and learning. There is no question that the stakes are high: the early childhood years lay the foundation for all of children's later learning and development. The strength of their positive outcomes is the responsibility of each and every early childhood professional; we simply cannot settle for anything less than the very highest quality practice! Our professional guidelines offer roadmaps and frameworks, but it is the assessment instruments that provide the practical evidence and data to more clearly direct our best efforts.

CONCLUSION

The NAEYC DAP and Code of Ethical Conduct statements serve as valuable partners in upholding the commitment to provide high-quality programs for all children. Ultimately, however, each individual must choose to take responsibility for embracing these ideals and principles in his or her own life and work. The satisfaction of knowing that this commitment will enhance the lives of countless children is a reward well worth the effort.

Embracing high standards of quality and ethics also calls teachers to develop a professional identity. Unlike in other levels of education, early childhood teachers endure public perspectives that do not endow them with the same degree of professional respect as other teachers (for example, classrooms referred to as "day care" and teachers referred to as "babysitters"). As a new teacher, you need to present yourself as a well-prepared, capable, knowledgeable professional. This is the only way we can continue making efforts to update and upgrade the view of early childhood education as an important profession pivotal in laying the foundation for later healthful development. This aligns with the view of teachers as reflective, deliberate decision-makers who use foundational theories of development and learning and current research in making individual instructional decisions. The heart of the DAP and Code statements seeks to do just this: to give you clear, articulate goals and strategies for developing yourself as a prepared, confident professional practitioner working on behalf of each and every child.

A final key element of today's professional practice is the systematic use of research-based assessments of instructional effectiveness. Rating scales such as the CLASS and Environment Rating Scale series provide evidence of what is working as well as direct improvement efforts. In concert, professional guidelines and practical assessments offer the direction and data to make sound decisions and ensure high-quality practice for each child. By basing your practice on evidence, knowledge, experience, and family input, you will be able to articulate a sound professional evidence base for your work.

SUMMARY

- The NAEYC promotes high-quality early childhood education programming through the publication of guiding frameworks and position statements.

- The DAP statement presents key principles that guide teachers' work with and for children and families by addressing basic knowledge of developmental trends and expectations as well as diversity among individual children.

- The important role of the family and community culture and collaborations with elementary schools present a newer facet to the statement, reflecting changes in early childhood education research and practice.

- The overarching principles presented in the DAP statement include a validation of play as an important vehicle for learning and balancing classroom activities between interest-based, or child-initiated, and skill-based, or teacher-guided, experiences.

- The Code of Ethical Conduct statement presents guidance for maintaining obligations to children, families, colleagues, and the community while handling situations in which these obligations may be in conflict.

- Using a clearly defined process for making evidence-based decisions in our practice serves to professionalize our work and ensure the best outcomes for children and families.

- Professional accountability and ongoing improvement is supported through the appropriate use of quality indicators, frameworks, and assessment instruments.

CHAPTER LEARNING GOALS SELF-ASSESSMENT

Use this chart to write down three to five key points for each learning goal that you learned from this chapter.

Identify role and purpose of professional associations.	
Identify scope and key professional guidelines of the National Association for the Education of Young Children.	
Create connections between professional guidelines and best practices.	
Discuss key features of evidence-based practice in professional decision-making.	
Examine features and outcomes of professional quality rating scales.	

APPLICATION ACTIVITIES

Discussion Prompts

1. What do you believe are the most important rights of children, parents, and professionals?
2. What key principles of the DAP or Code of Ethical Conduct statements do you think would be the most challenging to implement? What can you do to alleviate those challenges?

In Class   In small groups, analyze the following teacher scenarios. Based on what you know about children's development, DAP, and the Code of Ethical Conduct, examine these situations and decide what you would do and why. Identify specific principles and ideals from the Code (available on the NAEYC Web site in the Position Statements link) that helped guide your decision-making.

Holiday Play   The teacher in the 5-year-olds' room in your center is preparing to present her annual holiday play. She has written a long script with parts, lines to be memorized, and group songs. The children have been spending 90 minutes each day practicing their lines, moves, and songs. When you pass by, you see some children rolling on the floor, and some are standing in front of the teacher, emotionlessly repeating the lines. Two children are standing at the window, looking at the playground. You notice that on her posted schedule, this is the children's outdoor time. With the performance only one week away, however, the children have to focus on rehearsals.

Craft Project   The assistant teacher in the 4-year-olds' room has spent 15 minutes reading the story of Fredrick to his class. Then he directs the children to the tables where he has laid out various precut shapes of colored paper. The children sit at the tables and watch the teacher as he instructs them about how to assemble their mice from the precut shapes. All children are instructed to complete the project in the same way, although some children seem to be struggling with managing the glue and with grasping and placing the small paper pieces. The teacher redirects their efforts with the same instructions, pointing out that other children are able to complete the task without problem. He finishes by reminding the struggling children that they are "big boys and girls" and should keep working until they finish their craft projects. In the end, he completes the project himself so each child has something to take home at the end of the day.

Student Teaching   You are student teaching in a preschool class, and your classroom teacher gives you a lesson about Egyptian mummies that you feel is not age appropriate for the children in the class. Feeling obligated as a student teacher, you start the lesson. After several minutes, a few children indicate that they are scared by the activity and don't want to continue. The teacher tells them that they're fine and that you should continue.

In the Field   Using the Internet or your local phone book, locate a family services agency in your area. This may be listed as child welfare, maternal child and health, family assistance, healthy communities, or a resource and referral agency. Find the contact information and make an appointment to interview a representative. Ask the representative about the program's services, how families access programs, and what resources are available and gather any printed information (brochures) that are offered. Write a brief summary of your conversation, the scope of the services for families, and the materials you gathered. These resources will be useful to you as a teacher and are also items you can include in your portfolio to demonstrate professionalism and awareness of community resources.

For Your Portfolio   Locate the NAEYC Web site and explore their online list of position statements located under the Position Statements link (www.naeyc.org/positionstatements). Make some notes about the kinds of topics that are reflected therein. Locate and print the DAP and Code of Ethical Conduct statements. Read them through and make notes summarizing the statements and some personal reflections about how the statements affect your practice with children and families. Create an informational brochure to highlight and promote the values and guidance for practice in the statements, as if you were creating an advertisement. This activity can be added to your portfolio in the section on professionalism.

RELATED WEB LINKS

National Child Care Information Center
www.csrees.usda.gov/nea/family/part/childcare_part_nccic.html

National Association for Family Child Care
www.nafcc.org

Association for Childhood Education International
www.acei.org

ZERO TO THREE
www.zerotothree.org

CHAPTER 4

Influential Theories: Bioecological Model and Constructivism

Chapter Learning Goals

- Explore key aspects of a bioecological model.
- Identify important elements of constructivist learning theory.
- Compare and contrast branches within constructivism.
- Examine opportunities for theoretical applications in practice.

Education is a field in which theory and practice are continuously evolving through dialogue, reflection, synthesis, and experimentation. For centuries, educators have been attempting to create learning environments that maximize children's potential in terms of skills, knowledge, attitudes, developmental outcomes, and lifelong habits.

Family-focused and learner-centered theories of teaching have contributed to the landscape of classroom experience in powerful ways that have great potential to positively shape practice.

For the past two decades, early childhood practice has been influenced by several important theories of development and learning, especially ecological systems theory and constructivism. This chapter presents an overview of the theory of constructivism and an analysis of the possibilities and challenges of applying the theory to educational practice. Strategies for meaningfully making the theory-to-practice leap are presented as a starting point and as a guide to constructivist-inspired teaching and assessment.

84

BRONFENBRENNER'S BIOECOLOGICAL MODEL

An important function of theories in the early childhood professional's life is to provide ways of thinking about and approaching our work. Over the course of his long and celebrated career, developmental psychologist Urie Bronfenbrenner contributed one of the most influential and powerful frameworks for thinking about the context of children's development. Originated in the 1970s, his initial framework broadened the existing study of child development to more authentically reflect the multiple environments and influences at work in children's lives (Bronfenbrenner, 2005a). He described this as an ecological model of human development in which children develop amid a set of nested environments, relationships, and influences. Direct and indirect settings are often represented like a cross-section of an onion with arrows signifying interrelationships, as in Figure 4-1.

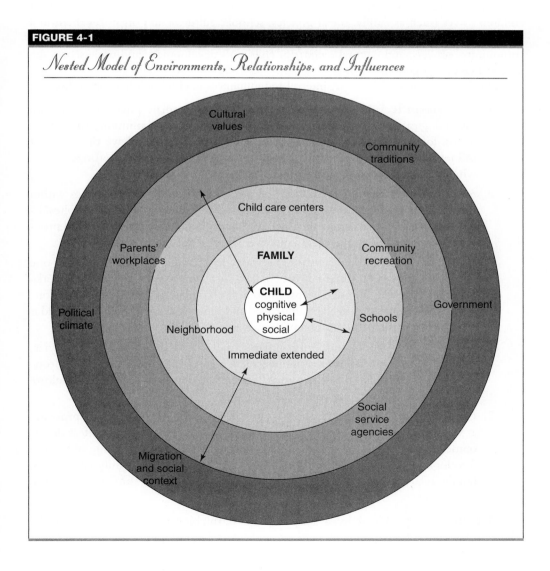

FIGURE 4-1

Nested Model of Environments, Relationships, and Influences

Bronfenbrenner continued to reshape and evolve his perspective to the more recent bioecological model of human development, which integrates the following key aspects of child development (Bronfenbrenner, 2005b):

- Developmental maturation (biological processes)
- Environmental influences
- Dynamic relationships among all aspects of children's lives
- Children's perceptions and experience of influences
- Influences both constant and changing across time
- Children influence their world just as they are influenced

Bronfenbrenner's work is especially meaningful to early childhood practice because of the prominence of family as well as multiple other systems operating within children's lives. It provides a structured organization to the complex context of children's development. This model both acknowledges the many direct and indirect influences that affect children's lives (such as family, social policies, schools, cultures) and organizes them in a flexible, bidirectional system of five structures. In essence, it provides a map of the family, community, process, and cultural *contexts* of children's development and underscores the importance of recognizing the many influences in children's lives.

The five structures of dynamic, interrelated influences in children's lives are as follows:

1. *Microsystems:* Relationships and activities in the immediate physical, social, and psychological environments of family, home, school, and community lay a foundation for development, learning, and social interactions and have the strongest influence on development. Microsystems are the face-to-face settings within which the child has direct experience.

2. *Mesosystems:* Links and interrelations between two or more direct settings within the child's life, such as how strong involvement between family and schoolteachers improves children's academic success. Mesosystems are connections and processes among people in the child's direct environments/microsystems.

3. *Exosystems:* Links and interrelations between direct and indirect settings, only one of which is part of the child's direct contact, such as how stress at a parent's workplace is felt in the home. The psychological connections among close relationships (in the microsystems) are influenced and influential even though the child is not directly participating in one of the settings.

4. *Macrosystems:* The overarching cultural patterns, values, beliefs, lifestyles, resources, and expectations that influence child and family life experiences. Bronfenbrenner referred to this structure as "a societal blueprint for a particular culture or subculture" (Bronfenbrenner, 1994, p. 40).

5. *Chronosystems:* The constancy and change of biological developmental processes as well as environmental experiences throughout the child's life that affect developmental outcomes. Chronosystems represent the influence of timing of life and developmental events including stability and change within family economics, family relationships, maturation, home and school environments, historical events, etc.

More than a simple hierarchy, a unique feature of the bioecological model is that the relative influence of these processes, settings, and interrelationships are dynamic and shift

FIGURE 4-2

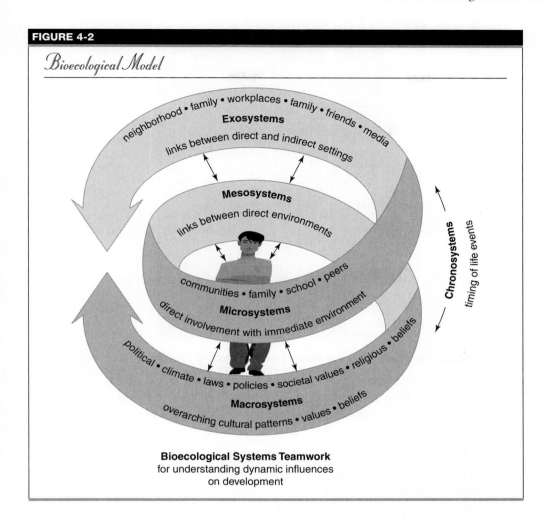

Bioecological Model

Exosystems
neighborhood • family • workplaces • family • friends • media
links between direct and indirect settings

Mesosystems
links between direct environments

communities • family • school • peers
Microsystems
direct involvement with immediate environment

Chronosystems
timing of life events

political • climate • laws • policies • societal values • religious • beliefs
Macrosystems
overarching cultural patterns • values • beliefs

Bioecological Systems Teamwork
for understanding dynamic influences
on development

and change over the course of the child's life just as influences are different from one child to the next. This model is about the interrelationships among people, settings, and experiences. Figure 4–2 represents an illustration of the relative strength and the fluid, interrelated nature and complexity of influences in children's lives.

IN YOUR OWN WORDS: YOUR OWN CONTEXT

Think about Bronfenbrenner's work in relation to your own life. Using small adhesive notes, write down each person, agency, institution, and system that influenced your life along its course. Once you have as many as possible down, organize them by how direct the influence was. Try to structure your organization, hierarchy, or map to convey the dynamic, fluid, interdependent way these influences helped shape who you are. Will you organize your notes like a timeline, spiral, web, flow chart, or other structure?

Another key element of Bronfenbrenner's theory that is particularly important for early childhood practice is that the influences are *bidirectional*. This means that the many influences shaping the course of a child's development are also affected by the child (Darragh, 2007). Many professionals are drawn to his framework because emphasizing

Traditions and activities of children's home lives are essential aspects of their identity and family experience.

the bidirectional nature of influences views children as a more empowered agent in their own development. Children can affect their world in the following ways:

- Parents' choices and decisions are based on goals for their children and their children's needs (living near extended family, schools, or health care).
- Employers often create policies in light of family needs (family leaves, family health insurance, flexible schedules).
- School district policy and practice are shaped by parent input and enrollment patterns.
- Community parks are placed in neighborhoods where children reside.
- Operation of child care facilities is based on family needs (schedule, cost, access).
- A variety of child-welfare issues are regular features of political platforms.
- Public funding and support for social service agencies serving children and families varies, in part based on parent lobbying.

Bronfenbrenner's dynamic, multidimensional model provides a way for early childhood professionals to carefully consider the many, varied influences in children's lives as well as the unique interactions in each child's particular contextualized experience. Bronfenbrenner's prolific writings and sought-after advice about family well-being policies and structures advocate a passionate and compelling message: ensuring successful development and outcomes for children demands that we value, support, and actively engage families in shared child-raising and education efforts (Bronfenbrenner, 2005b). Take a few minutes to see how one school community is coming together to support its members on behalf of their children in this **video**. For early childhood professionals, this translates into deliberate and intentional practices that both provide robust support *to* families and seek and access support *from* families. Examples of this reciprocity might include

- knowing and supporting family goals for children's development,

- promoting family activities that support program learning goals (such as take-home book packs),

- helping families access services and programs as needed (such as economic assistance or developmental screenings),

- seeking family input on program/school policies and activities,

- regular conferences with families about their children's experiences and progress in program or school,

- welcoming family participation in program/classroom activities (facilitating transportation or child care as needed),

- voting for and promoting family-supportive laws and policies, and

- dialoguing with families and community members about existing and needed programs and services that support child and family well-being.

OVERVIEW OF CONSTRUCTIVISM

With a long and rich history, including discourses in philosophy, psychology, and—more recently—education, the theory of constructivism continues to be dynamic and evolving. **Constructivism** is a theory about how people learn and understand their world with particular emphasis on the active process individuals undertake to develop complex knowledge. Originally formed as a developmental theory, constructivism is increasingly being applied to early childhood education settings. With a focus on individual and sociocultural processes of learning and an overarching valuing of interactive, personal engagement within the learning environment, constructivism is a natural fit with exploratory, hands-on, developmentally aligned early childhood practice. In the following classroom example, think about how children's knowledge is developing and the roles of children and the teacher.

Constructivism

A theory of knowledge and learning that posits that children actively engage with their world— people, experiences, materials—and build their beliefs and knowledge through interaction and internal processes.

CLASSROOM VIEW

Constructivist Teacher in Action

This morning a small group of second-graders are having an art class as part of their weekly school-community outreach program. The students' worktables are stocked with small baskets of glue, a variety of scissors, markers, and hole punchers carefully set out by the teacher, Gail. Gail will be their partner, teacher, and guide for a series of visual arts explorations. After telling the children to close their eyes, Gail takes the students on a guided imagery journey and asks them to imagine themselves in a place that is very special to them. They are asked to think about the time of day, the colors and light, what they see around them and in the distance, and how being in their place makes them feel. Gail uses words such as horizon, landscape, *and* contour *as guided imagery prompts.*

After a few moments, the students are asked to open their eyes and write down a few key words that describe what they saw and felt on their imaginary journey. Gail prompts the children to think artistically by using terms such as color, depth, light, hue, *and* shape. *Children are shown several prints of professional artists' landscapes, and their attention is focused on specific elements of line, color, shape, and composition. Contrasts among the different techniques, colors, and styles are discussed as the children comment on the pieces. Gail briefly discusses the color wheel, reminding them of colors that are neighbors and those that are complements.*

With pieces of tissue paper, children are asked to begin to choose a color palette that represents the colors they saw in their special place. The children are then invited to create a landscape collage with the papers to represent their special place. As the children begin to work, Gail moves around the room. At each table, Gail carefully looks at what the children are creating. After examining their work for a few moments, Gail comments on specific elements. She asks questions, uses artistic terms, and answers students' questions with examples of what some artists do or what else the child might want to think about. For example, Gail suggests to one child that she might want to include a thin contrasting line of dark color between her sky and ground to make the distinction stand out. Gail models teaching strategies for the classroom teacher, who is working alongside her children. Gail acts as a more knowledgeable guide and collaborator in the creative problem-solving. These are some of the comments she makes:

"Think about contrast as you work on this part. If you step back and look, do you think a darker strip in between these pieces would make it stand out more?"

"Think of your original color palette as a starting point. You may want to expand it as you work."

"I see you have made yours very textural. You've used a mosaic technique here with these small square pieces."

"Collage is about layers, building details, and making compositions with large and small shapes."

"Consider your point of view in this landscape. Are you looking from below, straight on, or from the sky?"

"Think about depth. Imagine that you were walking into the landscape."

After a little more than an hour at work on their landscapes, Gail encourages the class to wrap up their work and prepare for whole-group discussion. After about 15 more minutes, the class reorganizes as a whole group. Gail instructs the children to arrange their landscapes on a long table at the side of the room. The students then take several minutes to observe each other's work. They are invited to share their experiences with the activity.

Several children express satisfaction at working through the challenges of developing an idea and forming it on paper. Several comment that the collage technique is more familiar to them, so they feel more competent and are more pleased with their work. One child indicates things she would do differently now that she has stepped back and looked at her work. Gail facilitates this dialogue, but she now takes a secondary role to the students' interactions. She lets them drive the direction of the conversation.

Roles of the Learner

At the heart of the theory of constructivism is the belief that knowledge is constructed through an active process in which the learner engages in the following:

- Exploration with materials
- Inner processes of reasoning
- Interaction with peers and teachers

The learner is valued as an important part of the knowledge construction process, which is shaped by prior experience, learning, and beliefs. Constructivists believe that when ideas are challenged by new information, the learner interprets and makes sense of the new information in the context of previous experience. This process of making sense involves building a new cognitive framework that meaningfully incorporates the old and new information in ways that make sense to the learner (Davis & Sumara, 2002). When

Putting It Into Practice

Teacher–Child Interactions

The important influence of the way you talk to and interact with children cannot be overemphasized. Throughout your day, stop and take time to really listen to your children. Ask questions that reflect how attentively you are listening and how deeply you care about their lives. This is a foundation to demonstrating your respect and commitment to children.

constructivist theory is applied to classrooms, it generally involves engaging learners in a cognitive process that includes such activities as (Low & Shironaka, 1995; Schuh, 2003)

- asking and answering questions,
- making hypotheses,
- testing those hypotheses,
- dialoguing with teachers and peers,
- confronting challenges to one's own and others' thinking, and
- exploring and reflecting on results.

Learners in a constructivist classroom are not viewed as passive recipients of knowledge handed out by teachers. Rather, students are viewed as active partners in problem-solving through the asking, testing, considering, and answering of questions. Learning is viewed as a

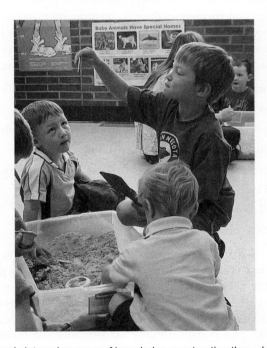

Teachers facilitate children's internal process of knowledge construction through hands-on experiences.

dynamic inquiry process (Gregory, 2002). At the core of this process is that the students are *thinking*. Students are not merely given answers, nor are they sent forth alone to face challenges they are not equipped to meet. Students are supported as they find ways to navigate through challenging and interesting problems and reflect on their own processing and solutions.

Roles of the Teacher

The nature of student-teacher interactions in the classroom observation at the beginning of the chapter is very different from such shallow complimentary comments as "That's pretty" or "Good job." Gail's comments are not the same as handing out directions about where to place cotton balls or precut shapes on paper and how much glue to use. Her comments, which include technical artistic vocabulary, are thoughtful and reflect both a careful analysis of the students' work and a sharing of ideas from a more expert knowledge base. Gail uses comments that are designed to encourage students to think about what they are doing. Her comments and questions encourage the students to become deliberate, thoughtful, and reflective about their artwork. She also prompts students to discuss their work together and share decisions they made about their creations. This teaching style illustrates an example of constructivist scaffolding, where the teacher acts as a guide and facilitator of students' thinking and activities within learning experiences. Watch another example in this **video** of a teacher and preschool children exploring the concept of patterns; listen to the prompts and cues the teacher uses to support children's emerging concept and skill.

By varying the degree to which she directly guides or indirectly supports the students' work and discussion, Gail embodies the careful balance of a constructivist teacher. At times she directs students' work and attention by teaching them strategies of artistic techniques, and at other times she steps back and lets the students discuss and reflect on their own processes and work. Through this balance of direct and indirect presence, Gail fosters a community among the students and encourages them to be thoughtful and engaged with their own work and with their peers. This thoughtfulness, reflection, and deeper cognitive engagement with one's own work and with one's peers are hallmarks of constructivist classrooms.

Constructivist teachers strive to balance their teaching style to include (Powell, 2000)

- posing engaging questions and challenging problems,
- giving students necessary information,
- supporting students' research to find information for themselves,
- prompting students to try new problem-solving strategies,
- focusing student attention on particular aspects of the activity,
- observing and considering students' actions and dialogue,
- promoting collaboration among peers and teachers, and
- assessing students' processing through careful dialogues.

In the constructivist classroom, teachers and students are viewed as partners in critically thinking about phenomena in their world and exploring them on a personal level (Castle, 1997; Richardson, 2003). This personal, active involvement is what makes constructivist learning meaningful, real, internal, interesting, and accessible to even the youngest students. To fully understand how teachers create learner-centered, constructivist-inspired classrooms, the origins and metamorphosis of constructivist theory should be briefly explored within its historical context.

Scaffolding

Scaffolding involves the dynamic and active assistance from the more expert partner, who relies heavily on verbal cues, prompts, and questions. The teacher provides clues that "nudge" the child's thinking or actions in solving a problem or completing a task. Be careful to give just enough help to avoid overriding the child's own process. Scaffolding requires that teachers know how children are capable of thinking—what their developmental level is at that moment. As children become more capable, the assistance is reduced. In this way, the teacher's help acts as a stronger support as children need more help and as a lesser support as they become more independently capable in the task.

CONTEMPORARY CONSTRUCTIVIST BELIEFS

In a broad sense, there are currently two main branches that use different lenses to view the nature of learning and knowing:

1. Cognitive-developmental constructivism
2. Sociocultural constructivism

Each branch has its primary advocate, Piaget and Vygotsky, respectively, and central perspectives (Simpson, 2002). Considered to be branches of the same overarching theory because they share several core beliefs, there is nonetheless a clear distinction between the two. **Cognitive-developmental constructivism** seeks to explain how learners shape their world, whereas **sociocultural constructivism** seeks to explain how the world shapes the learners (Davis & Sumara, 2002). The difference is one of perspective and position, and it is the differences, combined with the similarities, that present a more complete, detailed picture.

Cognitive-developmental constructivism

A theory of knowledge as an individual construct built through maturation and new experiences that challenge the learner's existing knowledge.

Sociocultural constructivism

A theory of knowledge as socially coconstructed then internalized; as such, the social and cultural environments heavily influence knowledge construction.

Piaget's Contributions to Constructivism

Within the cognitive-developmental perspective, heavily influenced by the work of Jean Piaget, knowledge is an individual construct built through maturation and new experiences that challenge the learner's existing knowledge. Recall that Piaget proposed that children actively seek to make sense out of their experiences. He felt that this active search for meaning is what leads to the child's developing ideas and changing them as new experiences bring

Piaget's Influence

Cognitive-developmental constructivists, such as Piaget, believe that children actively construct knowledge through cognitive processing of their experiences, driven by an innate desire to explore and manipulate materials in their world. More than just the sum of experiences or the sum of innate ideas, constructivists view knowledge acquisition as an active, dynamic cognitive process in which children build, rebuild, discard, and change their ideas.

new knowledge (Berk & Winsler, 1995; Davis & Sumara, 2002; Piaget, 1969). Piaget also suggested that as children mature, their thinking changes as their cognitive development goes through distinct stages: sensorimotor, preoperational, concrete operational, formal operational (Piaget, 1929).

Cognitive conflict

When new information contradicts currently held beliefs, which then prompts the child to rethink existing beliefs.

A key concept in constructivism is the notion of **cognitive conflict**, in which the individual child is made aware of discrepancies between existing beliefs and new information that presents a different perspective. In essence, cognitive conflict is finding out some new information that contradicts currently held beliefs. When this contradiction is realized, some testing of the old and new ideas happens to come to a new understanding. For Piaget, the processes and resulting changes associated with cognitive conflict are driven by the internal capacities of the individual, particularly assimilation and accommodation (Piaget, 1975).

Much of Piaget's theories of cognitive development arose from his extensive work observing children's processes and abilities as they worked to accomplish certain tasks at different ages. Piaget noticed that children's actions changed qualitatively over time as their development progressed through levels of understanding. He believed that these changes and activities contributed to the child's knowledge construction. He believed that development leads learning as children engage in spontaneous exploration and discovery using processes and abilities naturally available to them (Berk & Winsler, 1995).

Piaget's influence on current practice, particularly on the practice of teaching young children, is illustrated in the reliance on discovery centers as a primary vehicle for children's active exploration in the classroom. Think about observations you have made or videos you have watched of early childhood classrooms. You have probably seen children engaging in active explorations such as building with blocks, putting puzzles together, or mixing paint colors and drawing at an easel. As children become involved with their materials, they learn firsthand how they work, and they begin to develop ideas about cause and effect.

Although social exchanges are a part of the picture, they are valued in terms of the effect on the individual's engagement with ideas and materials. Piaget did not necessarily believe that social dialogues played as important a role in shaping children's cognitive development as active exploration of materials. Social interactions may provide the catalyst for the child's cognitive conflict and resolution when a partner provides new information based on his or her experience or understanding. Social exchanges may also serve as a forum for testing ideas when partners debate conflicting beliefs or jointly engage in testing new information (Richardson, 2003). The role of the social environment is a subtle but key distinction between the two branches of constructivism. This is also an area in which many current researchers and educators differ with Piaget's theory. Piaget himself, late in his career, began to question the universality of his earlier stage theory, acknowledging diversity in cognitive development based on diverse environment and experience (Knight & Sutton, 2004).

Vygotsky's Influence

Vygotsky's work expanded existing beliefs about constructivist theory. He influenced the sociocultural branch of constructivism, which believes that knowledge is constructed through active mental processes but is greatly influenced by one's social and cultural environment. The role of experience remains important, but interactions with people (such as teachers and peers) and society (cultural norms, traditions, and beliefs) are viewed as essential influences in knowledge construction.

Vygotsky's Contributions to Constructivism

Lev Vygotsky continued the process of shaping constructivist theory, but his work was particularly useful in applying constructivist principles to teaching (Davis & Sumara, 2002). For sociocultural constructivists such as Vygotsky, knowledge is socially coconstructed then internalized as opposed to being independently constructed within the individual working solely with materials (Berk & Winsler, 1995; Simpson, 2002; Vygotsky, 1978). Vygotsky's work represents a shift in constructivist thinking; he placed a heavy emphasis on the value of social collaborations, particularly with more expert partners. Within this framework, knowledge is a shared construct influenced by prior experiences, cultures, environments, people, and beliefs. Vygotsky believed that the purpose of learning was to lead development. As Vygotsky noted, "Learning awakens a variety of internal developmental processes that are able to operate only when the child is interacting with people in his environment and in cooperation with this peers" (Vygotsky, 1978, p. 90). When applied to classroom environments, this translates into teachers' engaging the children in discussions and activities a step ahead of their current developmental level. Vygotsky believed growth and learning occur only when appropriate challenge and support come together in the child's *zone of proximal* (or potential) development (ZPD). Working in the ZPD means working with more expert help on challenging activities that are neither too easy nor too hard (Berk & Winsler, 1995). The nature of learning and development is cyclical in that once the process is internalized, the teacher adjusts learning experiences to reflect a new zone of development.

IN YOUR OWN WORDS

Can you recall a time when you have been bored in class? (Though not this class, of course.) Did you feel tired or restless? Did you stop paying attention to what you were doing or to what someone was saying? Can you recall a time when you just didn't understand something, feeling as if it were way over your head? Did you get annoyed or frustrated because you could not figure out a solution or because someone was explaining something in a way that did not make any sense to you? In these situations, you probably did not learn much; maybe you cannot even recall what topic you were studying or the materials you were using. You probably "checked out" mentally and didn't think deeply or actively about what you were working on. For constructivists, deep cognitive engagement that is *appropriately challenging* is an essential part of the learning process. It is something that must be carefully and skillfully fostered by attentive, observant teachers.

Beyond Piaget: Social Learning, Language, and Culture

Inherent in the framework of the ZPD is the emphasis on the nature of the interaction with a more expert partner (a teacher in role if not in title). In a Vygotskian framework, the teacher deliberately assesses the child's level and provides interaction just beyond it, though still within reach. In Piaget's framework, the partner may unwittingly be a source of conflicting information so the child is thrown into the cognitive conflict–knowledge construction process. Vygotsky, on the other hand, viewed the partner as a deliberate actor in the purposeful engagement of the child's thought. It is an active role, one that requires expertise in both content and teaching technique.

The teacher must understand the child's current thought process to provide appropriate support for the child's method of working through challenging problems. Furthermore, the teacher must remain active and attentive during the child's processing so the form and level of assistance can be continually adjusted based on the child's place within his or her individual zone. Highly interdependent, this scaffolding is at the heart of a Vygotskian view of knowledge construction. Scaffolding relies heavily on careful verbal prompts and intentional interactions; underscoring the important connection between language and learning (Izumi-Taylor, 2013).

Vygotsky promoted the milestone of language use as the most influential event in shaping a child's cognitive development (Berk & Winsler, 1995; Vygotsky, 1978). Children use language to develop ideas socially, which are then internalized (Vygotsky, 1978). First, children think out loud verbally, which slowly becomes internal, private speech, which they use to organize thought (Dixon-Krauss, 1996). When children have a reasonable mastery over language, the dynamic of the learning environment is one of collaboration among children and adults in which the group negotiates meaning and socially constructs knowledge. For Piaget, the child's use of private speech was not particularly meaningful developmentally, and it was attributed to the child's cognitive immaturity (Berk & Winsler, 1995).

New research testing elements of Piaget's stage theory have led to modifications and expansions in beliefs about how cognition is influenced by culture (Knight & Sutton, 2004). Piaget believed that as a course of normal maturation, cognition progresses through distinct levels of processing. New research exploring thinking among individuals from diverse cultures—industrialized and nonindustrialized societies—indicates that the unique

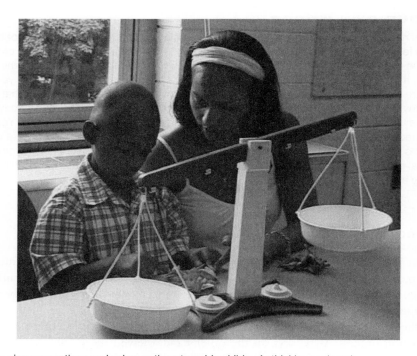

Teachers give suggestions and ask questions to guide children's thinking and work.

TABLE 4-1 Key Distinctions between Branches of Constructivism

Branch of Constructivism	Cognitive-Developmental	Sociocultural
Primary Advocate	**Jean Piaget**	**Lev Vygotsky**
Learner's role	Learners' explorations and actions shape their knowledge of the world.	Interactions with their world and the people in it shape learners' knowledge.
View of knowledge construction	Knowledge is individually constructed, shaped by processing new experiences.	Knowledge is coconstructed, shaped by interaction with people and influenced by culture and environment.
Role of peer/social partner	Peers can unwittingly provoke cognitive conflict (passive role).	More expert partner purposefully guides the exploration of ideas (active role).
Relationship between development and learning	Development leads learning.	Learning leads development.
Relationship between language and thought	Language–knowledge construction connection is not emphasized.	Language is promoted as strongly influencing thought.

experiences of specific cultures can greatly affect all aspects of development (Suizzo, 2000). Think about the important influence of culture on development and strategies for working with diverse children and families as you watch this **video** interview.

Although the Piagetian and Vygotskian branches of constructivism have different emphases, they nevertheless maintain several commonalities and present a more comprehensive picture of constructivist theory when explored together. Contemporaries familiar with each other's work, Piaget and Vygotsky traveled different theoretical paths within the same field. Both theories

- are learner-centered models of how thinking and knowledge acquisition develop;
- emphasize children as active creators of knowledge;
- recognize innate and social influences on thought processing;
- value the child's environment for its influence on thought (Berk & Winsler, 1995);
- view knowledge as a subjective, constructed reality (Richardson, 2003); and
- validate the child's internal motivation to explore and manipulate his or her world as a means of understanding it (Matthews, 2003).

When used in concert as complementary subsets of the overarching theory, cognitive-developmental and sociocultural constructivist views provide educators with a viable framework for both understanding children's developing thought and creating learning environments to support that development. However, just as constructivists promote the critical analysis of new information in relation to prior understanding, it is important for educators to carefully consider and reflect on any theory presented to them. As you read through all the chapters in this text and learn about any new aspects of educational theory and practice, you must continually reflect on what you are learning and examine how it fits into your own developing philosophy.

TRANSLATING THEORY INTO PRACTICE

There is challenge and potential in translating theory into practice under constructivist-inspired teaching. In spite of the challenges, for at least two decades, educational practice has adopted the vocabulary, interpreted the spirit of, and applied constructivist practices in effective classroom teaching. The key challenges in the application include how to support learning standards while encouraging individual knowledge construction, when to direct and when to allow choice, and how to preserve classroom organization while sharing authority with children.

The key principles of constructivist teaching can sometimes appear to leave teachers in the role of semiactive participants (Dewey, 1938; Simpson, 2002):

Constructivist Teaching Practice	Potential Criticism
Value children's conceptions even if they are misconceptions from the teacher's perspective	Looks as if teachers aren't correcting errors in children's thinking
Promote collaborative problem-solving where children can generate their own answers	Looks as if teachers aren't "teaching" (if observer defines teaching as transmitting information to children)
Work in partnership with students	Looks as if teachers aren't managing classrooms
Engage children's motivation through choice-making and negotiation	Looks as if teachers aren't in control of children

Based on the belief that knowledge is constructed within the learner through interaction with the world (material and social), constructivism supports the sharing of control over learning. Teachers and students bear collective responsibility for guiding learning (Ray, 2002). In other words, teachers are the ones with the right *questions*, not the right *answers*. Transmission models in which the teacher directly shares information are often regarded as contradictory to constructivist theory (Davis & Sumara, 2002; Powell, 2000). We can see the dilemma: If knowledge is individually or socially constructed through a collaborative inquiry or exploration process, what knowledge or information could teachers share directly? How should teachers evaluate whether a student's knowledge is valid, deep, and broad?

It's About Balance: Constructivism, Content Standards, and Assessment

Downplaying their role as experts or authority figures, teachers are in a quandary when it comes to judging students' progress. When teachers misunderstand the premise of learner-centered, constructivist teaching to mean there can be no direct instruction on core content or valid assessment of student learning, there exists a potential that children will not become competent in the basic set of standards deemed educationally necessary (Gregory, 2002). If you, as a new teacher, were attempting to embody a constructivist approach, you

---

Putting It Into Practice

Guidance and Room to Try

Remember from the classroom visit how Gail skillfully "danced" between giving the children directions and suggestions on their collages (whole group and individual) and giving them room to explore their own ideas and the materials? This is a great example of how this balance between teacher-directed instruction and child-directed exploration can be accomplished. It is the teacher's role to share expertise with the students, giving them skills, tools, and experiences that they can then use in their own active explorations.

---

would support children's questioning, curiosity, experimentation, and reflection. You would encourage children to explore challenging problems and work collaboratively to find solutions. What happens, though, if children's reflections and inferences from their experiments or solutions are simply not accurate or miss a key concept? How do you address core content and basic information?

Remember that guiding principles of best practices call for teachers to *balance* child-directed and teacher-guided activities. This requires skillful, intentional, reflective teaching. John Dewey, an influential Progressive and champion for the important connection between experience and education, recognized the need for some teacher authority and for widely accepted standards of skill and content within disciplines, and he saw these as existing in concert with inquiry-based, collaborative problem-solving learning environments (Dewey, 1938; Gregory, 2002). Equally compelling is the voluminous body of research that provides evidence of increased motivation and academic, intellectual, and attitudinal success in learner-centered, constructivist classrooms (summaries cited in Berk & Winsler, 1995; Bredekamp & Copple, 2009; Marcon, 2002; and Schweinhart, Barnes, & Weikart, 1993).

What these studies show is that a balanced approach, including some direct instruction paired with an emphasis on child-initiated exploration (including hands-on, problem-solving activities), leads to the biggest gains in a variety of developmental measures. Consider a Vygotskian framework in which teachers create environments that allow children to share ideas, test conceptions, and build meaning from experience—all while remaining active in scaffolding children's experience. The Vygotskian approach also validates the use of whole-group direct instruction on techniques, strategies, or use of new materials in moderate amounts as deemed appropriate by the teacher (Berk & Winsler, 1995).

Within this more compromising, balanced approach, children can engage in the meaningful, inquiry-based, constructive process while still gaining proficiency in a core set of standard content. At first glance, the constructivist teacher may appear to be less active than a transmission-style lecturer. In reality, he or she is continuously active, sometimes in the foreground, sometimes in the background, leading and following children's development in a collaborative, mutual, dancelike process. The constructivist-inspired teacher is skillful in multiple complex roles, including guide, facilitator, director, coach, supporter, provocateur, and observer.

STRATEGIES FOR APPLYING THEORY TO PRACTICE

The overarching goals of constructivist theory can translate into teaching pedagogy and shape practice in appropriate ways. Appropriate translations you can use include (Powell, 2000; Schuh, 2003)

- being an active participant with children ("Let's find out together");
- supporting children's connections to prior experience ("That photo looks like the bridge you were building with the long blocks last week");
- empowering children as contributing members of the classroom community ("That's a great idea; let's all see if we can figure that out together");
- facilitating children's questioning, testing, exploring, and reflecting ("What do you think will happen if/when . . . ?");
- observing and assessing children's ongoing processes;
- stocking the classroom with open-ended materials that invite exploration and multiple uses; and
- holding back from providing answers, solving problems, or resolving conflicts for children.

Interpreting constructivist theory from an educator's perspective yields several specific suggestions for practice.

Share the Road

First, believe the principle that classrooms can be communities of learners. This means that teachers must relinquish much of the control, power, and authority endowed in them in a

Teachers use systematic observations to assess children's progress and plan for future learning experiences.

traditional model (Low & Shironaka, 1995). Again, be willing to have more questions than answers. A willingness to share power in the classroom must start with mutual respect. Children respect teachers and peers, and teachers respect children, including children's ideas, prior experiences, and processing of new experiences. When children are validated as making valuable contributions to classroom learning, they are prompted and encouraged to share. You can encourage children to take an active role in the direction of their learning and the forming of the classroom community in many ways. Recall how Gail did this as she facilitated the students' reflection and let them engage in group discussion of their work. Observe how teachers use knowledge of and experience with the children in their classes to create authentic environments.

Using a simple chart or group web of what we already **know**, what we **want** to know, **how** we can find out, and what we **learned** (KWHL) allows children to share their knowledge and decide what new knowledge they want to explore. In keeping with constructivist theory on children's misconceptions, include all statements children make about what they know, even if they are incorrect. Through their own process of inquiry and exploration, they will come to see their misconceptions. The "what we learned" section of the chart can be a venue for highlighting new, corrected knowledge. The KWHL technique validates individuals' experiences, and it empowers children to shape future classroom endeavors. Asking children to generate ideas for how they will find out what they want to know places them more in control of their own learning activities. By reflecting on the KWHL chart, children can see the progress and transformation of their own learning.

KWHL Chart on Flowers, Pre-K

What Do We *Know*	What Do We *Want* to Know	*How* Can We Find Out	What Did We *Learn* (New Words in Bold)
• Grow from seeds	• How do they grow?	• Visit a flower shop.	• Bees do not eat them. Some other bugs do, such as beetles.
• Come in different colors	• Do they eat? What?	• Find some books.	• Flowers need sunlight, water, and **soil** to grow.
• Are tall and green	• Why do bees eat them?	• Grow flowers on the windowsill.	• Some are short; some are tall.
• Bees eat them	• How many colors do they come in? • Why do they die? • How tall do they get? • Where do they go in the winter?	• Ask a flower grower.	• Some grow from seeds; some from **bulbs.** • They can't grow in frozen **temperatures.** • The flower store had more red flowers than any other color. • There are many colors from all the rainbow colors. • Our class favorite flower color was yellow. • Our class favorite flower was the **sunflower.** • You can eat some flower seeds. • Some flowers grow fast; some grow slower.

Children can also direct the social climate of their classroom. For example, allow children to create desired classroom rules. This is an important part of creating a classroom that is psychologically safe and allows for risk-taking, mistake-making, exploration, and reflection. When children are empowered to create rules, they are more likely to internalize them, follow them, and remind each other of them (DeVries & Zan, 2003). When children understand and value the role of the individual within the classroom community, they are more likely to create fair rules that preserve the harmony of the community and serve the collective good. The experience of being a member of a cooperative, mutually validating system itself fosters positive moral development in children and is a primary benefit of constructivist classrooms (DeVries & Zan, 1995).

Refrain From Doing Too Much

Scaffolding can be used to increase children's self-regulation and autonomy in social interactions and task activity. When conflicts do arise or rules are broken, many teachers are quick to resolve the conflicts for the children. Imagine this situation: Two children are working with the blocks, and one grabs an item from the other, saying, "I need that!" The first child becomes upset and reaches for the item, crying, "Mine! I had it first!" The argument becomes louder, and both children reach for the block when you come over to intervene. The methods used to resolve conflicts in traditional classrooms often include the teacher's stepping in, separating children, reminding them of the rules, demanding an apology, and redirecting behavior. However, keep in mind that, in many ways, conflict is a prime opportunity for learning.

Constructivists view conflicts, particularly cognitive conflicts, as a necessary impetus for exploring and changing one's ideas and misconceptions (Piaget, 1975). By prompting children's dialogue instead of telling them what to do, using active listening as they explain their sides, and modeling respectful negotiating of a mutually satisfying resolution, children can learn to work through their own problems. Teachers can also start small- or whole-group discussions as a means to share ideas on how to resolve individual or group problems. Teachers start as facilitators, models, and mediators and ultimately reduce their presence as the children become more capable of resolving conflicts autonomously (Arcaro-McPhee, Doppler, & Harkins, 2002). This process embodies the scaffolding techniques used by constructivist teachers to promote children's self-regulation of learning as well as behavior.

Balance, Balance, Balance

A third suggestion for applying constructivist principles is to emphasize child-directed experiences but include instruction when necessary. This ensures a weighted balance of classroom experiences that allow children to act on their world to build understanding but also to learn conventional knowledge (DeVries & Zan, 1995; Schuh, 2003). Simply telling children things is not enough experience for them to build real understanding. They may be able to memorize facts but will not really understand what they mean or how they relate to their lives. It is the emphasis on this deeper, meaningful knowing that is foundational to constructivist theory and practice. Likewise, leaving children to journey without a map (guidance) also inhibits their learning.

Combine brief instruction with ample opportunity to explore, test, and manipulate materials. These experiences put abstract concepts into their hands and afford children the chance to understand concepts and phenomena (Richardson, 2003). Particularly when you are working with young children, it is always important to keep in mind their need to be active and explore their world with their own senses. If you find yourself continually reminding them to not touch something, sit still, or be quiet, you need to reevaluate your methods and environment. Chances are you are expecting them to behave and learn in ways that do not align with their naturally curious, social, active nature. Long circle time with too much teacher-talking time is often a disaster. Gauge your children's interests and read their cues. Give children plenty of time to engage in activities and with materials that they design and choose.

Authentic Assessment Is a Must!

Finally, teachers using a constructivist framework need to reconceptualize the type and use of assessment. **Authentic assessment** seeks to capture a richer picture of

- who you are;
- what you are thinking;
- how you have changed;
- your learning process and style;
- your ability to communicate through a variety of forms of expression; and
- how your experiences, thinking, and engagement with your world affect you.

Dissatisfied with focusing on only children's existing competency, as in standard testing, Vygotsky carried his ZPD concept from teaching through to assessment practices. *Dynamic assessment* strategies were developed to capture children's learning in motion. In keeping with the premises of the ZPD and the teacher's role as scaffolder, dynamic assessment uses a three-step system to gather information on how children complete tasks alone as well as how they respond to instruction (Berk & Winsler, 1995):

1. The children complete a new task alone.
2. The teacher intervenes with some form of scaffolding instruction.
3. Children then complete the task again.

The changes from step 1 to step 3 in the child's performance and process are explored to determine the child's potential for learning with adult assistance. Observational notes on the child's performance and transcriptions of the child's dialogue can be used to explore the child's task mastery and thought processing. Like dynamic assessment, performance assessment provides valuable information that can be included in overall assessments of children. In **performance assessment**, teachers record and evaluate children's responses on certain authentic tests (McAfee, Leong, & Bodrova, 2004).

The differences between the assumptions in traditional versus alternative assessments parallel the theoretical differences in traditional versus constructivist teaching. Traditional transmission models of teaching and assessment focus on decontextualized discrete skills and bits of information, the final product, objective facts and truths (a "right answer"), and assessment as a tool to document previous learning.

Alternative or constructivist assessment focuses on (Anderson, 1998)

- context and individual,
- past changes and future potential,
- subjective meaning of experience and information,
- the processes students employ to make sense of their world, and
- learning as an active process and assessment as a tool to facilitate learning.

Authentic assessment

Methods of assessing children's progress, knowledge, and accomplishments within a naturalistic context. Portfolios, observations, and work samples are examples of authentic, contextualized assessments.

Performance assessment

Methods of evaluating what children know and can do by observing their performance and responses on authentic (real-life) tasks.

Authentic assessment techniques include teachers observing children during typical activities and analyzing their performance.

One of the more widely used alternative, authentic assessment formats is the portfolio. Just as children are involved in creating classroom rules and guiding interest-based learning activities, children are also involved in the creation of their portfolios. Teachers and children together decide on the samples of work to be included—samples they both feel appropriately represent the child's learning process. This might include drawings, stories, paintings, photos of sculpture or block buildings, collages, journals, and so on. Teachers also select observation reports, anecdotal records, notes from children's conversations, developmental checklists, or notes from family conversations (Ediger, 2000). By gathering key pieces of authentic work spanning a variety of activities over a period of time, a more richly detailed picture of the child's growth in progress can be captured.

One drawback to the use of portfolios, aside from the time needed to gather and sort the work, is that they are more subjective than most standardized tests. The interpretations from one evaluator (parent, teacher, etc.) to another as to the rate and direction of a child's progress can vary widely. To standardize or grade a portfolio, teachers develop rubrics that identify key elements and broad levels of competence. **Rubrics** are expectations of what you want to see in an activity, performance, or assignment. The highest grade or points are given to work or performance that meets or exceeds expectations. Partial or no points or lower grades are assigned when some or no expectations have been met (see Figure 4-3, and Appendix E for sample rubrics).

With the use of rubrics to evaluate portfolios or other kinds of learning activities, the process, depth, and detail remain a part of the assessment while standard criteria and a placement within broader expectations provide important information about the child's development. For early elementary-age children, rubrics can be useful to clarify activities for children and families, as in this **video** example. Simple checklists based on developmental expectations and performance goals can also be used to evaluate children's progress and performance (see Appendix F for a sample checklist). Children can also use simple rubrics to self-assess their work, such as the first-grade writing rubric in Figure 4-4.

Rubric

An outline of expectations for assignments, including evaluations of basic, moderate, and advanced performance or quality.

FIGURE 4-3

Preschool Social Skills Rubric (Partial)

Sample Rubric Used to Assess 4-Year-Olds' Social Development

Skill/Milestone	Advanced—3	On Level—2	Emerging—1
Plays well with other children	• Plays collaboratively with individuals and groups • Creates and engages in complex play scenarios	• Plays with others • Engages in simple to complex play scenarios	• Plays next to others • Interrupts others' play when seeking companionship
Follows classroom rules	• Always follows classroom rules • Reminds other children of rules	• Follows classroom rules most of the time • Needs few reminders of classroom rules	• Needs 3+ reminders of classroom rules and routines much of the time
Initiates and maintains conversations	• Skillfully integrates into groups using appropriate requests • Listens and responds appropriately to several members of a group • Engages several members of a group in conversation	• Appropriately asks to play with others • Understands conversation patterns, knows when to interject • Is able to take turns in conversation	• Approaches others or groups but does not yet use language to request integration • Interrupts others, not yet taking turns in conversation
Expresses wants/needs with words	• Able to create solutions to conflicts over wants/needs • Understands effect of own wants/needs on others	• Mostly uses appropriate words to express wants/needs • With prompts, understands effect of own wants/needs on others	• Uses few words to express wants/needs • Uses physical actions to express wants/needs

FIGURE 4-4

Simple Writing Rubric for First Grade; Students Self-Score Using the Rubric

Writing Rubric: Circle One Point for Each Completed Item	
My name is at the top of the page.	1
I used three details in my story.	1
I used capitals and periods.	1
I proofread and corrected one error.	1
Total Points:	

Putting It Into Practice

Portfolios

Now you are familiar with the basics of the portfolio; perhaps you have even started to put one together for yourself. If not, you will soon! Even if you don't need it for school, you can definitely use it when you apply for jobs. Review artifacts that you would put into a binder or folder as if that portfolio were all you had to use to describe yourself. Make a list of items that you would include. If you already have one, write down what is in it. Review your list and write a few sentences about why you selected each item in your portfolio. For example, perhaps you put a résumé in to show people what work experience, education, and skills you possess. Maybe you included an observation report or a paper on which you did well to demonstrate your writing and analytic strengths. Perhaps you put in photos of a learning center you created with an accompanying lesson plan to show your competence as a teacher. Just as important as doing a portfolio in the first place is that you choose which items to include *deliberately* and you reflect on them. You may want to even attach your why statements. These things not only show your deeper reflections but also are handy topics to talk about during an interview.

In this way, teachers can use assessments to glean insight into children's ongoing processes and interests as well as their progress on defined learning goals. This twofold use for alternative/authentic assessments allows teachers to use the information gathered to plan instruction and guide children's learning while also documenting the outcomes of their classroom experiences.

From an overarching understanding of constructivist theory, more specific strategies of teaching and assessing can be developed and used. Vygotsky's framework, in particular, provides inspiration for many learner-centered, constructivist teaching strategies. Specific theoretical principles with related teaching and assessment strategies are presented in Table 4-2.

CONCLUSION

For many teachers, being in the role of cocreator, jointly learning from students while skillfully guiding their explorations, is exciting and refreshing. The possibilities for reinventing the classroom climate as a place alive with activity and enthusiastic learners are vibrant within constructivist theory. Unlocking that potential is possible with thoughtful, collaborative translations of theory into practice. Appropriate application of constructivist principles to teaching practice requires that teachers be empowered with the knowledge, skills, tools, and room to renegotiate the classroom into a collaborative community of learners. When teachers consider the realities of classroom life; children's development; and the effect of interactions with peers, adults, and their environment, principles of constructivist theory dovetail nicely with the overarching goals of education.

TABLE 4-2 Constructivist-Inspired Teaching and Assessment Strategies

Constructivist Principles	Teaching Strategies	Assessment Strategies
Children learn through guided problem-solving of challenging tasks.	Determine each child's developmental level and ZPD. Present interesting tasks and challenging problems within their ZPD, and form groups to work through them collaboratively.	Keep observational records of children's responses to challenging problems. Note how much help they needed at periodic points. Use labeled photographs of children's work in stages to chronicle process.
Children use language to organize their thinking.	Model self-talk, active listening, and problem-solving dialogue. Encourage children's dialogue. Facilitate children's dialogue when needed. Ask children higher level questions (open-ended, seeking elaboration).	Capture children's dialogue through transcripts. Analyze their conversations for clues of cognitive processing. (For example, ask children how they arrived at a solution or observe dialogue between children as they explain their reasoning.)
Scaffolding involves using verbal cues, questions, and prompts to engender inquiry.	Use open-ended, higher level questioning. Ask children to make predictions and hypotheses, explain observations, and elaborate on ideas of self and others.	Record child-teacher conversations and code for evidence of higher level responses. Document number and complexity of responses to open-ended questions.
The goal of education is to lead to increasing self-regulation and independence.	Begin by exploring new problems together; slowly reduce help as children become more capable.	Use children's work samples and anecdotal records to document progress toward independent task mastery. Use performance assessment to demonstrate independent task mastery.
Overbearing, authoritarian adult influence minimizes children's active exploration, problem-solving, and social relationship building.	Remain in the role of guide and facilitator, providing challenges, assistance, support, and resources as needed. Determine need by carefully observing children's activity and language. Keep the classroom climate free, allowing children to take risks, make mistakes, and share authority over making decisions. Allow children to make classroom rules and meet as a group regularly to discuss children's feelings about classroom community.	Reflect on the nature of interactions among teachers and children and children and children. Record group discussions to assess children's feelings about the tone of the classroom. Use photos of children interacting paired with dialogue transcripts to capture children's process and progressions.
Children's conceptions and misconceptions are all part of the knowledge-construction process.	Validate children's attempts to understand and accomplish tasks. Use children's errors to assess thought progress and direction. Pose questions that guide children in different directions if they are off track.	Ask children relevant questions and ask them to support their ideas with rationale. The children themselves may discover misconceptions as they explain their thinking. Observe and record children's responses and reactions.
When children are interested in the tasks at hand, learning is more meaningful.	Present tasks, experiences, and materials that relate to children's individual and group interests.	Keep notes during small- or large-group discussions for clues to children's interests. Ask children to identify prior knowledge and current questions. Record children's responses. Use children's prior knowledge to inform the group and connect to current experiences. Revisit the list when explorations are in progress. (Using a KWHL chart is helpful.)

SUMMARY

- Bronfenbrenner's bioecological model of development acknowledges the many direct and indirect influences that affect children's lives (such as family, social policies, schools, cultures) and organizes them in a flexible, bidirectional system of five structures.

- The dynamic framework of this multidimensional model provide a way for professionals to carefully consider the many, varied influences in children's lives as well as the unique interactions in each child's particular contextualized experience.

- Constructivists believe that knowledge is constructed within the individual, shaped by experiences with the materials, phenomena, and people in their world.

- Scaffolding involves teachers skillfully providing more or less support as needed, encouraging children to become deeply engaged in the cognitive process.

- The roots of constructivism can be traced back to early philosophers, but more recent contributions from Piaget and Vygotsky have shaped current constructivist theory and practice.

- Vygotsky believed that the role of the teacher was to scaffold children's learning by providing varying support and guidance as children work through challenging tasks within their zone of proximal development.

- To Vygotsky, language served as a primary vehicle for both communication and organization of individual thought.

- Among the potential challenges of applying constructivist theory to classroom practice is the ability of teachers to find a careful balance between learner-initiated activities and teacher-directed lessons.

- In the same way that learning experiences are structured to be authentic and meaningful to children, assessing their processes and progress toward goals must be authentic and meaningful.

CHAPTER LEARNING GOALS SELF-ASSESSMENT

Use this chart to write down three to five key points for each learning goal that you learned from this chapter.

Explore key aspects of a bioecological systems framework.	
Identify important elements of constructivist learning theory.	
Compare and contrast branches within constructivism.	
Examine opportunities for theoretical applications in practice.	

APPLICATION ACTIVITIES

Discussion Prompts

1. What elements of a constructivist-inspired classroom do you most agree with? What aspects do you disagree with? Why?

2. Think about things you recall from your own education or things you have seen during classroom observations that you particularly liked or disliked. What were they, and why did you think of them as positive or negative?

3. Think about a time when you were allowed to choose a topic to explore—perhaps a group presentation or a report. How did you feel about this? Was your ability to choose the topic meaningful?

In Class   Constructivists believe that one way knowledge is more deeply understood is through the process of teaching. With a small group, take a key concept from the chapter and create a demonstration that teaches the main components of the idea or concept. You can be creative with this one; think about a short skit, media tools, documentation panels, activities, songs, or whatever other strategies come to mind to engage your audience in a learning experience about your concept. Topic ideas include Piaget's contributions, Vygotsky's contributions, assessments, and classroom community.

In the Field   Observe a program for young children in your area. Identify elements that align with constructivist theories of learning and teaching. For this assignment, you should take a broad view as you observe, keeping in mind the following questions:

- How would you describe the teacher's role?
- How would you describe the children's roles?
- How are materials displayed and used?
- How are learning experiences presented and implemented?
- How are conflicts handled?

Take notes on these and any other elements you feel are important. Prepare a brief presentation on how the program you observed compares to the constructivist practices you have read about.

For Your Portfolio   Choose either older toddlers (2–3 years), preschoolers (3–5 years), or kindergarteners as your target age group, and create a series of simple rubrics or checklists you could use to assess children's performance on tasks in the following learning centers: literacy corner, block area, and **manipulatives** (which are hands-on materials that are designed to illustrate and demonstrate important physical concepts). Think about expected performance, advanced responses, and responses that would fall below age expectations. Create sample responses that would earn advanced, average, and below-average ratings. Keep in mind that milestones represent broad expectations but that some variation in children's responses and performance is expected.

In a book and writing corner, children may have access to physical books, audiobooks, paper, crayons, markers, pencils, magazines, and puppets. In a block area, children

Manipulatives

Hands-on materials that are designed to illustrate and demonstrate such concepts as shape, series, categorization, grouping, and so on.

may have access to different-shaped blocks, cars, and animal and people figures. In a manipulative center, children may have access to sorting bears in different sizes and colors, colored connecting beads, puzzles, lacing cards, matching and memory games, plastic building blocks, peg boards, unit blocks, and geometric-shaped blocks with pattern cards. Start this project by researching classroom materials. Refresh your memory about expected developmental milestones in language, cognition, social, fine motor, and gross motor skills for your selected age group. (A child development textbook, early childhood journals such as *Young Children* from www.naeyc.org, and observations can assist you in this. In addition, the following Web sites may be useful: www.pbs.org/wholechild/abc/, www. howkidsdevelop.com/developSkills.html, www.growingchild.com/milestones.html, and www.zerotothree.org). Share your rubrics in class, and discuss them in groups. Your rubric series can be an artifact in your portfolio section on observation and assessment.

RELATED WEB LINKS

Developmental Checklists for Ages 2 Months to 5 Years
www.cdc.gov/ncbddd/actearly/milestones/index.html

Developmental Checklists for Children Birth through 5 Years
ecdc.syr.edu/wp-content/uploads/2013/01/Developmental_checklists_Updated2012.pdf

CHAPTER 5

Families and Children Today: Diversity in Today's Classrooms

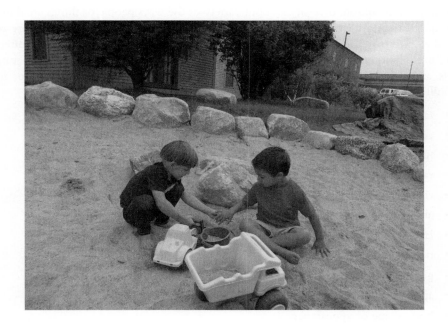

Chapter Learning Goals

- Identify essential elements of diversity and culturally competent practice.
- Examine family structures and composition.
- Explore characteristics of racial, ethnic, and linguistic diversity.
- Discuss the scope and effect of socioeconomic diversity in children's lives.
- Describe goals and effective practices in today's inclusive classrooms.
- Apply multiple intelligences theory to the classroom.

C hildren and families in today's schools, programs, centers, and classrooms represent a wide array of different backgrounds, cultures, languages, traditions, beliefs, family structures, values, and ways of thinking. At the core of all professional practice with children and families is a need to value, appreciate, embrace, and welcome each and every child and family. Today's early childhood policies and practices center on ensuring equity (fairness) and equality (equal access) for all children and families. And as such, being knowledgeable and competent in appreciating diversity is a key aspect of professional preparation and work. This work begins by becoming aware of the scope, context, and definitions of diversity and continues with the development of skills and strategies for actively valuing each child and family. This chapter presents definitions of key concepts related to diversity, background on the context of family life in the United States today, and strategies for sensitively and meaningfully engaging with all children and families.

DEFINING DIVERSITY AND CULTURALLY COMPETENT PRACTICE IN TODAY'S EARLY CHILDHOOD CLASSROOMS

Diversity

The many ways people differ from one another.

Diversity is the focus of a great deal of professional research, discourse, and policy and is a reality of daily teaching practice. We hear and read about the term *diversity* related to many different concepts, settings, and practices. Diversity is highly complex, personal, and rooted in personal and shared history. Definitions and experience with diversity hold different meanings for individuals and groups. Exploring and valuing diversity involves understanding and appreciating individual uniqueness, group affiliation, social justice, and committing to equity for each child and family.

What Is Diversity?

In its simplest definition, diversity is about variety or the ways people or things are different or unique. In child development and education settings, definitions of diversity are more layered to refer to "the human differences between people including, but not limited to, shape, size, ability, gender, age, skin color, sexual orientation, family background, spiritual beliefs, and political affiliation" (York, 2003, p. 262). The attributes that help shape identity, influence development, and characterize the context of our lives can include:

- family structure and composition,
- economic resources/socioeconomic status,
- nationality/geography,
- race/ethnicity,
- religion,
- ability,
- language,
- thinking/learning style,
- gender identity,
- age, and
- body shape or appearance.

Clearly diversity is closely connected to each person's sense of self, identity, and connection or belonging in a family, group, or community. The attributes in the list above may not all be equally influential or important to a person's sense of identity, just as several attributes at once may be extremely important and influential in a person's life. From infancy, children are internalizing the messages from their environments and from their families in particular. Infants and toddlers demonstrate behaviors and preferences that reflect family and community values and expectations. Early childhood professionals must be aware of how sensitive young children are both to cultural patterns from families as well as messages from outside the family. Specifically, young children will pick up on positive and negative attitudes about their family culture, both of which can have an effect on their sense of self and relationships with their family, among peers, and with teachers. Listen to this teacher talk about valuing cultural diversity in classrooms in this **video**.

The child's developing identity and connection to communities is strongly influenced by home and family culture at first, and later also by the culture of the various settings within which the child lives. **Culture** refers to everything that potentially influences our lives and shapes our identities (Bucher, 2010). Culture is about ways of thinking, beliefs, expectations, traditions, behavior, and sense of belonging, which are socially transmitted among members of a group. Cultural identity and practices can hold great personal and family value for people. When families' cultural values are disrespected, marginalized, or devalued, even unintentionally, it can cause great hurt and damage to the child and family-professional relationships. For professionals, it is essential to be aware that children and families may feel very strongly about one or many of the attributes that shape their sense of their culture and identity, and to be prepared to welcome and honor each person's culture. Intentionally using skills and behaviors to sensitively and responsively work with diverse families is part of being a **culturally competent** professional. Intentional classroom, school or program, and system-wide culturally competent policy and practice are essential elements of multicultural education.

Culture
Everything that potentially influences our lives and shapes our identity.

Culturally Competent Practice and Multicultural Education

Being a culturally competent educator able to teach to diverse ways of thinking, dual-language learners, children with diverse abilities, and children from different family backgrounds is considered a professional expectation as you enter the field of teaching. Professional educational associations and teacher preparation standards unanimously recognize the importance of professional preparation, which clearly recognizes and values diverse populations. Cultural competence means being knowledgeable about diverse cultures, aware of your own values and judgments, and deliberate in using positive professional skills and behaviors to promote inclusive, welcoming practices. Cultural competence includes:

Culturally competent
Intentionally using skills and behaviors to sensitively and responsively work with diverse families.

- communicating with families in accessible and preferred ways (print, digital, verbal, home language);
- using inclusive language ("Welcome Families" instead of "Welcome Moms and Dads");
- understanding different communication styles and norms (direct, indirect, body language);
- offering vegetarian lunch options;
- refraining from religion-specific holiday activities or integrating a wide variety of holidays;
- creating physically accessible environments (ramps, wider paths, Braille signs, automatic doors);
- displaying authentic materials reflective of each family's home life and background;
- planning activities that engage children through different modalities (visual, verbal, physical);
- implementing activities accessible for children at different ability levels; and
- providing opportunities for children to explore and represent ideas and experiences in a variety of ways (using words, art, bodies, music, different languages).

Multicultural education
School- or program-wide effort to meaningfully integrate children's home cultures into the classroom and program or school setting.

Multicultural education (ME) involves a school- or program-wide effort to meaningfully integrate children's home cultures into the classroom and program or school setting (Gollnick & Chinn, 2009). ME strategies embrace social justice, inclusion, and equality to support reciprocal relationships and full participation among each child, family, and professional. ME is about recognizing differences, valuing them as strengths, and actively working to ensure all children are provided with equal, equitable, discrimination-free educational experiences. ME is about school reform and requires not just commitment from individual teachers but curriculum, policies, and cohesive action across the span of educational institutions, and it engages all members of the school community (Banks, 2006).

A first step in being able to effectively implement inclusive culturally responsive programs for diverse children and families is to explore broad categories of ways that we differ. First, a word of caution: it is important to understand that looking at differences can lead us to try to generalize or define people into groups and make assumptions about *all* people we categorize in that group. There can be great harm in using generalized themes to make stereotypes or inappropriate assumptions about all people sharing characteristic(s). It is essential that we are sensitive to valuing the ways that some people feel similar to others but also how people with some shared characteristic differ. Each person and family will experience association with certain attributes in unique ways. Our job is always to get to know each child and family individually, along with background knowledge of broader themes and trends in diversity. It is ultimately valuable to learn about some of the characteristics that may be shared by groups of people who may associate themselves with these characteristics. Indeed, expanding our knowledge of various families' cultures, traditions, and styles is an essential element of becoming a culturally responsive professional. It is part of our ethical responsibility to acknowledge and understand group *and* individual differences as we journey to valuing and celebrating the diversity among us.

FAMILY STRUCTURE AND COMPOSITION IN TODAY'S DIVERSE HOMES

Exploring snapshots of the demographic context of families in the United States today is a helpful part of beginning to understand the context within which children are growing up. Remember that the foundation for developmentally appropriate practice always begins with three key pillars:

1. Knowledge of developmental theory
2. Knowledge of each individual child
3. Knowledge of family and cultural contexts

Building a strong knowledge of family and cultural contexts is supported by exploring trends and data on today's family life. From there, your task will be to intentionally learn about the demographic context of the specific community and school or program you work in, since national trends and data are just a backdrop and will probably not fully reflect the particularities of each and every community.

Variety in Family Structure and Composition

Family life in the United States has changed a great deal over the past several decades. Changing legal, political, and sociological perspectives contribute to an evolving and expanding definition and scope of what it means to be a family. Today definitions of families recognize the more complex, pluralistic, and changing nature of how we live; consider individual variations in experience; and may take into account legal, emotional, financial, religious, political, functional, and structural aspects of what it means to be a family.

The following section presents some of the most commonly framed family structures with children, including a snapshot of the percentages of children living within these types of families, based on the most recent available data. Some categories are not mutually exclusive; for example, a single-parent household may also be an adoptive family, or a two-parent household may also be same-sex parents. Figure 5-1 provides a graphic representation of variety among family structures and configurations. The following descriptions are not meant to be used to exclusively define families or categorize children you work with, but rather are to provide a broader background knowledge for understanding dynamic and diverse characteristics of today's modern families. In addition, professionals must recognize that warm, nurturing parenting with reasonable, consistent, and appropriate guidance and discipline (an "authoritative style") is related to positive child outcomes in any family structure.

Nuclear families include a married mother, father, and biological children living in the same household (married, cohabitating). Decades ago, this type of family structure was generally considered the mainstream, accepted family composition. Families made up of other structures were not afforded social, legal, or political status. While recognition of much more variety in family composition has emerged, some preferences and status remain associated with a nuclear family structure.

Nuclear families

A married mother, father, and biological children living in the same household.

Two-parent family represents a similar, yet expanded definition of family household relationships and is the term used frequently in data-collection surveys of family life in the United States. Two-parent families may include biological parents and children (married or unmarried), and can also include families joined through divorce, remarriage, or new cohabiting relationships.

- 64% of children live with two married parents (biological, adoptive, stepparent)
- 4% of children live with two unmarried, cohabitating parents (U.S. Census Bureau, 2013)

A **blended family** refers to adults and children who have become a family through cohabitation, close relationship, or remarriage (sometimes referred to as "reconstituted family"). "The presence of a stepparent, stepsibling, or half sibling designates a family as blended" (Kreider & Ellis, 2011, p. 1). Blended families or stepfamilies are the fastest growing form of family structure in the United States (Greeff & Du Toit, 2009). This generally involves a biological parent who forms a relationship with a new partner who becomes an involved, responsible party to the parent's child(ren).

Blended family

Adults and children who have become a family through cohabitation, close relationship, or remarriage.

- 8% of children living with two parents live with a biological parent and a stepparent (U.S. Census Bureau, 2013)

Extended family generally means relatives other than parents and siblings and can include grandparents, aunts and uncles, cousins, etc. Often these extended family members have a strong role in children's daily lives, though as immigration and family mobility has changed over the past many decades, more families are living at a distance from extended family. Grandparents or other relatives also may be the child's primary caretakers, serving as the parent role either in absence of the parent or when adult children and grandchildren move into the grandparent's home.

Extended family

Relatives other than parents and siblings.

- 2–3% of children live with grandparents or other relatives (not biological or stepparents) (U.S. Census Bureau, 2013)

Many single-parent families are created when couples with children divorce or separate. Some are created when unmarried or noncohabitating couples have a child but do not choose to reside together. And some are created when single people have children and choose to raise them on their own, through assisted fertility procedures, for example.

Families today come together, grow, and change, representing a wide array of diverse experiences.

- 34% of children live in single-parent families (Kids Count, 2012)
- 24% of children in single-parent families live with their mothers (U.S. Census Bureau, 2013)

Foster parents and families

Relatives or nonrelatives appointed as temporary guardians and serve as the child's caretakers.

Foster parents and families can be relatives or nonrelatives who have been appointed as temporary guardians and serve as the child's caretakers. Usually foster parents and children are brought together under stressful conditions such as abuse, neglect, abandonment, or other life crisis that makes it impossible for the biological parent to care for the child(ren). Fostering is generally a temporary measure until family stability can be regained or until parental rights are terminated and children can be adopted into a new family. Foster families sometimes seek to adopt children and take on permanent parenting responsibilities. Foster children and families benefit from extra support due to the stressful nature of family crises, often in the form of interdisciplinary therapies in psychological, developmental, and health care treatments.

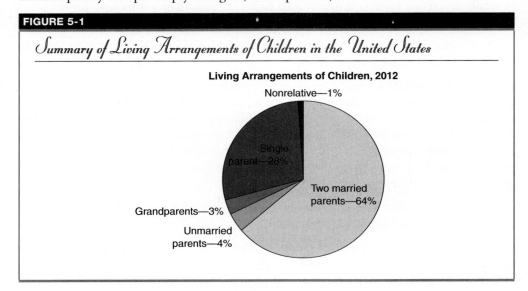

FIGURE 5-1

Summary of Living Arrangements of Children in the United States

Living Arrangements of Children, 2012

- Nonrelative—1%
- Single parent—28%
- Two married parents—64%
- Grandparents—3%
- Unmarried parents—4%

- 1% of children living with a nonrelative are in foster care (U.S. Census Bureau, 2013)

While still a relatively small but growing percentage of families in the United States today, gay and lesbian (same-sex) parents or adoptive parents may be represented in any of the categories listed above: two parent (married or unmarried), blended, single parent, grandparent, nonrelative. Adoptive families may be formed as a result of biological parent crisis (such as if the child is removed from the biological parent's custody) or as a result of biological parents' decision to seek a more stable family life for the child. When trauma or family stress is part of the adoption history, ongoing support services can have a positive

Putting It Into Practice

Culturally Responsive Strategies Related to Family Diversity

- Include many children's books that represent a wide variety of family transitions, structures, and compositions.

- Invite families to share photos, stories, or artifacts of their family and aspects of their home traditions; share these in beautiful and respectful ways.

- Use "families" instead of parent or mother/father in interactions with children and families and in bulletin boards and communications; shift from "mother" or "father" to "parents" or "caregivers."

- Dialogue with children about broader definitions of families, being prepared for potential confusion about families with same-sex parents, guardians, or extended family caregivers (challenges to typical, narrow ideas about mother/father family).

- Provide many ways for children to explore and represent life in their families, being cautious about personally sensitive experiences or transitions.

- Value and validate the many ways families share traditions, routines, and time together.

- Encourage and validate the different ways families may participate in the classroom and program: sharing materials, volunteering, guest story reading, governance or curriculum planning, paperwork, fund-raising, mailings, etc.

- Seek information from families about home life and their goals and experiences with their children, promoting communication as a "two-way street."

- Create a family resource center as a comfortable, personal space designated just for family use, and include resource information, refreshments, "swap-table" sharing, or lending library materials as space permits.

- If a child experiences the death of someone in his or her life, educators must actively support the child's processing (Schonfeld, 2011):

  - Offer explanation using simple, clear language such as *dead* or *death,* not *gone to sleep* or *in the clouds.*

  - Support children's participation in mourning activities (funeral, memorials) as they are comfortable and families allow.

  - Accept children's grieving process, including emotional expressions and talking about the deceased.

  - Continue to assure children they will be cared for and their needs will be met.

  - Give children time, space, and materials to explore and express their emotions (books, art materials, dolls).

  - Provide accurate information and limited details as needed to satisfy children's questions, fears, or need for information.

effect on the new family relationship and outcomes for children. Gay- and lesbian–parent families may be formed through adoption, new relationships, or assisted fertility procedures. As the population of same-sex parent families continues to grow, so does the research base that indicates the potential for healthy child and family outcomes in same-sex parent families. Current research demonstrates that the single most important predictor of children's overall well-being is to be raised with loving, responsible adults and family stability (especially economic). In essence, children with loving, supportive, stable families of any composition or structure are able to achieve healthy and positive developmental outcomes (APA, 2005; Gatrell & Bos, 2010; Houston & Kramer, 2008).

RACIAL, ETHNIC, AND LINGUISTIC DIVERSITY AMONG TODAY'S FAMILIES

Racial, ethnic, and linguistic differences represent attributes of diversity that have also increased markedly over the past several decades in the United States. Race categories, such as black, Asian, or Pacific Islander, are defined by social constructs, rather than based on a biological basis. Race categories are generally based on geographic and sociopolitical features. The U.S. Census Bureau has been defining and revising categories of race in population surveys over the past 200 years. Population survey reports conducted every ten years demonstrate trends in increasing racial diversity, as well as recognition and increase in multiracial respondents. Table 5-1 outlines the current census definitions of race (among U.S. adults) and the breakdown of individual self-identification on the six race categories

TABLE 5-1 Definitions of Race Categories

Race (Specific Terms Used by the Census)	Definition of Race Category	Percentage of Population	Increase from 2000 Census
White	"Origins in any of the original peoples of Europe, the Middle East, or North Africa" (p. 3)	72.4%	5.7%
Black or African American	"Origins in any of the Black racial groups of Africa" (p. 3)	12.6%	12.3%
American Indian and Alaska Native	"Origins in any of the original peoples of North and South America (including Central America) and who maintain tribal affiliation or community attachment" (p. 3)	0.9%	18.4%
Asian	"Origins in any of the original peoples of the Far East, Southeast Asia, or the Indian subcontinent" (p. 3)	4.8%	43.3%
Native Hawaiian or other Pacific Islander	"Origins in any of the original peoples of Hawaii, Guam, Samoa, or other Pacific Islands" (p. 3)	0.2%	35.4%
Some other race alone	Includes responses not listed above, and written-in responses such as "multiracial, mixed, interracial, or a Hispanic or Latino group (for example Mexican, Puerto Rican, Cuban, or Spanish)" (p. 3)	6.2%	24.4%
Two or more races	Used for individuals who self-identify with more than one of the above categories, which are written into the census form by the respondent	2.9%	32%

along with changes from the 2010 census (Humes, Jones, & Ramirez, 2011). These changes are important indicators of growth and trends among the total U.S. population, with important implications for educators.

The 2010 Census report also includes a section for all respondents to indicate Hispanic origin status, which is defined differently than race. The U.S. Census uses the following definition: "*Hispanic or Latino* refers to a person of Cuban, Mexican, Puerto Rican, South or Central American, or other Spanish culture or origin regardless of race" (Ennis, Rios-Vargas, & Albert, 2011, p. 2). The identifiers *Hispanic* or *Not of Hispanic Origin* come before the question about race, with an explanatory note that the Hispanic Origin categories do not relate to race. In other words, a person can identify as Hispanic origin and also identify with any of the six race categories. Data from the 2010 report reveal that 16% of the U.S. population identifies as Hispanic, and growth of the Hispanic origin population accounted for more than half of the total population growth in the United States (with most Hispanic origin respondents identifying their race as White). Hispanic status is considered a form of ethnicity. **Ethnicity** is defined as "membership based on one's national origin or the national origin of one's ancestors" (Gollnick & Chinn, 2009, p. 406). Framed in this way, we all have national origins and ancestors with national origins. This is an important element of exploring diversity: we are all a part of the diversity conversation. Exploring diversity is not just about *others;* it is just as much about our own background and identity.

Ethnicity

Membership based on national origin or the national origin of ancestors.

As the percentage of individuals of color and with multiracial backgrounds continues to increase, it becomes increasingly important for early childhood professionals to be culturally competent in all of our work with each and every family. When Hispanic Origin status is separated from racial identification, the population distribution changes significantly. Population distributions among children represent trends toward increasingly balanced percentages, demonstrating the pressing need for all teachers to value and effectively support diverse children (U.S. Census Bureau, 2012) (See Figure 5-2, with ethnicity reported separately from race.)

Children with diverse racial and ethnic backgrounds benefit from teachers and curricula that recognize, understand, and meaningfully integrate their racial and ethnic diversity throughout their early experiences. In particular, as multiracial and multiethnic families

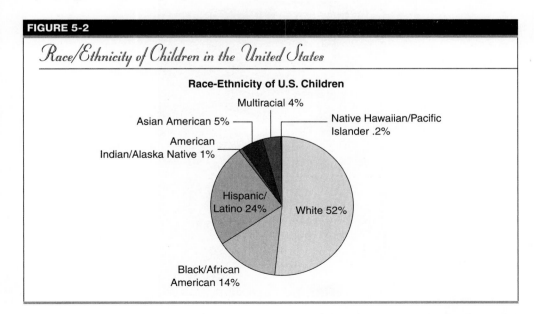

FIGURE 5-2

Race/Ethnicity of Children in the United States

Race-Ethnicity of U.S. Children

Multiracial 4%

Asian American 5%

American Indian/Alaska Native 1%

Native Hawaiian/Pacific Islander .2%

Hispanic/Latino 24%

White 52%

Black/African American 14%

continue to increase, early childhood professionals and curricula must robustly recognize and support the development of children's self-identity in multiple group associations.

Linguistic Diversity

Children from linguistically diverse backgrounds may have little or no proficiency in English and may be in varying stages of learning English, but some children may be proficient speakers and literate in English even if family members are not. And yet other families may be fully fluent in English while using another language as the primary language in the home. The percentage of children who speak a language other than English in their home (dual-language learners [DLL]) continues to increase.

- Currently 21% of all school-age children are DLL and 5% speak English with difficulty (Snyder & Dillow, 2012).
- Nationally, Spanish-speakers represent more than 77% of the DLL population, and Spanish is the top language spoken by DLL children in 43 states (Batalova & McHugh, 2010).

In some areas the vast majority of non-English-speaking children and families share a common language. In other areas, a regional dialect or nonstandard form of English is spoken in homes and communities. Some of our language differences are due to regional pronunciations, immigration from other countries, and family culture. Even within some schools and programs, there may be dozens of different languages spoken by children. Successfully teaching and caring for linguistically diverse children does *not* require that all teachers become fluent in many languages, but success does begin with valuing multilingualism as an asset to the classroom and children's lives. Listen to the educators in this **video** describe teaching strategies for engaging all children, DLL in particular.

For many children and families, the home language holds deep connections to family culture; it's about more than just communication but also a sense of family identity. The close

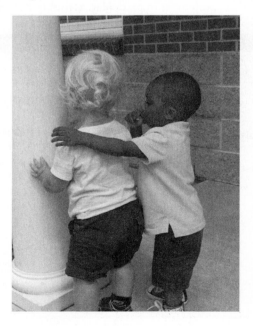

Authentic friendships are a powerful way to promote appreciation for diversity.

tie between language and culture can pose transition challenges for children who are new to English and/or new to the United States (immigrant families). For example, nonverbal communication rules vary greatly from one culture to another, as with eye contact, physical touch, how close people stand, etc. Recent immigrants may not yet be familiar with these norms and conventions of U.S. communication and may have quite different cultural expectations of nonverbal communication. The intimate connections among language, identity, and family culture make it particularly important that professionals engage children in activities that extend and preserve the home language. For families who do not speak English well, communications about the children's day in the classroom need to be presented in ways the family can understand. Teachers might rely on human translators, computer translation programs, community members, other family members, or phrase books to convey important information.

Putting It Into Practice

Culturally Responsive Strategies Related to Racial, Ethnic, and Linguistic Diversity

- Include a range of skin tone shades in art materials.
- Integrate children's books with positive images and messages about race, racial identity, and linguistic similarities and differences.
- Facilitate children's reflective explorations about "who am I?" and other self-descriptive projects (self-portraits, poems, stories) (such as in Table 5-2).
- Ensure that materials (particularly books and stories) include positive, empowering messages about diverse races and ethnicities.
- Create activities that explore fairness, equity, and inclusiveness.
- Select and use ample materials that are authentic and appropriate as representations, avoid simply adding one "token" image or item and those that are stereotypical (such as an egg roll in the kitchen section or a sombrero or feathered headdress in the dress-up area).
- Integrate authentic materials into curricular experiences to support children's exploration and understanding of diverse traditions and ways of life.
- Encourage children to share their ideas about skin tone, race, and terms and labels they have heard and dialogue together about context and meaning within a frame of valuing differences. (Observe and listen carefully to children's dialogues, especially during play.)
- Prepare for sensitive conversations about the messages children may have heard about race, skin color, or ethnicity.
- Practice responses (scripts) that open up dialogues about complex and sensitive topics, such as "I just heard you mention that Chen talks funny. Were you talking about how he and his mother were speaking a different language this morning at drop-off?"
- Integrate audio books and music in different languages. Ask families to record stories in home languages.
- Label classroom areas, schedules, and materials in different languages and with symbols/picture cues.
- Adjust verbal interactions for children learning English, using simpler words and phrases and slower pace as needed while comprehension develops (being cautious not to overwhelming children).
- Give dual-language learners time to process and speak. Avoid finishing sentences for them.
- Use important words and phrases in the child's home language.
- Use visual cues, drawings, and pictures to convey meaning and for children to process and represent their thinking.

TABLE 5-2 Learning Experiences Related to Race and Ethnicity Understanding

Sequenced Learning Experience Goals and Age-Related Considerations (Follari, 2014)

Learning Experience	Infant–Toddler	Preschool Age	Kindergarten–1st Grade	2nd–3rd Grade
Who I Am Goals: • Identify attributes of self • Categorize attributes as internal and external • Create representations of self	• Prompt awareness of external image with mirrors and dress-up items • Describe caring behavior and how friends act toward each other • Use child's name and attributes in rhymes	• Guess games using attributes to guess child's name • Make all-about-me books • Write who-am-I riddles • Read books with predicting and guessing prompts about attributes	• Trace child's body, have child write and draw aspects of themselves inside (around edge for external and in center for internal) • Create "I am . . ." fill-in-the-blank poems	• Create more intricate external/internal descriptions and representations of how children see themselves • Expand vocabulary with synonym strings
Self-Portrait Images: painting Goals: • See physical appearance from an artist's eye • Identify unique elements of physical appearance • Create and compare unique skin tone to others	• Consider using more photos of children as a start • Prompt children's dialogues about their physical characteristics • Match similarities and differences among children • Paint mixing and blending is a prelude to mixing skin shades	• Mix and blend with a variety of materials • Explore paint chips from a hardware or paint store to see the spectrum of shades in related colors • Use mirrors to look closely at specific features	• Create stories and poems about own skin shade and the process to create it • Make equations about how much of each paint color was used to mix (e.g., 1 drop tan + 3 drops nutmeg) • Use magnifying glasses to look closely at skin and hair textures	• Keep graphs and tally charts of skin shade mixing • Create comparative charts or Venn diagrams of similarities and differences • Explore stories and literature with overt discussion of skin color and multiracial and multiethnic people
Exploring Our Rainbow: skin tones and labels Goals: • Encourage children to share things about themselves • Engage in creating multiple representations of self	• Blend and mix paints of similar colors to make subtle shades • Include paint chips in color families to focus on subtle differences	• Display all the unique shades • Count and recognize all the differences and similarities • Discuss how we are the same and different • Emphasize the beauty of the "rainbow of us"	• Make patterns and mosaics from all the shades • Identify items in nature that also have a range of shades (tree bark, grasses, stones, etc.) • Discuss connections to naturally occurring shade variations	• Mix skin tone shades for family members; compare to class's • Sort and chart other found materials with naturally occurring shade variations • Explore up close with microscopes or magnifying glasses • Identify other similarities and differences among us

TABLE 5-2 *(Continued)*

Learning Experience	Infant–Toddler	Preschool Age	Kindergarten–1st Grade	2nd–3rd Grade
Equality Means Respect for Everyone Goals: • Encourage children to share things about themselves • Engage in creating multiple representations of self	• Integrate key vocabulary such as *fair, needs, equal, value, caring* • Comment on children's taking care-taking actions and acts of fairness • Connect feelings with actions about fairness and caring	• Focus on feelings related to acts of caring and kindness • Demonstrate how we stand up when things are unfair (for ourselves or others) • Share stories about how we feel when things are fair or unfair	• Read stories about people who have advocated for fairness and equality • Identify laws that are written to provide for equality • Explore how rights and needs are different • Connect to equality and equity	Engage with community guests or family members who are part of advocacy groups or efforts to promote equality and equity • Identify ways children can take on advocacy work in their community (letter writing, resources drives) • Read stories about people who have worked for social justice

SOCIOECONOMIC STATUS AMONG TODAY'S FAMILIES

Socioeconomic status (SES) is widely used as a gauge of family stability and includes measures of family income and the context of the child's life outside of the immediate family and home, including neighborhood and social resources. Family income is typically a key determinant of access to resources for meeting children's basic needs such as nutrition, health care, housing, and education. The factors specifically considered in determining a family's SES include:

- parent employment status (employed, unemployed, seasonal, temporary, migrant);
- type of employment (professional, service, labor, self-employed, etc.);
- family income level;
- poverty levels around the family's neighborhood/community; and
- parent education level.

Family SES may be higher or lower, depending on the factors listed above; SES is not specifically negative. There has been much attention paid in the research base to the effects on children of living in lower SES homes, but it is important to note that SES is not synonymous with living in poverty. Poverty is a specifically defined income threshold assessed annually by the federal government, outlined in Table 5-3 (USDHHS, 2013). Family income is related to access to health care and health insurance, nutrition, cognitively stimulating interactions and experiences, and parenting quality (connected to maternal depression) (Wood, 2003). It is estimated that the low-income threshold is the very minimum needed to just meet a family's basic needs for food, shelter, and health care. When family resources are severely limited, children's development and school success are

Socioeconomic status

Measures of family income and the context of the child's life outside of the immediate family and home, including neighborhood and social resources.

TABLE 5-3 2013 Federal Poverty Guidelines

Persons in Family/ Household	Poverty Guideline (Income Threshold)	Low Income Threshold (200% of Poverty Guideline)
1	$11,490	$22,980
2	$15,510	$31,020
3	$19,530	$39,060
4	$23,550	$47,100
5	$27,570	$55,140

significantly affected, often due to impoverished and under-resourced neighborhood and school conditions. Due to the kaleidoscope of these related quality-of-life factors, living in a family whose income is close to or under the poverty level is a major risk factor for negative developmental outcomes in children.

- Nearly 50% of all young children in the United States today live in low-income families, and 25% live in families whose income is at or below the poverty level (Addy & Wright, 2012).

These startling (and growing) numbers point to a major need for both specialized family support programs as well as careful preparation for early childhood professionals who will invariably be working with children from economically stressed backgrounds.

The early years are a critical time for growth and development, which can make this time especially vulnerable to the negative effect of lacking resources to meet basic needs. Adequate nutrition and rich stimulation through responsive interactions with caregivers, materials, and safe environments lay the foundations for later development and learning. When families lack resources to provide these things for children, developmental outcomes can suffer. Participation in high-quality early childhood programming can help, but unfortunately the costs of quality child care are often simply too great. Early intervention programs such as the Chicago Child-Parent Centers and Head Start and Early Head Start are designed specifically for children living in poverty (and sometimes qualified as low income). Other programs, such as free and reduced school lunch, nutrition subsidies such as WIC (Women, Infants, and Children), and Temporary Assistance for Needy Families are instrumental in providing basic needs to income-qualified families. Early childhood professionals must be knowledgeable about these and other federal and local supportive programs to be able to assist families in gaining access to these services.

Early childhood inclusion

Programs, policies, and practices that support each child's right to meaningfully participate in home, community, and educational settings.

INCLUSION AND DIVERSE ABILITIES IN TODAY'S CLASSROOMS

Today's best practices in early childhood education strongly promote the value and importance of inclusive practices and settings. "**Early childhood inclusion** embodies the values, policies, and practices that support the right of every infant and young child and his or her family, regardless of ability, to participate in a broad range of activities and contexts as full members of families, communities, and society" (DEC/NAEYC, 2009, p. 2). Above

Putting It Into Practice

Culturally Responsive Strategies Related to Socioeconomic Diversity

- Include materials and books with a variety of types of work (out-of-home employment, homemakers, job seekers) as well as a variety of types of homes and shelters in which families live.

- Use food for eating only; avoid being wasteful with food resources.

- Frequently engage children in activities that focus on their strengths.

- Validate and recognize children's accomplishments: "I watched how carefully you set out the napkins for snack. Thank you!" "I see how hard you worked to make the letters in your name neat and evenly spaced!"

- Hold appropriately high expectations and convey confidence in children's capabilities: "I know this feels like a big task, but I've seen how well you are able to put together big puzzles, and I know you can do this. Let's start with the outside pieces first."

- Promote opportunities for peer friendships by focusing on collaboration, teamwork, and partnerships.

- Offer and validate many different ways for families to participate in children's classroom experiences (volunteer, record audio stories, create materials, help in planning activities, advisory boards).

- Plan for family needs for child care, alternate scheduling, or transportation to participate in conferences or program events.

- Create take-home learning lending bags to extend learning activities into the home (materials, books, games, simple activities with directions and notes from teachers).

all, the right of each child to meaningfully participate in natural settings (home, program, school, community) permeates inclusive values. Professional guidelines identify three core components of high-quality early childhood inclusion (DEC/NAEYC, 2009):

1. *Access:* Create equal access and membership in the community group (be it a classroom, care center, or other early childhood setting) for each child.

2. *Participation:* Design all programs (indoor and outdoor) to maximize each child's strengths and capacities and ensure full participation.

3. *Support:* Identify and implement systemic support, including professional development training, scheduled time for collaborations, and structures for family-professional collaborations.

Inclusive practices value each child as an individual, each with diverse abilities, unique strengths, and different areas of need. Framing our perspectives of children around the concept of *diverse abilities* has a particular purpose. Diverse abilities are not necessarily just about disabilities or atypical patterns of development (called *red flags*). Each and every person has a unique array of capabilities, strengths, needs, and abilities that fall along a spectrum of levels. Approaching our work with children with the recognition that each child is unique and deserves individualized instruction is an inclusive approach to our professional responsibilities. Meaningful inclusion and individualized education for infants, children, and adolescents with identified disabilities is the law, as set forth by the Individuals

Inclusive practices value each child and support meaningful participation of every child.

with Disabilities Education Act (IDEA). IDEA serves as the funding provision for special education services for children from infancy through 21 years old as well as outlining eligibility for services (OCR, 2011). In particular, the role and influence of families on children's development and educational experiences is emphasized throughout the regulations. There are several key provisions in IDEA law:

- Unequivocal access to a free and appropriate public education (referred to as the FAPE standard) for all children with disabilities ages birth to 21 in the least restrictive environment in or as close to a regular education setting as possible or in the home
- Protection of the rights of infants, children, youth, and parents/guardians
- Ensure involvement of parents/families in educational decisions
- Require the creation of individual learning and support plans called **individualized education programs** and **individualized family service plans**, including integrated plans with goals, objectives, and supports
- Assess the effectiveness of programs, services, and children's progress
- Provide funding for appropriate accommodations

In the context of educational settings, diverse abilities are generally referred to as **exceptionalities**, referring to a child's functioning in a variety of areas interrelated with life inside or outside schools, including:

- academic achievement;
- cognitive and intellectual development;
- speech, language, and communication;
- emotional or psychological functioning within specific contexts;
- physical and motor functioning;
- health condition; and
- social skills and interactions.

Individualized education programs

Plans developed by interdisciplinary teams of families and professionals that outline strengths, supports, and services for children with disabilities.

Individualized family service plans

Plans developed by interdisciplinary teams of families and professionals that outline strengths, supports, and services for infants and toddlers with disabilities.

Exceptionalities

Development that falls above or below typical developmental milestones or expectations.

A child who is developing or performing above a typical range is labeled *gifted,* and a child who is developing or performing below a typical range is labeled *child with a disability.* IDEA outlines 13 categories that describe specific characteristics of a child with a disability, along with two conditions: educational performance is adversely affected and specialized services related to the condition are necessary (GPO, 2012). Early childhood professionals are often among the first professionals to work with young children, and so often we are the first to observe developmental red flags or potential areas of need. Because of this influential role, it is imperative that professionals understand foundations of developmental theory, resources for families and children at risk for disabilities, assessment options, and support services and systems.

Important considerations about identification and assessment processes include focusing on the following (DEC, 2007):

- Child- and family-centered context (attention to family's linguistic and cultural background)
- Involving interdisciplinary teams (teachers, specialists, therapists, administrators, families)
- Comprehensive information sharing among team members, especially family members, in language and terminology families understand
- Integration of relevant information from a variety of sources (using reliable and valid screening tools)
- Use of authentic assessment measures related to the child's everyday routines (play, interactions with familiar people, routines)

We must approach assessment in the early years with awareness that young children's development progresses through relatively predictable trends, though at widely varying paces. In this way, children's development is characterized as universal and also highly diverse.

Programming in inclusive settings is built upon the same characteristics of all quality practice. All high-quality early childhood programming begins with an ultimate goal of equity in access and participation. "To benefit all children, including those with disabilities and developmental delays, it is important to implement an integrated, developmentally appropriate, universally designed curriculum framework that is flexible, comprehensive, and linked to assessment and program evaluation activities" (DEC, 2007, p. 3). Well-designed programs and curricula can be individualized through adjustments to materials, schedules, or routines (accommodations) or alternatives for outcomes, expectations, criteria for performance, or assessment (modifications) as needed. Observe the benefits of effective early childhood inclusion in this **video**. Families play a central role in collaboratively designing accommodations or modifications with professional teams.

- Currently, more than 13% of all children in kindergarten through 12th grade and 3% of all infants and toddlers are receiving disability services (Snyder & Dillow, 2012; OSEP, 2012; respectively).

Developing an overarching curriculum framework and individualizing for instruction and assessment are essential components of quality inclusive early childhood practice. Specific practices that integrate multiple modalities, individualization, accommodations, and modifications

Putting It Into Practice

Inclusive Teaching Strategies

- Adjust learning opportunities to increase access to content and experiences
- Provide materials, information, and experiences in varying levels of complexity and format
- Engage children through varied sensory experiences (hearing, seeing, manipulating)
- Provide many ways for children to express ideas and knowledge (different formats such as art, writing, drama, technology, structure, complexity)
- Create many different ways to engage children's interest and spark curiosity on a particular topic by presenting different displays, materials
- Provide and adjust challenge and supports as needed to capture and sustain engagement (scaffolding)

- Use flexible grouping (sometimes same-sometimes mixed-ability level) to tailor learning experiences and maximize each child's strengths
- Model and concretely label attitudes and actions that promote inclusion and respect for all children ("Giving everyone a turn is how we are fair here," "making space for everyone to reach the water table is how we include everyone in this classroom")
- Actively include families in decision-making about children's learning experiences (planning, implementation, and assessment)
- Seek and integrate family perspectives, goals, and ideas for their children's care and education

---

Differentiated instruction

Practices that integrate multiple modalities, individualization, accommodations, and modifications for each child's unique strengths, needs.

for each child's unique strengths and needs represents **differentiated instruction**. Table 5-4 outlines ideas for differentiating instruction for broad areas of diverse abilities.

SUPPORTING DIVERSE WAYS OF THINKING: MULTIPLE INTELLIGENCES THEORY

Traditionally educational settings focus much of children's time on language, listening, and logical thinking activities and problem-solving processes. For children who think and understand their world and problem-solve through these forms of processing, such activities make sense and feel comfortably accessible. But for children who think, process, and represent knowledge and understanding in different ways, much of the educational setting can feel uncomfortable and unwelcoming. Concerned by the discord of seeing many children who demonstrate keen thinking and strong competencies in other areas but who struggle or are labeled as "failing" in school, Harvard University researcher Howard Gardner examined and developed a broader framework for considering the many ways people are smart. This framework is the theory of multiple intelligences (MI) (Gardner, 1993, 2006). Gardner's definition of *intelligence* focuses on how individuals process information and experiences. Multiple intelligences describes the diverse ways in which individuals:

- think about their world,
- process experiences,

TABLE 5-4 Differentiated Instructional Strategies for Diverse Learners

Diverse Ability Area	Instructional Strategies and Considerations	What Children Can Learn About This Diversity
Attention and focus on learning tasks	• Integrate opportunities for focused physical movement in lessons, transitions, and throughout the day to expend excess energy. • Minimize loud background noise and environmental distractions. • Provide cues and supports to organize information, directions, and task steps (graphic organizers, planners, step sequence cards).	• Sometimes a person's body is more busy and needs to move. • Sometimes a person's brain notices more things at one time. • People organize information in different ways.
Cognitive and intellectual development	• Select a variety of books and materials at different complexity levels on the same topic to allow all children to explore the same topic together. • Give instructions and direction using varied levels of vocabulary and steps.	• People think about things in different ways. • People finish tasks at their own pace or in their own time.
Speech, language, and communication	• Use simple, clear directions. • Speak in an adequate tone of voice and articulate clearly. • When available, use a voice amplification/distribution device. • Provide visual and auditory cues and directions (signs, symbols, verbal cues). • Model patient, active listening, and teach children to wait for others to finish speaking.	• Some people listen with just their ears, and other people listen with their ears and a small device. • Some people talk with words, and other people talk with their hands, gestures, or written notes, or a machine talks for them. • People speak different languages.
Emotional or psychological functioning	• Maintain a calm voice and demeanor. • Use calming redirection cues ("Let's take a breath and work out a solution together"). • Provide a safe spot in the room for expressing strong emotions. • Offer materials for safely expressing physical aggression such as hand-held squish balls, clay or dough for squeezing or punching, or exercise bands for stretching.	• Everyone has a range of feelings. • We all have different ways of expressing feelings. • Sometimes we need help to express our feelings safely.
Physical and motor functioning	• Ensure access to and around the environment (ramps, lifts, bar-style door handles, open pathways). • Arrange desks or tables to allow ease of flow among activities (children using mobility support positioned on a clear pathway). • Use hook-and-loop tape, magnets, and rubber grippers on materials to support coordination. • Reconsider rules or expectations such as "raise your hand to speak"; consider an alternative cue to request attention.	• People's bodies move in different ways. • Many people move around in the environment using just their bodies, and many other people move around using their bodies and devices or equipment to support parts of their bodies.

(Continued)

TABLE 5-4 Differentiated Instructional Strategies for Diverse Learners (*Continued*)

Diverse Ability Area	Instructional Strategies and Considerations	What Children Can Learn About This Diversity
Health condition	• Know the physical limitations the condition may impose on the child, for example, what activity level is too strenuous. • Be aware of cues of limitations such as shortness of breath, flush, posture changes, onset of seizure, etc. • Provide quiet or small semiprivate space if children need rest or medication administration if a nurse's room is not available. • Maintain close communications with families to ensure updates on children's health.	• Sometimes a part of a person's body needs medicine or extra support to work properly. • Everyone's body gets a little sick now and then; sometimes a person's body takes longer to get well. • Health conditions (such as those listed under IDEA) are not contagious, and you cannot get sick from playing with a friend.
Social skills and interactions	• Provide structured opportunities for dyad or small-group interactions. • Coach children on specific steps for social interaction. • Use simple picture cues and directions for social exchanges. • Practice social interactions in structured learning experiences. • Provide children with self-talk prompts to cue themselves. ("First I ask if I can join the group. I make eye contact. Then I wait for a response.") • Practice with children responses for when inappropriate social exchanges occur. ("We keep our hands to ourselves." "I don't like it when you call me names like that.")	• Some people prefer small, quiet groups or working alone sometimes. • Some children are learning how to play and work together appropriately. • We can all help each other follow the rules of our classroom community by using clear and friendly reminders.

• solve complex and authentic problems, and

• function within their own daily lives.

Gardner recognized that although one or more types of intelligence may be particularly more developed or a natural preference, we all possess varying strengths in many or all of the intelligence areas. As educators, it is particularly important for us to develop an understanding of all the ways in which people are smart. Observe a 1st grade differentiated math lesson in the following **video**. The current list defined by Gardner (see Table 5-5) offers a snapshot of diverse types of human intelligence (Gardner, 1993, 2006).

Supporting Diverse Ways of Thinking and Learning

Three primary goals for applying MI theory in the classroom are:

1. to recognize diversity in how children think, solve problems, and represent ideas;

TABLE 5-5 Summary of Gardner's Eight Intelligences

Intelligence Type	How People Demonstrate Intelligence
Verbal/linguistic (word smart)	Well-developed language skills and a sensitivity to the sound, meaning, and rhythm of words
Logical/mathematical (number smart)	Ability to think abstractly in concepts and to discern numerical patterns
Musical (music smart)	Appreciation for or the ability to produce rhythm, pitch, and tone quality
Visual/spatial (art smart)	Thinking in pictures or images or the ability to visualize abstractly
Body/kinesthetic (body smart)	Ability to use and control one's movement or a sensitivity to handling and manipulating objects
Interpersonal (we/people smart)	Awareness and sensitivity to the moods and motivations of other people
Intrapersonal (me smart)	Self-awareness and a connection with one's own feelings and thought processes
Naturalist (nature smart)	Appreciation and ability for recognizing and sorting objects in nature

2. to broaden learning opportunities to ensure natural preferences are accessed; and

3. to support and build experience and capability in many ways of thinking, problem-solving, and representing understanding.

The most important caution when applying MI theory to the classroom is to avoid testing or evaluating children's specific intelligence area(s) then tracking them into activities related to their intelligences. This misapplication serves to narrow and limit children's range of thinking and learning, the exact opposite of the key goals of using MI theory.

Teaching to multiple intelligences is about expanding classroom experiences for all children and not about classifying children's processing styles. The teacher's role is to provide rich, meaningful, and varied opportunities that support and encourage all learners

Space, time, materials, and environmental design are ways that teachers support children's many forms of thinking and representation.

Putting It Into Practice

Using Observations

Careful observations of children's choices and approaches to solving problems can guide teachers in their planning for children's learning. For example, a child who spends most of the time in the science discovery area grouping animal cards or figures into classes of species (naturalist) but who rarely explores the musical instruments and listening area might be encouraged to explore music by classifying different pieces by such categories as soft, fast, sleepy, or energetic or by categorizing the instruments according to the kind of sounds they make when played by fellow classmates. In this way, the child is able to engage with music and instruments through his or her preferred thought processes and also engage with a new peers group.

Or consider the solitary child who enjoys listening to stories, scribbling in the writing center, and spending time in the book corner (verbal/linguistic, intrapersonal) but who rarely engages with other children and prefers to sit on the bench during outdoor time. This child might benefit from activities in which he or she is able to explore stories about nature and go on a nature story hunt outside. One idea is to have a group of children go on an expedition to hunt down a story either through chronicling their own outdoor adventures or by searching for and gathering printed words or pictures that the teachers have hidden on the grounds. After the words or pictures have been collected or phrases from the adventure have been dictated to the teacher, the children can gather inside to create poems and stories using the materials from their hunt. Encouraging the children then to illustrate their poetry and story can further engage and develop their visual/spatial intelligence.

(Gardner, 1997). Teachers embracing an MI approach view their roles as (Armstrong, 1994; Gardner, 1995; Stanford, 2003):

- facilitator of children's explorations, with promoting questions;
- coach and guide of children's investigations and problem-solving processes;
- deliberate decision-maker, creating opportunities to support and expand children's thinking and learning based on emerging interests and capabilities; and
- observer and researcher, documenting children's experiences.

Differentiating instruction to support diverse learners can yield positive results in terms of children's classroom experiences as well as improvements in standard assessments, as this teacher describes. *"When I started teaching, things were very different. The standards movement was huge, and the whole school was really focused on skills, standards, and testing. Things were getting pretty stressful for the children and teachers. In our January staff meeting, the principal talked about a program that used a multiple intelligences curriculum and mixed age grouping to support diverse abilities. She asked if a pilot group wanted to explore the possibility of us doing that. I signed up, and the journey began! Over the past 3 years, we've continued to expand schoolwide. It's been a big learning curve but a great growth experience for us. The best part is that even though we've adopted a portfolio assessment method, the state test scores are also improving. I've seen how we are able to meet all our state standards in a rich, meaningful way that really engages the kids' strengths in different ways and multiple levels."*

Putting It Into Practice

Supporting Diverse Learners

- Balance individual, pair, small-group, and whole-group activities.
- Value many formats for representing knowledge: talking, writing, drawing, charting, demonstrating, sequencing details, mapping concept connections.
- Integrate ample hands-on manipulatives and sensory or tactile experiences.
- Use picture and word labels on shelves, classroom areas, schedules, and name charts.
- Create flexible and predictable routines, allowing for movement breaks between transitions.
- Create indoor and outdoor spaces designed for gross-motor movement (especially important for toddlers and preschoolers).
- Create spaces for children to be alone and together.
- Include mirrors for children to notice self-expression and emotions.
- Use carefully selected music to signal transitions or create a mood.
- Facilitate planning and reflection sessions to organize children's thinking about classroom activities.
- Create leadership roles along with observer and participant roles.
- Outline the inquiry process approach to problem-solving and learning experiences: observe, predict, pose questions, explore/ test, observe, reflect.
- Present organized collections of natural and manmade materials such as stones, shells, pine cones, recycling materials, varieties of bottle caps, and beads.

The extensive list in Table 5-6 provides ideas for learning experiences that support thinking in diverse ways. These can be used as suggestions for starting the process of developing activities and experiences based on the specific interests, capacities, and strengths of individual children.

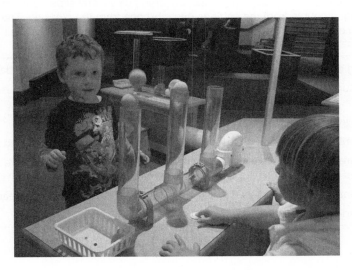

Exploratory, hands-on learning centers allow children to test different ideas using diverse learning styles.

TABLE 5-6 Activities to Support Multiple Intelligences

Key Skills	Activities and Experiences to Support Verbal/Linguistic Intelligence
Listening	• Reading and telling stories and poetry aloud • Listening games • Sound-discrimination games such as guessing among various objects in a shaker or guessing the instrument being played • Listening to recorded stories • Giving directions, plans, and instructions verbally or in song/rhymes that allow for playing with words
Speaking	• Repeating chants and rhymes • Reading stories • Storytelling • Allowing classroom and individual discussions • Asking many open-ended questions • Allowing show-and-tell, word plays, and riddles • Creating dialogue with children • Allowing dramatic play • Allowing group activities
Writing	• Dictating stories • Tracing letters in sand or stencils • Forming letters out of dough • Using journals, either dictated or written, to let the children reflect on their day and plan for tomorrow • Making paper bag stories (Label bags with the words for characters, settings, and plots; then ask children to come up with suggestions for each element of the story and place them in the bag. In groups, children pull several slips from the character bag, a couple from the settings bag, and one from the plot bag. The children then combine their elements to create an original story to write or tell the class.)
Reading	• Incorporating quality children's literature into the curriculum several times a day • Supporting curricular concepts with stories, songs, and rhyming games that relate to subjects • Playing recognition games and "word hunts" • Integrating written language into classroom materials such as food boxes and menus • Making picture-word association boards where preliterate children can create stories using pictures and can pair select words with the pictures • Taking student dictation to create a class story or poem for the children to read • Modeling reading behaviors

TABLE 5-6 (*Continued*)

Key Skills	Activities and Experiences to Support Logical/Mathematical Intelligence
Calculating	• Counting • Measuring • Number corresponding • Cutting out geometric shapes • Cooking • Sorting • Providing pattern blocks and cards, puzzles, blocks, and measurement devices for children to explore • Recognizing series of sizes
Strategies for Problem-Solving	• Using open-ended questions and materials that support many possible solutions • Predicting outcomes • Engaging children in deep, investigative projects and experiments that allow them to hypothesize, research, test, and explore their world • Having children make charts or graphs to categorize, compare, and represent information • Creating games with rules • Identifying patterns or creating new ones with various blocks • Explaining actions • Creating treasure or scavenger maps • Creating sand and water activities that explore different-sized containers to see how many it takes of one to fill another; volume; cause and effect

Key Skills	Activities and Experiences to Support Musical Intelligence
Listening	• Developing songs for transitions or directions • Discussing different sounds, combinations of instruments, styles, speeds, etc., from selected audio recordings • Discussing how certain sounds, instruments, or pieces make us feel • Arranging a class trip to a performance • Going on a "listening walk," where children are instructed to collect as many sounds as they can (like a nature walk collecting leaves and things) • Using music strategically; constant background music may prompt children to tune out
Singing	• Singing favorite songs as groups and at transition times • Chanting and humming to feel different sensations of vibrations • Instituting "singing-only time," where, for a limited period of time, everyone must use lyrical utterances to communicate
Composing	• Allowing children to create their own musical works (but do not pressure them into too many structured lessons) • Allowing children to create rhythms, patterns, melodies, and songs • Going on a "composition walk," where children play materials such as tapping on a tree trunk or clinking on a fence to create an original song • Making up songs to favorite rhymes

(Continued)

TABLE 5-6 Activities to Support Multiple Intelligences (*Continued*)	
Playing	• Providing a variety of instruments and having children make their own to be used individually and as a group • Trying to re-create sounds heard in nature by making and playing child-created instruments • Exploring authentic instruments from various cultures
Key Skills	**Activities and Experiences to Support Visual/Spatial Intelligence**
Visualizing, Mental Imagery	• Using guided imagery • Describing the images in the child's mind's eye • Using imagination and make-believe games • Describing hidden objects by touching—"feely" bag/box
Working Visually and Spatially	• Giving children pattern blocks and cards to visually represent concepts in geometry, math, etc. • Letting children develop a treasure-hunt map using the school/playground as the parameters then follow the map • Recognizing shapes • Using mazes, mapping, and puzzles • Building with blocks, creating towns, solving traffic problems with blocks and ramps • Playing spatial navigation games that allow children to move around the room/space • Making flowcharts or maps to outline information • Using a camera to select and take pictures
Making Images, Visual Art	• Creating their own storyboards or illustrations for stories • Using paper, paint, crayon, pencil, etc., to create pictures from their mind's eye after a guided-imagery journey • Allowing children to make whole-class murals to depict a class trip or story • Using graphic symbols to represent a process, flowcharts, graphs • Creating 2-D art using drawing, painting, collage, printing • Creating 3-D sculpting/modeling
Key Skills	**Activities and Experiences to Support Body/Kinesthetic Intelligence**
Motor Skills and Coordination	• Navigating obstacle courses • Using large-motor equipment • Playing games such as Head, Shoulders, Knees, and Toes and the Hokey Pokey, which allow children to use their bodies to identify body parts • Taking exercise breaks to focus on energy release/energizing
Hands-On Activities	• Using materials such as sandpaper letters to allow children to feel the shape and use their tactile sense and motion to understand the letters • Creating sensory projects and games such as shaving cream tracing • Using tools • Cooking • Creating touchy-feely boxes that allow children to guess what they are feeling without looking at the object • Going on nature walks • Gardening • Sculpting with various forms of dough and clay • Using manipulatives

TABLE 5-6 (*Continued*)

Using Body for Expression	• Having children paint or trace letters or short words on wall-mounted, mural-sized paper, which requires a full range of motion of their arms • Dancing to different tempos, rhythms, and sounds to integrate abstract concepts into physical experiences • Providing props and time for creative movement experiences so children can develop their own choreography and dances to stories • Playing the writing a letter/word on your back game, where children have to guess what you've written only by feeling the shapes you trace with your finger on their backs • Forming parades, marching to rhythms • Using gestures, pantomime • Role-playing, acting, dramatic play
Key Skills	**Activities and Experiences to Support Interpersonal Intelligence**
Using Social Skills	• Modeling prosocial skills by teachers • Feeling games such as "Guess what I'm feeling by my expression" • Playing active listening games, encouraging children to listen and paraphrase what they heard • Practicing conflict resolution with puppets and role-play • Allowing the children to define and agree on classroom rules • Using collaborative learning to remove win/lose emphasis • Sharing classroom responsibilities • Allowing show-and-tell time, where children can share and learn about one another
Working In a Group	• Allowing plenty of time for working in small groups on project-oriented activities that allow children to investigate, explore, and solve problems together • Playing team games and scavenger hunts • Playing group sports • Having class meetings, where children plan their activities, engage in their play, then regroup to review and share their experiences • Role-playing and dramatic playing, where children learn to divide roles and responsibilities, work out conflicts through play, and redefine social norms and rules • Mural making by the whole group • Making a class quilt, where children collect information about themselves and turn it into a square in the class quilt • Collective story and poetry writing, where each child contributes a line • Creating paper bag stories (described in verbal/linguistic activities) • Creating enjoyable, collaborative learning with discussions, brainstorming, planning together, and majority-rule decisions • Using peer tutoring/coaching

(*Continued*)

TABLE 5-6 Activities to Support Multiple Intelligences (*Continued*)

Key skills	Activities and Experiences to Support Intrapersonal Intelligence
Self-Identity, Self-Management	• Setting goals, planning activities, reviewing experiences • Identifying self-control strategies • Developing self-care skills such as hygiene habits • Exploring books, pictures, and materials that convey diverse identities and cultures • Working independently, providing individual activities and centers, along with nooks where children can go to be alone for a few minutes • Playing "My favorite thing about you is . . ." game, where children toss a soft ball to the peer next to them while telling him or her the favorite thing about the person • Acknowledging and respecting each child each day • Viewing children as active participants in the running of the classroom
Making Personal Connections	• Journaling, reviewing choices and experiences • Providing support for children's poetry writing, taking dictation for prewriters • Identifying likes and dislikes • Playing "Imagine if you were . . ." game, where children close their eyes and imagine to be something/someone other than who they are; discuss their vision and feelings as a group • Discussing how new knowledge personally affects them
Processing Emotions	• Identifying and expressing emotions • Recognizing appropriate and inappropriate responses to emotions • Exploring emotion puppets or masks • Playing board games that identify emotions and behaviors • Including art activities as a means to express and explore feelings in an effort to develop intrapersonal intelligence. (This can include not only hands-on activities but also discussions about professional art and music and how different pieces make us feel.)
Key Skills	**Activities and Experiences to Support Naturalist Intelligence**
Observing and Using Senses to Gather Information	• Recognizing plants and animals • Describing and recording observations using graphs and charts • Creating patterns to classify objects • Using microscopes, binoculars, telescopes, and computers to study organisms • Watching processes and cycles, such as in growing plants • Sorting sequenced picture cards displaying natural processes such as the life cycle of a butterfly
Interacting with Nature	• Caring for a classroom pet • Caring for the environment—recycling, composting • Creating a school garden by finding a plot of land, tilling and preparing the soil, discussing and deciding what to grow, sowing and watering seeds, weeding and fertilizing, and harvesting • Going on nature walks, collection walks • Taking field trips to the zoo, planetarium, arboretum, park, aquarium, museum • Exploring collections of natural materials in the science area, including rocks, shells, seeds, leaves, cleaned feathers, pictures, fossils

TABLE 5-6 *(Continued)*	
Making relationships and connections	• Sorting natural objects • Classifying and categorizing • Matching and comparing • Arranging objects to form associations and connections • Identifying relationships among species using picture cards • Creating charts and webs to represent information and relationships

Source: Adapted from Campbell, Campbell, & Dickinson, 2004; Carlisle, 2001; Gardner, 1993; Nuzzi, 1997; Reiff, 1996.

CONCLUSION

In every early childhood community, whether in a home-based, center-based, or school program, each child and family will bring a unique and richly diverse background of experiences, identities, values, and context. Among families with shared characteristics and attributes, there may be connections and similarities along with different personal experiences. Experiences with the varying attributes of family diversity are essential aspects of personal identity and family culture. Early childhood professionals can truly be effective in supporting success for each child only when family culture and individual diversity are robustly integrated into all aspects of our practice.

By balancing the kinds of activities, teaching strategies, curricular goals, interactions with children and families, and materials, you can ensure that all children use their strengths and engage in activities that help them develop to their fullest potential. In the course of teaching and assessment, personalizing instruction and evaluation to maximize individual and group identity, background, and diversity is the only way to ensure success for each child. By maintaining a commitment to value and celebrating the rich diversity in each child, you can begin to unlock each child's potential for successful learning and development.

SUMMARY

- Diversity is about the ways people differ and can include many attributes that reflect our personal identity and family culture.

- Culture is about ways of thinking, beliefs, expectations, traditions, behavior, and sense of belonging that are socially transmitted among members of a group.

- Culturally competent practice means being knowledgeable about diverse cultures, aware of your own values and judgments, and deliberate in using positive professional skills and behaviors to promote inclusive, welcoming practices.

- Families today represent a wide range of structure and composition, including single-parent homes, blended families, adoptive families, nonrelative care, and extended-family arrangements.

- Racial, ethnic, and linguistic diversity in the United States continues to increase as the percentage of children of color, multiracial, multiethnic, and dual-language learners increases across the country.

- In many classrooms, dual-language learners reflect multiple languages and ethnic backgrounds, while on average the most popular language of dual-language learners is Spanish.
- Today nearly 50% of all children live at or below the low-income threshold, with one quarter of all children living in poverty.
- Experiencing economic stress and significantly limited resources can have negative effects on children's growth and development.
- Early intervention programs for families living in poverty provide important comprehensive resources and support for children and families.
- Inclusion represents intentional, system-wide policies and practices that promote access and meaningful participation of all children.
- In inclusive classrooms, each child is valued as an individual, each with diverse abilities, unique strengths, and areas of need.
- Inclusion is guided by professional commitment and legal regulations through the Individuals with Disabilities Education Act (IDEA).
- Multiple intelligences theory describes how children think and learn through at least eight different ways:

  1. Verbal/linguistic
  2. Logical/mathematical
  3. Musical
  4. Visual
  5. Body/kinesthetic
  6. Interpersonal
  7. Intrapersonal
  8. Naturalist

- Responsive, differentiated practice involves recognizing the many ways children differ and responding appreciatively and sensitively to adjust interactions, programming, teaching, and environments to strengthen and support each child and family.

CHAPTER LEARNING GOALS SELF-ASSESSMENT

Use this chart to write down three to five key points for each learning goal that you learned from this chapter.

Identify essential elements of diversity and culturally competent practice.	
Examine family structures and composition.	
Explore characteristics of racial, ethnic, and linguistic diversity.	
Discuss the scope and effect of socioeconomic diversity in children's lives.	
Describe goals and effective practices in today's inclusive classrooms.	
Apply multiple intelligences theory to the classroom.	

APPLICATION ACTIVITIES

Discussion Prompts

1. Describe three benefits and three challenges faced by professionals working in classrooms with much diversity represented among the children and families.

2. Describe three benefits and three challenges faced by professionals working in classrooms with less diversity represented among the children and families.

3. Reflecting on your own educational and workplace experience, identify specific experiences you have had with diverse individuals. Describe these experiences and how they can inform your professional practice as an early childhood educator.

In Class   Working in teams or small groups, design an inclusive early childhood indoor or outdoor environment and sample list of materials that supports all aspects of family diversity. Use an 8" × 8" square of standard-sized paper or a larger square on poster paper to represent the room or play yard area. Be sure to think about all of the aspects and attributes of diversity described in this chapter in your planning.

In the Field   Visit an early childhood classroom (pre-K through 3rd-grade) and discuss diversity with the classroom teacher. Ask the teacher to describe how he or she makes accommodations and modifications and engages in culturally competent practices to support all children and families. Using the following categories, identify specific designs and decisions that reflect responsive practices based on the various aspects of diversity presented in this chapter (family structure, race, ethnicity, language, socioeconomics, abilities, and ways of thinking).

Environment	
Displays	
Curricular goals	
Lesson plans	
Instructional strategies	
Technologies	
Other	

For Your Portfolio   For educators, recognizing diverse ways of thinking and learning is as much about understanding your own ways of thinking, problem-solving, and representing. Since we all have preferences and intelligence strengths, we may have the tendency to "teach to our strength" without realizing we are leaving out other ways of thinking. Understanding the profile of strengths, preferences, and ways of thinking you can develop further will help you understand potential imbalances in your teaching.

Visit the Literacyworks Web site (www.literacyworks.org) and search for MI assessment for overviews of the multiple intelligences and a free interactive self-test, which returns immediate feedback on your intelligence strengths.

Reading your results and thinking about how you approach solving problems, what learning experiences you enjoy the most, and what kinds of activities you like to do in your free time, think about which intelligence areas you believe are your strengths and which are areas you do not feel are as strong. What effect do you think your MI profile might have on your teaching? Write a brief description of your MI profile, and identify three ways your specific strength(s) are evident in your life (school, work, with friends or family, etc.).

RELATED WEB LINKS

Edutopia is a Web site dedicated to promoting innovation and improvement in K–12 education. There are numerous resources on ideas and strategies for supporting diverse learners.
www.edutopia.org

Teaching Diverse Learners is a Web site of resources and information about effective instructional strategies to support dual-language learners and increase culturally competent practices.
www.alliance.brown.edu/tdl

The Foundation for Child Development (FCD) Web site provides information and resources to expand professionals' capacity to support all children and families with particular emphasis on resource information for children from disadvantaged backgrounds.
http://fcd-us.org/

CHAPTER 6

Head Start and Early Head Start: Empowering Change from Within

Across the nation, there are families and communities suffering under adverse conditions including poverty, unemployment, and poor access to community services. These conditions, existing in urban, suburban, and rural locales, may put children at risk for later school and life problems. Research on early brain development has revealed the importance of healthful environments and experiences for young children as well as the benefits to society of raising strong, healthy children. Children with special needs or disabilities are also considered to be at risk for developing later school problems. In an effort to combat poverty and increase all children's chances for

Early intervention

Comprehensive programs for young children who are living in conditions that include one or more risk factors for possible future school or life problems.

life success, national initiatives and programs have been created. **Early intervention** is the term widely used to refer to the comprehensive programs for young children who are living in conditions that include one or more risk factors for possible future problems in school or life. The overarching goals of early intervention programs are to provide developmentally appropriate, stimulating, individualized learning experiences and comprehensive health services for families and children living in poverty or with disabilities.

This chapter traces the history of early intervention programs in the United States, explores definitions and effects of risk factors, assesses the current status of children living with risk factors in the United States, and identifies specific elements of current early intervention programming. The federally funded Head Start and Early Head Start programs and policies are presented to illustrate key components of intervention programming. Research on the effectiveness of Head Start in reaching program goals is presented, and current trends and changes to federal policies are reviewed.

OVERVIEW OF HEAD START AND EARLY HEAD START

Head Start

Comprehensive programs for families living in poverty, including education, health and wellness, and nutrition services for 3- to 5-year-olds.

Early Head Start

Comprehensive programs for families living in poverty, including education, health and wellness, and nutrition services for pregnant women and infants through 3-year-olds.

Head Start and **Early Head Start** are federal grant-funded early education and comprehensive care programs specifically designed for children of families living in poverty. Head Start serves 3- to 5-year-olds, and Early Head Start serves infants to 3-year-olds. While Head Start and Early Head Start are most well known as early education/preschool programs, they are actually comprehensive services integrating all areas of children's education, health, and wellness. Since its inception, Head Start program goals have taken a holistic view of children's needs, maintaining a broad perspective on all areas of children's development. "Head Start's commitment to wellness embraces a comprehensive vision of health for children, families, and staff" (Head Start Bureau, 1997, p. 5). Head Start addresses these goals through comprehensive, structured services, including

- physical health and wellness;
- nutrition;
- mental health;
- medical and dental care;
- social, emotional, and cognitive stimulation in infant, toddler, and preschool education programs;
- parent support, including education and networking; and
- community-based service provisions.

Listen to professionals describe highlights of Head Start programs in this **video**. Visit a Head Start program in the vignette below to gain a sense of the environment and programming that Head Start early intervention provides.

CLASSROOM VIEW

Today you are visiting a small preschool program operating out of a community church in an urban neighborhood. The center has three rooms, each with 15 preschoolers and 2 teachers. There is a small playground, which is fenced in on the other side of the parking lot. The church is a small stone building with long windows at the top of the walls. These windows provide plenty of natural light but afford no view to the outdoors. The church also serves as a community resources center, with counseling services in another room down the hall. A smiling face pops out of a doorway and welcomes you to the school. An African American woman with gray streaks in her dark brown hair gives you a wave. "Hi there! I'm Ida. The kids call me Grammy Ida. Come join us!" She laughs in a warm voice.

The preschool teachers invite you to sit at the small table and observe a typical morning in the "threes room." The children are finishing their snack of fruit salad and milk. The teachers encourage the children to serve themselves fruit and use their small spoons to eat by themselves. Some children are using their fingers to hold the fruit on the spoon, and some are using their hands to eat while they hold the spoon in their free hands. The teachers do not correct the children but rather model eating with a spoon themselves. They have lively chats with the children about their morning and what activities they will be doing for the rest of the day. Occasionally a child proudly holds up a spoon loaded with fruit, pleased at being able to keep the fruit on the spoon. The teachers cheer the children in their efforts to master the utensil.

When they finish, the children take their bowls and spoons to the low sink while the teachers wash the tables. The teachers thank the children for being such good helpers and remind them about washing hands after eating. There is a procedure for cleanup: The tables must be sprayed with disinfectant and allowed to sit for 2 minutes before being wiped clean, and the children must wash their hands for 15 seconds. These health and hygiene regulations are mandated by the state. The teachers and children sing songs to count the time.

After snack cleanup, the children move around the room and choose activities. They have 45 minutes of uninterrupted time, during which the teachers support children's play and use of such materials as blocks, push toys, clay, books, counting bears, and puzzles. Teachers are particularly focused on supporting children's social engagement and ability to regulate their emotions. After this free-time segment, the group will go outside. Today the teachers have brought in a large basket to collect items that interest the children during a community walk. The mother of one of the children is a local artist and is coming to class tomorrow to help the children create a mural with their collections. Their walk will take them through a downtown area and a local park. The children routinely visit

Promoting community connections is important for all children.

some of the shops (the Spanish and Korean food markets, the bakery, the butcher, the florist), and the shopkeepers talk to them about their work.

"These places are a part of the children's home lives, so it's important that we integrate them into school activities too. The store owners love having the kids come around. They have even visited the classroom. We can barely keep up with the children on those days. They are all talking and sharing stories so fast! They really love investigating the stores on a deeper level."

During the children's choice time, one of the teachers sits at the table and makes notes in a few of the children's files. She is using observations from snack time to document children's developing self-care, social, and fine-motor skills. The file seems thick. You ask her about paperwork, and she comments that it sometimes seems like a lot. But she quickly adds that it really helps when she's meeting with parents and program supervisors. She can readily find plenty of examples of how children are developing and what they have been working on. She also uses the files to help plan for new materials or activity ideas. "We make general plans for the group, but we also make individualized plans," she explains. "The individualized plans can be simple, such as introducing a new material to the child. Sometimes they are more complicated and involve therapists. It all depends on the specific child and what they're working on at the moment. Having all these notes about what a child said one day or did another helps me get ideas about what skills they need to work on and what things are interesting them."

Just then one of the girls starts screeching and crying. It looks as if every muscle in her small body is tensed up; her face is deep red, and her screaming rings through the halls. The other children look at her for a moment but quickly go back to their work. They don't seem surprised by her behavior. One of the teachers goes over and speaks softly to her. The child begins to slam her legs against the floor. The teacher puts her arms around the screaming child and holds her gently but firmly. The child flails her arms and legs for a few moments then begins to quiet. After several minutes, her body relaxes into the teacher's rocking and soothing voice.

Ida smiles and explains that this child's family is working with a therapist referred by Head Start because of her emotional disturbances. The therapist also comes into the classroom to work with the teachers and show them the techniques the family is using at home with the child, such as the embrace. "This kind of consistency among all the networks in the child's life is so important. At Head Start, being a teacher is just one role we play. We have lots of trainings on things like special needs and community resources. Most times we are the first and only contact for the families. They need me to guide them to health and welfare networks. Doctors, dentists, therapists—we help families find whatever services they need, especially families who don't speak English. Most of the teachers here speak Spanish or Portuguese too, so that we can communicate in a way that is comfortable and effective for them. We're all from this neighborhood, so we know what's what here. And I need them to keep me included in family plans. We're really lucky that family partnerships are such a focus from day one. It benefits the children more than anything we could do alone."

Soon all the children are busy working in their chosen areas. Some are building structures with blocks and driving the cars around them. Four girls are preparing dinner in the kitchen area. Ida works with one child on a puzzle. Three children are working together on a collage of their favorite foods, sparked by a recent trip to the food market. They page through old magazines and newspaper circulars, tearing and cutting out pictures of foods for their collage. Periodically they call out to the teacher, "Mira! I found carrots. I found pollo! I found ice cream!" The teacher responds by rubbing her stomach and saying, "Mm! Try to put the different foods in sections, like we see at the market. Then we'll have to show Mr. Ramirez the collage when we visit the market later."

This visit highlights Head Start teachers' efforts to keep the curriculum balanced, culturally relevant, and individually tailored to each child's particular developmental level. A strong emphasis is placed on authentic assessments of children in the form of observations, portfolios, and parent meetings.

HISTORICAL PERSPECTIVE: THE START OF EARLY INTERVENTION

Social renewal has been a goal for educators throughout the centuries, but it wasn't until the 1960s that current early intervention preschool programs were formalized in the United States. At that time, new research fueled a growing belief among American policy makers, civil rights activists, psychologists, and sociologists that a strong start early in life could have lasting positive effects on all children (Bloom, 1964; Gershoff, 2003). This applied especially to children from low-income backgrounds. With this growing aware-ness, the early intervention movement received support over the following decades (Kagan, 2002; Schweinhart, Barnes, & Weikart, 1993). It was during this time that the Head Start initiative was created. Other early intervention programs, such as the High/Scope Perry Preschool Project, were also designed at this time. High/Scope is an educa-tional research foundation and model preschool program signed to address the unique needs of children living in families experiencing economic stress. The High/Scope cur-riculum is also used in programs serving families from all economic levels. Currently a significant number of Head Start programs use the High/Scope curriculum. The impetus for programs focusing on improving outcomes for disadvantaged children was also closely tied to the overarching social climate of the time.

Influence of the Social Climate of the 1960s

The late 1950s marked a new, growing demand for equality for all people, beginning with the emotionally charged struggles for racial equality. Other socially marginalized groups, one being the women's movement, then began to voice their opposition to being treated unfairly and insist on equal freedoms and rights. Advocates championed expansion of educational and employment opportunities for women, which were previously afforded to only men. Along with increased employment opportunities for women outside the home came the need to expand early childhood programs quickly to meet the requirements of a changing society.

   Half-day nursery schools catering to the interests of wealthier families were not appealing to a working mother who needed all-day care for her children. Many families, especially families from lower socioeconomic-status (SES) backgrounds, did not have access to high-quality programs. Placing children in low-quality care that lacked appropriate stimulation only amplified the problems facing children living in families with limited income. Many programs lacked rich language environments, materials to manipulate, indoor and outdoor play spaces, and appropriate curricula taught by trained teachers. The concern over quality in early care environments was further fueled by research in the new field of brain development.

Influences of Brain-Development Research

Researchers in the 1950s began to investigate the idea of *critical periods,* also called sensitive or key periods, in human development. New connections were made between genetically influenced development and how environmental stimuli affect the outcomes of those crit-ical periods. These influences are often referred to as *nature* (biological influences) and *nurture* (environmental influences, including relationships). Researchers carefully observ-ing large numbers of children promoted the belief that there are key times, especially in very young children, in which the brain is primed to make certain developmental leaps (Bloom, 1964; Diamond & Hopson, 1998).

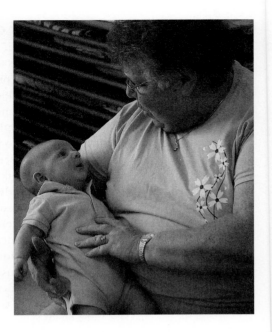

Stimulating experiences fostered through relationships with caring adults are essential for optimal development from infancy.

For example, at birth infants are unable to clearly see things in their world. Their visual focus sharpens over the first 8 months or so. With adequate visual stimulation in the first year of life, most infants will achieve nearly adult-level visual acuity during this time (Vander Zanden, 2003). Conversely, visual development can be hampered by a lack of stimulation, such as living in perpetual darkness or not having interesting objects to look at and reach for. The first year of life, then, would be considered a critical period for the development of aspects of vision.

Likewise, anyone who has been around a toddler can attest to the amazing leaps in physical and language development that occur between infancy and the preschool years. Researchers, including Jean Piaget, Erik Erikson, and Maria Montessori, made major contributions to our understanding of the periods and stages through which children develop. The discoveries in brain research continue to shed light on the complex nature of human development, offering practitioners clues to optimizing children's developmental paths.

Research evidence mounted during the decades following the 1950s and supported the belief that appropriate stimulation in the early years was critical to positive developmental outcomes and later school success (Bloom, 1964; Gershoff, 2003; Hanson, 2003; Kagan, 2002; Nord & Rhoads, 1992; Peth-Pierce, 2000; Schweinhart et al., 1993). Evidence also emerged from early High/Scope research that suggested children growing up in families with limited incomes were more likely to continue to need costly welfare and special education services (Muennig, Schweinhart, Montie, & Neidell, 2009; Schweinhart et al., 1993). Educationally based programs for families with limited incomes were created in response to achievement and behavior gaps in school-age children (Kagan, 2002).

Early Intervention Programming Takes Shape

Government intervention efforts to address gaps in socioeconomic status as well as children's achievement became part of the national agenda in the 1960s. Political goals focused on keeping America globally competitive, whereas social welfare plans focused on decreasing poverty. In 1965 and 1966, the government passed a large number of laws that targeted such social issues as voting rights, urban renewal, subsidized medical care, and improved education. Part of President Lyndon Johnson's War on Poverty initiatives, the first Head Start pilot program appeared in 1965 (USDHHS, 2002a). The primary goal of the Head Start initiative was to alleviate the risks to children and families associated with living in poverty (later including children with disabilities). This goal was addressed through comprehensive health, wellness, family involvement, and education programming. Watch how children engage in family-style meals and explore healthful nutrition in this **video**. Key goals for the programs were to (Smith, 1988)

- increase children's developmental outcomes,
- focus on social and academic achievement,
- meaningfully integrate families into the early education program, and
- strengthen families' status within the community.

From early in Head Start's history, programs have been tailored to diverse communities, including American Indian (AI) tribal communities, migrant families, and Alaska Native (AN) communities. Unique challenges, such as remote rural locations and limited transportation, are issues these programs alleviate to provide comprehensive services to AI and AN families with limited incomes. Throughout changes in administration of program funds, of primary importance in the AI-AN program is to preserve community involvement and governance. To that end, tribal governments remain active in grant money authorization (USDHHS, 2006). By addressing unique challenges while preserving control within the community, Head Start programs validate the key role community members play in the empowerment cycle. Despite reauthorizations in the legislation and funding concerns, Head Start has always maintained a commitment to innovation and responsiveness to changing trends in the field. The inclusion of children with disabilities is an example of this responsiveness.

Putting It Into Practice

Suggestions From DAP

The Developmentally Appropriate Practice (DAP) framework calls for teachers to base their teaching on a solid knowledge of child development. The awareness of critical periods aligns with this belief. To maximize toddlers' blossoming language of development, for example, you must be aware of what trends, norms, and milestones to expect at different ages. Knowing what to expect enables you to plan stimulating activities, experiences, and environments that support and lead development as it is ready to unfold. Another example would be basing instruction on the awareness that preschoolers and kindergarteners are ready to refine their fine-motor control through focused activities, whereas toddlers need more support for gross-motor development. Keep in mind that you must use your understanding of universal trends in development together with expected variations between individual children to plan optimal learning environments and experiences to suit each child.

Expanding the Scope of Head Start: Inclusion and Infant/Toddler Programs

When racial segregation practices of "separate but equal" became unacceptable after the civil rights struggles of the 1950s, parents of children with disabilities began to demand equal educational opportunities for their children. Supported by strong advocacy of parent groups, federal legislation was enacted in 1968 to provide adequate educational experiences for young children with disabilities. This law was originally titled the Handicapped Children's Early Education and Assistance Act.

Head Start programming has always been based on comprehensive services for families with limited incomes. In 1972 Head Start initiatives were expanded to include comprehensive educational and welfare services for children with disabilities. Providing adequate services for children with disabilities, integrated into programs for all children, continues to be at the forefront of today's Head Start educational goals. By law, at least 10% of enrollment must be children with disabilities (USDHHS, 2008). In 2012 children with disabilities constituted 12% of Head Start enrollment across the nation (USDHHS, 2012a). Research continues to emerge that demonstrates increased positive outcomes for children with disabilities who have access to intervention before age 5 and who are included in classrooms with typically developing peers (Hume, Bellini, & Pratt, 2005).

On the heels of continuing research on the critical nature of the early years in terms of children's development came a new initiative, developed in 1994, to serve pregnant women and infants. Early Head Start marked an expansion of programs and services and underscored the importance of optimizing the earliest years of development, even prenatal development, to ensure later positive developmental outcomes (USDHHS, 2002b). Early Head Start programs maintain a strong emphasis on family education and prenatal health care services.

Individuals with Disabilities Education Improvement Act

Further evolutions of federal legislation emerged with the 1975 Education of All Handicapped Children Act (later renamed the Individuals with Disabilities Education Improvement Act of 2004). Combining earlier legislation for preschool-age children, revisions in the 2004 act govern how states provide early intervention services for infants, young children, and school-age children with disabilities. Provisions call for ongoing improvements in the access to free appropriate public education for children with disabilities, specifically including (IDEA, 2004; Lascarides & Hinitz, 2000)

- teachers and parents to jointly create individualized plans for children,
- children to be educated in the least restrictive environments,
- high expectations for all children,
- schoolwide support and aid to ensure maximum success for children with disabilities,
- fair educational decisions for all children,
- accountability of professionals to children and families, and
- high-quality preservice teacher education designed to prepare teachers to meet students' unique and diverse needs with research-based teaching approaches.

RISK FACTORS: CONTEXT AND DEFINITIONS

While professionals strive to maintain a positive, empowering perspective of children and families, research continues to demonstrate the greater potential for negative developmental outcomes when children live within certain contexts. These contexts are described as *risk factors,* and children experiencing risk factors are described as *children at-risk.* As early childhood educators, we believe all children have tremendous promise and potential within them. It is our responsibility to provide opportunities, environments, and experiences to help them realize that promise and potential, particularly in the face of family stress and risk factors. Research on preschool and early intervention programs designed to mitigate risk factors show success in strengthening child and family resiliency (ability to overcome stress and risk factors) (Hall et al., 2009; USDHHS, 2010).

Risk Factors and Impact

Although it is impossible to draw up one complete profile to fit every situation, it is possible to establish commonalities shared by many families living in low socioeconomic situations. Research has identified the following factors that may pose challenges to optimal developmental outcomes (Knitzer & Lefkowitz, 2006; Robbins, Stagman, & Smith, 2012):

- Living at or below the federal poverty guidelines or at the low-income threshold (200% of federal poverty level)
- Living in a single-parent household
- Being born to a teenage mother
- Low education level of parents
- Non-employed parents
- Low birth weight
- Living with a disability
- Living in a family with four or more children
- Family having changed residences one or more times in the past 12 months

The potential effects on a child living within these conditions can be lifelong and severe. It is important to remember that simply living with one or more of these factors does not necessarily determine a child's school or life outcomes nor are all children experiencing one or multiple risk factors destined for negative outcomes. These factors represent the potential for increased school and health problems. Living with more than one risk factor compounds the potential for negative outcomes. Whereas half of American preschoolers face at least one risk factor, 20% of young children are coping with three or more risk factors (Robbins et al., 2012).

Poverty as a Risk Factor

Most young children who demonstrate negative effects of one or more of the risk factors noted previously were living in poverty (Knitzer & Lefkowitz, 2006; Robbins et al., 2012). Poverty is periodically assessed and annually defined by the U.S. Census Bureau and the U.S. Department of Health and Human Services (USDHHS). In 2013 the

USDHHS national poverty guidelines were defined as follows (guidelines are slightly higher for Alaska and Hawaii):

2013 National Poverty Guidelines	
Size of Family Unit	Income at or Below
1	$11,490
2	15,510
3	19,530
4	23,550
5	27,570

Source: USDHHS, 2013.

The term *poverty* is defined by these thresholds. The term *low income* is used to refer to families whose income is at or less than twice the federal poverty level (Robbins et al., 2012). For example, a single mother with two children earning less than $40,000 would be considered in a low-income category.

Family income is considered a crucial element in determining children's developmental outcomes because of several associated factors. Children living in poverty or low-income families more frequently suffer from inadequate nutrition, are more likely to be exposed to environmental toxins such as lead, may suffer abuse or neglect, and are the least likely to be placed in quality child-care settings (Aber & Palmer, 1999). Finding safe housing, providing adequate nutritious foods, and being able to afford quality child care can be a challenge for any family, but for families experiencing economic hardship, the stresses are even greater. You may be surprised to learn that young children living with a parent who works full time year round make up 45% of the low-income population and more children living in rural areas live in low-income households than those in urban areas (57% and 47%, respectively) (Addy, Engelhardt, & Skinner, 2013). Sometimes parents work more than one job to try to make ends meet, which diminishes the time they can spend with their children and increases the family's stress. After a period of decline, the rates of children living in poverty are now increasing. Statistical data from 2011 reveals that more than 46% of children age 6 and younger are living in low-income households, and more than 25% of those are living at or below the federal poverty level (Addy et al., 2013). The numbers of children living in families with income at or below the low-income threshold continues to increase steadily and is connected to race/ethnicity.

Child Race/Ethnicity	Percentage of Children Living at the Low-Income Threshold or Below
Asian	30
White	35
Black and African American	70
American Indian/Native American	70
Hispanic/Latino Origin	67

Putting It Into Practice

Knowing Your Children

The rise in child poverty rates only underscores the importance of knowing your children's family and home context. You know it is important to support linguistic and cultural diversity, but support becomes even more urgent when families are struggling to provide food, shelter, or medical care for their children. Making connections between homes and schools requires that teachers embrace family-friendly practices, understand the child's home context, and be knowledgeable about access to resources and supports. The following are strategies you can use to get to know your children and families:

- Invite parents into the classroom; find ways for them to contribute meaningfully.

- Encourage dialogues.
- Share helpful resources (first of all, be knowledgeable about local resources).
- Offer sensitive responsiveness when parents do talk about life at home; don't judge their parenting skills.
- Welcome and promote family participation in the classroom and program/school
- Maintain professional confidentiality.
- Participate in a home-visit program.

The disparities in family income level with respect to family race/ethnicity reveal a very troubling, persistent difference in the experience of families in the United States, often described as *persistent racism*.

There is additional evidence that being raised in a low-income household increases the likelihood that children will exhibit behavior disorders (Elliot, Prior, Merrigan, & Ballinger, 2002; Halle et al., 2009). Remember the child's outburst during the classroom visit? She was not yet able to handle conflict with a classmate and lost control. She deteriorated into disruptive and unsafe behaviors (yelling, kicking) when the stress of social conflict, on top of the stresses of home life, was too much for her. Lack of coping skills, social skills, and the ability to handle classroom conflicts compounds school problems for children from homes facing economic stress or limited resources. Social maladjustment further exacerbates problems with schoolwork and forming social connections with teachers and peers. These impediments to successful classroom interactions, particularly underdeveloped social skills, all increase the likelihood for school problems.

Increasing children's social competence and ability to regulate emotions and impulses has been identified as an essential area of development for children's school success. The ability to get along with diverse groups of people, to accept new people into their world (both adults and children), and to be comfortable trying new activities in small and large groups are all rated as the highest priority in terms of kindergarten and 1st-grade readiness skills. In keeping with their mission to grow and expand as children's needs do, Head Start programs place a strong emphasis on social competence (Powell, 2000).

Other Factors Contributing to Risk

More than half of the children in families receiving public assistance have mothers who began childbearing when they were teenagers. Teenage mothers are also more likely to

Learning to work together and develop strong social skills is an essential part of Head Start programs.

have only a high school education level, compounding risk factors for their children. Being a child of a teenage mother itself appears to be a risk factor for later school problems, health problems, and behavior problems. Young mothers are less likely to seek prenatal medical care, and they are less likely to maintain healthful habits during pregnancy. Inadequate prenatal and neonatal care can lead to lower birth weight (a risk factor for negative developmental outcomes) and undernourishment (Blair, Peters, & Lawrence, 2003). These insufficient prenatal care habits may be due in part to lower education levels, lower income, fewer support networks, or a lack of awareness of healthful self-care and parenting skills (Nord & Rhoads, 1992; Peth-Pierce, 2000). Early Head Start seeks to address these issues as early as possible during pregnancy through comprehensive health and education support services.

Children of immigrant parents are also more likely to be living in low-income households: 65% versus 46% for children of native-born parents; (Addy et al., 2013). These statistics illustrate the importance and need for intervention programs that target children and parents as early as possible and within their own community and cultural context. Many immigrant families do not yet have strong English-speaking skills. This can limit their employment options as well as their access to social services. Also, even when immigrant parents held professional jobs in their home countries, the transition to a new job market can track them into lower paying jobs. Simply focusing on addressing children's needs, independent of the family unit, is not an effective way to address larger social and economic issues. It is important to validate the child's home culture, parent involvement, and unique background in an effort to support success for the whole family.

Many families who are receiving some form of public assistance are struggling with a combination of the risk factors mentioned or even struggling with some factors not mentioned. In light of this reality, it becomes clear that families living with risk factors are in need of high-quality, comprehensive early intervention services. What specific elements constitute a successful, quality early intervention model? Let's turn to the Head Start program as a successful, national example.

HEAD START AND EARLY HEAD START PROGRAMS

Project Head Start has become the country's largest provider of education and medical services to disadvantaged children and families with limited incomes. As of 2012 statistics, Head Start and Early Head Start programs serve more than 1 million children annually, and more than 30 million children have participated in programs since its inception. The annual national budget for Head Start is now nearly $8 billion, although threats of budget cuts continue to be part of political debates. Forty-five percent of grantee programs provide both Head Start and Early Head Start services (USDHHS, 2012a). Even with these impressive numbers, Head Start programs are serving only roughly half of all eligible children (with Early Head Start serving 4% of eligible children) owing to limits in funding (Schmit & Ewen, 2012a, 2012b). Eligibility for program enrollment is most closely related to family income. Children who are homeless and families with income at or below the federal poverty level categorically qualify, and under the 2009 reauthorization, programs are able to serve families with incomes less than 130% of the poverty level up to 35% of the program enrollment (USDHHS, 2008).

The kinds of early experiences that are identified as the most suitable to foster healthful early development for all children include (Bredekamp & Copple, 2009; Smith, 1988)

- developing warm and caring relationships with care providers who model positive behaviors, such as compassion, cooperation, and curiosity;
- exposure to authentic literature experiences daily, such as reading stories together, noticing signs, and using maps and menus;
- exploring materials, such as blocks, water tables, and clay, in a hands-on way;
- plenty of child-initiated play and choice-making;
- some teacher-directed, skill-based learning experiences, such as fine-motor art lessons, cooking experiences, and crafts; and
- interacting with both children and adults in relaxed social groups.

This framework is true for all early childhood programs; however, it becomes especially important in early intervention settings where the program is attempting to combat the effects of poverty or other risk factors. The early intervention programs that have proven to be the most successful are those that (Marcon, 2002; Parke & Agness, 2002)

- are comprehensive (education and health components),
- balance teacher- and child-initiated learning,
- are based on developmental theories,
- seek to support families and involve them meaningfully in children's school life, and
- are implemented by trained and educated staff.

Overall health and wellness, learning experiences, family involvement, and community partnerships are four pillars of Head Start and Early Head Start practice. Table 6-1 outlines the comprehensive scope of programming within these four key pillars of practice. Observe how this teacher integrates dental care lessons into the learning program in this **video**.

TABLE 6-1 Four Pillars of Comprehensive Head Start Services

Health and Wellness	Learning Experiences	Family Involvement	Community Partnerships
• Adequate nutrition: 2/3 of children's daily nutritional needs provided in full-day program	• Views children's learning and development holistically	• Families are valued as the child's first teacher and primary influence	• Reducing the effect of poverty must have a community-wide focus
• Medical, dental, and mental health screenings happen for each child within 90 days of entrance into program	• Curriculum planning organized through the Head Start Development and Learning Framework	• Families are welcomed through early home visits	• The community context and culture are woven into each program
• Medical and dental care: checkup visits coordinated through program; office visits may occur as part of program day	• The Framework integrates all broad areas of learning and development, but does not dictate specific activities or outcomes	• Parents are encouraged to volunteer in the classroom	• Community members often volunteer and act as classroom guests and field trip sites
• Screening for developmental progress or disability within 45 days of entrance into program	• Learning activities are centered around children's play	• Program mandates require family members hold a majority of governing board positions	• Head Start programs serve as an employment base by hiring from within the community
• Ongoing assessments throughout school year	• Teachers balance child-initiated activities, content/theme center-based play, and teacher-guided instruction	• Job skill training, adult education, parent education, and English learning education are often provided on-site for parents	
• Referrals as needed to network of physical and mental health providers as well as disability specialists	• Many Head Start programs use the High/Scope curriculum or other research-based, scientifically validated learning program	• Many Head Start parents move into paid positions within programs	
• Health and wellness knowledge and behaviors are also integrated into the learning environment	• Ongoing assessment and reporting of children's learning and developmental progress are essential parts of program guidelines	• Family culture and home language are integrated into programming	

These examples of a more comprehensive, family- and community-centered vision illustrate the philosophy behind Head Start, Early Head Start, and early intervention programs in general. It is a philosophy that employs a *change-from-within* process. This is based on the belief that real social change can be effected only by empowering individuals to take control of their lives while working together to overcome adverse conditions (Rappaport, McWilliam, & Smith, 2004). Understanding this focus is crucial in recognizing how these programs have the potential to ameliorate widespread social problems as well as empower individual children and families.

Head Start Development and Learning Framework

The Framework outlines the essential areas of development and learning that are to be used by Head Start programs to establish school readiness goals for their children, monitor children's progress, align curricula, and conduct program planning." (USDHHS, 2011, p. 2). The content of the Framework is solidly based on research on children's developmental needs and foundations for school success and integrates 11 overarching areas of development and learning. The 11 broad domains are:

1. Physical Development & Health
2. Social & Emotional Development
3. Approaches to Learning
4. Language Development
5. Literacy Knowledge & Skills
6. Mathematics Knowledge & Skills
7. Science Knowledge & Skills
8. Creative Arts Expression
9. Logic & Reasoning
10. Social Studies Knowledge & Skills
11. English Language Development (specifically focused for dual-language learners)

Each of the domains is described and includes sub-categories, or *domain elements,* which further define types of learning and activities within each domain area. The Framework does not provide a list of specific benchmark achievements or skills. Instead, educators are cautioned to base outcome expectations on research on developmental milestones and children's individual capabilities and family culture. This emphasis reflects current research on developmentally appropriate practice, which calls for all early childhood professionals to responsively integrate knowledge of

- developmental theory and practice,
- individual child characteristics and capabilities, and
- family and community cultural contexts (including dual-language learners).

The Framework serves as a guide to ensure that learning experiences are meaningful, appropriate, and comprehensive in terms of supporting all of children's learning and developmental areas. Teachers then design and implement practices in the classroom that reflect an emphasis on active, integrated, child-centered programming. "Investigation and exploration; purposeful, engaged play; and intentional, scaffolded instruction based on the developmental level of each child are essential elements of appropriate practice in Head Start programs" (USDHHS, 2011, p. 4).

Active, integrated, child-centered programming is a key feature of Head Start programs.

DOES HEAD START WORK? EVIDENCE OF EFFECTIVENESS

One of the biggest challenges faced by early intervention programs such as Head Start is the reality that children eligible for Head Start and Early Head Start services are often lagging behind their peers in many areas of development (Robbins et al., 2012). Scores on tests of cognitive development and language and literacy skills show consistent differences for children based on family income status. Children from families with limited incomes fare worse on these measures than their more affluent peers (Caputo, 2003; Champion, Hyter, McCabe, & Bland-Stewart, 2003; Children's Defense Fund, 2003; Rauh, Parker, Garfinkel, Perry, & Andrews, 2003; USDHHS, 2003). Some researchers point to cultural biases within the test instruments; however, it is generally believed that children from homes experiencing economic stress or limited resources lag behind their peers developmentally (Champion et al., 2003). So the question remains: Can Head Start programs help?

Results: Social Skills and Language Skills Strengthened

Improving children's social competence is a key Head Start program goal. The mission to help children be ready to learn in school *(school readiness)* hinges on their social

Putting It Into Practice

Forming Parent Partnerships

Here are some ideas for forming parent partnerships:

- Ask for parent input. Parents know more about their own children than anyone else does. Learning from them makes your job easier and validates their role as their children's first teachers.
- Support parents' decisions for their children. Let parents know that their goals, beliefs, values, and choices are important to you. When there are conflicts between your practices and parents' goals (such as in academic expectations), discuss these. Start by listening. Share your beliefs and your rationale for your practice. Find ways to integrate both views. Communication is a two-way street!
- Let parents know that your door is always open and they are welcome at any time.
- Communicate freely with parents about when their child has a good day, not just when there are problems. Send home "Great Moments" notes celebrating positive classroom experiences or funny anecdotes.
- Communicate in ways that are comfortable and accessible for families: home language, format (written, digital, verbal), formally or informally, etc.
- Let them know your position: We're in this together!

competence and ability to regulate their emotions and impulses. Earlier research has demonstrated significant gains were found in Head Start participants in social development, reduced hyperactive behavior, and increased cooperative behaviors in the classroom (USDHHS, 2006). The importance of developing positive social skills as a precursor to being successful in later educational environments is a key foundation of all preschool programming, but it is especially important in a program that is seeking to ameliorate delays or achievement gaps prior to kindergarten. The effect of healthy social-emotional development in infants and toddlers is perhaps even more significant than in preschoolers. Strong attachments and healthy social-emotional development in infancy and toddlerhood lay the foundation for being ready and able to learn in preschool classrooms.

Recent years have seen an increased emphasis on the rigor and reporting of data on the effects of Head Start and Early Head Start programs. The Head Start Impact Studies are ongoing analysis and reports of important indicators of Head Start effectiveness. The most recent reports reveal the following key general findings comparing children attending Head Start for 1 or 2 years and children who did not attend Head Start (but may have been enrolled in an alternate preschool experience) (USDHHS, 2010):

- Much stronger language arts skills
- Strong emergent literacy skills reported by parents
- Closer and more positive relationships with parents
- Improvements in behaviors, social skills, and positive approaches to learning
- Positive effect on child health insurance coverage and health status

Overall, children attending Head Start programs accessed higher quality early childhood settings, as measured by environment rating scales and teacher credentials. In addition, families of children in the Head Start attendance group report positive effects on children's social-emotional development and parent-child interactions. The follow-up study revealed that there were no differences in quality of early elementary setting children attended after the initial preschool-age study (USDHHS, 2012b).

These key findings reveal that, although children do enter Head Start programs significantly behind national averages in literacy and social skills, the gap is narrowed during program attendance. However, the most recent data, follow-up at 3rd grade, reveal that gains made in the preschool years are generally not sustained over the early elementary years.

Program Effects Over Time

A primary concern of Head Start and Early Head Start program evaluators is the fading of positive effects over time. There have been reports emerging for many years that show improvements in children's development have faded by 2 years after leaving the program and/or entering public school (USDHHS, 2011). In particular, the most recent comparison of program participants and nonparticipants in the Head Start 3rd Grade Follow-Up study revealed mixed results of some lasting gains as well as fade-out of gains:

- no evidence of effect in cognitive domains at the end of kindergarten
- some evidence of positive effect on children's vocabulary scores at 1st grade

- some evidence that Head Start children were promoted through the early grades less than nonprogram participants
- some evidence of positive effect on 3rd-grade reading assessment
- parents report higher social-emotional skills and positive approaches to learning
- no significant effect for math, prewriting, or teacher reports of children's school accomplishments or social-emotional skills
- early gains in health status faded consistently over the early grades
- positive parenting practices emerged during the Head Start year(s) and persisted through 3rd grade

Some people point to these results as a failure on the part of Head Start programs to produce sustained benefits over time (Lee, Brooks-Gunn, Schnur, & Liaw, 1990). Other researchers, however, point out that the comprehensive services provided under the auspices of Head Start are not necessarily continued through the public school years. As children enter classrooms with many more children and fewer teachers, the time and attention they need may not be available. In addition, access to health and welfare services may not be included in school programs in the same way. This drop-off in intervention services and supports is a factor that must be considered when interpreting the fade-out of initial positive effects (Rauh et al., 2003).

Despite the fade-out and concerns about sustaining effectiveness of the program, deeper data analysis has revealed lasting gains for children from high-risk households in some cognitive development and social-emotional development areas (USDHHS, 2011). Additional recent studies of adults who attended early intervention programming as children are demonstrating positive gains, which appear later in life, as well as overall improve-

Cycle of Stress

Imagine a young single mother, living alone and struggling to maintain two low-paying part-time jobs while raising a toddler. She is often stressed about how she will provide food and shelter for herself and her child. Adding to her stress is the child's consistent fussiness; he often cries and refuses to be comforted by her. The more she is unable to console him, the more inadequate she feels as a mother. The more inadequate she feels as a mother, the more she herself withdraws from her child. The more she withdraws from her child, the more he is unable to be consoled by her. Soon this small family is entangled in an unfortunate, vicious cycle. Many parents may lack the knowledge, skills, and support networks necessary to handle the stresses that can be associated with poverty. Research has found that by specifically focusing on improving the dynamic of the mother-child relationship, early intervention efforts can have positive effects on the quality of that relationship (Blair et al., 2003). Improved relations between the mother and child then set the stage for a healthier social-emotional development that positively influences later social relationships. Given that strong parent support and involvement in the child's life are two of the best predictors of positive developmental outcomes, parent support and involvement are key features of most early intervention programming (Kagan, 2002).

ment in later life outcomes for participation in high-quality early childhood programming (summarized in USDHHS, 2011). The mixed results point to a clear need for ongoing research both early and throughout the lifespan to continue to illuminate the relative effects of early childhood education on children and adults.

Current Trends in Head Start Programs

Originally the Head Start curriculum focused more heavily on developing children's social competence. Previous years have seen the focus expanded to include a strong emphasis on language arts development. As national goals for school readiness become more defined (for example, specific skill expectations such as knowing 20 letters and recognizing letters in one's own name), Head Start child and program outcomes and learning frameworks are continually revised to reflect these trends. The latest education program revision is the Child Development and Early Learning Framework that presents a comprehensive, holistic view of the developmental and learning goals for Head Start programs (USDHHS, 2011). And while strong parent involvement has always been a key feature of Head Start, in recent years emphasis has been placed on strengthening involvement of fathers and community collaborations.

Trends in Teacher Credentials

Improving program quality through curriculum reviews, increasing teacher credentials and salaries, and striving to reach all children in need of services are historic and current goals for the program (Jacobson, 2004). The 2004 reauthorization called for all Early Head Start teachers to have a child development associate (CDA) credential by 2010, at least half of all Head Start teachers nationwide to earn a bachelor's degree by 2013, and all Head Start teacher assistants to have a CDA by 2013 (USDHHS, 2008). (The CDA, a credential that combines minimal education and experience, was created as an entry-level credential for teachers and assistants.) As of 2012, 62% of Head Start center-based teachers held baccalaureate or higher degrees, surpassing the goal set. An additional 31% of teachers held associate two-year degrees (USDHHS, 2012a). Head Start program guidelines and funding continue to support improving teacher credentials and professional development. Improving the professionalization of Head Start teachers is a complex issue involving concerns about funding and timeliness but is a goal that is widely accepted as a viable means of improving quality programming for children. Remaining at the forefront of the field and supporting innovations in best practices have been part of Head Start programming since its inception.

Trends in Program Implementation: Emphasis on Accountability

Periodic reauthorizations of the Head Start legislation also mean that the program is continually under review, which ensures timeliness, relevance, and responsiveness to changing

Programming for children's nutrition includes engaging in warm social interactions during meals and snacks.

trends and community needs. The 2007 reauthorization included several key changes, including (USDHHS, 2008)

- grant renewal required every 5 years;
- expansion of American Indian/Alaskan Native and migrant/seasonal programs;
- prioritizing homeless children for enrollment;
- if space allows, enrolling children whose family income is between 100% and 130% of the federal poverty guidelines; and
- all Early Head Start teachers must hold a CDA credential at a minimum.

On the heels of data that prompt questions about the short- and long-term effect of Head Start programming, an increased emphasis is now being placed on both individual program assessment and national system effectiveness. Recently Head Start programs have implemented a new competition process for grant funds that involves stricter procedures for assessing program compliance and quality. Program and classroom quality rating scales have become a major feature of Head Start assessment. Data collection and reporting are now priorities at the national and local levels. These new changes to the funding process and use of assessment cut-off scores to determine compliance are creating some stress for established providers (Samuels, 2013), but the pressure to make data-driven decisions continues to mount. The debates continue as educators and policy makers seek fair, reliable, and accurate assessment parameters and procedures.

CONCLUSION

Responsibility for ameliorating negative outcomes for children living with one or more risk factors is carried by all members of society. Current research promotes the idea that the most effective way to address social problems of poverty and inequality is by providing comprehensive support services to children and families. Head Start and Early Head Start programs have remained at the forefront of the long-standing effort to combat poverty and give every child the best chance for success. Through research and responsive program implementation, Head Start also remains a leader in shaping future practices in early childhood education.

The implications for educators from Head Start policy are clear: it is essential to understand, validate, and support children's development within the context of the family and community through individualized, appropriate, comprehensive programs and services. By identifying and addressing children's and families' needs as early as possible, we stand the best chance for improving children's developmental outcomes. Also by improving children's developmental outcomes throughout school and later life, we stand the best chance of repairing torn communities and strengthening society as a whole.

SUMMARY

- Head Start and Early Head Start are national grant-funded early education and comprehensive care programs specifically designed for children of families living in poverty.
- Research on child outcomes in the 1950s and 1960s underscored the divide in developmental outcomes between children from lower income families and their more affluent peers.
- In response to the growing developmental gap between socioeconomic classes, Head Start and Early Head Start were created in 1965 and 1994, respectively, to close the gap and help prepare all U.S. children for success in school.
- Risk factors include a variety of aspects of children's household and family context that increase the potential for negative developmental outcomes, particularly living in poverty.
- Other risk factors include low parent education attainment, parent unemployment, maternal age, living with a single parent, and living with a disability.
- Head Start and Early Head Start programs strive to ameliorate the negative effect of risk factors through comprehensive early intervention programming:
  - Children learning within the interrelated contexts of the family, community, and school environments
  - Strong partnerships with families and community members
  - Comprehensive health, wellness, education, and sociocultural elements
- The Child Development and Early Learning Framework provides 11 broad, overarching areas of focus for children's learning.
- Recent evaluations of the programs' effects on children's developmental outcomes yield marginally positive reviews, with concerns about fade-out by 3rd grade.
- Increases in teacher qualifications, changes to the curriculum guidelines and funding procedures, and a commitment to accountability for program quality all seek to initiate positive changes in program implementation.

CHAPTER LEARNING GOALS SELF-ASSESSMENT

Use this chart to write down three to five key points for each learning goal that you learned from this chapter.

Describe key features of Head Start and Early Head Start programs.	
Examine important historical trends in early intervention programs.	
Discuss risk factors in the context of children's development.	
Identify key features of Head Start and Early Head Start programs.	
Analyze data on Head Start and Early Head Start effectiveness.	
Explore current changes and trends in Head Start and Early Head Start legislation and implementation.	

APPLICATION ACTIVITIES

Discussion Prompts

1. List at least five things you believe are necessary for children's healthful overall development. Consider what you believe to be the optimal home, school, and community environment for children.

2. Who do you think should be responsible for providing food and medical care for children (access and cost)?

3. How do you feel about welfare or social service programs such as food stamps, housing subsidies, and child care tuition subsidies?

4. Can you foresee any problems with the administration of early intervention programming (for example, diverse cultural values and talking with parents about sensitive issues such as poverty and employment status)?

In Class   In small groups, review the resources and information on the Head Start Early Childhood Knowledge and Learning Center Web site: eclkc.ohs.acf.hhs.gov/hslc/ecdh/eecd. Select any of the topics that sound interesting to you, and explore the linked content. There is a wealth of information available on the Web site that can be used by any teacher in any program.

In the Field   Arrange a visit to a local Head Start program. Use the Head Start Web site, eclkc.ohs.acf.hhs.gov/hslc, to locate programs. Try to identify strategies the teachers are using to provide comprehensive supports to children and families. Talk to the teachers about their perspectives on working with families (including home visits), inclusion of children with disabilities, curriculum goals, and assessment.

For Your Portfolio   Locate a current early intervention journal article on one of the following topics:

- Early intervention programs for preschool children from homes experiencing stress or limited resources
- Bilingual education for young children
- Preschoolers with special needs

After reading the article, include the following sections in your two-page, double-spaced, typed review:

1. Complete reference in APA format
2. Brief summary of article (between half a page and a full page), including the purpose and topic of the article, the main points, and the major findings
3. Your reaction to each article (between half a page and a full page), including what you learned and whether you agreed with the author (article can be added to your portfolio in a section on child development and learning or knowledge of the field)

RELATED WEB LINKS

Early Head Start National Resource Center
www.ehsnrc.org

Head Start information
acf.hhs.gov/programs/ohs/

CHAPTER 7

The High/Scope Foundation: Models in Curriculum and Research

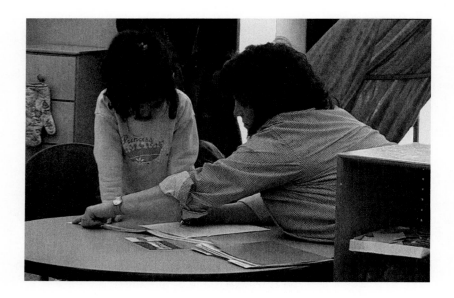

Chapter Learning Goals

- Describe learning activities in High/Scope classrooms.
- Identify important aspects of the High/Scope curriculum approach.
- Examine key roles of the High/Scope teacher.
- Discuss elements of child and program assessment in High/Scope.
- Discuss implications of ongoing High/Scope research projects.
- Explore diversity and inclusion in applying High/Scope principles.

The High/Scope Educational Research Foundation encompasses a lab school, teacher-training program, and robust research agenda. The High/Scope early childhood and elementary education curriculum is based on Piagetian beliefs and constructivist learning principles. Developed as an intervention program for children from families with limited incomes, the curriculum seeks to instill in children a deliberate, active approach to learning. High/Scope teachers facilitate children's self-directed planning, which the children then carry out and later take time to reflect on. High/Scope is much more than just a curriculum model, though. The High/Scope

166

Educational Research Foundation also publishes child and program assessment tools and conducts research on the effects of a variety of early childhood approaches and programs on children's later school and life success.

OVERVIEW OF HIGH/SCOPE

Since 1970, the High/Scope Educational Research Foundation has been creating, implementing, and researching high-quality early childhood programs specifically targeting children living in poverty. High/Scope publishes an extensive array of informational training videos and books and coordinates teacher trainings nationwide. The foundation also conducts research on the effects of High/Scope and other early childhood programs and has been collecting data for more than 40 years. Above all, the foundation seeks to inform practice and advocate for the right and need for all children to have access to high-quality early childhood programming.

The High/Scope demonstration preschool includes the following key elements:

- A core curriculum that includes specific elements but encourages following children's interests
- A three-phase "plan-do-review" learning cycle
- Assessment tools and strategies

In the following classroom view, identify where you notice teachers scaffolding and facilitating children's play and how you see play being used as a primary vehicle for children's learning.

CLASSROOM VIEW

The rain is lightly falling as you pull up to the large facility that encompasses a High/Scope program in a small urban area. Through the swish of your windshield wipers, you note that the long driveway with the brick buildings on the hill makes it feel more like an old college campus than a preschool program. Most of the old buildings house other social service agency programs. The one that houses the preschool programs is new and boasts an inviting playground with large, wooden climbing equipment and flower gardens. You park your car and ring the bell outside the locked glass doors. Once inside, you are met with a smile, sign in at the reception desk, are given a visitor badge, and are escorted to the classroom that you will be observing. Although the safety of the children is clearly important, the program staff makes every effort to make invited visitors feel welcome. The classroom at the end of the hall has a small observation room with one-directional windows and speakers hooked up to the classroom, allowing unobtrusive observations. You settle in at the observation windows as the teacher is preparing for the children's arrival.

The classroom is quiet now, and you can see that the room is set up in distinct learning areas. Materials are grouped on low cubby shelves that are all labeled with pictures and words in English and Spanish. There are numerous open-ended materials, including blocks, dramatic play props, empty boxes and bottles, water and sand toys and tables, and art supplies. There is also an inviting book corner with disc players and headphones. In each learning area, posters are hung on the wall with descriptions of the kinds of developmental skills promoted by the area. Neat displays of children's work abound, and each one has a separate note card describing how the child completed the work or something the child said about it. There are several large display boards with photos of the children and their families around the room. The teacher is busy setting the tables with laminated place mats that include each child's name and outlines of eating utensils. Trays of cereal, juice, and milk are on the tables, ready for the children to eat breakfast.

The early morning quiet of the classroom soon gives way to a buzz of activity as children arrive from their buses and are walked to the room by the assistant teacher. A few children are brought to the classroom by their parents, but most children arrive by the buses provided by the center. As the children enter, they deposit their coats into individual cubbies, wash their hands, and take their seats at one of the four tables with the place mats. The teachers and children (19 children present) eat breakfast together, along with another support staff who is visiting for the day. They all talk naturally and openly about life at home and their busy mornings getting ready for school. Several children speak in Spanish with the assistant teacher, who responds in Spanish. He then follows with English translation for the non-Spanish-speaking children to fill them in on the conversation. He encourages the children to use both languages, and he encourages non-Spanish speakers to repeat some of the Spanish words. You notice that the non-Spanish-speaking children appear to be interested in the new words, and the Spanish-speaking children are eager to praise their peers' efforts. The classroom feels warm and respectful.

After the children finish eating, they clean up and gather together on an open carpet space. The teacher brings over a large poster listing (with words and pictures) all the available centers and activities. The children begin to discuss which areas and activities they want to play with and work on for the morning. The teachers engage the children in dialogues about their choices and their plans.

KARISSA: *I want to work with the blocks.*

TEACHER: *Karissa, you want to work with the blocks again like yesterday? What do you want to do with the blocks? Are you going to build something today?*

KARISSA: *I want to build a bridge for the cars to go under.*

TEACHER: *A bridge? Great! What kind of blocks do you think you will need?*

KARISSA: *Um . . . long ones for across I think. (Pause.)*

TEACHER: *OK. How do you think the cars will fit underneath the long—*

KARISSA: *(Bursts in.) And tall ones for the sides!*

TEACHER: *OK. So you're going to the block area to build a bridge for the cars to go under, and you're going to try using long blocks and tall blocks. Great! Let's see how it works!*

Karissa puts her nametag next to the blocks section on the chart and hurries off to carry out her plan. The rest of the children make similar choices during conversations with the teachers, each with specific plans. Before leaving the rug area, the children are reminded about the daily schedule, also written with words and pictures. After breakfast time, there is always a planning time, followed by individual and small-group activities for nearly 2 hours. After work time, the schedule indicates that all the children will come together again for a reflection time.

For now, the teachers circulate with the children as they carry out their plans, and the assistant teacher works with a small group of children who are planning to put on a talent show in the music area. They are listening to recordings of children's songs and singing and playing along with musical instruments.

One child excitedly talks about how he recently went to his cousin's school play and they gave them a paper (a program). The assistant teacher talks about programs and what information they provide for the audience. He asks the talent show group if they would like to design their own

By guiding children's planning through dialogue and questioning, teachers can indirectly promote more complex thinking and more in-depth play in children.

programs for their performance. They excitedly begin to make plans for using the writing center, and one child decides to make a collage from old magazines in the art area for the cover. Another child cautions her, "Don't forget to just look for pictures of music and instruments. This is a music performance." With a nod, she is off to gather magazines.

As the group continues their project, the assistant teacher talks to the teacher about a possible large-group activity involving singing and dancing. It would tie in to the talent show group's interest and encourage other children as well. He mentions that Javier was able to apply classification concepts when he reminded Maria to look for only music pictures. The teachers discuss the progress he is making from his last observation report. Wanting to build on the children's interests, they agree to write up a music-related lesson plan for tomorrow. The teacher mentions the book on bridges she has brought in for large-group time today to connect to Karissa's ongoing interest in cars and bridges. She seems as excited as Karissa as she tells the assistant teacher about how the child is integrating more complex structures into her building and has begun using arch-shaped blocks as tunnels for the cars.

As work time winds down, children begin to gather at the table with the teachers. They talk about their experiences in their choice time, but it is more than just a review. Just as the teachers prompted children to make more detailed plans, they encourage deeper reflection during review time.

TEACHER: Karissa, I noticed you started using some different-shaped blocks today. Why did you decide to do that?

KARISSA: I saw a picture in the Thomas book of a bridge for the trains. Underneath it was where cars go. But the tall parts weren't just straight like my tall blocks on the sides. They were curved in the book.

TEACHER: And you wanted to make the tall part of your bridge look curved like the book?

KARISSA: Yes.

TEACHER: How did you do that?

KARISSA: I remembered those curved blocks. Well, they have a curve on the underneath part, but the top part is flat. Just like in the picture. So I got some from the shelf and put them under the long blocks. It made it just like in the book!

TEACHER: I could see that! I took a picture of your bridge structure, so we can put that in your portfolio. You know, I also found another book about bridges I think you might like. We're going to read it together after rest time.

KARISSA: OK!

TEACHER: Can you think of anything else that you would like to put into your portfolio section on bridges?

The interactions between the teacher and Karissa are typical of those you hear with all the children. The classroom is abuzz with conversations; there is a lot of discussion happening in this classroom. You've observed active learning environments before, but with the deliberate planning and reflecting, these children are not only learning through hands-on activities but are actively in control of and aware of their own learning. As the children clean up the room and prepare to go outside, you look forward to sitting down with the teachers and hearing more about the High/Scope model.

HIGH/SCOPE CURRICULUM

The High/Scope curriculum is rooted in more than 50 years of program implementation and research of effectiveness. Recently updated and revised, the curriculum strengths include the following:

- Developmentally aligned: based on important milestones of learning and development
- Research-based: integrates a wide array of research data on program effectiveness
- Child-centered: balances play- and interest-based activities that extend children's thinking and social interaction
- Family-centered: includes home visits and family involvement

The alignment of curriculum and assessment with developmental indicators, inclusion of several levels of ability for each indicator, and overall structure of the learning experience are key aspects of High/Scope's effectiveness. Listen to educators talk about the underlying philosophy, approach to learning, and organization of the environment in the High/Scope model in this **video**.

Key Developmental Indicators

Key developmental indicators

Fifty-eight learning goals that serve as a foundation to the High/Scope curriculum.

The High/Scope preschool curriculum is based on 58 **key developmental indicators** (learning goals) (High/Scope Education Research Foundation, 2009b) and is organized in five curriculum areas covering nine content areas:

- Approaches to learning
- Language, literacy, and communication
- Social and emotional development

- Physical development, health, and well-being
- Creative arts
  - Mathematics
  - Science and technology
  - Social studies

Within each learning area, specific skills and behaviors are identified that are appropriate outcomes for preschool-age children. These 58 key developmental indicators serve as the foundation for teachers' planning and design of the learning environment and material selection. Each of the five curriculum areas is composed of a number of specific key developmental indicators. Teachers use the extensive key developmental indicators to ensure that children are provided with opportunities to grow and develop fully in all learning domains and skill areas. Teachers base their assessment of children on these milestones. High/Scope infant/toddler programs also include separate key experiences appropriate for that age group.

Putting It Into Practice

Infants and Toddlers

High/Scope also includes programming for infants and toddlers. The infant and toddler curriculum includes 41 key experiences covering the following content and developmental areas (High/Scope Educational Research Foundation, 2009a):

- Sense of self
- Social relations
- Creative representation
- Movement
- Music
- Communication and language
- Exploring objects
- Early quantity and number
- Space
- Time

Although the nature of teacher-child interactions is important at all levels of education, it is perhaps most important when working with infants and toddlers. Infants come to know about their world through active exploration. But this is made possible only when infants are encouraged and supported in their explorations by adults who love and care for them and who respond to their verbal and nonverbal cues.

Adults must be in tune with infants' patterns of behavior, gestures, vocalizations, and eye movements. Looking toward sounds or objects indicates to the watchful caregiver that infants are interested in something. Looking away or raising hands to the face can be an indication that they are not interested in something. Infants will also indicate different needs through different cries. Their willingness to explore their world is heightened by being surrounded by adults who learn how to read their signals and respond quickly and sensitively to their needs. This sensitive responsiveness is essential for infants' healthful attachments and willingness to explore. Visit an infant-toddler center and learn about the unique aspects of teaching our very youngest children in this **video**.

In addition, infants and toddlers thrive in environments where adults engage them in conversations and interactions with words, gestures, and eye contact. Being an infant and toddler teacher in a High/Scope classroom involves much more than ensuring that children's needs are met. It is also about developing warm, reciprocal relationships with the children in your care, an essential foundation for learning (Girolametto, Weitzman, van Lieshout, & Duff, 2000). Relationships are important for all learning environments, but for infants and toddlers, education *is all about relationships.*

Plan-Do-Review Structure

The companion piece to the key developmental indicators in the High/Scope curriculum is the plan-do-review routine. The overarching emphasis here is on encouraging children's active learning and meaningful involvement in their own education. The plan-do-review sequence is the mechanism by which learning goals are met (Schweinhart, 2003).

Time to Plan   As you read in the observation visit, the teachers and children gathered together prior to choice or center time and discussed their goals for themselves. The teacher prompted Karissa to make specific plans about which blocks she would use in her bridge building. In this way, Karissa learned to elaborate on her general plan to build a bridge. The teacher also helped expand Karissa's thinking about the bridge by including photos and making connections between the child's work and the books. During planning time, children are encouraged to

- make plans,
- think about how they will use materials,
- consider ways to work together with other children, and
- make predictions about what they expect to happen as they carry out their plans.

It is through this thoughtful planning phase that children learn to be deliberate, active agents who are able to direct the course of their own learning. This is truly an empowering experience for children. Children see that they are in control of their time and actions and that their choices are respected. The planning phase also promotes higher order thinking and problem-solving skills as well as deliberate, purposeful action (Epstein, 2003). When children are in the driver's seat in terms of choosing activities, teachers find there are fewer discipline problems and are free to interact with the children as partners (Child Care Information Exchange, 2002). Many center programs offer children a free-choice time where they are allowed to choose among materials or learning centers, but High/Scope's method takes the notion of children's choice-making to another level. Here the emphasis is on intention, thinking ahead, discussion of ideas, and more detailed planning. This thoughtful planning can lead to a more deliberate use of the materials and a deeper engagement with peers and adults.

Time to Do   When children are given choices about materials and activities to engage in, they are naturally empowered and more interested in their learning. When children thoughtfully plan details about their choices, they *think* more about their actions. There is a sense of ownership that comes with directing their actions. This ownership promotes autonomy (independence), initiative (willingness to try and do things), and industry (interest in being busy and active). Erikson's theory of socioemotional development states that achieving positive outcomes in these areas is essential for healthful development throughout life.

An important feature of the activity time is that children are given long periods to carry out their plans. By allowing children ample time in the "do" phase (nearly 2 hours in the observation classroom), teachers ensure that children have time to really get into their play and learning. Children are encouraged to engage deeply in their activities, revising and extending their plans as their play and work progress. They are encouraged to use materials from different centers—housekeeping, writing, blocks, and manipulatives—to add richness and detail to their play and work. In the opening classroom visit, the talent

Typical High/Scope Preschool Classroom Daily Schedule

8–8:30 A.M.	Arrival and Breakfast
8:30–9 A.M.	Self-Serve Breakfast for Latecomers
8:30–8:45 A.M.	Group Meeting: Planning Time
9 A.M.	Center Activities
10:45 A.M.	Wrap Up Learning Activities
10:50 A.M.	Group Meeting: Reflection Time
11:15 A.M.	Outside on the Playground
12 noon	Prepare/Lunch
1 P.M.	Rest/Quiet Activities
2:30 P.M.	Group Activities
3 P.M.	Outside on the Playground
4:30 P.M.	Prepare to Go Home

show group combined materials and activities in the music, writing, and art centers to elaborate on their play. Throughout the do time, teachers were actively participating with children in their play. Through interactions with peers and teachers, children are prompted to think actively about their learning experiences.

Time to Reflect and Review   When it is time to wrap up do time, teachers and children come together again to recap their experiences, reflect on how their predictions

Teachers are active partners in children's dramatic play; participating and extending, helping them implement their plans.

and outcomes aligned, and share the excitement of learning with peers and adults. Once again teachers encourage dialogues with children by

- asking open-ended questions;
- making connections to prior learning;
- extending children's ideas with suggestions for future plans; and
- pointing out similarities with projects other children have undertaken, encouraging collaborations.

Teachers ask children cognitively challenging questions that reflect the children's activities and interests. This helps to promote language, social, and cognitive development (Trawick-Smith, 1994). In these conversations, children are encouraged to make connections between predicted outcomes and actual events. In this way, casual yet meaningful interactions become a teaching tool that can be applied throughout the day to enhance children's skills and promote positive adult-child bonds (Child Care Information Exchange, 2002).

As children and teachers reflect on and analyze the do-time activities, children are encouraged to reflect and represent their experiences in a variety of ways. They may dictate a story, make a drawing, write or draw in a journal, or discuss their experiences. Through this review phase, children learn that

- their actions have effects and consequences;
- they can direct their learning;
- adults and peers are interested in their discoveries; and
- language is a powerful tool for reflecting on experiences, describing events, and organizing thought.

There is a growing body of research that shows the importance of responsive interactions, including authentic and conversational dialogues, for children's optimal development (for discussions, see File & Kontos, 1993; Girolametto et al., 2000). Through the active learning experiences, open-ended materials, responsive interactions, and personal goal setting, children's learning is supported on their own levels and at their own paces. With the plan-do-review sequence and the emphasis on social dialogues throughout the day, the High/Scope curriculum has integrated hallmarks of good practice into the structure of the model. To prepare teachers and ensure that the model is applied appropriately, High/Scope also provides initial and ongoing training, teacher certification, and regional and international conferences, which focus on the curriculum and importance of the teachers' roles.

HIGH/SCOPE TEACHER ROLES

The primary role of the teachers in High/Scope classrooms is to facilitate children's active learning. This means providing hands-on learning experiences and materials as well as encouraging children's active thinking about their learning. Teachers use the plan-do-review sequence as a framework to promote children's deliberate, active involvement in learning. Teachers also use a lot of discussion to encourage children's thinking and build relationships. Recall from the observation vignette how the teacher prompted Karissa to make her block-building plans more specific and encouraged her to predict what would happen to the cars when she used the long blocks. The teacher also encouraged Karissa to reflect more deeply on how her bridge building went by asking open-ended questions, such as, "Why did you decide to do that?" Through their discussions with children and participation in their play, High/Scope teachers strive to increase children's thinking and active roles in their learning. The rich language environment that is created by these in-depth discussions is also a key ingredient in promoting language and literacy development. The processes of predicting and assessing children's own work assist in developing their logical thinking (Epstein, 2003).

High/Scope teachers are also active partners in children's play and learning experiences. For example, when children are engaged in a dramatic play scenario, adults may play a part in the stories. They may act as playmates or extend the child-directed play. Teachers do not take over children's play or try to direct it. Instead, they participate actively but in the background, taking advantage of moments to extend children's thinking by

- suggesting new materials,
- expanding children's ideas with questions or comments, and
- supporting children's social interactions with peers and adults.

It is also important for teachers to watch and listen carefully to children's interactions, play, and work with materials. Through this keen observation, teachers are able to assess children's emerging interests and meaningfully integrate new materials, ideas, and activities that will maximize their internal motivation. The teacher in the opening observation did this by bringing in new books that related to a few children's interest in bridges and transportation. By integrating new materials that align with children's current interests, teachers facilitate children's deeper exploration of topics. This validation of children's interest promotes personal, authentic learning. These are the hallmarks of the High/Scope approach (Epstein, 2005).

Dovetailing with the teacher's role as an active participant and listener is the teacher's role as an observer. Observations are every teacher's best tool for

- getting to know children,
- understanding children's needs and interests,
- planning meaningful instruction,
- individualizing instruction/materials, and
- assessing children's progress.

When teachers are not engaged in children's play or running group learning activities, they take time to watch children in action. They are careful to record children's language, details about their play, and their use of materials. Observations are essential for creating learning environments that reflect the individual children's unique lives and interests. When making choices of materials, designing classroom space, and even making the daily schedule, it is imperative that teachers use their knowledge of their children. Listen to how this educator organizes the centers in her classroom to support children's learning through play in this **video**. Through observations and open, two-way communications with families, teachers are able to learn much that they can use to plan engaging learning experiences for all children and document children's development and learning.

Home visits are an important component of intervention programs such as Head Start and High/Scope that foster strong family connections and involvement.

ASSESSMENT IN HIGH/SCOPE CLASSROOMS

For observations to be effective as an assessment tool, they must be conducted systematically over time at routine intervals. They must include key details and broad generalizations. They must also be related to developmental theories to determine children's healthful growth and progress toward age-appropriate milestones as well as to highlight unique paths individual children follow. In High/Scope programs, teacher observations are implemented with the help of the **High/Scope Child Observation Record** (COR). The COR includes informational packets, especially designed for families, to assist teachers and families in working together to facilitate and assess children's development.

High/Scope Child Observation Record

The assessment checklist, completed over time, which appraises children on 30 developmental outcomes in all domains.

Child Observation Record

The preschool COR is a checklist that is completed over time and assesses children on 32 developmental outcomes (28 on the Infant/Toddler COR) in all domains (socioemotional, cognitive, language, and physical). The items align with the key developmental indicators (Schweinhart, 2003). Teachers use one checklist form for each child, and each checklist includes space for three separate observations over time. This allows for progress to be charted easily over time on one form. Each item includes five examples of behaviors, milestones, or skills teachers might observe from children at different levels—from simple to complex. Each item also includes space for open-ended notes. Here is an example of the progressive range of sample behaviors in the COR for 2.5- to 6-year-olds in the social relations category (High/Scope Educational Research Foundation, 2005):

1. Child expresses an emotion.
2. Child comforts another child.

3. Child talks about an emotion.

4. Child represents an emotion through pretend play or art.

5. Child identifies an emotion and gives a reason for it.

As teachers observe children at play in natural and authentic situations, they make notes about the highest level of behavior or skill being exhibited by the child. Teachers are cautioned not to make the completion of the COR into a test situation unrelated to children's normal activities; rather, the COR is to be used as an authentic assessment during children's natural activities. In this way, teachers and children feel less pressure than when completing more formal, structured tests, and the results more accurately represent how children are actually developing and performing in their daily activities.

Most teachers use anecdotal records as the primary source of information for completing the COR. **Anecdotal records** are short, focused notes about a moment in a child's day. They are quick and easy to complete, which makes them particularly appealing in the busy day of a teacher. Key information to incorporate in an anecdotal record includes the child's name, part of the day/time, setting (center or area), and a 1- to 2-sentence description of the event. Include a specific quote if the child spoke. Capturing the child's specific language is an important part of documenting their thinking. Anecdotal records are like a snapshot of the child's development. Alone, one record doesn't convey much about the child, but combined with a few records each day over time, a rich and detailed picture of the child's learning and development is painted. Figure 7-1 is an example of blank and

Anecdotal record

A brief note about a child's action, interaction, or milestone; a snapshot from the child's day.

FIGURE 7-1

Anecdotal Record Form and Sample

Child's name:_____

Date/Time:_____ Observer: _____

Setting: _____

_____

Others involved: _____

_____

What did the child do/say:_____

_____

_____

_____

_____

_____

_____

Developmental or learning domains:

_____

Child's name: _Greisan_

Date/Time: _4/28/13, 10:15am_   Observer: _Jackie_

Setting: _upper loft, with hospital materials_

Others involved: _Alice_

What did the child do/say:

Greisan entered loft and began wrapping his ankle in a bandage. Three other children joined. Greisan: "I broke my leg. I need a doctor!" Alice: "It's OK. It's OK. I'm here Gee-san. Dotter here. First you need shots." Greisan: "No! [pause] OK. But I get candy then." Alice gives Greisan a shot and then hands him a pretend candy. Alice: "Here you go. All better." Greisan: "All better. Back to work. Anks.doc."

Developmental or learning domains: _Social-role play, collaborative play, care-taking; cognitive-aware of health care activities, sequence_ completed anecdotal record forms, sized to one quarter of a standard page. The small size makes them easy to fit in a pocket; left as a four-to-a-page full sheet they can be clipped to a clipboard for easy access and portability. An essential aspect of effective documentation is to make it as easy as possible to complete, thereby increasing the consistency of note taking.

Program Quality Assessment

In addition to the COR, which is for use with individual children, High/Scope publishes a program assessment packet called the High/Scope Preschool Program Quality Assessment (PQA). The purpose of the PQA is to "evaluate the quality of early childhood programs and identify staff training needs" (High/Scope Education Research Foundation, 2003, p. 1). Completing the assessment includes conducting observations of individual classrooms as well as across the center. Interviews of teachers, administrators, and even children provide important information that could be missed in a single observation. All aspects of the program are reviewed, including the following (High/Scope Educational Research Foundation, 2003):

- Learning environments
- Schedules
- Interactions
- Curriculum
- Family involvement
- Staff development
- Program management

Each category includes several items, which are individually rated on a 5-point scale. Items marked with a 1 indicate poor performance and a need for improvement. Level 5 indicates high-quality programming. The PQA is designed to assess programs using the High/Scope or other curriculum model as well as align with Head Start performance standards. It can be a useful self-assessment tool for identifying strengths and weaknesses in a program and for identifying staff-training needs. The inclusion of several specific items addressing staff credentials, orientation, and ongoing training is a unique feature of this assessment tool compared to other rating scales. This emphasis reflects High/Scope's strong teacher-training programs and belief that increasing teacher credentials and training are keys to improving early childhood programming (Epstein, Schweinhart, & McAdoo, 1996).

HIGH/SCOPE RESEARCH

In addition to comprehensive academic programs, educational research and publication are important parts of High/Scope's efforts to empower children and families. A great deal of research has been published under the auspices of the High/Scope Educational Research Foundation. The reports shed light on outcomes for lower socioeconomic status children as well as on the efficacy of developmental-constructivist curriculum models in general and High/Scope programs in particular. Although some early research indicated a lack of significant effect of preschool curriculum models on children's outcomes (cited in Marcon, 1992), more recent reports indicate a stronger correlation between curriculum approach and child outcomes (summaries in Quindlen, 2001). High/Scope researchers have published results from studies of program quality and effectiveness as well as evaluations of program effect on child outcomes (Epstein et al., 1996; Muennig, Schweinhart, Montie, & Neidell, 2009; Schweinhart, 2003).

Results indicate positive short-term and long-term outcomes for children attending High/Scope and other high-quality early intervention programs in all developmental domains and general adult health (Muennig et al., 2009). Research projects include exploring teacher-training effectiveness and comparisons of curriculum models; however, High/Scope's best-known research project is the Perry Preschool Study (Bracey, 2003; Schweinhart, 2003).

Perry Preschool Study

"The **High/Scope Perry Preschool Study** identified young children living in poverty, randomly assigned them to a no-preschool group or a high-quality preschool program using the High/Scope Curriculum at ages 3 and 4, and collected data on them throughout their childhood, adolescence, and young adulthood" (Schweinhart, 2003, p. 8). The study, conducted during the children's preschool years from 1962 to 1965, included 123 African American children who attended preschool 5 days per week in addition to receiving weekly home visits. Data on various academic, developmental, and lifestyle outcomes continued to be collected from program participants and parents annually during childhood and periodically through middle adulthood. This form of long-term data collection on one participant sample is called longitudinal research. The most recent report includes data from age 40 (Schweinhart et al., 2005). As research results have been published throughout the years, especially with the report at age 27, more and more attention has been drawn to quality early childhood programming in general and to early intervention programs in particular.

High/Scope Perry Preschool Study

The longitudinal research project that tracks school and lifetime achievements for randomly assigned program or no-program participants.

Several features of this research project make it especially important in the field, including elements of the research design and data-collection methods that are indicators of quality research:

- Random assignment of participants (so any differences between the program and no-program group are more likely to be due to the program, not sample bias)
- Longitudinal design (tracking the same participants over time, thus ensuring results are true to the intervention, not to differences between people)
- Low attrition rate (very few participants dropping out of the study; data collected from a high percentage of the original participants)

These are the behind-the-scenes quality indicators, so to speak. It is the actual effect on the program participants that has stolen the spotlight since the powerful "age 27" report. Researchers gathered data on school performance measures (special education services, graduation rates) through adolescence and lifestyle indicators (employment status, arrest rates, homeownership) through the most recent data-collection point at age 40. One of the most eye-catching components of the reports is the cost-benefit analysis: the actual dollar amount of return on the public investment in this early intervention program. Findings from the study are summarized in Table 7-1 (Schweinhart et al., 2005). General conclusions of the study indicate that there are positive lifetime effects of high-quality early intervention preschool programming for children of families living in

TABLE 7-1 Summary of Key Findings of the High/Scope Perry Preschool Study Through Age 40

Outcome	Program Comparison Criteria	Performance Comparison Data	Savings to Public
Education: In general, the program group required fewer special services for educable mental impairment; scored better at some data collection points on standard tests of intelligence and language; had more positive outlooks on school; and program parents had higher goals for their children (attending college, for example).	Special education services required	Program: 1.1 years No-program: 2.8 years	$7,303
	Attitude toward school (participants reporting preparing schoolwork at home)	Program: 68% No-program: 40%	
	Graduated from regular high school	Program: 65% No-program: 45% (higher program graduation rates due to much higher percentage of program females graduating vs. no-program females)	
Crime Rates: In general, participants in the program group were arrested fewer times; were arrested fewer times for violent, drug, or property crimes; and spent fewer months in prison or jail.	Average number of arrests	Program: 2.3 No-program: 4.6	$171,473
	Arrested 5 or more times	Program: 36% No-program: 55%	
Economic Welfare: In general, in middle adulthood significantly fewer program participants reported receiving social welfare services; held higher paying jobs; owned and paid more per month for residences; owned a car.	Employed at age 40 (continued trend from previous data collection)	Program: 76% No-program: 62%	$16,846
	Median annual salary	Program: $20,800 No-program: $15,300	
	Owned own home at age 40	Program: 37% No-program: 28%	
Health/Family: In general, program males reported better relationships with their families; raised their own children; and were married.	Male participants raising their own children	Program: 57% No-program: 30%	
	Males reporting getting along "very well" with families	Program: 75% No-program: 64%	
Total Cost-Benefit Ratio: In general, savings to the public for program participation was highest in reduced crime rates and associated costs (88%), increased payment of taxes from higher earnings, and reduced need for special education services. Reduced dependence on welfare services also contributed to public return. Worth noting is that male program participants account for 93% of the public return.		Cost of Program	$15,166
		Total return/savings of program at age 40	$195,621 to general public
		Return to public on program investment at age 40	$12.90 per dollar (compared to the $7.16 cost-benefit ratio at age 27)

poverty. Furthermore, these lasting effects influence school performance, economic welfare, and social functioning into adulthood.

Researchers caution, however, that the results should not be generalized too broadly (Schweinhart et al., 2005; Sylva & Evans, 1999). For example, many people compare the High/Scope Perry Preschool Program to Head Start programs and mistakenly assume the results also apply to Head Start programs. It is important to understand the specific elements of the High/Scope Perry program that are thought to be the key factors influencing the lifetime effects:

- The program was a 2-year education program for 3- and 4-year-olds living in families with limited incomes.
- The curriculum and schedule supported child-initiated learning and included small- and large-group activities.
- Program teachers held bachelor's degrees and teaching certification.
- Teachers received ongoing training and support in implementing the model.
- Each teacher served five or six children.
- Weekly home visits were conducted by classroom teachers.

To expect the same positive lifetime benefits seen in this study, other programs would have to be comparable, that is equal on these specific elements. While there are many connections to Head Start's mission and practice, there are some differences. Head Start policy has only recently started working toward requiring bachelor's degrees of a percentage of its teachers. Also, Head Start programs usually have higher teacher-child ratios, which align with state requirements but do not compare with the 1:6 ratio of the classrooms in the Perry study. Interestingly, many Head Start programs across the country use the High/Scope curriculum and assessment tools, and High/Scope materials include connections to Head Start performance standards. Although the Perry research results cannot be generalized to all Head Start programs, there is some connection between High/Scope and Head Start history, goals, and implementation.

What researchers say can be concluded in a broader sense is that all children living in poverty should have access to high-quality early childhood programming with reasonably similar features. With other quality early intervention programs also producing research results with similar positive effects, the importance of investing in quality early intervention programming continues to be emphasized. The most basic implication is that we must continue to provide high-quality programming for the children who need it most. This call to action starts with early childhood professionals committed to high-quality programming, is supported by research results such as the Perry study, and opens much-needed dialogue at local and national levels. The returns to program participants specifically and to society in general prove that the improvement of quality early childhood programming is everyone's business.

DIVERSITY, INCLUSION, AND APPLICATIONS OF HIGH/SCOPE PRINCIPLES

The overarching framework of High/Scope's developmental-constructivist practice can guide practice in any setting. These applications can improve program quality and increase children's positive outcomes. The key is to maintain the emphasis on child-initiated play that is facilitated and scaffolded by supportive adults. With roots in the social reform movement of the 1960s and initial focus on early intervention, High/Scope programs are designed to meet the needs of diverse families. Underscoring High/Scope's commitment to quality is the belief that unique family culture is to be valued and preserved. Families and children are viewed as individuals, not defined by comparisons with others. As you read in the COR example, the expectations of children are broad and represent a range of abilities. Children scoring mostly at level 1 are not necessarily viewed as deficient but rather as being at different developmental points (Shouse, 1995). With an emphasis on viewing children as individuals within a broad developmental stage, teachers are able to value and support all children. Observe how this teacher engages a child with language delay in meaningful dialogue using scaffolding in this **video**.

Another aspect of High/Scope's early intervention roots is the importance of meaningfully involving families in children's development (Schweinhart, 2003). High/Scope strongly advocates the use of home visits as a vehicle for developing open relationships with families. Family members are validated as the child's first teachers. High/Scope teachers seek to support families as well as rely on families to support their work. Family literacy programs are also currently being implemented to encourage parents and children to learn together. With open communications, facilitated by outreach programs and formal and informal reports, each child's unique family culture is welcomed into the classroom.

Teachers also strive to maintain connections to the dual-language learners home language (Maehr, 2003). Remember the breakfast conversations in the opening classroom observation? The teachers were having conversations in Spanish with Spanish-speaking children and English with English-speaking children. They also involved all children in group conversation by translating between the two languages. The teachers do not try to push children to speak English; instead, they engage in conversations in Spanish. By speaking in the children's native language, they are able to have more elaborate and meaningful conversations.

Just think about how limited the depth and meaning of conversations would be if the children could use only a handful of English words. These limited words and phrases could not adequately express the complex ideas they are capable of thinking. The difference between their thinking and speaking would leave these children at a great disadvantage in the classroom. Remember Vygotsky's work in promoting the connection between thought and language? He believed that children use language to organize thinking. To limit children's language by suppressing the use of their dominant language is to also limit their thinking. The preservation of the family's home language while the child and family learn English is an important part of supporting overall language development (NAEYC, 1995).

The core structure of the plan-do-review sequence can be implemented whenever children are given time to engage in learning centers. Providing open-ended materials and ample time to explore them individually or in small groups is a hallmark of developmentally appropriate early childhood practices. Adding the child's own direction and responsive adult interaction strengthens the active learning environment.

Just as important as having children guide their own learning experiences and having teachers who actively support children's learning is having teachers systematically assessing children's interests and development. Accomplishing this important task is most effective when teachers and parents are able to build close relationships that include open communication. Teachers use classroom observation reports, notes, and work samples to share with parents to show how children are doing in school. But that's only half the story.

Putting It Into Practice

Strategies for Supporting Linguistic Diversity

Young children come to centers and schools with a variety of family culture and linguistic backgrounds. All children, regardless of their home language, bring with them a wealth of diverse experiences, knowledge, interests, and capabilities. Our responsibility, as early childhood educators, is to work to maximize each child's development and support each family's success. Children's home language is closely tied to their individual and family identity as well as their cognitive development. It is essential that all teachers remain sensitive and responsive to the unique family culture of all children. "For the optimal development and learning of all children, educators must *accept* the legitimacy of children's home language, *respect* (hold in high regard) and *value* (esteem, appreciate) the home culture, and *promote* and *encourage* the active involvement and support of all families, including extended and nontraditional family units" (NAEYC, 1995, p. 2). NAEYC recommends the following strategies for appropriately working with linguistically and culturally diverse children and families:

- Recognize the connections between home culture and cognition and emotion.
- Understand that increasing proficiency in the child's first (home) language contributes to learning a second language (English).
- Promote the many ways (or "languages") children use to share and represent their knowledge (including arts, movement, gesturing, etc.).
- Support and encourage family involvement in the classroom and English-language learning, while validating the importance of maintaining the home language.
- Become aware of available resources to help you, the children, and their families communicate together. This may include translators, dictionaries, translation software, and so on.

For more information, print and read the NAEYC position statement on responding to linguistic and cultural diversity from www.naeyc.org/position-statements

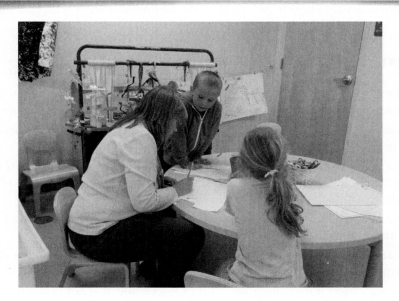

Systeamtic assessments include notes, photos, quotes from children, and samples of children's work.

Teachers also need to seek out more complete information from parents and validate the role of the parents as their children's first teachers. It is important that teachers take responsibility for encouraging parent involvement in a variety of ways that respect the home culture. Explore children's home life in open, nonjudgmental ways. Invite parents into school to share something special about their family culture. Opening the doors between home and school allows teachers to integrate authentic cultural experiences from a child's home life into the classroom. This is a key ingredient in making learning meaningful for children and validating for families.

CONCLUSION

The work of the High/Scope Educational Research Foundation serves as an example of what is possible when early childhood professionals maintain an unwavering commitment to children. With an emphasis on respecting children's interests and abilities to take an active role in their own learning, the High/Scope curriculum lays a foundation for the ability of children to grow into deliberate, responsible people.

High-quality early childhood programming continues to demonstrate significant benefit for families with limited incomes, but High/Scope's curricular approach provides a road map to achieve high standards of practice for programs serving all diverse families. As professionals and advocates, all early childhood teachers must continue to remain current with new research. The High/Scope research projects and reports provide a place to start. The emphasis on meeting the needs of children living in poverty makes much of the High/Scope research particularly important for all teachers. The poverty rates among children continue to rise. Teachers in nearly every center or school setting will work with families facing economic stress or living with limited resources at some point in their careers. With such compelling evidence that quality early childhood programming can ameliorate the risks associated with living in poverty, it becomes the responsibility of all educators to understand how to give children the best possible chances for lifelong success.

SUMMARY

- The High/Scope Educational Research Foundation is an organization that promotes best practices through research, training, and a published curriculum model.
- Based on a constructivist learning perspective, the High/Scope curriculum was originally designed as an early intervention program.
- The plan-do-review sequence encourages children to be deliberate in selecting activities and materials to work with, active in implementing their plans, and reflective in their subsequent review.
- The extensive key developmental indicators guide teachers in planning a range of activities to enhance all areas of development and skills.
- Teachers use sensitive scaffolding techniques to guide and facilitate children's learning through social interactions and play.
- Formal observations, using the Child Observation Record, form the basis for assessment.

- The longtime research efforts conducted through High/Scope, the Perry Preschool Study, have contributed to our current knowledge base and practices.
- Long-term effects of the Perry Preschool Study indicate significant positive outcomes for children in high-quality early childhood programs that last into middle adulthood.
- High/Scope practices are uniquely suited for applications with diverse children and families, validating a range of ability levels and cultural backgrounds.
- High-quality teacher-child interactions, intentionality, and family involvement are hallmarks of High/Scope principles in action.

CHAPTER LEARNING GOALS SELF-ASSESSMENT

Use this chart to write down three to five key points for each learning goal that you learned from this chapter.

Describe learning activities in High/Scope classrooms.	
Identify important aspects of the High/Scope curriculum approach.	
Examine key roles of the High/Scope teacher.	
Discuss elements of child and program assessment in High/Scope.	
Discuss implications of ongoing High/Scope research projects.	
Explore diversity and inclusion in applying High/Scope principles.	

APPLICATION ACTIVITIES

Discussion Prompts

1. Think back to the observation at the start of the chapter. What lesson plan suggestions could you give the teachers to build on the music group's interests? Think about the key developmental indicators, the development of preschoolers, and their interests.
2. Why do you think researchers suggest that there are fewer discipline problems when children learn through the plan-do-review sequence?
3. In what ways do you think the plan-do-review sequence might contribute to later prosocial behavior (less crime, for example)?

In Class   Go to www.highscope.org to the research link and then to the Perry Preschool Study link. Locate the video clip "Lifetime Effects—The Perry Results Through Age 40."

Watch the video, making notes about how the High/Scope program was designed to affect lives of children living in poverty. In small groups, discuss the research study results in light of the original program goals.

In the Field   Use the plan-do-review sequence in your own learning experience. Design an appropriate lesson plan integrating at least four key developmental indicators. Include predictions of how the children will respond, potential problems and solutions, and desired outcomes. Implement the lesson plan at a local child care facility or with a personal acquaintance or family member. Write up and present a review of your experience to the class. Include connections to your predictions, analysis of how your implementation went, and a representation of something you learned from the experience (use any media or format you choose).

For Your Portfolio   Select a key developmental indicator learning area (creative representation, initiative and social relations, etc.), and design a learning center that supports each of the key developmental indicators associated with that learning category. Be sure to align with High/Scope's theoretical framework of developmental constructivism as well as goals for active learning experiences. Include a drawing of your learning center, list of materials, description of your goals, and purpose of the design. This activity can go in your portfolio in a section on learning and teaching.

RELATED WEB LINKS

High/Scope Educational Research Foundation
www.highscope.org

Information on the Child Observation Record
www.highscope.org

The Project Approach: Active Inquiry in Early Childhood

The idea of child-centered curricula is not new. The importance of creating authentic learning environments—those that are real to children and flow naturally from the context of their daily experiences—cannot be emphasized enough. Creating authentic learning environments is the most effective way to fully capture imagination and engage children's senses. Within the context of children's interest and authentic experiences, learning can come alive. Many teachers struggle to keep children interested in classroom activities and feel challenged by disruptive behavior. All teachers strive to foster in children an internal (intrinsic) motivation that will keep them engaged in learning. The Project Approach is a framework that maximizes children's interests, supports higher level thinking, and engages children in contextualized learning experiences. Teachers act as guides and facilitators to engage children in personally meaningful, interesting investigations that promote intellectual and social development. In Project Approach classrooms, children are valued as the driving force in their learning process and are empowered to engage thoughtfully with their world.

This chapter presents an overview of the Project Approach, including structure and process of learning experiences. Challenges and opportunities are also explored with an emphasis on appropriate applications in any classroom setting.

BACKGROUND OF THE PROJECT APPROACH

Historical Context

Many of the key elements of the Project Approach are not necessarily new or exclusive. The use of project-based curricula was influenced by the work of educators in the British Infant Schools in the early 1900s. A project method was also used by John Dewey in his lab school at the University of Chicago and promoted by William Kilpatrick during the Progressive Era. This emergent curriculum framework (coming from children's interests) of active inquiry and hands-on investigation has been practiced internationally for many decades. Considering the pendulumlike swings in educational practice, it is not surprising that project work has had periods in favor and periods out of favor within the field of education. Once considered at odds with more academic, skills-oriented instruction, project work was seen as conflicting with established formal education models. As the field now moves away from an "either/or" type of thinking toward a "both/and" philosophy, project work is once again finding favor in the field (Katz & Chard, 2000).

Teachers at both preschool and primary grade levels are now making strong connections between project learning and state standards (Mitchell, Foulger, Wetzel, & Rathkey, 2009). With the integration of a balance of skill-based and interest-based activities and a focus on broad learning goals, the Project Approach is finding its place as a viable method for engaging children in meaningful, purposeful learning activities. Visit a classroom using the Project Approach and notice how the teacher and children are jointly engaged in an integrated curriculum investigation.

CLASSROOM VIEW

To more clearly envision what project work looks like, let's visit a first-grade classroom in which the children are learning through inquiry and investigation.

In a mid-sized public school in a shore community, the children in Miss Michelle's first grade have spent the past 2 weeks investigating the types of creatures that inhabit the seashore. Being an integral part of local culture and geography, the seashore is a topic that builds on widely shared experiences of both the children and their families. The shore is often a topic of conversation among the children as well as a popular spot for family vacations and class field trips. The catalytic event for this particular study occurred 3 weeks earlier. Miss Michelle explains, "It all started when Chaelia came to school one Monday with a collection of shells and a horseshoe crab shell after a weekend trip with her family. The children were just enthralled with her treasures. They wouldn't stop talking about them! We call that kind of spark a **catalytic event**. *It can be anything that sparks children's interest and that motivates them to want to know more."*

Catalytic event

An experience or material that sparks children's interest and motivates them to want to learn more.

Many of the children expressed interest in the shells and began asking questions about how Chaelia found them and about the nature of the creatures that had inhabited the shells. When questions and discussions dominated several days' group time and dramatic play, Miss Michelle decided to make a list of the children's questions and a list of what they already knew about seashore creatures. "We always start projects with a discussion about what the children already know about the topic, and then we discuss what they want to know more about. This is the beginning of the KWHL chart" (what we know, what we want to know, how we can find out, what we learned).

*On the fourth day of discussion, Miss Michelle began making a **concept web** with the class centered around the main topic of life at the beach. The web included subtopics such as animals with shells, plants, fish, and birds. Additional branches of sub-subtopics radiated out from these, forming a web of ideas and possible research areas. Children were interested in animal life both in and out of the water. The planning web also included the children's questions and initial ideas about how to find answers to those questions. (See Figure 8-1.) Miss Michelle explains that the web serves to guide the children's research and document the earlier stages of their understanding. "But the assistant teacher and I also use the web to document which state standards are being met. When the children are in the investigation phase, where they are actually doing their research, we go through our standards and mark down which ones are being addressed by which activities. It's a great way for us to see immediately which areas are being covered and which standards we may need to target during a teacher-directed activity. We keep making notes as the children complete new representations too. It's really another assessment tool for us as well as being a planning tool for the children."*

On the day of your visit to the classroom, some of the children are preparing for a visit to the beach, where they will conduct investigations in small groups. They all have clipboards, pencils, and paper. One group of children, who express interest in gathering shell specimens, will be collecting actual shells as well as making field sketches (drawing items they see on their field trip). Another group that wants to count the number of different kinds of birds they see will be listing and graphing their findings. Armed with a picture encyclopedia, they have marked the types of birds they predict they will see at the shore. A last group of children has been exploring the nature of tides and how the waters move in and out. This group will be taking measurements of the tide lines over the course of the field visit to note changes. Several parents are on hand for the trip, and Miss Michelle explains that many other parents have been involved in the development of the project by donating most of the materials the children are now using.

In addition to the children who are preparing for their field visit, another group of children will remain in the classroom. They have been working on representing their experiences from a recent aquarium trip, and they are currently engaged in transforming a section of their classroom into a replica of the aquarium. As you scan the walls behind an art area, you notice several paintings and drawings of different kinds of fish and shells, all labeled with the species names and parts. A picture dictionary and other photo books, lying open on the table, are being used along with the children's photos and sketches as references.

Three children are sitting in the art area, having a discussion about their plans for their aquarium replica. The children have drawn and painted several different kinds of fish and crabs and have sculpted shells out of clay. They are now trying to figure out how to replicate the water. Mr. Dean (the other teacher) is sitting with them, transcribing their conversation in an observation notebook.

MICHAEL: *We need to have our fish and shells look like they are in the water.*

GREISAN: *Yeah, we need the water to be blue and see-through.*

NICOLA: *We could use blue paper.*

GREISAN: *(Pausing) No . . . paper isn't see-through. We looked through the water at the fish and shells in the water. The water was right up against the glass and the fish were behind it.*

NICOLA: *So we need something clear but blue also.*

GREISAN: *Yeah, and shiny. To make it look wet. (The children pause and look around the room.)*

Concept web

A visual mapping strategy that creates a web of related ideas.

FIGURE 8-1

Life at the Beach Project—Phase I Planning Web

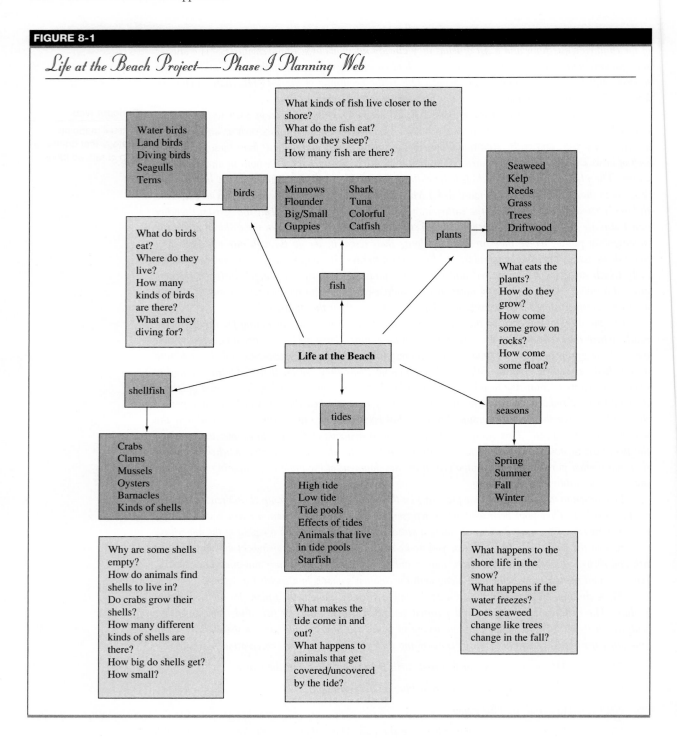

MICHAEL: *What about the blue plastic paper we painted on once?* (He was referring to blue cellophane that was provided in the art area.)

NICOLA: *Yes! That was clear and blue and shiny. Just like the water behind the glass at the aquarium.*

GREISAN: *Yeah! Let's use that!*

Miss Michelle explains that keeping records of the children's discussions along with samples of their work and pictures of them investigating are all important pieces in their documentation. *"We're lucky to have a video camera, digital camera, and tape recorder. We use all of those to record what the children do and say. But the children also use them to record things they think are important. I know it may seem odd to let the children use this kind of equipment, but we show them how to properly use and handle it. They know it is expensive, but they also know that the work they are doing is valuable. We respect them as capable of properly using the equipment, and in turn they respect class belongings."*

By recording the class's activities and conversations, the teachers are able to capture their learning and progress. The children are also able to document for themselves the things that sparked their interest and thinking along the way. The children use the photos, work samples, videos, and transcriptions to revisit their experiences as their investigations progress. This process of revisiting and rerepresenting is an important part of how the children, parents, and teachers are able to see children apply their growing knowledge and skills. Miss Michelle emphasizes the term apply, pointing out that through this method, children are using their abilities as they are also learning and developing.

You look around the room at the documentation of the children's investigation journeys. You notice with some surprise that all the children are active and excitedly engaged in a variety of activities. Some are building the aquarium structure; others are writing signs for the aquarium, drawing fish, and sculpting shells from clay. Others are engaged in dramatic play, acting like crabs and fish. Some are categorizing and labeling the classroom shell collection. It really seems that all the children are actively exploring and representing in unique ways that satisfy their own styles. Everyone in the room seems engaged and abuzz with activity and discovery, and you take a few moments to just take in the whole scene.

Project work can include individual, small, and large group work and supports children's learning through first-hand experiences.

WHAT IS THE PROJECT APPROACH?

According to the Project Approach framework, children's learning experiences are optimized when they are actively engaged in meaningful, authentic explorations of their day-to-day world. As the classroom view indicates, children who are learning through the Project Approach actively investigate topics that are meaningful to them. Topics can emerge from their own experiences or can be introduced by a teacher who has gleaned insight into the children's interests through observations. Whatever the topic of study, the basis of any good project is that the children are actively driving the investigation process while teachers support and facilitate the children's learning. "A key feature of project work is that it is an investigation—a piece of research that involves children seeking answers to questions they have formulated" (Katz & Chard, 2000, p. 2). Teachers and children work together to generate lists of questions and map out how concepts relate to one another within the scope of the project topic. Teachers use their ongoing observations of children to continually assess their abilities and interests, both to identify possible project topics and to evaluate the children's learning as they engage in project work. Listen to teachers describe the purpose and focus of integrated, interest-based projects with young children in this **video**.

At the heart of the Project Approach is the premise that children's learning is optimized when they are intellectually engaged in the learning environment (Katz & Chard, 2000). Children who are able to work on meaningful activities that allow them to explore topics of interest to them are, by definition, *interested*. Being interested is a powerful internal motivator that strengthens children's desire to explore, to ask questions and seek answers, and to be excited at discovery and sharing. Remember the children who were problem-solving the aquarium design? They were focused on finding the best possible way to represent what they had experienced during their field visit. They were very clear about creating a representation that was as close to their inner vision as possible. The dialogue they went through as they sought to re-create their aquarium as accurately as possible illustrates their excitement and motivation to represent what they had learned and experienced. This emotional aspect of children's learning in project work (being excited, motivated, interested, etc.) is one of the four key learning goals addressed in the Project Approach. It is also an area that is often neglected in educational environments.

In project work, the following four learning goals are each equally essential to promote authentic, meaningful learning (Katz & Chard, 2000):

1. Knowledge
2. Skills
3. Dispositions
4. Feelings

Knowledge

It is a widely accepted goal that children learn certain content, facts, concepts, and information that are part of the standard knowledge base (Gregory, 2002). This knowledge is the foundation that helps students grow into functional members of society. Standard concepts children learn through preschool and the early primary grades include

Putting It Into Practice

Sparking Interest

As you read in the life at the beach project, the children's interest was sparked when one child shared the collection of shells she found on a family trip to the beach. Sometimes worthy project topics flow easily out of children's lives: a walk through the park and a child sees a bunny family; a walk down the street and children see a fire truck or ambulance; a child has to visit the hospital; a family pet goes to the vet. Sometimes you can gently guide children's interest into a new topic. Perhaps you went to a new museum exhibit over the weekend. Bring in some artifacts to share with your children. Your ticket stub, brochure, postcard prints, or posters may just catch their attention as you vividly tell them about what you saw and did there. Or maybe you have a friend or parent in the class who works at a supermarket and can be a guest in the class and arrange a store tour. Parents can be great resources with their work and hobbies. You can also try bringing in a unique item such as a horseshoe crab shell or special stones. By sharing your own interests, you may spark your children's next project.

differentiating colors and shapes; understanding concepts in arithmetic; local geography; understanding the relationships among sounds, words, and sentences; and so on. Often related to state or national curriculum standards, the particular knowledge set to be explored at certain ages should be decided based on developmental appropriateness and children's readiness.

Skills

Skill development and mastery are also familiar elements of educational settings. When children perform certain tasks, they are using their skills. Being able to cut with scissors is a fine-motor and coordination skill. Drawing an object from the environment or a scene from the imagination demonstrates motor, cognitive, and aesthetic skills. Being able to use written words to communicate and number sense to add items shows a growing competence in literacy and numeracy skills. Children also learn self-care skills, such as learning to use a spoon to eat fruit salad.

Dispositions

Perhaps a less familiar learning goal, building positive dispositions in children relates to temperaments or habits toward learning and experiencing new things. Although we may be familiar with the desire to develop in children a love of learning, an interest in reading, or a willingness to take on challenges, many educational approaches do not clearly address these goals. The child-driven, meaningful, authentic nature of project work ensures that children's interests are engaged. Their excitement about exploring and representing knowledge is fostered by their internal motivation. Project work provides the opportunity for children to build dispositions in the following ways:

- Continually make predictions (through initial webbing and dialoguing about a topic).
- Actively explore and test those predictions (through fieldwork).
- Synthesize information (through representing and sharing newfound knowledge).

Sometimes it is a challenge for teachers to motivate children, to hold their attention, and to control their behavior. Resorting to using such external rewards as stickers, points, or candy may seem like the only way to keep them focused. One of the biggest benefits teachers find in using projects, however, is that children are naturally more focused because the work comes directly from their interests and their own ideas and questions. Teachers often report fewer behavior problems as a result of the children being more in control of their learning.

Feelings

As a learning goal, promoting positive feelings about classroom experiences is difficult to overtly address. Simply teaching children about feelings of self-esteem, competency, acceptance, and comfort does not actually promote those feelings in them. Children need real, authentic opportunities to engage in classroom experiences that serve to promote those feelings. A key criterion for selecting topics is that the children have some familiarity with the topic, that is, that the topic is a meaningful part of their lives. This familiarity allows children to begin an investigation in an empowered position of existing knowledge, thereby increasing their self-confidence.

The children discussed in the classroom visit at the beginning of the chapter live near the seashore, and the topic of life at the beach is one that is familiar to nearly all of them. Conducting an investigation on this topic allows the children to start from a place of confidence and competence; they have some personal experience with this topic and knowledge to contribute to the project. Through the initial planning, webbing, and listing of what the children know and what they want to know as with a KWHL chart, children's existing knowledge is highlighted and valued. Through the engagement in child-selected activities, children apply skills competently to new situations. This strengthens their feelings of accomplishment and satisfaction.

Four Learning Goals Are Interconnected

Through their in-depth investigations, the children engage in a wide variety of activities. They work in groups, all together as a whole class, or individually on tasks that support their growing knowledge base and skill development, promote positive learning dispositions, and increase emotional satisfaction. Children in the life at the beach project are learning meaningful knowledge about the ecosystem at the seashore by learning names and parts of different animals and exploring the nature of tides. In the same project, we saw children using skills such as counting and classifying, drawing, and language to interview experts and dialogue with each other. Children's dispositions to be inquisitive, interested in exploring, and able to actively problem-solve as they develop new ways to represent their research findings are strengthened as their project unfolds.

The aquarium group exemplifies this problem-solving and persistence as the children generate ideas of how to achieve their goal of representing the water. One of the most

Putting It Into Practice

Projects and Classroom Management

"Once our camping project got under way, I could barely keep up with the children! They were really into it—really thinking about what they were going to do to set up their campsite in the dramatic play area. Children were telling stories, like campfire stories. Some children were making a collage mural on the wall. They made one part out of darker papers and put on stars and a moon. On the other part, they used lighter papers and put on a sun and birds. One child painted a dog and attached it to the mural at the bottom when the other children were done. They made rocks out of papier-mâché, and I helped them tape blue paper on the floor where they wanted to make a stream. There were so many little projects going on at once, you know, that it would seem hard to manage, but really it was like they were managing themselves. We gave them materials, made suggestions when they needed help to construct their vision, and helped them find resources.

One of the parents drove his camper to school for the children to go in. We were able to take some space on the playground and 'camp' there one afternoon for lunch; then we napped in tents. After that trip, the children made a graph of who preferred tents or campers. When they learned that tents didn't have bathrooms, most of them voted for campers! One small group decided to build a camper from a clothes washer and dryer box. With so many subprojects going on, all the children found something that they were really into. We [the teachers] were able to watch it all unfold and document their learning and excitement. The parents even had a good time when we invited them for a campout lunch to wrap up the project!"

special elements of project work is the positive emotional climate generated by the children's satisfaction, feelings of competence, and group acceptance. Children's individual styles of processing and representing are valued through the many different project activities and forms of representation. Each child's place in the group is strengthened as each individual contributes something to the whole. Through this variety of activity and expression, project work celebrates, values, and supports the many diverse ways in which children think and process information and experiences as well as supporting each child at his or her own ability level. This support for learner diversity is a prime feature of project work that makes it particularly attractive as an integrated, inclusive approach to learning (Hertzog, 2007). Listen to teachers talk about diverse learners being supported in a project on eggs and birds in this **video**.

PARTS AND PROCESS: HOW PROJECTS COME TOGETHER

When you think about children working on projects, perhaps you think about sitting together at a table with a variety of materials where children are making some kind of teacher-directed craft activity. Perhaps you think about a science fair–type process in which children independently design and create a display to illustrate a particular phenomenon. Under the framework of the Project Approach, however, the children's experiences progress through a more structured system. One of the great appealing features of the structured system is that it provides teachers—even novice teachers—with a clear framework within which to implement projects.

As soon as a topic has been selected, teachers and children engage in activities structured in three distinct phases. Although each project will inevitably entail different kinds of activities and representations owing to the specific group of children doing the investigation, the categories remain the same:

- Phase I: planning and questioning
- Phase II: investigating and researching
- Phase III: concluding and culminating

It is important for teachers to keep detailed records of the children's activities during each phase of the project. As Miss Michelle explained in the opening story, these records will

- chronicle the path of the project;
- illustrate the process the children went through on their project journey; and
- provide authentic documentation of the children's learning, including standards covered.

Let's explore each phase in more detail, including how projects get started and examples of children's activities and strategies for teachers to use as they support and document children's progress.

Getting Started

Often referred to as a *catalytic event,* many projects begin with an experience that sparks a great deal of interest with all or a part of the class (Chard, 1998a, 1998b). There may be a shared group experience, such as seeing a fire truck during a walk (Helm & Katz, 2001) or children getting haircuts over the weekend (Gallick, 2000). By observing children's play and dialogues, teachers are able to determine the level of children's interest and potential for the project topic. Documenting children's questions and things they wonder about the topic is an important start to any project by providing direction and ensuring that the investigation is based on the children's interests. It is worth keeping some anecdotal records about how the initial interest was generated—whether it was through a whole-class or individual experience or even a teacher-prompted topic.

Phase I: Planning and Questioning

Phase I marks the official beginning of the project, where the project really starts to take shape and definition. Teachers may observe children expressing interest in a topic through discussion, questions, manipulating materials, or even by reliving an event through dramatic play. As teachers take note of the children's interest and excitement building around a worthy topic, planning can begin (Edwards & Springate, 1993). A hallmark of the Project Approach is that children drive the investigation process with support and, sometimes, leadership from adults. One way that the children truly direct the project is by generating the questions that will shape the course of the investigation. Teachers and children work together to write down the children's questions along with statements about what they already know or think they know. Often this process reveals misconceptions on the children's part, but it is important that those misconceptions are still included in the lists. Documenting all the children's initial conceptions allows teachers to address erroneous beliefs as children's misconceptions are challenged through their own investigations. This initial thinking about the topic can be facilitated and documented with a KWHL chart.

KWHL From the Life at the Beach Project, Phase I

What Do We *Know?*	What Do We *Want to Know?*	*How* Can We Find Out?	What Did We Learn?
• Shells live at the beach • Fish live in shells • Some shells are empty • Fish need water to live • Some birds fly; some birds swim	• Why are some shells empty? • Why do some fish swim and some live in shells? • What do fish eat? • Do birds eat fish? • What are the shells on the rocks; what happens when the water covers them? • How many kinds of shells are there? • How big do shells get? • How do fish breathe under water?	• Go to the beach • Ask a marine biologist (one of the children's parents; most children did not know these words) • Books • Internet • Go to the zoo (aquarium)	

While the children's questions and conceptions are being chronicled, the class can begin to map out their investigation. *Concept webbing* is a visual way to represent ideas and the relationships between those ideas. Beginning with the main topic in the center of a large piece of paper, children and teachers brainstorm as many related subtopics as possible. These are then written on the paper in a radiating web that lays out progressively more specific related concepts. (Figure 8-1 from the opening classroom view is an example of a concept web.) The initial web serves as a visual guide to where the children's investigations can take them, but it also acts as a documentation of the preinvestigation beliefs. As the investigation progresses, the web can be revisited, modified, and added to as children's knowledge and experience grows. This can be quite an involved process, so it helps to start with a big piece of paper.

As children are generating questions, making predictions, and planning out how they will investigate their topic, teachers are busy gathering resources to fuel their inquiry. An essential element of project work is the use of primary sources of information. In **primary sources** children gather firsthand experiences. Primary sources include field visits where children personally engage with places and materials as well as experts. Experts are the people who provide firsthand information through interviews and visits. This is also the optimal time to encourage parent involvement. A letter home can engender parent support by sharing the children's interest and excitement and outlining ways in which parents can help with the unfolding project. Often parents can serve as primary sources and make a guest visit to the classroom. Sometimes parents can even provide ongoing help with children's representations and classroom constructions.

Books and online sources, or **secondary sources**, are used in concert with primary sources to round out children's understanding. It is important that the content of books be as realistic as possible to provide accurate, authentic information. A photo-rich picture dictionary, nonfiction texts, and simple encyclopedia are key resources to have in the classroom. With a roster of children's questions and a handle on the resources that are available, the investigation can begin.

Primary sources

Firsthand sources of information, such as field visits and expert interviews, which allow children to interact personally with the information source.

Secondary sources

Secondhand sources that provide information in a one-way flow, such as books and other printed materials.

Primary sources—those with which children can interact face-to-face—are essential in project investigations and help children learn on a more meaningful, personal level.

Phase II: Investigating and Researching

Phase II activities generally revolve around the children's research of their topic and questions. This is the heart of the investigation of the topic. This is the time when children go on field visits and interview guest experts. Children seek out answers to their questions and use a variety of media to represent their knowledge and re-create their experiences. Children investigate the topic on field visits by seeing, touching, drawing, manipulating, counting, measuring, taking things apart, and fully engaging with the environment at the field site. Field visits can also offer chances for children to interview and dialogue with experts. During a project on a fire truck, the preschool children's field visit to a firehouse allowed them to explore all the ladders, hoses, buttons, and levers of the truck and question a firefighter about his job and his life. The children were able to try on the coat, hat, and boots and role-play being a firefighter (Helm & Katz, 2001). This role-playing provided the children, especially the younger children, with a means to explore the related topic more deeply.

Another important aspect of Phase II work is the children's representations of their experiences. As the children in the life at the beach project explore the seashore during their field visit, they are able to document from their firsthand experiences a more in-depth understanding of how shore creatures live. Although they may have spent time at the shore before, through their research and investigation, they are constructing a far more detailed knowledge of their community. They are also applying a host of skills that are being strengthened by their meaningful application to real-life situations. The classroom view provides a snapshot of Phase II activities. In the course of the project, children are actively learning by

- graphing,
- measuring,
- drawing,
- labeling specimens from encyclopedia sources,

Building and Representing Knowledge

Project work often lends itself to the building of some kind of group construction. This offers a valuable opportunity for children to engage in three-dimensional representation. For example, the children in a camping project decided to build a camper from large boxes. The older children built the frame and added lots of the details. The younger children enjoyed driving it and sleeping in the back. Through construction and dramatic play, children of different developmental levels were able to represent their knowledge in diverse ways.

- writing signs,
- role-playing,
- problem-solving,
- seeking answers to their questions, and
- building replicas of what they have seen.

Teachers' Roles in Phase II   Through the children's revisiting and revising of their earlier representations, children, teachers, and parents all are able to see how their understanding has changed over the course of the project. Being able to demonstrate changes over the course of a project is another important reason teachers have to be diligent and systematic about chronicling the children's representations, activities, and dialogues (Edwards & Springate, 1993). This is also the time when teachers can guide children's explorations to help them uncover misconceptions that may have been revealed during Phase I. For example, through the visit from a parent-expert in the beach project, the children learned about the differences in mollusks and fish. This related directly to their own questions about fish and shells. By continually reviewing the progress of the children's project, teachers are also able to notice content or standards that need more emphasis.

Teachers are active in orchestrating the children's activities and encouraging their dispositions to question, investigate, and problem-solve. They are often coordinating multiple small-group projects within the larger project, keeping track of needed materials and resources. Teachers are also continually staying in contact with parents to update them on the children's progress as well as to continue to seek their involvement (Beneke, 2000). Teachers assist children in recalling their field experiences when they are back in the classroom, and they prompt children's questions and exploration should they need it. By encouraging frequent drawing (in field sketches and later representations), teachers are able to capture illustrations of children's changing knowledge and abilities. By analyzing and comparing children's drawings and representations over time, teachers make children's learning visible.

Children are engaging with each other and the community to share ideas, challenge beliefs, and create new understandings. There is a real potential for strong bonds to develop in the classroom community through this kind of experiential learning. Through field visits, children are also making strong connections between content they are learning in the project and the real world around them. See how a field trip enhanced children's investigation of birds in this **video**.

As the children's questions are being answered and their investigations begin winding down, teachers develop a sense that the project is ready to be concluded. This is the opportune time to shift into Phase III activities, which give children the chance to wrap up their investigation and share what they have learned.

Phase III: Concluding and Culminating

Just as the project began with children and teachers dialoguing about the shaping of the project, the decision to wrap it up can be made together. As teachers notice that children's investigating and playing are diminishing, it is a good point to ask the children if they would like to review and wrap up their work (Katz & Chard, 2000). This has been a big undertaking for the whole class, and a satisfying culminating process is important. This allows the class to reflect on the journey and take pride in sharing what has been learned. By posing the question to the children about how they might like to share their project, their satisfaction with the closing phase will be enhanced. After all, this has been *their* project all along, so it follows that the culminating phase should stem from their ideas.

In the same way that initial brainstorming revealed questions and beliefs about the topic, a group discussion session can reveal creative ways for the children to share the project. Ideas for a culminating event might include (Helm & Katz, 2001)

- museum opening with children's work displayed,
- documentary book,
- documentary movie,
- family and community open house, and
- slide show.

The possibilities are numerous, and together teachers and children can explore the execution of the most popular suggestions. The goal of Phase III is to realize the journey, share what they have experienced, and provide closure for this particular project

Teachers use children's work samples and documentation panels to share their learning with parents and involve them in class projects.

(Edwards & Springate, 1993). Keeping a record of the culminating event is another way for teachers to gather evaluative data on the children's progress. Video cameras and digital cameras are indispensable equipment that can capture children's progress and help them remember trips and expert visitors. Using audio recorders regularly also allows teachers to capture authentic samples of children's dialogues. Transcripts of children's conversations can reveal great insights into their thinking processes.

The following points on engaging in the Project Approach with young children are important considerations to keep in mind in regard to how this approach fits into current frameworks about best practices in teaching young children.

CHALLENGES AND POTENTIALS IN USING THE PROJECT APPROACH

Based on what we currently know about developmentally appropriate practice, constructivism, social learning, and diverse learning styles, there are several ways in which the Project Approach dovetails with many of the current beliefs about how young children learn best. Generally accepted frameworks of good practice embrace the following practices:

- Balance skill and interest-based classroom activities
- Foster an atmosphere of curiosity and discovery
- Provide ample opportunities for active, hands-on learning experiences
- Maintain responsive and supportive social interactions among children and between children and teachers
- Maintain an open link between school and home
- Support children's play as a vehicle for learning

We know that children are active explorers of their environments from their earliest days. We know that as toddlers, they are full of questions and can become enthralled with exploring even the smallest details. We know that children need positive guidance and careful scaffolding from adults to reach their full learning potential (Vygotsky, 1978). And we know that young children need more concrete experiences that are meaningful to their own lives and provide continuity among time, content, and environment (Katz & Chard, 2000). All these elements can be found within project work.

Proponents of the Project Approach promote the idea that children need to learn some basic skills through teacher-directed activities but also become engaged in many child-initiated and child-directed activities (Katz & Chard, 2000). By allowing the path of the project to emerge from children's own interests, children's motivation remains high and learning remains meaningful. Also, by keeping the focus of projects centered on topics that are a part of their lives, the context remains authentic. This also allows for easier parent involvement, because topics are also a part of families' lives and communities. The nature of in-depth investigations of familiar topics also ensures that there is continuity between children's lives in and out of school (Trepanier-Street, 1993).

Think back to the children in the life at the beach project. The topic was a familiar feature of their family and community life, one that parents and children alike had experienced. Consider how their curiosity and natural inclination to find out more was fostered through their project work as they made predictions and discoveries throughout their field visits. Some children were wondering about bird life, making predictions from their encyclopedia research, and testing those guesses with their real data. Because the direction of projects springs from children's own questions, their inquisitiveness is naturally encouraged.

Beyond Play: How Is the Project Approach Different?

One of the contrasts between the Project Approach and other play-based approaches lies in the emphasis on the value of play as a primary vehicle for children's learning. Often a play-based philosophy is grounded in the belief that early learning environments should be solely child centered as opposed to strictly teacher directed. A worthy mission, keeping children at the center of educational planning is certainly an accepted hallmark of good practice and also a part of the Project Approach. However, whereas project work is child initiated, the emphasis is placed more heavily on engaging the child's intellect and developing the four prime learning goals: knowledge, skills, dispositions, and feelings. Project Approach proponents also believe that children's play is natural, is necessary, and has a key place in early educational settings. However, they also point out that play is not the only way to engage children in the deeper intellectual activities of questioning, problem-solving, researching, and representing. Focused, active inquiry is combined with play to ensure deeper engagement and learning in developmentally appropriate ways.

Challenges in Implementing the Project Approach

Teachers sometimes describe challenges in implementing the Project Approach in terms of the context and expectations of their school, mostly centering around emphasis on standards-driven lesson plans, schedules, and expectations of what "teachers do" in transmission-style classrooms (Hertzog, 2007). Sometimes young children are not viewed as capable of intellectual engagement, sustained attention, or the focus that an in-depth investigation takes. Many times, these challenges are more a function of teachers' lack of preparation or awareness of actual implementation strategies of the Project Approach. When teachers are provided the training, support, and opportunity to engage children in in-depth projects, the results are quite remarkable. A key part of teacher support for project work is in training, time, and materials to carefully document children's learning. It is also through this documentation effort that clear connections to effectively meeting state and national standards can be made.

Children are certainly capable of inquiry-based learning, researching, and active investigation, but too often their capabilities are underestimated and teachers make decisions for them and limit their intellectual engagement. It is through inquiry-based project activities that positive dispositions and feelings are promoted and strengthened. And it is through the balance of skill-based instruction, interest-based activities, play, and socialization that the four learning goals are integrated into the learning environment in meaningful ways.

APPLICATIONS WITH YOUNG CHILDREN

Selecting Topics

Although the balance of project activities remains key to successful learning outcomes for children, the selection of the project topic is perhaps even more important. Teachers maintain responsibility for making a decision about the project topic; however, most of the time they base the initial idea for the topic on the real or potential interest of the children. There are several important criteria teachers need to keep in mind as they weigh the value of a particular topic in addition to the children's interest (Helm & Katz, 2001; Katz, 1998; Katz & Chard, 2000):

- Are there opportunities for primary sources of investigation, including field sites and experts?
- Is the topic worthy of teachers' and children's time and effort? Is there enough to generate an in-depth investigation?
- Does the topic engender an interest in making an in-depth investigation?
- Is the topic relevant to the children's day-to-day life? Is it something they can get their hands on?
- Do many of the children have shared experiences that provide a starting place?
- Will the topic contribute to curriculum standards and learning goals?
- Does the topic lend itself to representations through a variety of media?
- Is the topic neither too broad nor too narrow (for example, are children engaged in a project on a fire truck, which is concrete, not the topic of fire safety, which may be too abstract for young children)?

With these main criteria in mind, teachers use their dialogues with and observations of children to determine suitable topic options. In addition, projects will be enhanced by the teachers' own interests, experiences, and knowledge about the topic. This may mean that teachers need to conduct some research on their own while the children's interest in the topic is building in the early phases (Katz & Chard, 2000). Being knowledgeable about the topic and available resources (consider parents and community members and sites) is an important teacher responsibility and one that will help in the planning and successful implementation of projects. Listen to this teacher talk about the emergence, evolution, and teacher/child roles in a project on hospitals in this **video**.

Cultural Responsiveness and Inclusiveness

Projects are based on children's worlds and emerge from their lives, interests, and conversations. From the start of Phase I discussions, children share their personal family experiences and knowledge, empowering them as important sources of information from the beginning. Children may share family norms, events, and traditions as part of the groundwork of KWHL and brainstorming sessions. Although children may have very different life experiences, the emergent nature of projects embraces this diversity. This authenticity provides a perfect opportunity for individualized, inclusive learning through

- integrating home, community, and school into the classroom;
- valuing the context of each child's unique family, culture, and abilities;
- tapping families and community members to bring their expertise to the project;
- valuing all children's contributions equally; and
- validating what children already know.

As children get into the heart of investigations during Phase II, the many ways to represent their thinking support varying abilities. Some children might enjoy literacy or numerical

Putting It Into Practice

Listen

To identify topics that are meaningful, interesting, and reflect children's lives, teachers must become adept listeners. Listen to children's conversations. Listen to their play. What themes, topics, ideas, or events are they talking about? Their spontaneous play can provide clues as to what they are most interested in at the moment. Those are the topics you can seize for potentially great projects.

activities; others might prefer dramatic play or sensory activities. Each child can engage in activities that demonstrate his or her own capabilities. This bolsters children's confidence to continue investigating and wondering about the world, no matter what level their learning or scope of their ability. Working in groups allows children to share tasks, problem-solve together, and build on each other's strengths. One child's strengths can support another child's weaker area. It is the supportive, collaborative nature of project work that enables all children to participate in their own unique ways. It is essential that all teachers remain vigilant about facilitating participation at a variety of levels so all children feel competent and valued.

Assessment

Assessment is a constant activity of teachers in a project classroom. Right from the very beginning, artifacts are being created that are useful tools in documenting children's learning. The first conversations, webs, and KWHL charts indicate where children are starting from; revisited at the end of the project, they provide a great comparison to show

Teachers create documentation panels with photos of children working, quotes from children's conversations, and notes, all carefully laid out on large posters or wall space.

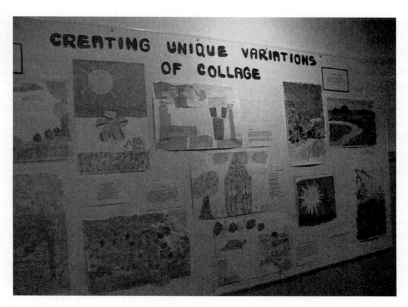

Documentation panels or walls create attractive and informative displays, both showcasing and chronicling children's process and work.

how far the children's learning has progressed. Teachers act as data collectors from the very first catalytic event through the close of the culminating activity.

The variety of children's investigation activities and knowledge representations provides a rich array of authentic assessment documentation. Teachers can use portfolios to compile and chronicle project artifacts such as

- drawings,
- graphs or charts,
- photographs,
- transcriptions of dialogues,
- notes from expert interviews (children's) and notes from observations (teacher's),
- field sketches, and
- stories from children and families.

A more public way to chronicle active learning is the use of documentation panels. **Documentation panels** are carefully designed displays chronicling the progress of the children's projects and the process they went through in their explorations. They can be created on cardboard trifold presentation panels or poster board, or they can be mounted directly on an open wall. The panels include photos of children working, webs, work samples, drawings, paintings, other graphic representations, teachers' notes, and transcriptions of children's dialogue.

Documentation panels

Displays of children's work, conversations, photos, and teacher notes that describe the process children engaged in throughout a project.

CONCLUSION

Project Approach teachers strive to create learning environments that truly value and support children's capacities for complex thought. At the heart of the approach is the goal of engaging children in interesting, personal, meaningful investigations of their world.

Through a three-phase structure and web-planning strategies, teachers support and foster children's active explorations. Because the project topics emerge from children's interests and are driven by the children's questions, this approach can be tailored to any age level. From toddlers to elementary school children and beyond, project work provides an opportunity for truly active learning.

SUMMARY

- The Project Approach has origins deep in the progressive era, particularly influenced by the emphasis on experiential education advocated by Dewey.
- According to the Project Approach framework, children's learning experiences are optimized when they are actively engaged in meaningful, authentic explorations of their day-to-day world. Children's interests and inquiry drive these explorations and in-depth investigations of emergent topics.
- The investigations promote positive outcomes on four main learning goals: knowledge, skills, dispositions, and feelings.
- Engaging children in project work integrates curricular learning goals and standards and maximizes children's natural curiosity and internal motivation.
- Implementation of the Project Approach follows three distinct phases that help organize the children's journey: planning, investigation, and culmination.
- Through a careful balance of skill- and interest-based classroom activities throughout the project process, teachers can successfully address all areas of children's learning while supporting children's diverse learning and representation styles.
- Projects permit children to work together and sometimes individually to satisfy their inquiry and interact with their authentic environment.

CHAPTER LEARNING GOALS SELF-ASSESSMENT

Use this chart to write down three to five key points for each learning goal that you learned from this chapter.

Describe the historical roots of the Project Approach.	
Examine important features of the Project Approach.	
Identify the structure and process of Project Approach activities.	
Discuss how the Project Approach reflects today's best practices.	
Examine strategies for applying a Project Approach framework.	

APPLICATION ACTIVITIES

Discussion Prompts

1. How can we teach children to be inquisitive and curious?

2. Reflect back on your own classroom experiences. Describe times when you felt empowered, excited, and interested in what you were doing.

3. How is learning from primary sources different from learning from secondary sources in terms of the children's constructing meaning and understanding for themselves?

In Class   One of the benefits of engaging children in project work is the ability to support diverse processing styles and the many different ways children can represent their learning through integrated content activities. Using the opening project story (life at the beach) or the bridge project that follows, analyze the investigation, children's activities, and representations to identify different kinds of thinking/processing styles. Consider the following questions after you have read the project descriptions:

1. In what ways did the teachers integrate the topic across curriculum areas?

2. What content or subject areas were integrated?

3. Brainstorm at least three other topics that can be integrated across the curriculum, making notes about key activities in several content/subject areas. Share these with your group.

Next, use Gardner's multiple intelligences framework or another learning style model to categorize the children's activities. For example, did you notice activities that would support verbal processing? Mathematical or logical processing? Naturalistic? Spatial? Feel free to use the following chart to analyze the diverse array of activities in the target project.

Processing Style	Supporting Activities or Representations

Sally and Barbara's Class Builds Bridges

One morning Luci came into the class with one of her favorite books. It was a book of paintings by impressionist painter Claude Monet. She had marked her favorite page, a print of an arching bridge over a pond with water lilies *(The Water Lily Pond).* Luci shared her picture during circle time. Teachers Sally and Barbara were excited at the idea that the children might become interested in exploring the life and work of Monet.

But the children's interests took a different turn. The children became very interested in the bridge, asked questions about it and the water underneath, and shared stories of when they had walked on bridges. Following their lead, the teachers encouraged this questioning and sharing throughout the circle time. The next day, when children's interests were still high, Sally and Barbara began making lists of children's questions and began a concept web. Soon the children decided they wanted to find more bridge pictures.

They started sketching their own bridges and replicas of bridges from books, including the Golden Gate Bridge in San Francisco. The children learned new words such as *truss, suspension, cable,* and *foundation.* In addition to sketching, some children began making tally mark charts, counting the number of foundation legs, the number of cables, and so on. Some children wrote stories and journals about their own experiences with bridges, sharing stories from family vacations and trips around town. Children began constructing models from blocks and craft sticks. This evolved into beginning to build a small, straight bridge from scrap pieces of wood. The children made plans and decisions about how it would be elevated and how to make it strong enough for people to walk on.

The teachers began planning for a field trip to a small footbridge on the grounds of the school. On the field trip, the children took videos and photos and sketched what they saw. Some children measured length and height, marking the arch and other dimensions on large butcher paper. Sally and Barbara also discussed the developing project with the parents. One of the parents, Marty, who works in construction, volunteered to assist with the project. He was also able to facilitate donations of supplies from a local lumber yard.

Marty became an integral part of the project and facilitated the children's planning and building of a life-sized footbridge to go in the children's play yard and garden. The children interviewed Marty, asking questions about how bridges were built and general building questions. With Marty's help, the children explored the building process, including tool safety, blueprints, and plans, through to actual construction. Several children, who took charge of overseeing various aspects of the project, became project managers. They facilitated class decisions about design, size, shape, and placement. When the children had designed their bridge, several weeks of construction began. The children were involved in all aspects of the construction. They took turns and used authentic tools.

One small group of children went back to the original inspiration print and began to find interest in the flowers. This group embarked on a subproject of designing flower gardens to go around the bridge in the play yard. They reviewed garden books, spoke to gardeners, and enlisted parent help in finding plants and bulbs. They decided to plant one area with vegetables and one with flowers.

The children's bridge construction, with surrounding gardens, culminated their Bridge Project.

They made sketches, selected color schemes, and ultimately worked on planting the actual garden in raised beds built by another family member.

Throughout the project, Sally and Barbara were busy providing resources as the children's interests evolved. They located materials, planned the trip and parent involvement, and supported group and individual activities. They also carefully documented the process. Sally took photos, Barbara collected work samples, and both teachers made notes about children's dialogues and questions. Ultimately the teachers created a large documentation panel to chronicle the project. When they reflected on their documentation, they highlighted each of the developmental domains and state learning standards areas that were fostered with each activity. They smiled as they spoke about how children's personal family stories (through vacation stories and photos) were integrated. They also nodded as they talked about how each child, regardless of abilities and skill levels, had an important role and made valuable contributions in his or her own way.

When the children's bridge was complete, the class came together to decide how to share what they had learned and created. The children chose to hold a garden party, where families, children, teachers, and visitors could come and traverse the bridge and see the artifacts of the project. On party day, the children excitedly shared their experiences, reliving the project and revisiting their work.

In the Field   In the spirit of engaging minds in meaningful, constructivist learning, one of the best ways to really understand the structure, process, and potential of the Project Approach is to actually *do* a project. As a class or in groups, consider topics that are interesting and worthy of in-depth study. Keep in mind the same criteria teachers use to decide on topics to investigate with children.

For each topic, begin documenting what members of the group already know and generate questions that address what you want to know more about. View this segment as a webbing/KWHL brainstorming session. Come up with as many related ideas, concepts, and questions as possible. Ask one person to keep a running list to document responses.

Begin to organize ideas into a web to see possible directions and relationships between responses. Once the web begins to take shape, smaller groups may want to break off to explore particular ideas or concept branches.

In small groups, explore possible primary sources where you could conduct your investigations. Think about possible field visit sites and possible experts to talk to. Continue Phase I activities until you and your group feel ready to embark on your investigation. Move into Phase II, remembering to keep notes and records of activities and investigations as they take place. Keep photos, notes, sketches, writings, and transcriptions of interviews and dialogues for your documentation panel and/or culminating event. Let your initial questions from your KWHL and web guide your investigations. Move into Phase III as time dictates or as your investigations begin to wind down. Plan and implement your culminating event as a whole class or as small groups. Your culminating event should answer this question: How can we share what we've learned and how we learned about our topic?

For Your Portfolio   When you have completed your project, reflect on the following questions in a brief paper:

- Were you surprised by how much you knew about your topic or how many questions you had while you planned in Phase I?
- How did Phase I activities help guide your investigations?
- How did you feel as you engaged in your investigations?
- Was a certain energy or excitement generated by your group?
- What can you say about the experience of getting out in the community to do fieldwork? How was this different than using secondary sources?
- Did you find out new information through your investigations? Describe it.
- What kinds of representations did you enjoy? Did you find yourself using a variety of skills and knowledge?

As a final group activity, make notes on your documentation panel, web, or KWHL chart about which of your state standards were covered. You will need to find your state learning standards for K–3 or preschool. If your state does not have standards for your age group, consider using another state. (Pennsylvania, Colorado, Arizona, and North Carolina are some states with extensive early learning standards.)

Include photos and descriptions from your project in your reflective paper. This artifact can be added to your portfolio in a teaching and learning section.

Related Web Links

Project Approach home page
www.projectapproach.org

Illinois Projects in Practice
http://illinoispip.org/

9

The Schools of Reggio Emilia: A Child's World

In the small, wealthy, northern Italian town of Reggio Emilia, a community of early care and education centers embodies the epitome of exceptional practice in teaching young children. Numerous books, exhibits, and observation reports have been published about their approach in the past two decades. The international educational community has become captivated by this aesthetically beautiful, professionally collaborative place. From the first illustrations of life in the Reggio schools, early childhood professionals in America have developed a vision of Reggio practice as a romantic ideal. With core values affirming a deep respect for children's capabilities and families' influence and an attention to beauty and detail, the Reggio philosophy, teaching methods, and environment are highly attractive yet also require tremendous effort. This chapter presents an introduction to the history, philosophy, and practice of the infant through preprimary schools of Reggio Emilia, Italy. Challenges and possibilities for successfully integrating the Reggio spirit and inspiration into U.S. programs are also presented.

OVERVIEW OF THE REGGIO EMILIA PHILOSOPHY

Overarching everything Reggio teachers do is the guiding belief that children are capable and competent. The educational system is based on an overriding belief that children, teachers, and parents each have core *rights* within the community. In the powerful Charter of Rights statement, founding member Loris Malaguzzi describes the Rights of Children:

> Children have the right to be recognized as . . . both source and constructors of their own experience, and thus active participants in the organization of the identities, abilities, and autonomy, through relationships and interaction with peers, with adults, with ideas, with objects, and with the real and imaginary events of intercommunicating worlds. (Edwards, Gandini, & Forman, 1996, p. 214).

Children are viewed as capable of responding to each other and to richly detailed, authentic artwork. They are able to create complex, beautiful, meaningful work either individually or in collaboration with teachers and peers (Gandini, 2002). Although the Reggio philosophy integrates developmental theories, their perspective is on each child's potential development rather than norms of ages and stages (Warash, Curtis, Hursch, & Tucci, 2008). In other words, the Reggio approach is based on seeing each individual child as capable of much more than expected when provided the right opportunities for engaging with his or her world in creative ways. Reggio teachers take children's aesthetic (sense of beauty) development as seriously as their development in every other domain. It is this respect for and valuing of the arts and beauty in children's lives that make possible the uncommonly expressive, aesthetically striking representations created by Reggio children.

Reggio Emilia schools focus learning experiences on allowing children to experience the world with all their senses. Teachers give children the opportunity and tools to explore the world at their will—to be the captains of their own learning. In turn, Reggio children's understanding reaches deeper and becomes much more personal to them. The themes of their study can last for months, continuing as long as the children need to squeeze all the juice out of the topic and feel satisfied that they have a real understanding of it (Seefeldt, 1995). The depth of their comprehension is most evident in the rich detail, variety, and maturity of the expressive works used by the children to give form to their individual awareness.

Small-group interaction is also an important element of the Reggio approach. Class-rooms are busy places where groups first engage in discussion and debate then embark on the task of exploring the topic of their discussion (Gandini, 1997). Throughout their investigations, teachers carefully document the children's process so all—teachers, children, and parents—are able to see children's learning and revisit and reflect on their process (Warash et al., 2008). This is a great example of the social construction of knowledge you read about in the constructivism chapter. In this environment, children's unfolding thought processes lead to the advancement and testing of their understanding. This is possible because the teachers and children promote an environment of value and respect for each other's ideas, differences, and expressions.

Reggio teachers, who teach in an area rich in traditions of art and social relationships, take great care in preparing children's environments to be places of beauty, complexity, comfort, and visual interest (Edwards, 2003). Teachers focus on aesthetic elements of light and shadow, texture, shape, dimension, color, and composition in the design of displays, presentation of materials, project experiences, and selection of classroom furnishings. The

Ressio-inspired programs take great care in presenting children's work, demonstrating respect for children as artists.

environment is viewed as the third teacher and, as such, is given careful, deliberate consideration (Danko-McGhee & Slutsky, 2003). Most important, teachers carefully focus children's attention and provoke interest through choice of material and classroom display.

Materials may be found, purchased, donated, or natural, but they are all displayed in organized, organic, unusual groupings that draw the children into activity with them. Teachers select, prepare, and present materials to challenge children "to respond deeply to the natural world, their cultural heritage, [and] to their inner worlds" (Tarr, 2003, p. 37). Through the use of materials, displays, and conversations, teachers act as **provocateurs**, seeking to provoke children's thought.

A full understanding, appreciation, and knowledge of the Reggio Emilia approach (REA) require an awareness of the forces that built and shaped the schools as well as of the motivations and efforts that perpetuate them so successfully. Before you launch into the historical overview, take a moment to visit a Reggio–inspired school.

Provocateurs

Teachers as provokers of thought by posing engaging questions and presenting interesting materials.

CLASSROOM VIEW

A Visit to an American Reggio-Inspired Classroom

In a small, close-knit town, the director of an established child care center became intrigued by the richly detailed, beautiful images publicized by the schools of Reggio Emilia. What transpired over the course of several decades embodied the emergent, dynamic, reflective, collaborative nature of the Reggio Emilia spirit. The center's transformation was made possible by a passionate commitment to the community, to the children, and to the beauty that could be created together.

Imagine you are visiting this center early one sunny, cold, winter day. The center is located in what looks from the outside like a house, now converted to a preschool. There is a welcoming entrance foyer with a couch, tables of informational pamphlets, and reference books on Reggio Emilia schools. The lighting is soft, and the room feels lush with several floor plants. There is a small table with tea and coffee near the couch. An office adjoins the space, allowing visitors to be greeted upon arrival. A hallway leads from the entrance to three classrooms, accompanied by a large community room and an art studio. Throughout the center, the walls are painted white and the wood floors gleam in the streams of sunlight shining through the many windows. The sound of children engaged with each other is immediately noticeable; many conversations and bubbling laughter echo through the hall.

From the entrance and throughout the center the walls are adorned with framed, lit prints. With such care given to the placement, framing, and lighting of the work, the space resembles a museum. These carefully displayed works are, in fact, representations the children have created using a variety of media in the course of their long-term projects. Near many of the pictures are small plaques of transcriptions of children's dialogue to serve as accompaniment and provide additional information.

Framed photos of children at work creating sculptures, drawings, and paintings; engaging in dialogues; and observing their world with rapt attention punctuate the project documentation. The expressions on their faces begin to reveal the deeply personal, authentic, engaging atmosphere that has been carefully and deliberately created by the teachers. This is clearly a child's world. It is made beautiful, nurturing, and exciting by a group of teachers who have committed themselves to valuing and celebrating the amazing potential of children.

The first classroom down the hallway is empty; the children, bundled against the cold, are outside in the snow-covered garden. A small group of children is gathered around a pine tree. They are pointing to a bough heavily weighed down with snow. They turn and talk to one another and the teacher nearby. Other children are busy scooping snow and shaping it into sculptures. You see animals and towers, not just the usual snowball snowman. One little girl takes deliberate steps and looks back to see her footprints in a patch of untouched snow. She creates a dotted pattern by varying between big and small steps. She laughs and sings in time to her stepping.

*Inside, the classroom is lit by a full wall of windows on one side and three large windows on the other. There is a large, open space on one side of the room, with several small alcoves and three clusters of small tables and chairs. Adjoining the room is a small art room, called the mini **atelier** in Italian. This studio room is lined with floor-to-ceiling shelves. One entire wall of shelves is stocked with clear jars holding collections of items, including naturally found items such as shells, stones, pinecones, leaves, twigs, sawdust, nuts, and seeds as well as manufactured materials, including flat wooden sticks, cotton balls, pom-poms, scraps of fabrics, sequins, glitter, pipe cleaners, yarns, cookie-cutters, wire, and beads. Recycled materials fill another series of jars: bottle caps, various packing materials such as Styrofoam peanuts, starch noodles, and pieces of bubble wrap. Other shelves hold baskets of artists' instruments, including clay tools, paintbrushes of all sizes, sponges, pens, pencils, crayons, pastels, different forms of paint (water color, tempera, powdered, acrylic, finger), paper of all sizes and colors, clear plastic bins of clay, small trays, and small jars and cups. On one shelf, children's paintings are still drying; other paintings are hung by clothespins from a string stretched across the room. The classroom illustration (on following page) depicts this room.*

The children's paintings are a study in composition. They are all done in shades of white and light gray, blue, and lavender. These are the colors the children chose to represent the snow outside and their experiences with it. There are two sinks, one low for children and one higher for adults, and a counter and cabinet for teachers' materials. In the center of the room is a long, wide, low table with small chairs around it. Despite being filled with objects, the small room appears organized, spacious, and inviting. Materials are grouped in collections and arranged in an orderly fashion.

In the main classroom, evidence of typical preschool centers appears in the form of blocks, dramatic play clothes, kitchenwares, a pillowed alcove surrounded by bookshelves, a table with puzzle racks, and low shelves housing manipulatives, dolls, cars, paper, and pens. An overhead projector and a screen are set up in a corner near a basket filled with a variety of items of different shapes and opaqueness. A tank with one fish is located in the far corner of the room. A class book has been placed next to the tank. You flip through the book and read the children's story about the death of one of the class pets. The book includes scanned pictures of the children discovering the fish in the morning, the fish's funeral and burial, and children's drawings of their memories of the fish. Quotes of children's comments and dialogue, printed alongside the pictures, include memories of the fish and feelings about the loss. The teacher later explains that this two-day project was discussed

Atelier

Art studio space—within the classroom or in a central location—that provides the children with space to create over time.

with families first and that they had all decided to let the children experience this loss as an opportunity for authentic learning.

As the children return from their snowy outing, there is a sound of dialogue from the large art studio (atelier) down the hall. Children use the studio to work on long-term projects. The large art studio is similarly well stocked, but it has larger collections of supplies and materials. There are several long, wide tables with groups of small chairs and a higher table for the art teacher (**atelierista**). A long wall of windows with wide ledges allows for plenty of natural lighting. The ledges are lined with pinecones, acorns, and smooth river stones. These collections of materials were found by the children on a recent nature walk.

Atelierista

A teacher who is also trained as an artist.

In the middle of one of the tables, there is a book of bridges, opened to an overhead view of the cables on the Golden Gate Bridge in San Francisco. Two children are seated around the book with large, thick paper and a variety of pencils and markers. They are intently focused on drawing their own bridges, attending to the shapes and lines of the cables and the overhead perspective. One teacher, who is sitting with them, shows the children how to use a smudging technique with their fingers to create soft shadows.

At another table, three children have gathered a variety of pieces of flat wooden sticks, string, toothpicks, and brown river stones. They are deep in debate about how to create three-dimensional models of their own bridge. They are talking about how to make it stand tall enough to span the stones. Another teacher is cutting ample pieces of clay for two children to use to sculpt more bridges. Three other children are gathered on the floor near a window, where they are working on a weaving they began yesterday. Integrated into the alternating strips are twigs, leaves, pinecones, and other found items. The children chose soft hues of greens and blues for their strips to represent the way the colors of the water and the grass looked when they blended at the riverbank on a recent field trip to a nearby footbridge. They talk as they work, animatedly describing qualities of each shell, seaweed, and twig as though it had a personality.

"This little pinecone is a baby; let's tie it on by its mother."

"This piece of wood looks like it is dancing. Turning, turning, turning." The child moves the small piece of wood in a spiraling motion.

"This leaf is blowing bubbles under the water. Blub, blub, blub." The child runs her hand along the bumpy surface of the large leaf.

Reggio-inspired classroom.

Sample Class Schedule

8:30 A.M.	Arrival and greeting, play
9 A.M.	Circle meeting and project discussions
9:20–10:40 A.M.	Children's choice, project work, art, play (may be outdoors)
10:40 A.M.	Snack together
11 A.M.	Outdoors
11:30 A.M.	Prepare for lunch (bathroom, washing, setting table)
11:45 A.M.–12:45 P.M.	Group meal
12:45–1:30 P.M.	Rest time
1:30–2 P.M.	Snack
2–3:20 P.M.	Play, choice, art, project work (may be outdoors)
3:20 P.M.	Clean up, come together, story, reflect on day
3:45–5 P.M.	Outside, play
5 P.M.	Pick up, good-byes

The building of a personal relationship with the things they encounter in their world is considered a valuable part of the learning process and is encouraged by Reggian teachers. "We believe in the power of the relationships children create with their world," the teacher explains. "It's not strange that they talk about pinecones and twigs as if they had personalities. To the children, they do. They are living elements in their daily lives, characters in their stories. This personal relationship makes their learning, their engagement with their world, so much more meaningful to them." The children and teachers will continue their explorations of building bridges as they work toward designing and building their own footbridge in the play yard. This kind of long-term project is fueled by the children's interest and motivation to process and represent new experiences in their world. In many ways, the projects undertaken by Reggio children align with the principles presented in the project approach, as with this bridge project.

HISTORY AND CONTEXT OF THE SCHOOLS OF REGGIO EMILIA

During World War II, Italians witnessed firsthand the tragedy and decimation of the war. The citizens of Reggio Emilia played a significant role in the anti-Nazi-Fascist movement. They were active in working to restore order from the chaos that followed the end of the war (Caldwell, 1997). Spurred on by a vision and dedication to reconstruct their society as a place of freedom, equality, and community, a group of parents set out to build new schools and a new world for their children (Gandini, 1997). Using proceeds from the sale of abandoned war equipment, parents secured the resources needed to begin forming their schools. In 1945 the first parent-run preschool of the common people opened in Reggio Emilia (Gandini, 2002).

Loris Malaguzzi, then a teacher and student of education and psychology, soon became committed to the effort. He was impressed with the passion of the parents and attuned to the vision of education as a force for social change (Day, 2001). With Malaguzzi's organization, additional schools soon opened. After nearly two decades of advocacy, in 1963 the city of Reggio Emilia instituted support for opening the first municipal preschool and within 5 years had played a major role in establishing a national early education system (New, 2003). Continuing a tradition of reflection and study, the Reggio teachers remained active scholars in education and related fields. Influenced by theorists such as Piaget, Vygotsky, Bruner, and Dewey, they became involved in exploring and promoting innovations in education, which garnered public support in the 1950s and 1960s (Gandini, 1997).

In 1968 national legislation was passed in Italy providing for public funding for preschools for all children from 3 to 6 years of age (Hewett, 2001). This public funding structure is very different from that of most preschools in the United States. Adequate funding for facilities, programs, and teacher salaries is an ongoing challenge for many U.S. early childhood centers today. Many teachers feel hopeless about being able to apply Reggio principles in other contexts, particularly without ample resources, but many programs are currently finding inspiration from Reggio and successfully embracing the spirit of their approach. In many ways, the Reggio community relies on the creative use of available resources, even when they are scant. Recall their humble beginnings financed through the sale of cast-off war equipment and fueled by the efforts of volunteers and their reliance on "found materials" to stock classroom shelves.

Amid the backdrop of the grassroots efforts to create a place of beauty and learning for their children, the schools of Reggio Emilia continue to self-reflect and evolve in pursuit of that goal. They remain fueled by the dedication and involvement of parents. Now with more than 36 preschools and infant-toddler centers, roughly 50% of the city's preschool children and 35% of infants and toddlers are enrolled in the municipal schools (Hewett, 2001; New, 2003). Nearly 99% of the young children in Reggio Emilia attend some kind of schooling (municipal, private, or parochial) (Gandini, 2002). These impressive numbers demonstrate a firmly entrenched family and community commitment to optimizing children's development. This is one city that truly embodies the African proverb, "It takes a village to raise a child."

In response to a growing interest in their schools, in 1981 Malaguzzi and the Reggio Emilia school community created an exhibit illustrating the spirit of their school. Echoing their belief that children have multiple ways of communicating, they titled the exhibit *The Hundred Languages of Children*. The exhibit traveled internationally, and along with the documentary book, brought attention to the philosophy, culture, and practice of Reggio schools (Edwards et al., 1996). Malaguzzi's final effort to disseminate information about the Reggio schools came with the 1994 formation of the Reggio Children organization. Malaguzzi died the same year (Gandini, 1997). Reggio Children continues to promote the REA through books and videos and sponsors annual study tours to the Reggio schools. Through all these efforts, their guiding principles of collaboration and emphasis on the value of relationships are promoted and encouraged among professionals in the field.

Italian Influences: A Cultural Context of Caring

Successfully translating Reggio Emilia values into the unique U.S. educational context requires careful, critical reflection and a rethinking of traditional norms of practice. This is no small task for new teachers, although it is one that is worth your effort on behalf of all children. Many U.S. educators have tried to import the REA into their classrooms, with varying success. Teachers in Reggio are the first to caution that the importance of cultural context cannot be overlooked. Their unique cultural surrounding is foundational to their approach.

Italy is a country with a long tradition of appreciating beauty, art, food, family, and communication (Edwards, 2003). Architecturally the country is filled with simple, ancient dwellings and churches still in use, as well as cosmopolitan cities demonstrating new and ornate designs. Geographically diverse, the mountainous north falls away to rolling, fertile hills and ends in the hot, rocky southern "boot" and the island of Sicily, both encircled by the brilliance of the Mediterranean Sea. Beauty surrounds Italians in the picturesque countrysides, the plethora of museums, and the murals and mosaics in local churches. It also lives in the warm closeness of family, the heart of the Italian way of life.

Of utmost importance in Italian culture is the celebration of the family as the core of any community. Children are celebrated as the promise of a beautiful future. Given this context, it is no surprise that the schools are carefully and thoughtfully designed to be places where children and adults alike cultivate a sense of wonder as they learn to look at, listen to, and feel the world around them from infinite perspectives (Caldwell, 1997).

Evolving Practice, Enduring Values

Reggio teachers consider their current philosophy to be a reflection and reinvention of innovations in education. They continue to be inspired by a variety of theorists and borrow pieces from traditional and contemporary educational approaches. You are doing the same thing here by exploring a variety of theories, frameworks, methods, and approaches and deciding what aspects of each work with your own personal philosophy of education. The guiding framework in Reggio schools is heavily influenced by social constructivist theory, which is embodied in their belief that learning is based on relationships (Edwards, 2003). The key principles that were the motivation for starting the schools remain foundational to current practice. The REA is "a tightly connected, coherent philosophy, in which each point influences, and is influenced by all the others" (Gandini, 2002, p. 16). Thus, the interrelatedness of the REA does not lend itself well to having its parts separated from the vision of the whole. However, a more in-depth look at the key elements of the underlying views on children, teachers,

Light Tables

One of the materials employed in the Reggio Emilia schools as a provocation is the light table. In the classroom visit, you read about the overhead projector and screen setup. Projectors, screens, and light tables are used to provide children with an interesting space to create compositions focusing on shadow, shape, light, dark, and levels from opaqueness to transparency. By placing items on the lit surface (lit either from above or below, like the light table), children are able to focus on the bulk or shape, not all the three-dimensional details. This is just one way that materials provoke children's visual perception and promote aesthetic development.

Light tables are used to explore light and shadow and create tabletop shadow compositions.

and the community, within the context of the program as a whole, serves to illustrate guiding values:

- *Rights and capabilities* of children, teachers, and parents
- *Collaboration* among all members of the school community
- *Relationships* among children, teachers, families, experiences, and materials

Listen to educators describe their experience with practice inspired by Reggio Emilia schools in this **video**.

VIEW OF CHILDREN IN REGGIO EMILIA SCHOOLS

To fully appreciate the REA, visitors are first introduced to their image of the child. Reggio Emilia educators validate all children as competent, resourceful, and curious (Gandini, 2002). Inspiring everything Reggio teachers do is an immense respect for children's potential to

- interact with their world (people, events, and materials);
- develop personal, meaningful relationships in their world; and
- construct new, complex meanings and knowledge.

Children's rights and capabilities are respected through the sharing of power and control over classroom experiences. This respect for children includes teachers allowing children to fully participate in all facets of classroom life and drive the topic and length of group projects. Children are viewed as powerful and capable of generating complex, meaningful ideas. The environmental design, the selection of materials, and the interactions and guidance in activities are all interrelated to an utmost respect and appreciation for the capabilities of all children (Bredekamp, 1993). The deeply held value that each child is uniquely capable and endowed with individual strengths results in a particular capacity to welcome and support children of varying ability levels. Recent research has demonstrated the success of a Reggio approach in supporting children with diverse abilities (Massey & Burnard, 2006) and dual-language learners (Zhang, Fallon, & Kim, 2009).

A visit to a Reggio infant-toddler center will reveal toddlers sculpting with wire, clay, and small beads. These materials would be forbidden in U.S. centers on the basis of safety. Likewise, preschool children, in investigation of a large lion statue in a town square, freely climb atop the 6- or 7-foot statue. They want to see what the top looks like, feel what it is like to ride on the lion, and experience the lion's perspective (Reggio Children, 1980). Reggio teachers support them in their interest. Concerns over safety would prevent U.S. teachers from allowing children to experience such perspectives (Tarr, 2003). Thus, a key area of U.S. teachers to consider would be how to adapt the core values for application in our own unique context.

Overarching all teaching practice is an emphasis on fostering children's learning to look at their world and see it in as many ways as possible. In essence, children are encouraged to look at, and really *see,* their world. It is this carefully trained eye, tied closely to an inner vision and imagination, which allows children to engage in deeply involved explorations and relationships. Reggio teachers remain present, involved, and ready to provide support and guidance as needed, but they make every effort to interfere as little as possible in the work of the child. Any such interference would deny the child's role as a powerful and capable individual (Reggio Children, 1994).

Children are also validated as unique individuals within a social group. They are provided with space and time to work alone and in small groups and also to come together as a community. Most of their classroom time is spent working in naturally forming groups. Teachers encourage collaboration through the design of the classroom (group tables, for example). They also embody a collaborative spirit by working together as a centerwide team and with the families and the community. In the bridge project, for example, a parent was enlisted to help with the construction of the children's life-size bridge. A contractor by trade, he was knowledgeable about tools and architecture. As a father, he was keenly aware of safety issues and supportive of having the children take an active role in planning and construction. He continued his collaborative relationship by working with the children on other projects.

The relationships children create with peers, adults, their environment, and materials are viewed as the very heart of education. The relationships among teachers, children, parents, and administrators are valued and promoted through active interaction and open dialogue. Collaborations between school staff and parents are firmly ingrained in the school culture, and parents are viewed as valuable resources and supports. Parents are routinely welcomed to the center for open-house events and are continually participating in project activities.

ROLES OF THE TEACHER IN REGGIO EMILIA SCHOOLS

Teachers are viewed as partners within children's learning, not as the external forces directing it. They provoke children's thoughts, ask open-ended questions, display materials that satisfy children's requests or extend their thinking (called provocations), and continuously observe children's progress (Caldwell, 1997). Through careful, systematic observations and recording of children's conversations, teachers pick up on key topics of interest to the children. Using this information, they may present materials or plan a trip around the unfolding interests. In this way they are able to position children as creators and coconstructors of their own ideas and enhance their natural curiosity about their world. Their participation may be more or less active, depending on the stage of children's processing at the moment. In addition to facilitating projects, the other two primary roles of the teacher—observing and listening to the children—define their level of activity and nature of involvement in children's activities (Danko-McGhee & Slutsky, 2003).

When they are not facilitating children's project work, teachers are carefully documenting the unfolding process of the children. Even when they are engaged in children's work, they often use audio recorders to capture children's dialogues to be transcribed later. The important learning revealed in listening to children's dialogue is always present in the teachers' minds (Caldwell, 1997). In this way, teachers also act as researchers. They are continuously gathering data, analyzing it, and reflecting on it in collaboration with other teachers and the children themselves (Gandini, 2002; Hughes, 2007).

The guiding principle of "education as relationships" also holds true for teachers. Teachers work in close relationship to children, fellow teachers, parents, and the community. They engage in a reflective self-discovery learning process alongside the children. Special time is set aside in the regular schedule for teachers, *atelieristi* (art directors), and **pedagogisti** (pedagogical coordinators) to come together to discuss their practice and the children's work. These honest, open exchanges often include confrontation and conflict over certain issues. However, the culture of respect and collaboration encourages these open dialogues as being necessary to the work of reflection and evolution. Suggestions are met with openness, just as they are offered in respect.

This level of passionate, respectful exchange, a natural part of Italian culture, is not routinely experienced in U.S. culture (Caldwell, 1997). Imagine yourself facing a conflict with a colleague at work. It probably does not conjure up pleasant feelings and may be something you would prefer to avoid. Reggio teachers embrace the potential for growth that is inherent in conflicts, and they negotiate through them respectfully and openly. This perspective allows teachers to learn from each other just as conflicts in the classroom can be great opportunities for children to grow. Remember how Piaget felt that cognitive conflict, in the form of challenge to existing ideas by new experience, was essential for development? This perspective certainly rings true for Reggio teachers.

Pedagogisti

The pedagogical coordinators who help teachers extend children's learning experiences and projects as far as they can go in meaningful, worthy directions.

Weaving Provocation

The teachers in the Reggio-inspired classroom visit noticed their children were becoming interested in entwining strings. They would twist them and showed the beginnings of weavings. Wanting to support and extend this, the teachers decided to create a weaving provocation. They found a beautiful storybook about a South American woman and her granddaughter who create elaborate traditional woven blankets, and the teachers read the book to the children. The teachers placed the book next to a wall-hanging weaving station. At the base of the frame on the wall, they placed a basket with a variety of string, ribbon, fabric strips, twigs, leaves, beads, feathers, and other crafting items. They put this display in the hallway where all the children would have access to it. They showed the children where the display was and encouraged them to visit and add to the communal weaving. Over the course of several weeks, they noticed that the weaving was growing as children from all the rooms added pieces here and there. When the space was full, they talked about what they had created, took some photos, and unwove it so that they could start a new work.

A weaving provocation; an invitation to children to explore weaving.

Likewise, open dialogues are fostered with parents through informal exchanges during the day or meetings scheduled to discuss pedagogy, children's work, and community issues. The heart of these dialogues, indeed the heart of all endeavors in Reggio schools, is to be in continual reflection in the ongoing effort of self-improvement. Teachers' pedagogy of listening promotes reciprocal relationships with children just as it does with fellow teachers and parents. With the dedication to providing the best possible experience for children at the heart of their work, teachers are motivated to remain open, collaborative, and mutually supportive of each other (Gandini, 2002).

Most teachers in Reggio Emilia begin their work with minimal preservice education, and the schools are viewed as laboratories where teachers are learning as well as the children. This is viewed as desirable because all Reggio teachers work together and, in effect, all new teachers are mentored. In Reggio schools, the right kind of spirit, heart, and attitude are as important as formal credentials. Within the context of the collaborative school community and through professional development and experience, Reggio teachers develop an advanced degree of understanding of children's development and learning (Bredekamp, 1993). It was only in 1998 that Italy passed a law requiring college-level teacher education for early childhood teachers (New, 2003).

LEARNING AND DOCUMENTATION IN REGGIO EMILIA SCHOOLS

Teachers believe that children's learning is developed primarily through discourse, representations, and relationships. Reggio teachers operate within the philosophy that the focus of education must be on the social context of the child's world. This means that the child's relationships with peers, teachers, family, and the community shape his or her learning (Caldwell, 1997; Krechevsky & Stork, 2000).

Reggio teachers believe strongly in the instructive power of the learning environment. They view the environment as the child's third teacher (after parents and teachers)

(Gandini, 1997). Beauty and complexity as key components permeate the Reggio classrooms. The learning spaces are carefully designed with two overarching goals in mind (Edwards, 2003):

1. Encourage children to sense their world through new perspectives (see things differently, hear new sounds or combinations of sounds, think about something familiar in a new way, etc.).

2. Provoke their thinking, questioning, hypothesizing, representing, and sharing.

Much of the children's project work revolves around the life of their surrounding community. Viewed as interrelated to life at school or at home, the school grounds and surrounding city often serve as the spark of interest for a project. Children have become entranced by the birds in the play yard, the mother cat and kittens outside their window, the streets and buildings on their way around town, the crowds in the streets, and everyday events such as trips to the market (Edwards, Gandini, & Forman, 1996; Reggio Children, 1980). An Alaskan Eskimo village preschool using a Reggio-inspired approach embarked on a journey exploring how life in their village had changed over generations, and the children's investigative journey brought them to the tradition of fishing. The children explored frozen lakes, fishing tools, stories from families, and the rich history of this core part of life in their village (Hughes, 2007). The connection between their learning environment and life outside the classroom is viewed as an interrelated, interdependent one. Reggio teachers use these connections to maintain an emphasis on education as a series of relationships. See how teachers can validate importance of the environment and authentic topics in children's emergent projects in this **video**.

Learning as a Socially Negotiated Process

Opportunities for small-group investigations and discourses are continually presented by teachers and propelled by the children. Even the architecture of the building prompts dialogues: Small windows join adjacent rooms and a central communal play space, called the **piazza** in Italian. It is during small-group exchanges that Reggio teachers anticipate challenges and cognitive conflicts. These settings prompt the group members to explore concepts more deeply to create a new understanding (Gandini, 2002).

Piazza

The town square at the center of the village; in Reggio Emilia schools, a central space in the school that serves as a shared gathering place.

Throughout each day, fluid conversations happen everywhere. Children converse with each other, discuss things with teachers, and create conversations with and through their representations. Keep in mind that relationships overarch everything. Relationships spring from communication—from dialogues. Dialogues are supported through the opportunities for multiple representations and modes of communication: painting, drawing, dance, shadow theater, sculpture, discussion, music, and dramatic play. Each of these expressive activities allows the children to process their own experiences as well as share their thoughts with others. Through their art, the children dialogue with their ideas as well as communicate with those who view their work.

The spiraling process of verbal dialogue, graphic representation, more verbal dialogue, and so on is the communication cycle through which children act on information. It is through this cycle that they are deconstructing and reconstructing as they process and represent. Children are thus empowered in their world by being given a myriad of languages through which to construct meaning and to communicate with themselves and others. Remember the view of *the hundred languages of children*.

Reggio teachers believe that it is through graphic representation that children create order out of the chaos of new experiences (Reggio Children, 1994). You, too, might find that making notes, sketches, maps, or diagrams helps you make sense of new information. On one level, you might make those kinds of graphic representations to keep track of information or remember things. On a deeper level, you might use graphic representations to rethink something or reflect on your understanding using a language other than words.

In Reggio schools, long-term projects emerging from the children's interests are the primary vehicles for classroom learning activities. Ample space and time are given for children's unfolding projects. Because children are the directors of their group projects, they are empowered as negotiators of their own learning with teachers reflectively and thoughtfully supporting and guiding their explorations (Edwards, 2003). Reggio teachers believe that there are three keys to a worthwhile project (Reggio Children, 1994):

1. Have a high level of personal interest
2. Are thoughtfully carried out by the children with intention
3. Revolve around the potential for developing relationships with people and materials

The incredibly rich, complex, and authentic projects that children undertake are captured in stunningly vivid detail and description through a keen focus on careful documentation.

Documentation: A Tool for Learning, Assessment, and Planning

As projects unfold, teachers capture children's processes and developing and changing ideas through careful documentation. The documentation sources (photos, videos, drawings, transcriptions of dialogues) are then used to promote teachers' and children's reflections on their process. This, in turn, leads to new directions for investigation, discoveries of thinking errors, and future planning. The use of documentation as a reflecting and planning tool differs from the common U.S. practice of using documentation primarily for evaluation purposes (Turner & Krechevsky, 2003). One step beyond simply using documentation for teachers' planning purposes, artifacts from classroom experiences are used by the children themselves as tools for reflection and future planning (Warash et al., 2008).

Documentation Panels

Documentation panels are carefully designed displays that chronicle the progress of the children's projects and the process they went through in their explorations. The panels include photos of the children working, work samples, drawings, paintings, or other graphic representations, teacher's notes, and transcriptions of dialogue. Capturing children's dialogue is a primary way teachers glimpse children's unfolding thought processing, learn about children's interests, and glean insight into future possibilities (Tarr, 2003). Documentation panels may be as small as a few poster boards or spread over an entire school wall.

So just as teachers review samples of children's work to "see" their learning, children are able to do the same. The importance of careful documentation is evident in the Reggio teachers' belief that only through collecting and reflecting on relevant documents or traces of children's work does learning become visible and knowledge construction possible (Rinaldi, 2001).

Because of the emphasis on the whole child and the complex processes unfolding within them, paper-and-pencil tests are inappropriate for assessments. Teachers seek to capture richly detailed, personally meaningful pictures of the children at various stages of learning and growing. These assessment goals require much more in-depth observations and conversations than any simple test could provide. If you have ever been frustrated because you felt that you knew more than a single test could accurately reflect, you probably can understand the Reggio teachers' choice of authentic assessment techniques. They would agree with you that you are more than a number.

IN YOUR OWN WORDS

Now that you have explored the key principles that underscore the spirit and practices in the schools of Reggio Emilia, do any of these principles and practices seem applicable in your own work or future work? Are there any facets of Reggio practices that you think would pose challenges for early childhood educators in the United States? Take a moment to reflect on the observations you have made of early childhood classrooms and compare them to your developing vision of Reggio schools. What similarities or differences can you see? What changes could you imagine making to either setting that would improve the beauty, learning, and overall quality of the children's experiences? Keep these ideas in mind as you read about the applications of the REA in U.S. schools.

CHALLENGES TO REGGIO-INSPIRED PRACTICE IN THE UNITED STATES: LOST IN TRANSLATION?

One of the overarching premises of the REA is valuing and respecting the unique context of children's lives. Much of the framework of the REA, as well as its success in garnering support and respect for the framework, comes from working in concert with the beliefs, values, and goals of the surrounding community. To simplify the REA into a checklist of beliefs and technical elements would be contrary to the spirit of the schools, which focus on the unique cultural context of the school community. Attempting to simply transplant the Reggio framework into a U.S. context is counterproductive, futile, and strongly cautioned against by Reggio advocates (Linn, 2001). This contextualization of learning experiences within the community is often a challenge to appropriately applying a Reggio approach in other cultures. Understanding the REA as a flexible framework, a system of beliefs, and an example of a collaborative process is necessary to learn useful lessons from the approach.

REA: Is a Philosophy, Not a Curriculum

The first mistake many visitors to Reggio schools make is assuming that what happens in Reggio schools is a curriculum. The term *curriculum* has been defined as "an organized framework that delineates the content that children are to learn, the process through which children achieve identified curricular goals, what teachers do to help children achieve these goals, and the context in which teaching and learning occur" (Bredekamp & Rosengrant, 1992). The REA is fluid, emergent, dynamic, and responsive to the unique context of the children's lives and open to changes based on teachers' continued observation and reflection of children. There is not the kind of recipe for practice that would be the hallmark of a prescribed, preplanned curriculum.

Instead of viewing their program as a curriculum, Reggio educators suggest that the core beliefs and guiding principles be used as a means of generating reflection and dialogue among other educators in their own pursuit of a uniquely responsive approach (Goffin, 2000). When the parts that are interdependent and intertwined within the context of the school culture are viewed as a whole, valuable lessons and possibilities for inspiring U.S. practice emerge.

REA Requires Family Involvement

One of the most impressive characteristics of the schools of Reggio Emilia is the exceptionally strong support and interaction from parents and the community. Reggio teachers believe that parents have rights, just as children do. Parents are respected for being their children's first teachers and for having the right to participate actively and freely in their children's educational lives. This open collaboration is viewed as vital to children's emotional security and requisite for optimal learning (Gandini, 2002).

With its very foundation built on the tireless efforts of parents in the design of both physical space and philosophical beliefs, it is not surprising that parents remain highly involved and respected in the school collaborative. This level of involvement and respect may be a foreign concept to many American educators. Building bridges toward a true collaboration among school, home, and community is a challenge, but the possibilities are also there when schools and families build relationships of trust, mutual respect, and a shared goal of providing the very best care and education of their children. This collaborative relationship is even more important when working with children with special rights, as they are called in Reggio schools. For those children who may need adaptations, special attention, or modifications of some kind, close communication with families is imperative and can make all the difference in creating a fully inclusive classroom community (Gilman, 2007). The Reggio approach lends itself well to meaningful inclusion due to the emphasis on all children as competent, powerful individuals and the focus on child-guided activities and play (Zhang et al., 2009).

In several ways, the principles of Head Start programs are similar to Reggio principles. Both Head Start and Reggio programs share the following key principles:

- An eclectic mix of theoretical perspectives, including Montessori, Piaget, Vygotsky, Dewey, Froebel, and research from the High/Scope foundation, is synthesized to create a unique approach to educating young children.
- Continued self-reflection and critical analysis are viewed as necessary to keep teachers and programs current with research in the field.
- Staff are encouraged to learn from other related fields to ensure a comprehensive, holistic picture of children's learning in the context of their lives (psychology, social work, health).
- Space is reserved so children with handicaps can be fully included.
- An emphasis on family involvement is embedded as a core component of the program.

In the case of Head Start, parental involvement is mandated by national program guidelines (USDHHS, 2005). Some Head Start programs are also making changes to their program structures and practices in ways that align with Reggio principles (Hughes, 2007). Although teachers and parents report some challenges related to understanding about Reggio principles, many also report satisfaction with the changes in the program and their children's choices and interest in school. However, it is essential that teachers maintain a high level of communication with parents about changes in practice to ensure successful implementation of the REA (McClow & Gillespie, 1998).

REA Is About Context

Ultimately the lessons learned from Reggio Emilia concern context. The schools of Reggio Emilia enjoy a long history that is rich with the eloquent interplay of parents and teachers working together to create beautiful, enriching spaces for their children. They are founded on collaboration and a singular focus on creating the absolute best environment for children. Housed in a culture that historically values the family as a whole (children in particular) and is rich in beauty and generous in resources, Reggio schools thrive in part because of their context and history. Supported by national funding legislation, parent involvement, and staff commitment to ongoing self-reflection, the cultural context is one of the key relationships that shapes and perpetuates Reggio schools.

A major part of the REA is the validation of the context of children's lives and an unwavering effort to integrate that context into the learning environment (Strozzi, 2001). This emphasis on emergent, authentic learning does not necessarily align with a reliance on predetermined outcomes and universal standards. U.S. education systems rely heavily on the use of standards and preset curricula as tools to plan and evaluate learning experiences for children. This process of planning based on end results poses a real challenge to embracing an emergent learning model (New, 2003). Implicit in an emergent model is a respect for children's interests, motivations, and inner processes. Power is shared, and teachers focus on carefully listening to children's words and rhythms to guide learning. This level of responsiveness requires a great deal of ongoing reflecting and planning and takes up a fair amount of time.

The world surrounding children's school and home is an essential part of the curriculum.

For example, Reggio teachers embed 6 hours a week into their schedules for collaborative teacher planning and discussion (Gandini, 2002). That's almost an entire day's worth of hours. The time involved often feels like an insurmountable challenge for already stressed U.S. educators. It remains a key component, however, because emergent models take a great deal of planning and guiding despite seeming on the surface to require less planning on the teacher's part. The Reggio emphasis on taking time for thoughtful discussions and planning is another way of embodying its core belief that education is deeply entwined within social relationships.

In a broader view, U.S. early childhood professionals are continually battling for national validation and recognition, usually in the form of funding and professional credibility. Many caring, capable teachers leave the field, feeling frustrated, disempowered, and unable to effect positive change (Linn, 2001). This disillusionment arises when the divide between motivation to provide nurturing educational experiences and external pressure to conform to sometimes questionable standards feels unbridgeable. This negative cycle contrasts sharply with the Reggio approach. In Italy, early childhood education funding, extended family leave laws, and equal pay for men and women have been part of national legislation since the late 1960s (Gandini, 1997). Also, teachers there are part of a culture that respects them as thoughtful, deliberate, caring professionals (New, 2003).

Within this idyllic context, it is easy to dismiss the REA as simply not feasible within the U.S. environment. Even Reggio teachers are clear in their caution that the REA is not a recipe or a prescribed curriculum to be copied and transplanted elsewhere (Linn, 2001). Nevertheless, the spirit, core values, and guiding processes of the REA hold valuable lessons for all early childhood educators. And exemplary programs across the country have found inspiration and demonstrated great success for children through implementation of Reggio-inspired practice. At the very heart of the REA are the processes of

- social interaction,
- meaningful engagement,
- thoughtful reflection,
- respectful collaboration, and
- authentic investigations.

Think about these five key principles as elements of any learning process for a moment. Perhaps these are processes through which you yourself learn best: working in groups; sharing personally interesting and meaningful discussions; investigating authentic topics through hands-on activities; seeing connections to your previous experiences and learning; and being free to ask questions, wonder, try, and succeed. These are worthy endeavors for any student or teacher and are the inspirations educators from around the world are finding in the schools of Reggio Emilia.

INSPIRED APPLICATIONS: HOW SOME U.S. EDUCATORS ARE MAKING THE LEAP

Over the past few decades, U.S. educators have become increasingly interested in the practice and philosophy of the schools of Reggio Emilia. The intensely emotional response to the practices and agreement with the core values has sparked a passion and commitment that are driving a growing movement to integrate the REA in U.S. preschools and elementary schools. Preschools are demonstrating success in embracing the Reggio spirit through the translation and reinvention of key components:

- Careful meshing between school and community
- Validation of the reflective, analytic, and collaborative nature of teaching practices
- Willingness to take risks and learn from failures

Embracing core values and deriving inspiration from the beauty, relationships, and energy of the schools of Reggio Emilia are fitting ways to honor the commitment to provide children with the highest quality education possible. Watch how this school is using a REA and carefully integrating rich and varied art experiences for children to demonstrate their learning in this **video**.

Suggestions from the Field: Embracing the Spirit

The self-reflective exercise many U.S. teachers have engaged in since exploring the REA offers a starting point for the journey. First, educators must carefully consider their own vision of the child and what implications this has for their practice. Recognizing how deeply entrenched traditional deficit models of children and transmission models of teaching can be is an important part of freeing negative images and reenvisioning children, learning, and teaching in a more positive, collaborative light.

IN YOUR OWN WORDS

One way to start this awareness process is to consider well-known metaphors used to describe children and learning, such as children are sponges, the early childhood center should be a garden, or children are little angels. While reflecting on these metaphors, certain inherent implications may emerge. Regarding children as sponges may imply that they soak up their surroundings passively. How does this fit with a view that they actively deconstruct and construct their environment, experiences, and ideas in their formation of new knowledge?

If early childhood centers should be like gardens, the message may be that children need protected spaces in which they should be left to grow, although the role of the teacher is not so clear. Viewing children as angels may imply an innocence and a romantic notion that hinders their capacity to benefit from negotiating conflict, working through problems, constructing knowledge, and being present in the realities of life.

When children are viewed as powerful, capable, intelligent partners, possibilities arise for engaging in complex, authentic, worthy, meaningful experiences as part of a social group. Continuing to reflect critically on your beliefs is the first step in shaping or reshaping your practice.

Reflective Practice, Resourceful Practice

In reflecting on practice, teachers must consider what messages the environment conveys. The level of attention to detail (color, design, material selection and placement, aesthetics) sends a palpable message as to a teacher's level of commitment to children. Realistically, learning spaces may not be ideal homelike structures with lots of windows and light. The realities of early childhood practice are that centers operate wherever they can. The suggestion to carefully construct the environment does not imply building new centers or equipping classrooms with fancy, expensive furniture and materials. Resourcefulness is the first skill in any good teacher's toolbox.

An attention to detail, thoughtful design, and attractive arrangement of materials can happen within small budgets and architectural constraints. It is about the intention put forth. It is about the deliberate environmental design meant to convey a message of invitation, engagement, and genuine interest. This is possible with recycled or second-hand materials enriched by simple found objects such as collections of natural resources (sticks, stones, shells, leaves, nuts). In fact, interesting displays and combinations of natural materials spark children's interests more than just being handed a fancy toy. By participating in children's experiments and explorations of the world around them, teachers affirm the message that children are valued, respected, and empowered. Encouraging and facilitating children's representations through a variety of "languages" gives children the tools they need to process information and experiences more fully and deeply and to communicate ideas more skillfully. The goals of increased ability to process and communicate are timely and meaningful for all children, regardless of where they are living.

A final suggestion is to make connections and relationships with fellow teachers and parents. These are your partners in the quest to create the most beautiful, highest quality learning experiences for children. Relying on parents as resources for information and connections to the community expands children's learning. It also validates that the context of children's lives includes school, home, and community. As parents participate in children's learning, they should also participate in the documentation-reflection process. By engaging in a collective documentation-reflection process, each member of the team continues to see children and his or her own teaching from new perspectives (Grieshaber & Hatch, 2003). This process of seeing things in a new way is the heart of the REA. It is the result of careful, deliberate, collaborative reflection on the endless possibilities for improving practice for all children.

CONCLUSION

The schools of Reggio Emilia operate within a unique context that also shares many similarities with U.S. ideals and practice. There are challenges but also rich possibilities in exploring the REA as a way to reflect on and improve the status of U.S. early childhood education. To fully understand and successfully apply Reggio practices in U.S. schools requires that teachers explore lessons from Reggio within the context of the culture of their own area. By examining their beliefs about parents' role in schools and promoting reciprocal partnerships with families, U.S. teachers can begin the process of forging new, more open relationships between parents and schools. Although Reggio practice cannot be simply transplanted to foreign communities, the spirit of partnership, the emphasis on relationships, and the commitment to children's rights are all goals that can make any program more successful.

Acknowledging the REA as an example of a nurturing, emergent, collaborative, reflective, reciprocal learning environment allows educators to explore Reggio traditions as a catalyst for change in their own programs. The true inspiration of the schools of Reggio

Emilia rests in the ability of outside educators to embrace the spirit of the approach. The spirit is one that echoes all educators' goal of providing all children with a beautiful, respectful place. It celebrates the importance of social relationships and engenders meaningful, collaborative learning experiences for children and teachers alike.

SUMMARY

- The Reggio Emilia philosophy is based on an empowered view of children, viewing each individual child as capable of much more than expected when provided the right opportunities for engaging with his or her world in creative ways.

- The environment, materials, and projects are child-centered and carefully supported to engender meaningful relationships and learning.

- After the decimation resulting from World War II, a small group of families bonded together in defiance of then-current Nazi-Fascist regimes and created a school of hope, promise, possibility, and beauty.

- Nestled among the picturesque countryside of northern Italy and imbued with the traditions of beauty and family, the Reggio Emilia schools began as the vision of a group of dedicated parents and continue as a collaborative effort on behalf of all children.

- The schools of Reggio Emilia hold several core values at the heart of their practice:
  - Children are strong, powerful, and capable.
  - Children learn through active, social, constructive processes.
  - Art and beauty should be the foundations of the educational environment.
  - Families are essential partners in the education process.
  - Relationships are the foundation of learning.

- The deeply held value that each child is uniquely capable and endowed with individual strengths results in a particular capacity to welcome and support children of varying ability levels.

- Children in Reggio Emilia schools learn primarily through investigating emergent projects, through dialogues, and through representation and reflection experiences.

- The primary roles of the teachers are to observe and listen to children, to provoke their thinking, and to document their processes by collecting representative works and dialogues of the children.

- Teachers capture children's processes and developing and changing ideas through careful documentation of children's investigations and dialogues.

- Unique considerations when seeking to apply Reggio Emilia–inspired practices require that educators recognize the important cultural context within their own school community and actively involve families in children's learning.

- Educators in the United States have made successful applications of Reggio-inspired practice through embracing emergent teaching processes of negotiation, ongoing reflection, willingness to take risks, and engaging with children as true partners in learning.

Chapter Learning Goals Self-Assessment

Use this chart to write down three to five key points for each learning goal that you learned from this chapter.

Describe key values and practices of Reggio Emilia schools.	
Identify important historical events in the development and evolution of Reggio Emilia schools.	
Describe the view of children in the philosophy of Reggio Emilia schools.	
Identify key roles of teachers in Reggio Emilia schools.	
Explore the purpose and process of learning and documentation in Reggio Emilia schools.	
Discuss challenges to integrating a REA in the United States.	
Examine application ideas for using a REA.	

Application Activities

Discussion Prompts

1. List the core values of the REA. List your own core values relating to your own work with young children (current or future). Which elements are similar, and which are different? How did you determine your own values and beliefs about education?

2. After thinking about the environment and experiences in the schools of Reggio Emilia, what ideas do you have for infusing beauty and aesthetics into young children's lives in your own classroom?

In Class   Think about metaphors you have heard or other phrases that come to your mind that describe young children. While working in small groups, write down at least three ways that children and learning are described. Discuss what these phrases or words might be subtly conveying and how they might be affecting practice. Select your own image or metaphor, and create a visual representation to share your image of the child.

In the Field   With a heavy emphasis on aesthetics, or art experiences, Reggio schools seek to hone children's ability to really look at the world around them from many different perspectives. One activity you can do with children is to use 2-inch × 2-inch viewers to focus children's looking. Use an empty slide holder or make a viewer from a 2-inch × 2-inch card with a 1-inch square cut out of the middle.

Try it yourself first. Hold your viewer about 12 inches from your eye. Close one eye and look through the open space in the center of your viewer, focusing your attention on just the contents of your viewer. Look carefully and make some mental notes about what you see. Note shapes, lines, colors, forms, and so on. Once you have really looked, take 10 minutes to sketch what you see in your viewer. Do not try to reconstruct what the portion in your viewer is supposed to be (a table, a window) but rather just re-create the lines, shapes, colors, shades, and so on, from your viewer as though those parts existed separately from the whole. This exercise allows you to see something familiar in a new way, as a new piece of your world. It also takes your focus away from drawing a table or a window and prompts you simply to explore the composition of this isolated series of lines, shapes, and shades. Seeing a small part of something whole in your world makes you stop and really look at an item that you glance at or see only as a whole every day. In other words, you see it from a new perspective through your viewer. Keep refocusing your viewer around your world and find out just how much you can see!

For Your Portfolio   The underlying beliefs and values teachers hold about children are the driving forces for interactions, planning, and teaching approaches. These values serve to guide teachers but also ultimately affect children's experiences and learning. It is essential that teachers are clear in articulating their values and beliefs about children. In keeping with the Reggio approach to viewing all children as having rights, think about the very core rights that you believe *all* children should be endowed with. Many educators and communities think about this in terms of our own Constitutional rights. Review a collaboratively created version of a Children's Bill of Rights at www.newciv.org/ncn/cbor.html and http://educators.boulderjourneyschool.com/charter-of-childrens-rights.html for inspiration as a starting point to create your own statement. Your statement is a good addition to your professional portfolio in an introductory or professionalism section.

RELATED WEB LINKS

North American Reggio Emilia Alliance
www.reggioalliance.org

Boulder Journey School
www.boulderjourneyschool.com

Reggio Children USA
zerosei.comune.re.it/inter/index.htm

CHAPTER 10 Montessori Education: Environment, Materials, and Methods

Chapter Learning Goals

- Explore important events in Montessori's life and work.

- Identify important aspects of children's development and learning in Montessori classrooms.

- Examine essential roles of the Montessori teacher.

- Describe materials in the five key curricular areas of the Montessori method.

- Compare critiques, successes, and widely accepted applications of Montessori's work.

M ontessori education, a household phrase in the United States today, has had a significant effect on the fields of education and child development. Maria Montessori began her groundbreaking work with impoverished and developmentally delayed children and later devised methods and materials to use with all children. Her well-documented theories about the development of the child's will and intellect have been influencing teacher practice for more than a century. Many of Montessori's once-radical views have become accepted components of all good practice. Thousands of Montessori schools, some serving infants through high school-Age children, are found all over the world, with nearly 5,000 in the United States alone.

Because Maria Montessori plays such a key role in the way we think about and teach young children, it is important for educators to become more familiar with her as well as with her method of teaching. To truly understand her method requires that you have a foundational understanding of her beliefs about how children develop, how she came to hold those beliefs, and how her theories guided her practice in teaching young children. This chapter presents the historical background of Montessori and her theories and explores the key elements in her method, including the materials, environment, and teacher's role. Ongoing debates concerning divergent beliefs about the role of play in Montessori programs and other early childhood programs are also presented.

CLASSROOM VIEW

Montessori in Action

To better visualize the basic framework of Maria Montessori's method of education, take a moment to step into a carefully prepared Montessori preschool classroom. It is a bright, sunny fall day as we enter the houselike structure of the Montessori school. Today you are going to visit the 3- to 6-year-olds' mixed-age preschool room. The space is large and open, with a bathroom area sectioned off by half walls at one side of the room. There is also a mini kitchen space adjoining the bathroom that includes a sink and counter space for adults and a smaller one for children. Next to the kitchen, there is a small table on which orange quarters and a plate of crackers, small spreaders, and a tub of jam have been set out for an hour for those children who choose to help themselves to snack at their will.

The teachers explain that by letting children snack when they please, they do not have to interrupt children's work for a designated whole-group snack time. "As Montessori teachers, above all else, we are careful not to interrupt children's work," one teacher explains. "It is a way of respecting their process. We believe that the children's internal process is engaged when they work with the materials. I don't disrupt that because of a schedule we've set for them. We strive to allow close to 3 hours of

Montessori classroom.

children's choice time in the mornings. This allows children the time to get deep into their work. Here, the children drive their learning."

As you glance around the room, you notice the clean, pleasing appearance of the pink-and-white striped curtains and matching child-sized wicker sofa set. It is located in what seems to be a house area in the far corner of the room. The walls are white and are sparsely adorned with framed Monet and Van Gogh prints. The classroom space is well lit by both large windows and overhead fluorescent lights. The room has an overall feeling of order, brightness, and neatness. It strikes you as a little unusual for a room filled with preschool children in the midst of morning activity. It seems even quieter than the other classrooms you have visited.

As you continue to survey the scene, you notice that there are three-step climbers at one side and low shelves and small tables that divide the open space. There is a large, green carpet under a wall of windows. The carpet is lined with low shelves containing neatly stored block sets. Next, you begin to notice the children. Most of them are working individually with the self-correcting materials on trays placed on small carpet squares. They are intently focused on their respective tasks: Some are pouring water from one small glass pitcher to another. Others are stacking pink blocks of successively smaller dimensions into a tower. Others work at lacing, snapping, tying, and zipping. And still others intently focus on moving their hands over letters cut out of sandpaper with a gentler touch than you can recall ever seeing in a 4-year-old. In fact, you are surprised at the quiet intensity of all the children as they focus all their attention on the materials in their hands.

The teachers, too, seem to be unusually quiet, closely watching specific children who are intently and repetitively working. One teacher is slowly and deliberately modeling the correct use of a new material. She silently shows the child how to pick up a cylinder and place it in the empty space on the base. When she has completed putting the series of cylinders in their holes, she asks the child if he would like to try this work. He nods and quietly replicates her actions.

The children move about their space with care, quietly helping themselves to trays of materials stored on the low shelves. They deliberately and repetitively manipulate the materials. When the children decide that they are finished with a particular work, they return the pieces to the tray and return the tray to the exact location from which they took it. The materials look new, and you are surprised to later find out that they have been in this classroom for more than 15 years. The children clearly demonstrate that they have the utmost respect for their environment and understand that the materials will be used by children for years and years to come.

One of the teachers notices your surprise and explains, "Instilling in each child a reverence and respect for themselves, each other, and their environment is one of our most important tasks as teachers. A big part of each day is spent working on self-care skills and also work that takes care of this space. Children clean the tables and materials and dust the plants. They learn how to dress and serve themselves. Montessori considered these skills essential work for preschoolers."

After their rather intense period of mostly independent work, the children are called to the carpet space, where they converge with the teachers and participate in a circle time. Today the children are being

Children use knobless cylinders to develop fine motor skills and work on seriation.

Sample Daily Schedule

Montessori believed children should be allowed to work at self-selected activities with little interference from teachers. This translates into a long block of time for child-selected work.

8:00 A.M.	Arrival, bathroom, wash up, breakfast (if desired)
8:30 A.M.	Children select work (snack available)
11:00 A.M.	Circle gathering
11:15 A.M.	Outdoors—free play, gardening, exercise
12:15 P.M.	Clean up, set table, prepare for lunch
Lunch	
12:45 P.M.	Quiet rest
2:15 P.M.	Bathroom, clean up, outdoors
2:30 P.M.	Children select work (snack available), some free play
5:00 P.M.	Clean up, prepare for departure

introduced to a new object—a pineapple—and they are encouraged to feel and smell the fruit while the teacher talks about where it came from. Later the children will have an opportunity to taste the fruit in an afternoon snack. After a relatively brief circle period, the children and teachers get ready for an outing to their outdoor playground. After such an intense independent work time, the children and teachers alike are eager to enjoy the fresh air, sunshine, social interaction, and physical exercise of the climbing equipment.

HISTORICAL BACKGROUND OF MONTESSORI'S LIFE AND WORK

Maria Montessori was born in Italy in 1870 to a wealthy family, and even as a child, she became known for her superb intellect. In a time when women were not traditionally afforded the same kinds of educational or professional opportunities as men, Montessori demonstrated a competency and capability worthy of special recognition. While attending an all-boys technical school, she settled on the pursuit of medicine, although she had to complete clinical studies alone due to social decorum of the time relating to men and women studying together (Lascarides & Hinitz, 2000; Shute, 2002). Montessori quickly demonstrated unusual strength as a student and clinician even in her first year (Gettman, 1987). Thus began the recognition of her unusual capabilities.

Montessori became the first female doctor to graduate from the University of Rome. She subsequently spent a decade practicing surgical medicine and advocating equal rights for women (Gettman, 1987). As her studies and work branched out into psychology and she began teaching at the nearby psychiatric clinic, Montessori became intrigued with the so-called defective and insane children housed in the institution. In all likelihood, these children today would be classified as *developmentally delayed*. Montessori was deeply influenced by the work of Romantic philosophers Rousseau, Pestalozzi, and Froebel (Elkind, 2003) and the growing constructivist theory base (Edwards, 2002). But she was perhaps most profoundly inspired by the work of Jean-Marc-Gaspard Itard and his student Edouard

Seguin. Both physicians, Itard and Seguin promoted the radical belief that mental deficiencies were more problems of the way in which "defective children" were being taught and less a medical problem (Cossentino, 2006; Lascarides & Hinitz, 2000).

Montessori's Experiment with Education Begins

With a scientific rigor typical of Montessori, she observed and documented how the institutionalized children fought over the tiniest crumbs and dust fluffs. She set out to prove her hypothesis that these children were starved for stimulation and not biologically defective. Montessori began a 2-year experiment in which she observed the children engaging with a variety of hands-on materials that she created (Gettman, 1987). After 2 years of work with the materials, these defective children were able to pass age-level school competency exams as well as any typically developing child (Shute, 2002). This finding fueled her belief that stimulating environments and focused, purposeful activity could promote cognitive growth in any child. In this classroom observation **video**, learn about Montessori settings and materials.

Energized by this success, Montessori turned her attention to the current educational system. She believed that educational environments were stifling and suppressing the child's will, inner drives, and naturally unfolding development. She began to crusade for educational programs for young children that were not merely smaller-sized versions of the elementary education programs (Shute, 2002).

Absorbent mind

Montessori's description of how children soak up their surroundings and experiences.

Casa dei Bambini

Montessori's first Children's House, opened in 1907 as her first educational program for impoverished children in an area of Rome, Italy.

Montessori validated young children's instinct to touch any material they could get their hands on and soak up any stimulation in their environment (the **absorbent mind**). At the heart of her new model of early childhood education was the belief that children learn through purposeful work on sensory experiences and by absorbing their surroundings. This prompted her to be concerned with the careful design of the child's space and careful selection of manipulative materials. She also recognized the highly active, physical nature of young children and sought to celebrate this nature instead of try to suppress it. Montessori's first opportunity to work with community children came in 1906, when she was asked to take charge of nearly 50 undersupervised children of the families living in a low-income tenement area of Rome. Montessori regarded this as another opportunity to practice and expand her theories about children's learning and development. The opening of her **Casa dei Bambini** (Children's House) in 1907 marked the beginning of a theory and method of teaching that has had an enduring and significant effect on teaching practices for more than 100 years.

Putting It Into Practice

Make Your Own Sandpaper Letters and Numbers

Montessori created thin wooden tablets that had numbers or letters written in sandpaper to provide texture and sensory experience. You can easily stencil and cut out letters and numbers from medium-grit sandpaper and glue them to heavy cardstock or wood pieces. Invite children to trace the sandpaper shapes with their eyes open or closed. This experience gives them a physical, tactile sensation of the lines and shapes of letters and numbers.

Using Observation and Reflection to Hone Her Method

Montessori employed a scientific approach through the presentation of materials and objective observation of children's activity. Through her carefully documented observations, Montessori began to notice amazing discoveries. She found that these tearful, frightened children, ranging in ages from 2 to 6, could become intently engaged with her purposeful materials. She removed the irrelevant toys and found that the children preferred to work on meaningful tasks free from adult intrusion. She saw an inner calm come over them as they worked, repeatedly and with greater competence, with their chosen materials (Gettman, 1987). Building on her observations, Montessori refined the environment and materials to maximize each child's own spontaneous activity within a carefully prepared environment and structured materials. This system of *freedom with limits* became a hallmark of her method.

Montessori further chronicled the different activities and levels of competence in the children of various ages. Through these notes, she began to notice what she called *sensitive periods* in the children where they appeared more interested in particular developmental tasks. Montessori believed that maximizing development required sensitivity on the adults' part—an awareness that came from respecting the child's own inner forces and from observing the child freely engaged with materials of his or her own choosing (Montessori, 1966). Out of this belief came Montessori's view of the teacher as an observer and preparer of the environment, rather than an imparter of knowledge.

Montessori continued developing and promoting her method and was both applauded and criticized throughout her career. During her visits to the United States in 1913, Montessori's ideas were fairly well received by the public. In particular, her 1915 World's Fair exhibit, in which children silently and intently worked on independently selected activities with remarkable attention, caused a great public buzz (Sobe, 2004). Kindergarten advocates and teachers such as Patty Smith Hill and William Heard Kilpatrick, however, rejected the rigid, structured work children methodically repeated with the materials (Cossentino, 2006; Lascarides & Hinitz, 2000). Concerns were raised over the lack of creative expression, the absence of play, and the strict use of *didactic* materials. Although some upper-class families accepted the method and even founded several Montessori schools and a professional association, for the most part, the Montessori method remained an unpopular choice among early childhood educators in the Progressive Era.

Putting It Into Practice

Make Your Own Color Chips

Montessori created color chips of varying hues so children could discriminate from lightest to darkest. You can create your own by using paint swatches readily available at paint stores or home improvement stores. Get two of each color palette you choose. Cut one so each hue is separated. The task then is to match them, using the whole card as a template. Or for a more advanced work, cut one card in pieces and have the children seriate the shades (put them in order from lightest to darkest).

Montessori teachers demonstrate the correct use of materials and then observe children's work.

Her method did not become really popular until years after her death (in 1952), when, during the 1960s, three key shifts opened the door for new interest in her methods. At that time, more theorists were beginning to make connections between early experiences and later success, the early intervention movement for at-risk children was beginning to take hold, and educators were searching for a more scientific method of child development and education. With Montessori's strong science background, the emphasis on naturalistic observation, and the origins in special education, Montessori's method was once again in the U.S. spotlight in both the 1960s and again in the 1980s. Independent Montessori schools quickly opened under the auspices and direction of such agencies as the newly formed American Montessori Association and the Association Montessori Internationale (AMI). Both associations advocate close alignment with Montessori's writing. Although Montessori schools do not necessarily have to align with her method (there is no trademark on the name), those who are affiliated with one of these agencies will more closely adhere to Montessori's own design.

As more and more Montessori schools opened, public knowledge of Montessori's method increased. In recent decades, the number of Montessori-inspired schools has grown to around 5,000 in the United States, and Montessori methods have been implemented in more than 200 public elementary school settings (NAMTA, 2013; Lillard & Else-Quest, 2006). After Montessori's death in 1952, her only son, Mario, took over control of the AMI and continued to promote the Montessori method until his death in 1982 (Gettman, 1987; Henry-Montessori, n.d.).

Formalizing Her Method of Education

Throughout her career, Montessori took advantage of any opportunity she could to observe children in their natural environment. She made insightful connections from these extensive observations and began to be increasingly concerned at how adults seemed to be misinterpreting and thwarting children's needs and drives. A highly spiritual person, Montessori was concerned for the psychic well-being of children. She wrote extensively about her observations of children's distress when adults did not recognize the spiritual basis for children's outward expressions (Montessori, 1966). She was so committed to reinventing early childhood practice that she painstakingly documented her method with prolific writings, teacher training, and sometimes inordinate numbers of steps scripted for every activity in which children engage. She prescribed teacher's actions and words for every step of an activity—from the introduction, demonstration, and invitation to the child to try the work. Montessori insisted on strict adherence to her method because she was certain that her method was the single best way to maximize children's innate abilities to foster their own development (Goffin, 1994). Her method can perhaps best be understood by exploring the key principles that guided her work with children, which include Montessori's

- beliefs about children's development,
- vision of the teacher's role and function in the classroom, and
- original materials for which she has received much acclaim.

We explore each principle in turn as it relates to our overall understanding of Montessori's method and her contributions to the field of early childhood education.

MONTESSORI'S VIEW OF CHILDREN AND DEVELOPMENT

Montessori believed that children come into this world with a natural sense of spirituality, inquisitiveness, capability, and purpose, all of which act as driving forces in their development and learning. Montessori also believed that at birth children are in a state of internal chaos, out of which they strive to make sense and order. She believed this effort is manifested by their increasing purposefulness and productive behavior. A great deal of her writing chronicled her belief that the "secret of childhood" was that children, when unfettered by inappropriate adult demands, would naturally and spontaneously engage in activities that guided their development toward becoming ordered, productive adults. According to Montessori, development is an internally regulated process that requires carefully planned interaction with the environment and materials (Montessori, 1966).

Sensitive Periods

Montessori believed that children naturally pass through phases that prepare them for learning in certain areas. During these phases, called *sensitive periods,* the child is ready to master particular skills or concepts that cannot be fully mastered at other times. Beginning in infancy, these sensitive periods allow the child to soak up stimulation and cues in the world that, when subjected to the child's internal processes, result in developmental growth. In this way, Montessori viewed the young child's mind as *absorbent,* eager to take in, model, and imitate any stimulation that is put before it (Montessori, 1966).

We can see this idea illustrated in an infant's mimicking of a facial expression made by an excited caregiver, in a toddler's gleefully repeating a word or phrase just heard from an adult, or in a preschooler's imitation of an older sibling's physical actions. Through these examples, we see how a child is influenced by his or her environment. This also emphasizes what tremendous responsibility teachers have in presenting only the most appropriate model for children to imitate.

As we know from commonly observed milestones in development, an enormous amount of developmental growth is seen in the first 3 years of life. It is in this formative period that children learn to speak in their culturally accepted language and command their physical actions with relative control. Advances in these two major developmental domains enable the organization of all later cognitive, social, and emotional development. Thus, the early years represent a critically important period in terms of the child's later development. Montessori felt problems resulted from an adult's view of the infant as being completely dependent, resulting in an overbearing, overprotective—albeit loving—desire to do everything for an infant. She felt that doing too much thwarted the infant's own innate drive to make sense of his world. In turn, this would render the infant out of touch with his own tools of self-education. Out of respect for the child's inborn capabilities, Montessori sought to reempower infants and children to be able to guide their own development through self-sufficiency (Montessori, 1966).

Have you ever witnessed a battle of wills between an adult and a motivated toddler? Perhaps you've seen a child who refused to settle down into a stroller, insisting on walking instead. Or maybe you've seen an infant desperately reaching for food during feeding time, wanting to feed herself or perhaps smear food on her hair. If so, you can begin to understand that even young children have internal processes that are extremely important to them, even though they lack an adult framework for describing them. Montessori wrote passionately about what an offense to the child it was to exert unnecessary authority over the child in such a battle. She firmly believed in limits, but she insisted they be reasonable and not undermine the will and self-determination of the child. She viewed these as two essential components of development and learning (Lascarides & Hinitz, 2000).

Montessori also believed that the preschool years (3 to 6 years old) were years that were essential in developing a sense of order about the world that would lay a foundation for later rational thought. Although the belief that the child's early experiences have great influence on later functioning is now widely accepted, in her time Montessori's emphasis on the early years was met with skepticism. Ever the pioneer, Montessori maintained her conviction and developed materials and prescribed activities that would allow optimal natural development as it unfolded from within the child.

Burgeoning Independence and Will

Auto-education

Self-directed action using didactic (self-correcting) materials.

For the child's innate developmental plan to be realized, Montessori realized that the child needed to be able to function with independence. She defined this as the freedom for a child to take care of his or her own needs as well as the freedom from being dependent on assistance from others. She believed that, if children mastered some basic self-sufficiency skills, they would be at liberty to self-select materials, activities, and experiences. This self-direction using didactic materials, or **auto-education**, would naturally maximize the developmental outcomes of the particular sensitive period they were experiencing at the moment (Goffin, 1994). This belief served as the framework for the first phase of her curriculum plan, which she referred to as *practical life*. Practical life focuses on the skills of daily living: dressing, washing, and ordering one's environment. Watch in this **video** showing the child's focus and attention to her task as her mother encourages her to sort and classify a group of shells. Montessori was driven by observations of children's intense focus and attention to radically change existing perceptions about children's attention capabilities.

Montessori also observed that young children are innately driven to handle and physically explore their world and everything in it. She became increasingly dissatisfied with parents and teachers who always seemed to be at odds with their children who were not listening, sitting quietly, or keeping their hands off adult valuables. Ultimately convinced that these battles of will were detrimental to the child's naturally occurring sense of purpose, Montessori became outspoken in her disagreement with current practices of care and

Putting It Into Practice

Make Your Own Dressing Frames

Using purchased wood frames (discard the glass) and old shirts and jackets, you can create your own set of dressing frames. You can find old clothes at thrift shops if you do not have clothes with a variety of fasteners. Or you can sew zippers, buttons, and snaps onto purchased fabric. Cut the fabric/clothing to fit over the frame, hemming the tops and bottoms if desired. Use a staple gun or upholstery tacks to attach the clothing/fabric to the right and left sides of the frame, centering the fastener/closure in the middle of the opening. Children can unfasten and refasten the buttons, zippers, and other fasteners and develop self-care skills (learning to dress themselves) as well as fine-motor skills.

education for young children (Rambusch, 1992). For example, think about that toddler who resists being strapped into a stroller. Although a parent may insist the child remain there because the parent has a busy schedule and it is faster to push him, the child has a burning desire to test out his developing walking skills. The toddler does not necessarily understand the parent's schedule; instead, he is aware only that at this point in his life, he needs practice to master walking. Montessori would have advocated allowing the child to walk for a while, even though the parent's schedule would be delayed. Montessori reported

Children use work with the dressing frame or vest to learn self-care skills and develop fine motor skills like buttoning, zipping, lacing, or buckling.

that in these battles of will, when the child is once again on his own developmental path, there is an immediate shift in the child from inconsolable to joyful and bright eyed (Montessori, 1966). It is with this perspective in mind that we now explore Montessori's vision of the role teachers should play in the child's educational development.

TEACHERS' (DIRECTRESS'S) ROLES AND FUNCTIONS

Teachers in a Montessori program are carefully trained in a prescribed, approved Montessori teacher-training program. Here they learn the basic principles of child development and Montessori's view of children as well as the proper scripts to use when working with and talking to the children. Montessori's vision was that all schools and teachers would look and act in a similar way—carefully following her model.

Montessori constructed materials to act as the child's teacher, meaning that children could use the materials without teacher direction or assistance. She discovered that when children were properly introduced to the use of the materials deliberately and carefully, they could select and work with the materials at their own will (Montessori, 1965). This allowed the teacher to step back and let the child guide his or her own learning, serving as director of the classroom activities (thus her title of "directress") and observer. The teacher should remain a background part of the environment, guiding and supporting the child's unfolding development without pushing or imposing the teacher's own desire on the child. Montessori explained that "our intention in this marvelous process is *indirect;* we are here to offer to this life, which came into the world by itself, the *means* necessary for its development, and having done that we must await this development with respect" (Montessori, 1965, p. 134).

Along with the emphasis placed on the correct use of the didactic materials, the teacher, or *directress,* is an influence of primary importance in the child's life (Lascarides & Hinitz, 2000). The teacher's influence could have either positive or negative effects on the child's developmental and psychic outcomes. Montessori believed that the teacher should start with a tremendous respect for children's rights and abilities and be responsible for three primary functions:

1. Carefully preparing the environment
2. Appropriately introducing and modeling the didactic materials
3. Closely observing the children and documenting learning

Preparing the Environment

Although it may seem obvious to early childhood educators today, making the classroom and materials accessible to children was not a well-understood idea before Montessori. She insisted that children not be made to exist in an adult-oriented environment. To foster independence, she created classrooms for children that included lightweight, scaled-down furniture that could be easily moved about and from which children could easily take and replace materials (Mooney, 2000). Building on her beliefs that children craved order in their world, creating an aesthetically pleasing space that was neat, ordered, and free from undue clutter became a trademark of her vision.

Contrary to what we may commonly find in preschool classrooms today, Montessori did not believe in using intricate wall decorations and brightly colored paint. Her clean, white spaces presented an organized design in which carefully chosen materials and artwork were displayed in moderation. Montessori strove to provide an environment that was not overstimulating and distracting, but instead provided a clean backdrop for the internal work in which the child would engage. Shelves were to be stocked but not over-stocked, and materials were to be clean and in good condition. This order and visual harmony was extremely important to Montessori. She wrote passionately about her belief that children's development was strongly influenced by their environment and experiences as well as by their internal drives (Goffin, 1994). It was important to cultivate a psychological space in which children were respected and free. In this way there would be a great deal of individualization to children's learning.

Instead of supporting a laissez-faire, or hands-off, attitude, Montessori believed that it required great training and work to understand the child's innate drives and needs. She felt it demanded even more effort on the teacher's part to create a classroom space that offered appropriate experiences that could support drives and meet needs. This, she felt, was accomplished through

- setting clear limits,
- modeling proper use of materials, and
- backing away to allow the child to explore the materials and environment.

The Teacher as Model and Director

It may sound like a contradiction to talk about teachers as directors in a classroom where children are to be free from adult interference. Montessori was careful to point out, however, that the child is freed from dependence on others when he or she is able to act independently in his or her world. And independence is learned through skills acquired by imitating teacher directions. To support this independence in children, Montessori developed materials and instructions for their use that focused initially on developing self-sufficiency skills in children. Although many of her practical life materials address fairly common activities, such as dressing and cleaning, Montessori insisted that teachers follow her detailed method for introducing the work.

Knowing that young children are neither interested in sitting quietly in large groups for long periods of time nor capable of developing at the same rate, Montessori believed that individual instruction was the primary means to introduce the materials. Considering her preferred practice of mixed-age grouping, not all children would be ready to use the same materials at the same time; therefore, the introduction and use of materials was to be a very individualized endeavor. Specific materials were presented only to children who were ready and interested to receive them. Through their observations and insight into each child, teachers become familiar with each child's readiness for work with specific materials. If a material was introduced and the teacher observed that the child was uninterested or unable to work with it properly, the teacher was simply to remove the work, allowing the child to freely choose another work, and reserve the new material for another time (Montessori, 1999).

Also keeping in mind that Montessori viewed the child's work with the materials as the primary vehicle for learning (not the teacher's lessons themselves), she insisted that the introductory lessons were to be brief, simple, objective, and use as few words as possible (Montessori, 1999). A teacher slowly demonstrates the correct use of a material, such as the button dressing frame, by doing the following:

- Carefully removing the frame from the shelf
- Saying simply, "This is the button dressing frame."
- Placing it on the table with the child seated to her left
- Quietly announcing, "I will now show you how to button and unbutton."

Teacher Training

To ensure accurate presentation, Montessori insisted that all teachers who sought to teach through her method be trained under her own supervision. As the popularity of her method grew and as a way to maintain consistency after her death, approved institutions assumed responsibility for carrying on the work of teacher training. In addition to an emphasis on understanding the child, teacher training involved strict guidance in regard to exactly how teachers are to present the didactic materials. Remember that Montessori believed that children's minds were absorbent and highly influenced, positively or negatively, by their environments and adult interactions. Considering this framework, it naturally follows that the method of introducing the materials that will guide the child's development must be carefully and deliberately demonstrated. Visit www.montessori-ami.org to learn more about the history and practices of Montessori teacher training.

- Instructing the child. "Watch me do this work first; then you can try it if you like."
- Silently completing the button dressing frame work

Then the teacher slowly and deliberately demonstrates unbuttoning and rebuttoning the series of buttons, labeling both the unbuttoned and buttoned positions. When she has finished, she invites the child to try this work on his or her own, either at that time or later. Although the action of buttoning and unbuttoning may seem like a simple enough task, the teacher has 25 steps to follow according to Montessori's script for introducing this work. In fact, every lesson, including sweeping sawdust (34 steps), handling a book (42 steps), saying thank you (16 steps), and pouring between two jugs (26 steps), has a very detailed method of presentation to the child (Gettman, 1987). Limiting the amount of teacher talk is a part of Montessori's effort to free the children from undue teacher control (Cossentino, 2006).

After the presentation is complete, the teacher leaves the child to his or her independent work, either with the new material or with something else of the child's choosing. For the better part of the morning (3-hour work periods being ideal), children are independently engaged in working with materials of their choosing and are usually intently focused on their work. The child's independence, in turn, leaves the teacher free to address the last, equally important, of her primary tasks: the focused observation of the child engaged in work.

The Teacher as Observer

Throughout her career, Montessori fought against dissenting public opinion about her program model. One of the main arguments she made in favor of the validity of her approach was the fact that this was a scientific model (Rambusch, 1992). Her work was based on many years of work with children from a medical, psychiatric, and educational perspective. Montessori's emphasis on the teacher as a trained, objective observer was one of the main components of the professional, scientific model. She insisted that childhood was a special period and that children demonstrated unique processes, not merely scaled-down versions of adult needs and abilities (Goffin, 1994; Montessori, 1966). This intimate knowledge of children and the ability to observe them carefully were also aspects of prime importance in teacher training.

Putting It Into Practice

Make Your Own Smelling Jars

Use old film canisters or small bottles to create pairs of matching smells. Label one set with colored tape or some other distinctive mark so the child knows one is a tester and one is a matcher. Using a variety of extracts, spices, coffee grounds, or other safe items, put a scented cotton ball in each of two containers (making pairs). Glue a piece of mesh or screen over the can, fitting under the lid. Children then choose one match can and smell each of the tester cans to identify the correct match. You can use the same process to make sound cylinders. Use a variety of materials to make different sounds when shaken.

Only through the careful study of scientific methods of inquiry and observation and only through the complete divorcing of one's personality and ego could a teacher truly observe and see children's development unfold. This separation of one's self was critically important in the Montessori teacher. The Montessori teacher was instead trained to focus solely on the child as the director of his or her own development and learning (Swan, 1987). Although this may sound radical, in essence it is the same motivation in practice in today's child-centered programming. Consider how this Montessori teacher uses cooperative learning and focuses on each child's unique strengths and needs in this **video**.

First, the stage was set through the careful preparation of the environment and deliberate instruction on the self-correcting materials. Then the teacher was free to occupy her time not in detrimental interference of the child's work, but rather in watching the child's unfolding developmental path with reverence and care. Furthermore, having taken the time to witness this unfolding, the teacher was trained to carefully document her observations of the child's actions (Montessori, 1966). The teacher's analyses of the observations then served as a guide in the planning and assessing of instruction and material selection for each child.

This intense observation and documentation allowed the teacher to come to know each child's abilities and needs intimately. As with all quality early childhood practice, you can see the emphasis on using observations and documentation of children as a means of assessment and planning. It is hoped you are starting to see why your professors give you so many observation assignments in your classes!

MONTESSORI MATERIALS AND ACTIVITIES

This research-oriented practice elevated the status of the teacher's work from the more custodial nature of ensuring safety and care to the highly professional work of ensuring optimal, healthful development of the body, mind, and spirit. This attitude of professionalism, combined with the strict training teachers received, was necessary to maintain Montessori's vision just as she crafted it, even as her method was spreading internationally.

Perhaps compelled by the fact that her materials were carefully designed after years of observing children engaged with their explorations, Montessori was also adamant that only her original materials be purchased and used with her method (Goffin, 1994). Authentic, well-crafted Montessori materials can be a significant expense. Equipping a classroom with a complete repertoire of materials can cost up to $25,000 (AMS, n.d.). True Montessorians would not promote cutting corners; however, substitute materials can be crafted to achieve similar learning goals when expense is an issue. The high quality of well-crafted, well-designed Montessori materials and the emphasis on coaching children to properly care for their environment and materials does ensure that they will last for decades.

Over the years there has been much discussion about Montessori's self-correcting materials. Based on her observations and beliefs about children's development, the materials are purposeful, realistic, and concrete. They are designed and sequenced to provide children with experiences to satisfy their current developmental tasks. They are also designed to lay a foundation to prepare children for later academic and life tasks. When children enter the Montessori program, they are to begin with the simpler activities and progress to more challenging materials and activities as their own individual pace dictates, as observed by the teachers.

There are five overarching curricular areas that are addressed at increasing levels in the method and materials:

1. Practical life activities
2. Sensorial
3. Cultural
4. Language
5. Mathematics

Although most of the levels of activity include experiences in each of these areas, within the child's initial experience in the Montessori environment, there are no explicit mathematics activities per se. Instead, the child's experiences with some of the materials in other areas prepare the child for later mathematical activities (Gettman, 1987).

Practical Life Activities

Within the scope of early practical life activities, some of the tasks children engage in include tasks of pouring from one pitcher to another; completing simple dressing frames (buttoning, buckling); courtesy tasks such as saying thank you; self-care tasks such as hanging and folding clothes and brushing hair; and movement tasks such as sitting and rising from a chair, lifting and carrying a tray, and dusting. As children become more familiar with the Montessori environment, they progress to more advanced practical life activities such as polishing and cleaning different surfaces, being silent, greeting people, handling a book, using more difficult dressing frames such as tying and lacing, ironing, and simple cooking. Once children progress into the upper age of the mixed-age group, practical life activities include caring for and comforting younger children, caring for the environment, serving snacks and meals, and ultimately presenting early practical life activities to new children.

Throughout the sequence of practical life activities, we can see an emphasis on positive social behaviors, self-care, care of the environment, and consideration of others. The children's demonstration of respect for themselves, their environment, and the people around them often seems remarkable to visitors to Montessori classrooms. Remember from the classroom observation that the teacher described these qualities as essential and as being at the core of their classroom experience. When Montessori created her method for the impoverished children in the Casa dei Bambini, these skills were absolutely necessary for their success in life and basic health.

The Pink Tower develops sight discrimination and motor skills.

Sensorial Activities

Sensorial activities are designed to awaken and train children's senses. Montessori firmly believed that children learn best through their senses. Activities in the early sensorial domain include exploring size and dimension with a series of cylinder blocks that fit into precise holes based on their size; working with the pink tower (solid blocks in successively smaller units); using geometric solids, sound boxes, and bells tuned in a scale; and working with cubes and numeric rods. More advanced sensorial experiences include exploring a square of Pythagoras; discriminating a variety of fabrics by touch; exploring a mystery bag and other blindfolded discrimination work; using smelling jars and tasting cups; performing advanced sound work with the bells; and ultimately presenting early sensorial activities to younger children.

Even in the earliest sensorial activities, we can see the groundwork for later mathematical, logical, and spatial thought. Children learn to identify shape, order, size, and volume. As children progress to increasingly more difficult tasks and levels, as their development begins to move from concrete to more abstract, the emphasis shifts away from sensorial and practical life activities to the cultural, language, and mathematics domains.

Cultural Activities

Montessori advocated that humans learn not solely through biology, as other animals do, but through our shared culture and individual adaptations of our cultural experiences. These tendencies include affective characteristics such as curiosity and a desire to explore, the need to communicate and share experiences, an interest in calculating, and working toward lofty goals in the pursuit of independence. These qualities are indeed many of the forces that make us uniquely human. Within the cultural area, children explore concepts such as land and water formations, maps, classification pictures, past and present, air, gravity, sound, optics, plant life cycles, geography, and nature and human history and civilization studies. In this area, we can see how Montessori sought to address dispositional and affective needs of the child, along with instilling a respect for the environment and humankind (Williams & Keith, 2000).

Language Activities

In addition to these cultural qualities, our ability to master and use language allows us to connect in social groups; communicate and share on surface and profound levels; and organize our thoughts into coherent, complex forms. As we know from observations, the task of mastering language (in all its forms) is a major developmental endeavor of the young child. As such, it occupies a prime place in the young child's educational life. Montessori developed language activities that, in the early levels, begin with exploring pictures, books, and sounds. Later language experiences progress to exploring the written word through tracing sandpaper letters and metal shape insets and eventually to manipulating and outlining movable alphabet letters to make words and sentences.

Language activities ultimately culminate in the child's ability to write down thoughts and to read and understand the writing of others. Children in Montessori classrooms can be observed using their communication skills to engage in group dialogues and, in early primary grades, in fantasy play. Even though there are no dramatic play areas in the early classrooms (Montessori did not value fantasy play for young children), children still develop imaginary stories and tell them to each other (Soundy, 2003). Through the activities in this domain, children's linguistic and related cognitive skills are encouraged as the children are continuing to become more and more independent within their world.

Mathematics

The final area of Montessori activities falls within the mathematical concepts of counting and arithmetic. Montessori noticed, as many parents and teachers might, that children actually embrace activities of sorting, categorizing, quantifying ("His piece is bigger than mine!"), and performing basic arithmetical functions ("Now I'm going to take one away from him so I have more.") and have a natural inclination toward exploring many mathematical concepts. These natural tendencies are enhanced through carefully timed introduction of sequential number rods, sandpaper numbers, bean sorting and counting, number cards, memory games using numbers, more complex decimal counting beads, fraction exercises, more complex arithmetical functions with beads (subtraction, multiplication, and division), and the use of charts and boards to explore multiplication and division.

As mentioned previously, several of the earlier explorations with sensorial activities, such as geometric solids and sequential blocks, build a conceptual foundation for later, more abstract mathematical skills. Planning that builds earlier experiences as a foundation for later, more complex tasks is seen throughout the Montessori curriculum. The process of later skills building on previously accomplished skills is one of the hallmarks of any developmental program since this process is at work in all human development. (For example, we learn to balance upright prior to standing, then learn to walk, and walk prior to running, etc.) This is another example of how Montessori's method strives to be in balance with the child's natural developmental processes.

CRITIQUES, ACCOLADES, AND APPLICATIONS

Throughout our introduction to Montessori's unique method of working with young children, you may have noted some surprising elements that may have seemed contradictory or controversial. Think about what you know about lesson planning or perhaps your own teaching. Do you analyze every aspect to the degree that Montessori did in her detailed, step-by-step system? Do you notice a plentiful amount of verbal interactions and dialogues about materials and activities? Or perhaps you notice a discord between philosophy and practices that promote imaginative play as a primary way for children to learn. These are all aspects of Montessori's philosophy and method that have sparked debate and critical reflection among early childhood professionals—including Montessori teachers.

Contrary to the currently and widely held belief that children learn through meaningful play, Montessori viewed play, imagination, toys, and games as frivolous to learning. She regarded these activities as counterproductive to the young child's own drive to purposefully engage with realistic, practical activities (Montessori, 1966; Cossentino, 2006). Through her observations, she noted that children appeared to be entertained for a brief period by play and toys, yet remained somehow unsatisfied and easily drawn away from them when productive work and tools were available. She noted, "since a child always has some important thing at hand, he is not particularly interested in playing" (Montessori, 1966, p. 122). She believed that the adult ideal of learning through play and letting childhood be a time of fun and imagination was nothing more than that: an adult ideal that was in conflict with the child's need for productive developmental "work" (Gettman, 1987). Montessori considered frivolous play—as well as stifling advanced academic lessons—something the teacher ought to redirect children away from (Montessori, 1967). Born out of a tremendous respect for children's capabilities, Montessori's method seeks to value the child's ability to become intently and joyfully focused in productive exploration. She felt that it was these explorations that served a mysterious inner developmental need that arose within the child (Montessori, 1965).

Montessori's detailed procedure for presenting lessons with limited verbal exchange is another aspect of her method with which contemporary teachers and teacher education students may disagree. Montessori's restriction on teacher-child dialogues might feel at odds with many researchers who advocate for plentiful, warm teacher-child interactions. Many early childhood education programs today promote more of a busy, joyfully boisterous classroom environment in which children are encouraged to play, dialogue, and explore learning centers in small and large socially interactive groups. Play as the primary vehicle for children's learning and development is routinely promoted as a benchmark of high-quality practice. This ongoing tension and dialogue is an example of the richness of diversity among approaches and can offer an interesting source of professional debate.

There are many people in the field of early childhood education who show concern over the seemingly rigid, narrow way in which the children are directed to use the materials and de-emphasis of child-initiated and fantasy play. These concerns are not easily resolved, and as reflective practitioners, it is important for educators to continually analyze alternative methods and theories. Through your reflections and dialogues, you will find elements you choose not to use, but you will also find elements to embrace that enhance your own perspective and approach to teaching. This is your task throughout this text and your education studies.

Montessori's Enduring Legacy

Amid criticism, the Montessori method has contributed aspects worthy of recognition to nearly all early childhood classrooms. Her series of blocks in sequential order (short to long, low to high, thin to wide); geometric solids; sense-discrimination tasks (smell, touch, taste, hearing); dressing frames; and sorting tasks—to name just a few of the inviting sensorial works—are widely considered staples in most preschools. Her theories concerning children as active, sensory learners have also greatly contributed to current practice and understanding in the field. Her goals to have teachers carefully understand each child's development and individualize planning are keys to quality care and education within any approach.

Providing self-directed activities with purposeful work is a hallmark of Montessori practice and is integrated into many differing types of programs today.

Student Outcomes

Teachers and prospective teachers studying Montessori's method often wonder about comparative research exploring effectiveness of her programs. Although the research base is relatively small, one study reported higher academic achievement on math and science tests for Montessori graduates who attended Montessori public school programs from ages 3 to 11 (Gartner, Lipsky, & Dohrmann, 2003). Another study of 5-year-olds attending a public Montessori program demonstrated significantly higher achievement in language and math skills and, most notably, in children's reasoning, fairness, and social problem-solving (Lillard & Else-Quest, 2006). Montessori programs' emphasis on culture studies and conflict resolution, such as the use of a peace table for children to independently resolve social conflicts together, have been applauded as innovative contributions to positive social change and education for democracy (Williams & Keith, 2000). Watch this **video** of a peaceful conflict-resolution process at a classroom peace table for an example of how children can be actively involved in negotiating through conflicts.

Montessori wrote extensively about children deeply engrossed in their work, intently focused on an unfolding inner process. In essence, she reported that children seemed to get into a "flow." Recently researchers have taken an interest in this intent work, this flow, and have sought to evaluate this and other dispositional or emotional experiences in the classroom. A study of more than 300 middle school students' reports demonstrated higher affective (emotional) satisfaction in the Montessori programs (Rathunde, 2003). Montessori students reported feeling more comfortable, supported, and successful than their traditional school counterparts. Among these important findings were increased student reports of intrinsic motivation in Montessori programs. In other words, students in Montessori programs reported feeling more internally driven and personally satisfied with their schoolwork and school experiences. As the research base continues to build, more specific effects of Montessori education will be explored and identified.

Application Ideas

Some general applications of Montessori's method in any early childhood setting include the following ideas:

- Use trays, small baskets, place mats, or carpet squares to organize the environment to clearly define space for individual materials and individual children's work.
- Integrate materials that focus on addressing concrete self-help skill building (dressing, cleaning).
- Provide long blocks of time for children to engage with materials.
- Maintain an orderly, cleanly designed environment.
- Promote respect for environment, self, and others through caretaking messages and lessons.
- Take time to observe individual children, taking careful notes on their actions and language to determine developmental progress and plan for next steps.
- Provide materials and experiences in an array of curricular areas.

CONCLUSION

There is much to be learned from Montessori's philosophy and methods, which have endured for more than 100 years. Above all else, we can embrace the reverence and respect for children that is such an integral part of Montessori's theory and practice (Williams & Keith, 2000). Montessori's emphasis on a carefully prepared environment, deliberate interactions, and use of observations to assess and plan for children remain respected elements of quality, developmentally based practice. Through her careful documentation and prolific writing, she has reshaped the role of the teacher and the design of the child's environment to better reflect children's needs. Classrooms are now routinely places where children can independently choose and access materials. Materials and activities are sensory based, and teachers continue to carefully train themselves to be objective observers of children's independent, active engagement. Teachers use their observations of children to plan for them and guide their work with the materials.

Although some elements of her method might not fit in with your own personal philosophy, it is important to carefully consider her beliefs, philosophy, and practice as you continue to develop your own eclectic approach to teaching young children. Yours will be an approach that will combine key elements of many exemplary models and will be tailored to suit the individual children with whom you work. It is this sharing of ideas and individualizing of our approaches that make the professional practice of education a dynamic, progressive field.

SUMMARY

- Maria Montessori's work began with observations of institutionalized children's attention and interaction with her specially designed materials.
- Montessori opened her first early childhood center in 1907 as an intervention program for children from low-income families in Rome, Italy.

- Montessori observed that children develop through spontaneous, sensory activity that is free from undue adult interference.

- Montessori believed that children develop through sensitive periods when learning in specific domains is optimal.

- In Montessori classrooms, children's drive to seek order and structure in their world is supported through focused engagement with materials and in purposeful work.

- Montessori teachers serve three primary roles: carefully preparing the environment, introducing and modeling proper use of the materials, and observing and documenting children's learning.

- The specially designed materials cover five key curriculum areas: practical life, sensorial, cultural, language, and mathematics.

- Critiques of Montessori's method include concern for the prescribed nature of material presentation and use and debates over the role of child-initated imaginative play.

CHAPTER LEARNING GOALS SELF-ASSESSMENT

Use this chart to write down three to five key points for each learning goal that you learned from this chapter.

Explore important events in Montessori's life and work.	
Identify important aspects of children's development and learning in Montessori classrooms.	
Examine essential roles of the Montessori teacher.	
Describe materials in the five key curricular areas of the Montessori method.	
Compare critiques, successes, and widely accepted applications of Montessori's work.	

APPLICATION ACTIVITIES

Discussion Prompts

1. How do you feel about teachers being given detailed, scripted routines for presenting materials? In what ways could you see this helping or hindering the teacher and/or children?

2. Identify other teacher roles that you feel are important and plan to use in your own teaching.

3. How involved with children should a teacher be while observations are being conducted? Would there be a difference between actively teaching or refraining from contact during observations?

In Class   Working in pairs, identify three questions you would ask Montessori if you could have lunch with her right now. Write them down. Share them in class with your instructor. Using Internet sources, such as various Montessori associations and articles, as well as any local Montessori schools you may have available, try to find the answers to your questions.

In the Field   Arrange to visit a Montessori program in your area. During your visit, try to interview an administrator or a teacher as well as observe a classroom. If you do not have a Montessori center near you, arrange a phone interview. Is the center associated with a Montessori organization? What ages does the program serve? Are the teachers Montessori trained? If so, where did they complete their training? Identify aspects of the classroom and school that illustrate Montessori principles and methodology. Identify and describe authentic Montessori materials.

For Your Portfolio   Montessori insisted on the use of her commercially available materials, but many can be made on your own. Research her materials (try www.montessori-ami.org) and make substitutes for two of them. Try to make your own version as close as possible to her version.

For example, make your own shape inserts. (Purpose: Children learn shapes and can trace insert.) Using heavy cardstock squares, cut out exact shapes using a razor knife so the shape and frame are intact. Glue a small knob, such as a pencil eraser, small block, or bead, to the insert so children can pick it up out of the frame. Children then can remove the shapes from the frames and practice finding the correct frame for each shape.

RELATED WEB LINKS

North American Montessori Teachers' Association
www.montessori-namta.org/

Association Montessori Internationale
www.montessori-ami.org/

American Montessori Society
www.amshq.org/

11 Waldorf Education: Harmony and the Whole Child

Chapter Learning Goals

- Explore the history and philosophical foundations of Waldorf education.
- Identify key aspects of child development in Waldorf education.
- Describe major themes in Waldorf early childhood practice.
- Examine essential roles of the Waldorf teacher.
- Discuss the integrated, spiral curriculum in Waldorf education.
- Explore diversity in Waldorf practice.
- Compare critiques, success, and applications of Waldorf education.

Waldorf education is a unique approach that views children as complex, whole human beings developing in mind, body, and spirit—or head, hands, and heart. The Waldorf philosophy is based on this holistic approach to education and operates under the often-used principle of education toward freedom. Waldorf schools strive to foster an environment in which children are free to explore themselves and their world and ultimately develop into capable, competent, caring adults. This approach to education strives to develop children's ability to think creatively and analytically. In this highly creative model of education, early childhood classrooms are routinely abuzz with dialogue, storytelling, building, painting, creative fantasy play, and representation of individual knowledge and experience. Waldorf education is an approach that seeks to offer a model of education with the goals of social renewal and strengthening society.

Throughout the educational experiences of all students, Waldorf education is designed to develop well-rounded individuals. This chapter presents the key elements that make up the Waldorf education approach, including its history, philosophy, and pedagogy, with a particular emphasis on the early years.

CLASSROOM VIEW

The Waldorf Nursery-Kindergarten

Imagine a room softly lit by the early fall morning sunshine peeking through large, arching windows. The morning sun shines through the tall trees outside the windows, making dappled marks on the earth-toned area carpet. The windows are gently draped in a soft pink silk fabric. The walls are painted in a light peach color, using a fluid color-washed technique to create a feeling of blended waves of peach tones. Wooden support beams rise from the wooden floor to the high ceiling at obtuse angles, not the usual 90-degree angles. The gentle arch of the beams, roundness of the room, and soft colors foster an embracing feeling. The space smells warm, like bread rising, nearly ready for baking. All these sensations make the space feel very homelike: warm, gentle, cozy, and inviting.

The natural wood shelves, which line the space, are filled with rocks; crystals; pinecones; baskets of beads and blocks; soft, handmade dolls; and the occasional knitted gnome peering out from among the organic material. There are baskets cradling balls of soft-colored yarn. A child's kitchen area is sectioned off by low wooden dividers. The dividers are draped with colored silk fabric clipped with oversized clothespins. A row of small white slippers is lined up at the door near the children's personal cubbies. The cubbies are labeled with a hand-painted drawing with each child's name and a special design. There are a few low tables at one side of the room. In the open center of the room, there is a round, low tree stump topped with an unlit beeswax candle surrounded by rocks, sticks, leaves, and small felt gnomes. The children's chairs form a ring around the candle. You take in this

In the earliers years, adults create natural, beautiful spaces for children to explore and imitate gentle models and influences.

scene with a deep breath that both relaxes your body and spirit and fills you with the soft scents of bread, beeswax, and pine needles.

The children arrive, replace their shoes with slippers, and begin to quietly enter the room. The classroom teachers warmly greet every child individually in melodic voices. The children move about the room and begin to engage with materials of their choosing. Several children converge in the kitchen area, taking soft, faceless dolls from a shelf and beginning an imaginative play with them. Other children quietly gather around the teacher as she rocks in her rocking chair, sewing more felt dolls. She sings softly, and the children, who are gathering around her feet, take up vegetable-dyed yarn and begin finger knitting.

After all the children have arrived, the teacher sings a song to gently guide them over to their chairs around the candle. She lights the candle to help the sun bring light into the classroom. The children gather, settle into their seats, and wait eagerly while the teacher offers each child a piece of beeswax from a fabric-lined basket. The children take the sculpting material with reverence and delight, cup it in both hands, and watch the teacher as she finishes her round. She takes a deep breath, welcomes the children together, and introduces the story of the day.

While the teacher quietly tells the story of gnomes, fairies, and life in the forest, the children cup the beeswax, occasionally moving their hands as directed in the story. Their hand movements are deliberately directed to warm the wax and make it ready for sculpting. After the story concludes, the teacher brings the children's attention to the now-softened wax in their hands, and they are invited to begin to work with it. The teacher gently guides the children's sculpting: "Children, move the beeswax in your hands this way and that. Let it bend and stretch as the form waiting inside takes shape." As the children complete their sculpting, the teacher extinguishes the candle and talks to the children about their creations. Each sculpture is different. Some children make animals, one child makes a tree, and another makes a bowl-shaped object.

Thus begins a typical day in a Waldorf early childhood room. It is a day that is filled with nature, harmony, song, social interaction, play, and fantasy. This environment is full of reverence for life and nature. It celebrates the innocence and wonder of childhood and embodies the belief that children's play is of the utmost importance.

IN YOUR OWN WORDS

Take a moment now to reflect on some of the early childhood environments you have seen. Make some comparisons to the scene you created in your imagination as you journeyed into a Waldorf classroom. Think about these spaces and the emotional environment that you sensed.

- Do you feel any differences between this early childhood classroom and others you have experienced before?
- What are your beliefs about play and young children's learning?
- How does this environment compare with your own educational experiences?

THE HISTORY AND PHILOSOPHY OF WALDORF EDUCATION

The Waldorf education movement was born during a time of collective social crisis. During the chaos in the early decades of the 20th century, much of Europe struggled to cope with the devastation in the aftermath of World War I. It was during this era that Austrian philosopher Rudolf Steiner devoted his life to exploring human potential, spirituality, and growth and development. Steiner believed that human beings were truly complete only when the three main parts of their being—the body, mind, and spirit—were developed. In the wake of the devastation of World War I, Steiner embarked on a quest to educate the European community on the necessity to reunite the whole human being as a collective effort toward social renewal (Oberman, 1997). Steiner's golden opportunity came in the form of a request to develop a school program for the children of the factory workers at the Waldorf Astoria cigarette factory in Stuttgart, Germany.

A highly spiritual man, Steiner developed his own form of *spiritual science,* called *anthroposophy* (human wisdom). **Anthroposophy** is a movement described as the knowledge and awareness of humanity, with a belief that there is a spiritual world that can be accessed by the highest intellectual faculties (Steiner, 2005). It is a philosophy based on examining more deeply the three parts of the human being (body, mind, and spirit) and the connections that bond humanity together. Although anthroposophy forms the basis of Steiner's educational plan, it is not explicitly taught in Waldorf schools (Nicholson, 2000). Because he believed in a holistic (whole-person) perspective, Steiner asserted that life and education called for schools to address all three elements of the human being. The holistic educator strives toward "the cultivation of a receptive, compassionate awareness, an attitude of wonder, awe and reverence for life" (Miller, 2006 , p. 8). Based on his life's work, the educational curriculum he developed reflects his beliefs that

Anthroposophy
The knowledge and awareness of humanity, with a belief that there is a spiritual world that can be accessed by the highest intellectual faculties.

- children grow through three distinct developmental phases,
- the highest pursuit of education should be to develop the whole child to become a free and creative thinker capable of self-actualization, and
- all children should have the right and access to this form of schooling.

And so it was that the first Waldorf school was opened in Germany in 1919; the first Waldorf school in North America opened in New York City in 1928 (Nicholson, 2000). Steiner insisted that Waldorf schools operate under four key conditions, which were quite radical for the day:

1. The school was open to all children (race, class, ethnicity, ability level).
2. The school was coeducational (accepting boys and girls).
3. The K–12 curriculum was viewed as a unified, complete program.
4. The teachers bore the primary responsibility for control of the administration of the school, with minimal outside interference.

Steiner firmly believed that the social renewal that society so badly needed could be achieved through only the careful education of the whole child (Fenner & Rivers, 1995; Steiner, 1997). His purpose in developing this radical alternative education model "was to create a new impulse in education that would enable children from diverse backgrounds to develop the capacities necessary to cope with the demands and challenges of a postindustrial world" (Easton, 1997 , p. 88). Steiner believed that each school should maintain some commonalities but should also reflect the particular culture and needs of the community in which it was located. In this way, Steiner sought to ensure the relevance, authenticity, and service of each school as it responded to the unique community. Since the opening of the first Waldorf school in 1919, the movement has spread internationally and has become one of the largest independent school movements in the world. As of 2009, there were approximately 900 schools and 1,600 kindergartens operating in 83 countries worldwide. The Association of Waldorf Schools of North America (AWSNA) lists 107 Waldorf teacher-training centers worldwide and reports 250 Waldorf schools and 102 early childhood programs affiliated with the Association in North America alone (AWSNA, n.d.).

BELIEFS ABOUT DEVELOPMENT IN WALDORF EDUCATION

Steiner's theory of child development lays the foundational framework for the development of the curriculum, the design of the classroom space, and the general focus of the approach. As did several other key developmental theorists (e.g., Piaget, Erikson, Kohlberg), Steiner believed that children grow and develop through distinct stages:

- Early childhood (birth to 7 years old)
- Middle childhood (7–14 years old)
- Adolescence (14–21 years old)

The early childhood phase extends from infancy to roughly 7 years of age, when baby teeth are beginning to be replaced by adult teeth. Before this milestone of physical development, Steiner believed that children were still connected to the spiritual world from which they were born (Iannone & Obenauf, 1999). During this formative period, Steiner believed that children were deeply influenced by their environment. Evidence of this is the child's unquestioning imitation of adult models and susceptibility to external stimuli. Consider the toddler who crawls across the floor following the family dog or the preschooler who repeats everything he or she hears. Protecting the child from unhealthful, unnatural, or inappropriate experiences, models, and stimuli—while embodying a reverent teacher archetype—is of the highest importance for the adults in the child's world. As in any developmentally appropriate approach, the heart of Steiner's early childhood practice is focused on teacher-child relationships. Waldorf teachers achieve strong bonds with children through deliberate storytelling, dramatic play, and creative expressions (Mitchell, 2007).

Steiner firmly believed that, during the early years, children's energies needed to focus on developing their physical bodies and imagination. He strongly cautioned against pushing children's development of intellectual skills. This resistance to a so-called push-down effect, or early academic instruction, is supported by educators and researchers (the NAEYC, Lillian Katz), as well as education policy makers across the world (Clouder, 2003). For example, children's early literary experiences in Waldorf kindergartens include oral storytelling, not formal training in decoding words or forming letters. Informal literacy experiences that lay the foundation for structured literacy knowledge, also called **emergent literacy** activities, abound, however, through listening to teacher storytelling, fine-motor development through painting and sculpting, and children's own storytelling. These experiences are viewed as a foundation of thinking and feeling that enable later development in the academic skills required to read and write. The opening classroom visit illustrates the Waldorf emergent literacy process. There, you saw the children listening to a short story, learning about story structure and plot while creating images in their minds to illustrate what they heard. Their imaginary illustrations then came to life in their fine-motor work with the beeswax.

Steiner recognized learning and development as a lifelong process, and he was consequently resistant to pushing children into experiences that were beyond the scope of their naturally unfolding development. This is similar to Froebel's view of a child's garden. Steiner believed intellectual skill building would take the child's natural energies away from their endeavors in creative play, imitation, and refinements in physical development (Steiner, 1997). Steiner believed that the development of a healthy, coordinated

Emergent literacy

Ongoing development of knowledge and skills related to reading and writing that develop over time through informal language activities.

body was a necessary foundation for all later learning. He further explained that the child's innate intelligence of his or her developmental needs and energy to work on those needs must not be "siphoned off too early from this essential task [physical development] into intellectual learning. Therefore, in the Waldorf Kindergarten no academic instruction takes place" (Schmitt-Stegmann, 1997, p. 4). Instead, children's imaginative play in a carefully crafted environment serves as the foundation for later academic knowledge and skill building.

Middle Childhood

According to Steiner, as children begin the transition into middle childhood, which is marked by the transition from baby to adult teeth, their developmental process lies firmly within the domain of imagination. He believed that it was through imagination that children learn the cognitive tasks of concentration, mental imagery, and more complex thinking. It is during this phase that language is refined to adult levels, academic and intellectual work begins, and children are ready to experience their world on a deeper, more conscious level. Here teachers introduce alphabetic and numeric symbols, which are explored throughout all disciplines including literature, drama, stories, art, movement, and languages (Fenner & Rivers, 1995).

In this fully integrated curriculum, conceptual connections are made across disciplines and throughout the child's school years, thereby allowing for a deeper, richer understanding. Children are routinely engaged in creative, hands-on activities that allow them to hold and manipulate concrete examples of more abstract concepts (Nicholson, 2000). This can be seen in the emphasis on art; music; handcrafting (knitting, sewing); woodworking; and dance, which all align with academic subject matter. For example, as children learn basic mathematical concepts, they are simultaneously applying them in their knitting projects as they are planning and counting and increasing and diminishing stitches and rows. Geometric forms are being explored in math classes through painting, drawing, and sculpture and in a special form of dance called **eurythmy**, in which the arms reach out in different angles. Eurythmy is a form of dance in which body movements correspond to musical tones and spoken words. This careful integration of the body and mind is a hallmark of the integrated Waldorf curriculum.

Eurythmy
The art of movement that attempts to make visible the tone and feeling of music and speech.

Whereas the early years are focused on imitation of the physical surroundings, the middle childhood years emphasize explorations through language, feelings, and imagination. Throughout the Waldorf school experience, teachers embrace multiple representation methods for exploring content. Teachers routinely use storytelling, song, music, visual art, drama, movement, written word, and diagrams to present content (Nicholson, 2000). In turn, students are able to use multiple forms of representation to explore and share their understanding.

Adolescence

Often noted for its turbulent nature, adolescence marks the rocky transition from child to young adult. Steiner saw this as a time when youths are forming strength in their individual identity at the same time that they are developing feelings of social connectedness. It is during this time that youths could develop a deep and abiding love of humankind—a fraternity that would allow for the development of respect, morality, character, and social consciousness (Steiner, 1997). Although all the traditional academic areas are required parts of the curriculum (sciences, mathematics, English, arts, technology, foreign language, health, etc.), a holistic approach to learning continues throughout the high school years. Along with academic expectations, social consciousness remains a focus for Waldorf high school teachers today. This can be seen in the community service component of the high school curriculum and in the international exchange programs that are promoted in most Waldorf schools.

WALDORF EARLY CHILDHOOD PROGRAMS

In the nursery-kindergarten room, the Waldorf school classroom is designed to be a place of harmony, beauty, and gentle guidance. It is a place where the innocence of childhood is protected and revered. Specially trained teachers, who believe that the first phase children grow through is that of imitation, serve as the purest form of model. All the materials in the child's world are natural and inspire creative play. The foods served are organic, nutritious, and often grown by the class members themselves. Children are provided with long periods of outdoor play to encourage healthful physical development and a spiritual connection to nature. The open-ended, hands-on design of the materials and the aesthetic focus of the curriculum encourage development in all children, including children with special needs (Edwards, 2002).

Like Montessori, Steiner observed that young children unquestioningly imitate and absorb their surroundings. Thus, he believed that adults, through careful and deliberate action, should prepare and present an environment worthy of children. Unlike Montessori, however, he asserted that the child's early years should be a time of creative play and imaginative fantasy play. We could see this emphasis during the opening visit to the Waldorf nursery-kindergarten as the children transitioned to their beeswax-modeling activity after hearing a gnome story.

Other familiar characters the children come to know through the teachers' stories and displays include angels, fairies, fairy tales, and other stories about animals and woodland spirits. Traditionally, fairy tales are told from their original version (Grimm and Andersen, for example). These versions include graphic parts about death and suffering that may concern some early childhood teachers. In their storytelling process, however, Waldorf teachers skim such details in a matter-of-fact way that does not dramatize them or emotionally arouse the children (Astley & Jackson, 2000). Waldorf teachers prefer this authentic, gentle retelling as opposed to editing stories, which changes their deeper meaning and intentions.

Waldorf early childhood teachers are also adamant about not hiding academics in their curriculum or trying to mask academic lessons through play. Steiner believed that education should fit the child, not the other way around. Because he cautioned against pushing children before they are developmentally ready (Ogletree, 1975), there are usually no books, letters, or printed numbers in the nursery-kindergarten classroom. However, the nurturing of naturally unfolding development in young children is part of the complete academic curriculum for nursery-kindergarten to 12th grade. It is carefully constructed to develop strong cognitive, social, emotional, and physical development throughout the child's early life into young adulthood. Recall that one of Steiner's four key conditions set at the time he created the model was that the school be a unified K–12 program. The

Waldorf Nursery-Kindergarten

Sample Half-Day Daily Schedule

8:00 A.M.	Teachers prepare for children's arrival
8:20 A.M.	Children arrive, begin engaging with materials such as finger knitting; children gather with teachers for oral storytelling; may include beeswax modeling, movement and music, special celebrations
8:50 A.M.	Free play, dramatic play, cooking or baking activities
10 A.M.	Snack together
10:20 A.M.	Outdoors, free play, gardening
11:30 A.M.	Lunch together
12:30 P.M.	Prepare for departure

foundations that are laid in the early years are built on in later years and seek to instill a lifelong love of learning more than just attainment of certain skills. This big picture, or awareness of what lies ahead for the developing child, is always in the forefront of Waldorf educators' minds.

The experiences in early childhood are meant to develop a strong intellect through

- imitating exemplary models in carefully constructed environments;
- communing with nature through ample daily outdoor play and gardening;
- fostering the child's imagination through storytelling and play; and
- creative experiences such as painting, movement, and drawing, which build skills for later literacy.

Children's self-initiated play with natural, open-ended materials is viewed as the most appropriate means of development at this phase. Nursery-kindergarten materials include yarns, blocks, dolls, paints, sculpting materials, household artifacts, instruments, natural elements, and dress-up scarves.

These simple hand-knitted dolls, with their formless bodies and blank faces, are typical toys Waldorf teachers make for their children. The lack of form and expression is intentional, to encourage children to use their imaginations to create features.

Children's play is allowed to flow freely from the children as much as possible. They are given long, uninterrupted blocks of time and ample open-ended materials to engage in child-initiated social or individual play experiences. The children engage in a great deal of dramatic play, which may entail building tentlike homes from lengths of silk fabric and clothespins and caring for cloth dolls. Blocks (often made from smoothed slices of tree branches) and collections of natural materials are on hand for other constructions. Sculpting with beeswax, knitting, gardening, and sewing are routine activities. Teachers remain in the background, modeling such tasks as cooking, baking, knitting, tidying, and gardening; the children are free to move about the classroom at their will. There is a pervasive feeling of harmony, gentleness, dreaminess, and calm that surrounds children in the Waldorf nursery-kindergarten. This is promoted through soft lighting; muted colors; melodic singing; and the slow, deliberate actions of the teachers. Visit a Waldorf classroom and observe these elements in this **video**.

WALDORF EARLY CHILDHOOD TEACHER ROLES

Steiner observed that children were deeply affected by their surroundings and experiences. He became increasingly concerned with tracing later adult dysfunctions to negative experiences of children reared in a careless environment (Waldorf Kindergarten Association, 1994). Thus, especially in the Waldorf nursery-kindergarten, the role of the teacher is viewed as particularly important. As you explore this role more deeply by revisiting our focus on the early childhood years, keep the broader contexts of the whole child and unified K–12 perspectives in mind.

Teacher Preparations: Self and Environment

As mentioned previously, early childhood teachers recognize children's early years as a period in which children deeply absorb their surroundings and imitate the adults in their world. The teacher is entrusted with the task of serving as an ideal model (in action and words) and the protector of children's innocence. Above all else, teachers strive to provide children with a sheltered environment. Much preparation goes into being a Waldorf teacher. There are special training institutes, and a specialized teaching certification is required. Part of this training focuses on the philosophical underpinnings of Steiner's work. Another part of it focuses on nourishing the teacher's creative skills so that he or she may, in turn, model these qualities for the children (Oberski, Pugh, MacLean, & Cope, 2007).

During the Waldorf teacher training, in addition to learning about anthroposophy, the teacher would explore the roles of

- storyteller,
- embodiment of the parent figures,
- protector of the child's innate drives and creativity, and
- nurturer of children's play.

The teacher spends a great deal of time lovingly preparing the classroom environment to feel like a household. Teachers make cloth dolls and collect materials from nature to enhance the children's play. Teachers learn poems, stories, and songs to fill the children's day with fantasy and wonder. They create works of watercolor art to enrich the aesthetic beauty surrounding the classroom. Teachers learn how to knit, weave, sew, and create pictures using pieces of fluffy, colored wools (a handcraft called *felting* (Waldorf Kindergarten Association, 1993).

Teacher as a Model

Steiner envisioned an early childhood teacher as one who embodies the ideal parental persona: loving, deliberate, careful, watchful, supportive, and present but not imposing. Early childhood teachers express delight and inner satisfaction as they engage in daily activities that mimic home life: gardening, baking, woodworking, caring for the classroom space, and interacting meaningfully with the children (Fenner & Rivers, 1995). When the teacher wants the children to do something (clean up, gather together, prepare for an outing), he or she begins by modeling the action and gently using a song to verbally draw the children to the activity.

Teachers strive to maintain a harmonious, peaceful space by using song and story to direct the children. They would never use a harsh or raised tone of voice or a forceful movement. Indeed, all movements are deliberate and pensive, always keeping in mind that young children take every aspect of their surroundings into themselves and seek to preserve a dreamy quality. When watching Waldorf teachers, you have the sense of the movements of a graceful, deliberate dancer. All these aspects of the teachers' roles of creating the environment and being a model are carried out with care and reflection (Astley & Jackson, 2000). Waldorf teachers strive to be thoughtful in all their actions, always aware of the children in their care.

Teacher as an Observer

During the hours the children are in the classroom, the teachers engage in purposeful activity as well as careful observation of the children. Knowing each individual child is an essential aspect in the Waldorf teacher's role, and this is often accomplished through observation, strong parent relationships, and communication. It is through an intimate knowledge of each child's unique personality that the Waldorf teacher is able to support each child's growth and celebrate the individuality of each. To allow for the child's true spirit and nature to be exercised, as well as for ample teacher observation, the schedule in the early childhood classroom is fairly open.

Each day begins with a long period of free play, later accompanied by such outdoor experiences as gardening, nature walks, and playing on the school grounds. The class also comes together to share poems, songs, and a nutritious snack consisting of bread or soup made by the teachers or fruits or vegetables grown in the class garden (Waldorf Kindergarten Association, 1993). When space or season makes home growing of food impossible, the children are still given organic, whole foods from local farms. The closeness children feel to nature is preserved throughout all activities as well as in the selection of materials and foods.

The activities of daily life, focus on routines, and explorations of nature largely make up the basic elements of the curriculum in the early childhood classroom. As such, the teachers do not rely on standardized tests or intelligence measures to assess children's development. Beginning in early childhood, observations and portfolios of children's

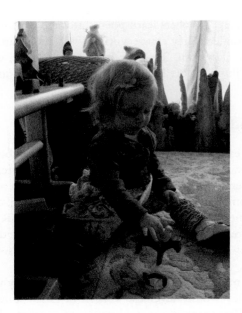

Waldorf teachers create beautiful spaces filled with natural materials to support and enrich children's play.

work are used. Teachers throughout all the grades write reflective statements about each child's progress, which are compiled with work samples to demonstrate developmental progress. It is important with any assessment plan that the methods used reflect the educational experience. By using authentic assessment methods such as observations and work samples, Waldorf teachers strive to validate each child's unique characteristics and progress.

WALDORF CURRICULUM

By working with their hands while gardening, modeling, painting, or sewing, children develop the capacity for later writing, dance, and visual lessons. Through their creative play and sharing of stories, children develop the capacity for later intellectual, social, and imaginative tasks. In this way, the early childhood teacher lays the groundwork for the child's later experiences in elementary classrooms. Teachers at all levels are intimately knowledgeable about the entire curriculum, and they are in close contact with each other. In keeping with Steiner's original condition that school administration be part of the teachers' role, teachers meet regularly to plan and discuss instructional and curricular goals. This is one small way in which teachers view their work as a part of a larger, unified program that is embodied in the view of the curriculum as an *ascending spiral* (Nicholson, 2000).

The curriculum in the Waldorf school is carefully and thoughtfully designed to be viewed as a unified whole from kindergarten to the 12th grade. Content, skills, attitudes, and knowledge areas are visited and revisited at different levels in what is referred to as an ascending spiral. This means that children explore topics and their world at earlier ages; similar topics are repeated and explored as the children's maturity levels change and their cognitive processes develop. This ensures that children are continually engaged in authentic experiences that are both familiar and new, and they are engaged at a level that progresses with them. In this way, the curriculum is developmentally appropriate and addresses the most important criteria required for learning to occur: that learning activities be meaningful and appropriate for children's age and developmental level. This also allows for later academic experiences to build on early experiences, giving children a frame of reference with which to better understand increasingly complex ideas.

Cultivating Imagination as a Precursor to Intellect

The early childhood classrooms are generally structured as a nursery school model, in which children come to school for the morning, sometimes only two or three mornings a week. In addition to presenting pure and idealistic models and protecting the innocence of childhood, teachers endeavor to celebrate and revere children's fantasy and creative play. To this end, teachers do not expose children to printed literature, which includes only illustrations generated by adults. As noted earlier, children are continually exposed to language through oral storytelling, which is believed to allow the mind's eye to create images of their own design. This resistance to early academics also means that children are not pushed to read and write in the early childhood classroom.

Formal training in reading and writing is reserved for introduction later in the second or third grade (Oppenheimer, 1999). However, children are routinely developing and refining their fine-motor skills and exploring shape through sculpting and painting and in their play. Young children draw with blocks of beeswax crayons, as opposed to stick-shaped crayons, which more closely resemble writing implements. They are routinely exposed to different forms of stories, characters, and authors through the storytelling. These experiences are viewed as the appropriate early foundations that support later reading and writing when the children's intellect is developmentally ready (Fenner & Rivers, 1995).

This point is often surprising to outsiders, and it can be a source of concern in today's academically focused early childhood world. Despite ample support by prominent early childhood experts on the potentially negative effect of pushing academics too early (referred to in Oppenheimer, 1999, and Clouder, 2003), some people are critical of this practice. Take a moment to close your eyes and conjure up an image of a talking mouse that has all kinds of adventures. Did you immediately think of Walt Disney's Mickey Mouse? Indeed, you would not be alone; many people would. But this image was just Disney's vision of a mouse, so why should so many of us conjure up the same image? Why are we not able to develop our own vision?

Waldorf educators believe that early exposure to print and media images can have detrimental effects on our ability to create our own ideas, vision, and imagination. When we are not allowed or encouraged to develop strong imagination skills, we may never

Block crayons are made from beeswax and designed to encourage shading, not line drawing.

hone this active, creative potential. This may leave us instead passively relying on someone else's vision through the variety of media forms that abound. Remember that Waldorf education seeks to develop independent, creative thinkers. Thus, the loss of our unique power of creative imagination is something that the curriculum is designed to prevent. Certainly, advocating for a resistance to early academics, technology in classrooms, and media influences such as television and movies may not be the most popular position today. On the other hand, it is important to keep in mind that Waldorf early childhood classrooms value children's play, social interactions, and inquisitive explorations of their world. And these are widely considered to be important characteristics of good practice that may be jeopardized when media and technology bombard the senses.

Recent research on academic proficiency of students attending four public schools using Waldorf methods found that although language and mathematics test scores of the Waldorf-method school second-graders were "far below their peers[,] by eighth grade, however, they were on par with the top 10 peer-alike public schools. Overall, the Waldorf eighth-graders often performed a tiny bit lower on the language arts (reading and writing), and moderately better on mathematics" (Oberman, 2008, p. 12). Furthermore, other studies of private Waldorf graduates revealed that the Waldorf school students earn SAT scores above the national average, but Waldorf schools also instill in students critical thinking skills, global awareness and concern for others, stronger relationships, and dedication to lifelong learning (Mitchell & Gerwin, 2007; Oppenheimer, 1999). Coupled with strong academic achievement in the later grades, these attitudes and dispositions are widely valued in schools and society.

The Integrated Curriculum

The Waldorf K–12 curriculum also takes an integrated approach, recognizing that content must be meaningful, applicable, and used in context. In this way, children explore content and topics through multiple modes, including foreign languages, literature, arts, movement, discussion, experiment, debate, and so on. A truly hands-on model, Waldorf education seeks to develop in all children the ability to engage with the world on a concrete level and later to expand that experience to an abstract, thoughtful, spiritual level. The curriculum allows for an exceptional degree of individual expression. This also contributes to the personal meaning and relevance of all studies. One of the ways in which Waldorf education integrates the individual into all learning is through the reliance on the student's writing and illustrating of his or her own "textbooks" (blank artist's sketchbooks), commonly called **main lesson books**.

Main lesson books

Blank books that each student fills with information and student-generated illustrations that align with each new course of study.

Much of the content in the elementary grades is explored through lectures, dialogues, body movements, and active experiments. Rarely will children be seen passively relying solely on a textbook as the main source of information (Nicholson, 2000). Rather, teachers and children actively explore their world, finding primary sources of information. Children chronicle their newfound knowledge in their blank sketchbooks, in which they write, draw, or paint as they represent their knowledge. Children prepare a new book for each new course of study they undertake (AWSNA, 1996). In this way, Waldorf education uses principles of project work both in the nature of classroom activities and in the myriad ways experiences are represented. Through the use of multiple modes of learning and representation, Waldorf education also aligns with principles of multiple intelligence theory.

Pages from an elementary Waldorf student's main lesson book.

Daily Structure

In the elementary schools, the schedule is constructed around a 2-hour block of study each morning. It is out of this focused study that the student's main lesson books are created. This allows for a more focused, intense experience in which children and teachers concentrate on topics covering all disciplines in turn. The rest of the day is generally divided into the familiar 50-minute periods in which courses in academic subjects such as languages, sciences, and mathematics, as well as creative subjects such as handwork, woodwork, dance, movement, and music, are studied (Fenner & Rivers, 1995). For the most part, all children participate in all classes together, strengthening their bonds as an extended family.

Throughout the first- through eighth-grade years, Waldorf teachers ideally remain with the same class. This practice is called *looping*. **Looping** refers to having the same teacher move through ages or grades with the same class for 2 or more years. This continuity of care is used in various programs from infant care through elementary school grades, although it is practiced more frequently in European and Japanese schools (Hegde & Cassidy, 2004). In Waldorf schools, teachers loop from first grade through eighth grade. Many teachers and parents report increased satisfaction because they are able to develop more profound relationships with each child (Cicala Filmworks, n.d.). Obviously not every Waldorf teacher remains with the same class. The same issues of relocation, staff changes, and so on can be found in individual schools, but looping remains the goal of all Waldorf elementary schools. Although this practice is not unique to Waldorf schools, it is certainly a notable feature of the approach resulting from the scope of the span of grades.

Many people new to Waldorf education are surprised by this practice, expressing concern over the ability of one teacher to provide comprehensive learning experiences for such a range of ages. Newcomers have also raised the potential for personality conflicts to fester for long periods of time as a concern of long-term looping. Imagine if you were in this situation, facing many more years with a student who routinely gave you trouble—

Looping

The practice of having the same teacher move through ages or grades with the same class for 2 years or more.

the one who just pushed your buttons every day. Or imagine yourself having to be an expert in the advancing content of 8 years of study. A daunting and exciting task!

Proponents of Waldorf education cite the practice of looping as a valuable asset in teacher satisfaction, in building social connections, and in managing the inevitable conflicts that arise from such close contact. When teachers or children experience social conflicts, it is not an option to passively wait until the end of the year to avoid resolving the issues. The last day of the school year does not mean "that child" will become someone else's problem in September. Teachers are keenly aware that personality conflicts among students or with them will have to be resolved directly. Through the productive resolution of problems as they arise, both teachers and children learn positive, necessary skills in conflict resolution and how to get along with diverse personalities. In terms of teacher satisfaction, many teachers report that the continual change in grade levels pushes them to continue to enhance their own knowledge and to remain creative in designing successively more skilled lesson experiences; in addition, it reduces the monotony of repeating the same content year after year. Many looping teachers report that this practice helps keep their teaching fresh and interesting (Fenner & Rivers, 1995).

DIVERSITY AND INCLUSION IN WALDORF EDUCATION

The Waldorf education model is well suited to serve children from families with limited incomes and children with special needs because of the

- hands-on manipulative activities prominent throughout the grades,
- focus on individual expression through the creative arts,
- integral part that music and eurythmy (used as a form of curative dance) play in the curriculum, and
- unified nature of the K–12 curriculum.

Today Waldorf schools are serving children from all socioeconomic backgrounds and are found in rural, suburban, and urban settings. The Waldorf model has been employed in public education at nearly 40 public schools, including an urban district in Wisconsin that was plagued by poverty, violence, and low student achievement. Soon after the school's opening, the school district, parents, community, and teachers witnessed remarkable changes in students' attitudes, motivation, abilities, and academic achievement scores (Byers et al., 1996). Called "healing education" by administrators and faculty alike, the hallways now ring with song and music, are veritable museums of students' watercolor paintings, and are no longer places of violence and tension (Cicala Filmworks, n.d.). Stories of such transformation are shared by educators in other schools as well (Mollet, 1991).

Additional intervention applications of Waldorf education in the United States can be found in California, where a juvenile correctional facility has adopted a Waldorf approach (Cicala Filmworks, n.d.; Oppenheimer, 1999). The results have been favorable. Teachers, students, and parents alike have praised the arts-based curriculum as having opened pathways of communication between once-rival gang members, troubled teens, and violent repeat offenders. Perhaps most meaningful to students, teachers, parents, and administrators is the sense of pride that the students begin taking in their creations. This feeling then spills over into the sense of pride and responsibility in themselves that is often lacking in children, whether at risk or at promise.

Several Waldorf charter schools in California have reported that the curricular methods specific to Waldorf education, such as integrating the arts into all subject areas, the hands-on methods of all subjects, and the social dynamics of the classrooms, have made learning English easier for their linguistically diverse students (Cicala Filmworks, n.d.). The variety of expressive activities, including music, dance, art, story, and handcrafts, allows children at all levels of language learning to find ways to communicate.

In addition to the modifications made to suit specific applications, such as public schools, the Waldorf education model has been used to address the wide range of needs of diverse students. Steiner called his approach *curative education,* emphasizing the powerful role education can have in healing and promoting development. This is similar to Montessori's early experiences with institutionalized children. Although some schools are not well equipped to handle children with special needs, for the most part, Waldorf schools welcome all children, and there are currently programs that exclusively serve children with developmental and physical disabilities in New Hampshire; that serve children in an impoverished community in South Africa; and that serve abandoned, extremely poor children in the most destitute area of Nepal.

CRITIQUES AND APPLICATIONS OF WALDORF EDUCATION

The vast majority of families and teachers involved in Waldorf schools report success and satisfaction with children's outcomes. Waldorf graduates are frequently referred to as *well-rounded people,* able to think, manage challenges, and lead successful adult lives (Almon, 1992; Mitchell & Gerwin, 2007). Some reports indicate that, in addition to being more reflective, deliberate thinkers and strong students, Waldorf students' Scholastic Aptitude Test scores are above national averages (Oppenheimer, 1999). In addition, roughly 94% of Waldorf high school graduates go on to 4-year colleges, an impressive rate compared to the national average of 64% of 2007 high school graduates attending 4-year colleges (Bureau of Labor Statistics, 2008; Dancy, 2004; Enten, 2005; Mitchell & Gerwin, 2007). Nonetheless, criticism of the application of the Waldorf philosophy in public schools integrates a tension surrounding some of Steiner's philosophical values of spirituality.

Criticism mostly centers around the argument for the division of religion and public schools. Although Waldorf educators do not promote any one religion, there is a strong spiritual component, grounded in the anthroposophy roots, that has contributed to the criticism (Ruenzel, 2001). Many of the traditional Waldorf songs and poems learned in the nursery-kindergarten and repeated throughout the years include reference to various gods and saints. Many of the rituals and festivals, so important to life in the Waldorf school, center around such events as Advent, solstices, and spiritual awakenings. Even such things as the use of candles during some festivals, the recitation of poems, and the celebrations of earth changes generally stray from mainstream religious holidays and are, therefore, sometimes surprising to people new to Waldorf education.

However, it is this separation from mainstream (religious) holidays that, Waldorf education proponents point out, makes them not a religious program. Proponents point to the differences between religion and spirituality. Religion is defined by specific texts and beliefs, and it is often exclusionary to other religions. Spirituality is a more personal set of beliefs and reverence for all life, and it does not necessarily align with one formal religion (Miller, 2006). When viewed in this way, spirituality—as an individual construct—allows for an openness and acceptance that some religious faiths may not have room for. Advocates of Waldorf education point to the emphasis on education that frees each individual to think for himself or herself as a counter to this criticism (Ward, 2005).

Waldorf teachers give children access to open-ended materials, outdoor play, and plenty of time for creating imaginary worlds.

Public school systems have circumvented this issue by successfully modifying the curriculum and practice to better fit their communities' needs and expectations. Some schools may refrain from using certain verses and celebrations. Most Waldorf schools, whether public or private, do not engage in formal religious teaching and do not tolerate discrimination or exclusivity. Recently the Waldorf education community crafted and adopted a statement against all forms of discrimination in any Waldorf school, referred to as the Stuttgart Declaration. The statement includes a commitment that "Waldorf schools do not select, stratify or discriminate amongst their pupils, but consider all human beings to be free and equal in dignity and rights, independent of ethnicity, national or social origin, gender, language, religion, and political or other convictions" (ECSWE, 2007).

Application of Waldorf Practices

When introduced to the foundational beliefs and practices of Waldorf education, many early childhood teachers find inspiration for their own practice in diverse early childhood education settings. Some simple ideas for Waldorf-inspired applications include the following:

- Integrate more natural materials into the classroom for children to explore and create with
  - Sections of tree branches
  - Collections of leaves, shells, stones, and crystals
  - Seasonal collections such as pinecones and boughs, flowers and dried grasses, moss-covered rocks, abandoned birds' nests, and gourds
  - Balls of wool yarns
  - Beeswax for sculpting
- Replacing finished, formed, plastic, or battery-operated toys with open-ended materials
  - Simple dolls sewn from organic cottons and wools
  - Large squares of soft material or silk scarves

- Homemade blocks from wood or fabrics
- Items and materials for sculpting and building
- Items reminiscent of home such as cooking utensils, simple tools, sized-down bedding, or dress-up items
- Encourage constructive, social play
  - Providing materials and prompts to foster imagination (What can we make out of this? What shape do you see hiding in that clay? I wonder . . .)
  - Giving children ample time, space, and freedom to build imaginary worlds together
  - Allowing fantasy play (fairies, gnomes, talking animals, etc.)
  - Sewing simple dolls with twist or braid yarn for hair
  - Making characters from natural materials (corn husks, twigs, pinecones, wool)
  - Baking and cooking nutritious snacks (bread, soup, fruits)
  - Providing outdoor time as much as possible, preferably with access to natural areas
- Slowing down your actions, being deliberate in gesture and voice
  - Integrating soft, slow songs throughout the day and for transitions
  - Moving in fluid, graceful gestures and deliberate movements (no yelling across the room or running down halls)
  - Modeling kind language and gentle touches of friendship
  - Integrating oral storytelling with simple props and hand gestures
- Deliberately greet each and every child as he or she enters the room in the morning

CONCLUSION

Waldorf education is a significant educational movement, and it has important implications for all educators. Many elements of this approach can influence practices in child development and learning, including

- the way adults structure the environment and teaching to protect childhood,
- the emphasis on preserving the developing imagination by resisting offensive media influences, and
- the view of education as a means of strengthening society.

Considering the foundational elements, you can begin to see the comprehensive, complex interplay between philosophy and practice. Waldorf is a philosophy that began with one man's vision of empowering individuals through holistic education. It has progressed into a worldwide, independent movement that is committed to the practice of educating well-rounded individuals ready to reshape and reform society.

SUMMARY

- Based on the work of philosopher Rudolf Steiner, Waldorf education is a unique kindergarten-to-12th-grade model that seeks to develop independent, creative thinkers.

- The first Waldorf school opened in 1919 in Germany and served children of factory workers.
- The school environment and curriculum are integrated, holistic, and carefully designed to nurture the whole child—head, heart, and hands.
- Waldorf education centers around a view of development in three phases: early childhood, middle childhood, and adolescence.
- In the early childhood years, the primary focus of education is on play and imitation.
- Waldorf early childhood teachers' roles are to preserve children's naturally unfolding processes in physical development and their awakening to the physical world around them.
- Teachers provide open-ended materials and model appropriate behaviors.
- Teachers hone their skills as observers and indirectly encourage children's play.
- The Waldorf curriculum emphasizes the use of hands-on learning and open-ended materials and integrates the arts throughout all subject areas.
- The unified K–12 curriculum introduces and revisits concepts and content in an ascending spiral model, thereby deepening children's knowledge and providing cross-content connections.
- Waldorf schools are increasingly being instituted in the public school sector and as intervention programs for youth at-risk.
- Critiques of Waldorf education mostly focus on concerns about spirituality or religion in the curriculum, particularly when Waldorf is used as a public school model.

CHAPTER LEARNING GOALS SELF-ASSESSMENT

Use this chart to write down three to five key points for each learning goal that you learned from this chapter.

Explore the history and philosophical foundations of Waldorf education.	
Identify key aspects of child development in Waldorf education.	
Describe major themes in Waldorf early childhood practice.	
Examine essential roles of the Waldorf teacher.	
Discuss the integrated, spiral curriculum in Waldorf education.	
Explore diversity in Waldorf practice.	
Compare critiques, success, and applications of Waldorf education.	

APPLICATION ACTIVITIES

Discussion Prompts

1. In what ways does the learning environment embody the philosophy of a school, teacher, or approach? What environmental elements might give you clues to the program's or teacher's beliefs?

2. Look back at the classroom view from the start of the chapter. In what ways can you identify aspects of the Waldorf philosophy illustrated in this classroom visit?

3. Are there elements that you strongly agree or disagree with about the philosophy and application of Waldorf education? Describe these.

In Class   Visit www.edutopia.org and do a search for "Waldorf Education." Find articles, photos, videos, and links to information on Waldorf schools, criticisms of Waldorf education, parent information, teacher trainings, and so on. Bring a copy of the source you found and a one-page summary of your findings. In small groups, share your reflections, what you learned, and your thoughts about Waldorf education.

In the Field   Storytelling is a key part of the early childhood classroom. All teachers can use some practice to hone their storytelling skills. For this activity, choose a well-written children's book and prepare a storytelling session based on the book. Practice using your tone of voice, facial expressions, and body gestures to bring the story to life. You may want to observe a storyteller for ideas. Locate a child care center, family care program, or library where you can present your storytelling session to a group of children.

For Your Portfolio   Interview an early childhood teacher from a local program in your area. This does not have to be a Waldorf teacher. Ask about the teacher's beliefs about the following concepts and compare the responses to what you've read about Waldorf education:

- Academic programming for prekindergarteners
- Development of literacy
- Young children and imagination
- Aesthetic environments for young children
- Teachers as role models
- Media and technology in the classroom

Write a two-page summary of your comparisons. This paper can be added to your portfolio in the teaching and learning or professionalism section.

RELATED WEB LINKS

Association of Waldorf Schools of North America (AWSNA)
www.whywaldorfworks.org

Waldorf Early Childhood Association of North America (WECAN)
www.waldorfearlychildhood.org

Waldorf in the Home
www.waldorfhomeschooling.org

12

CHAPTER

Bringing It All Together: Imagining and Becoming

Chapter Learning Goals

- Identify important professional dispositions.
- Create evidence of professional knowledge and skills.

You have taken a long journey through some of the events, research, trends, and practices that continue to shape the field of early childhood education. Set against the backdrop of a long history rich in discourse, innovation, debate, and challenges, your task now is to reflect on who you are becoming as an early childhood professional. I use the term *becoming* even considering the many experiences and skills you may already bring to your professional persona. I choose this word to convey the dynamic, active, transformational state in which all educators live. Through our continued reflection, risk-taking, trying, testing, inquiring, and introspection, we are all on the ever-stretching path to "becoming." This is the work of the caregiver, the educator, the advocate, the professional—the passionate, lifelong learner.

The people and practices in this book have shared with you what they have learned during their own course of becoming. Their stories and histories are like a lantern illuminating our shared history. Now it is passed to you to carry it forward into the as yet uncharted future. Standing on the solid foundation of our past, now it is up to you to imagine who you are becoming. Looking forward, there are some familiar topics that remain timely as well as some new issues that we face in our changing world. As technological and social advances have created an increasingly global society, we find ourselves with more access and open communications than ever before. Communications have indeed brought the world together in many respects. And yet we still see vast divides in economic classes; access to quality education; and cultural practices, values, and beliefs. Teachers continue to see dramatic changes in culturally and linguistically diverse student populations. Families and communities struggle to find successful schools and quality programs. In addition, we continue to advocate for increasing inclusion of children with broader ranges of abilities and needs in all classrooms. Teachers must be sensitive to the unique resources and needs of all of the families they work with while always respecting the increasing diversity of education environments. Professionals promote and demonstrate positive internal qualities, called "dispositions," which shape our dedication to high-quality practice for children and families. As you move forward in your journey, these commitments will be your companions and will guide the nature of your work.

PROFESSIONAL DISPOSITIONS: RESPECT, ENTHUSIASM, COMMITMENT

Dispositions guide decision-making and are made evident in behaviors and actions used in academic and professional practice. Dispositions are internal qualities such as integrity, valuing social justice and fairness, responsibility, commitment to ethics, initiative, reflectiveness, and dedication to ongoing professional development. These qualities are evident in the way you approach and complete academic and professional tasks, the nature of collaborations and relationships with others, and in behaviors related to working with children and families. Professional dispisitions are an essential aspect of educational practice and include the following internal qualities and examples of behavior:

- Commitment to learning: reflecting on own process
  - Respond productively and respectfully to feedback from peers, instructors, classroom teachers, principals, and supervisors
  - Reflect on teaching by various forms of feedback from instructors, classroom teachers, principals and supervisors; actively seek additional feedback
- Commitment to learning: engaging all students
  - Demonstrate and prompt inquiry through posing open-ended questions, engaging higher order thinking, and facilitating student problem-solving
  - Effectively use assessment to identify strengths and weaknesses in students and to individualize instruction
  - Demonstrate flexibility in modifying ideas, course assignments, materials, plans, lesson implementation, and schedule changes
  - Value diversity and ensure equitable access through selection and creation of inclusive materials, lessons, assessments, and inclusive environmental design to promote diverse students' participation and learning

- Commitment to collaboration and partnerships
  - Cooperate with peers, instructors/school personnel; resolve differences or misunderstandings respectfully and reflectively: maintain confidentiality, apply professional ethical guidelines when resolving conflicts
  - Demonstrate sensitivity to others' feelings, opinions, and cultures
- Commitment to professionalism
  - Present well-groomed appearance and demonstrate an understanding of appropriate, professional dress that adheres to the school's dress codes and professional expectations and allows for complete performance of duties
  - Display positive, professional attitude and enthusiasm for planning, initiating, and completing assignments and/or lessons
  - Respect and support ethical and professional standards, diplomacy, integrity, and commitment
  - Pursue ways to contribute to others in the profession, participate in professional development opportunities such as conferences and professional organizations

Throughout this book, you have engaged in reflective activities designed to deepen your self-awareness and professional skills. This process of being a self-reflective, deliberate professional will continue throughout your studies and career. Dedication to valuing diversity, enthusiasm, and commitment to professional advocacy will be lifelong companions on your journey.

Collaboration and Valuing Diversity

One of the most important guiding principles all teachers must bring with them is an awareness of and respect for working with diverse people. Many new teachers may not have experienced opportunities to interact with diverse people. It is natural to develop deeply held beliefs, habits, and biases based on your own experiences. As you move forward into the classroom as a teacher, how you teach will be greatly affected by how you were taught and raised. It is imperative that you continue to reflect on the connections between your past and your teaching style. You may make deliberate choices about how you want to teach, about how you want your students to learn, that are different from your own school experiences. You will be able to make these conscious choices only if you are aware of your past and you create a vision of your future.

Each child who comes into your classroom will bring a unique perspective and set of experiences. Finding ways to connect new learning with familiar experiences is a key to being a successful educator. To do this, you will need to get to know your children and truly value each child's background. Regular communication with families is the first step to integrating children's home culture into the classroom. Families have a wealth of resources to offer and are often flattered and proud to share them with your class. Just be sure to welcome their input in meaningful activities, not merely as an extra set of hands.

At different times in your career, you will also undoubtedly work with colleagues who bring very different backgrounds and beliefs to their teaching. You may not always agree with them, but there is always something to learn from the people who cross your path. As you read about in the chapter on the National Association for the Education of Young Children (NAEYC) Code of Ethics, part of being a professional educator is respecting and supporting colleagues. Seek out advice, share strategies, and develop open communications. Creating mutually respectful, supportive relationships in your center or school is a primary way to nurture your satisfaction and enthusiasm for teaching. Throughout many of the chapters in this book, you read about the importance of teachers working

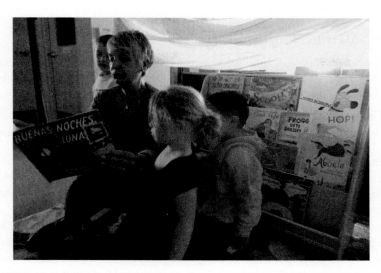

Great early childhood teachers carefully integrate meaningful activities and diverse materials to vibrantly reflect the unique family background of each child.

collaboratively. Making meaningful connections with families and colleagues is challenging at times, but it is at the heart of best practices.

Enthusiasm for Teaching

When you think about your experience as a student, the teachers who stand out as favorites are probably those who conveyed enthusiasm, energy, and genuine caring. The affective disposition you bring to your classroom sets the tone for all your interactions with your children. Children, especially very young children, need caring, energetic teachers. They need to feel that they are with adults who, first and foremost, want to be there with them. The way you tell and read stories, build villages from blocks, and play restaurant or house while skillfully negotiating conflicts, challenges, and collaborations conveys your enthusiasm for your work. Above all, the many ways you listen—truly *listen* by being genuinely present and in the moment with them—conveys the depth of your relationship and commitment to each and every child. Considering there will always be rough days, try to retain a childlike energy, curiosity, and wonder as you work with and for children. Cultivate a vivid imagination, just as your children are exploring theirs.

Being enthusiastic about your work not only benefits your children but also helps improve your own work satisfaction. When you feel that our work is meaningful and that your dedication is recognized, you naturally feel more personally and professionally fulfilled. Your energy and enthusiasm can also translate into a willingness to imagine, wonder, and try. Being open to new experiences in teaching, just as reading this book opened you to new methods and approaches, keeps your work fresh and interesting. Some ideas or strategies may not work the way you thought they would, just as some lessons will not go as planned. But even in the "flops," you learn and grow. You will develop new twists on old ideas and discover new directions for your teaching. This process truly gets at the heart of the lifelong journey of being a professional educator.

Professional Advocacy

The field of early childhood education has not always been a highly regarded profession. In recent decades, however, great strides have been made nationally to increase standards,

NAEYC Membership

Go to the NAEYC Web site at www.naeyc.org and look up the section on membership. Study the costs and benefits of being an NAEYC member. Think about the benefits listed on the site as well as others, such as the feeling of being part of a large national group with shared commitments.

teacher credentials, teacher salaries, professional development, and respect for this rewarding and demanding profession. It is essential that new teachers entering the field continue this important work. Teachers promote the increase in professionalism by carrying out their work with ethics and care and by continuing the learning process.

By now you have heard people encourage you to be a lifelong learner. This is also a call to be a professional. By attending conferences, joining professional organizations, networking with other professionals, and completing workshops and seminars, you can keep yourself current on new research and innovations in the field. As you gain classroom experience and research knowledge, you will be able to contribute to future research and innovations. This cycle of learning, growing, exploring, and sharing is the epitome of professional collegiality. As you can see, this is just the beginning of a long, exciting journey.

Congratulations on making this commitment to becoming a professional educator. Now let the real journey begin!

The important thing is not to stop questioning. Curiosity has its own reason for existing.

—Albert Einstein

Culminating the Text and Creating Your Portfolio: Application Activities

In the following series of activities, you will explore your ideas, beliefs, goals, and vision as you imagine and define yourself as an educator. These will help you not only synthesize what you have read about in this text but also continue to refine your vision of education and of being a teacher. You may decide that several of these activities fit into your professional portfolio and provide evidence of your teaching philosophy, style, and skills. Thoughtfully select and organize the work you choose for your portfolio based on categories or standards. The NAEYC standards provide a recognizable, professional organization for your portfolio and may be your college or university's preferred framework, particularly if your program is part of the Council for the Accreditation of Educator Preparation (CAEP) or NAEYC accreditation processes (Bredekamp & Copple, 2009).

Activity 1, Meshing Approaches   Using the charts in the appendices or another graphic organizer of your choice, identify key elements of each of the theories, frameworks, methods, and approaches you have read about. This will help you organize your ideas and will also help you pick out aspects of practices you agree with most and want to integrate into your own beliefs and practice. Highlight elements that speak to you, energize you, and empower you. Share your chart with a small group or your class, and compare which elements you highlighted.

Activity 2, Ideal Environment Visual   In small groups, decide what you believe educational environments for young children should look like. Think about how theorists have described ideal settings. Come up with some descriptions that you agree with from their work or your own ideas. Create a visual representation of your own ideal educational environment for young children using large paper and a variety of art supplies (markers, collage, sculpture, painting). Or if you prefer, create a skit/play to illustrate your vision.

Activity 3, Philosophy of Education   Throughout this book, you have stopped along the way and thought about your own beliefs and ideas about early childhood education. You may want to flip back to some of the starting or ending reflection questions in each chapter to refresh your memory. Using your responses to these questions, create your own philosophy of education statement. This statement is an important part of all teachers' professional identities, and it should be put in your professional teaching portfolio. As you gain more experience and learn more about the field of education, your philosophy statement will evolve. Think of this as a living, breathing, working document. This is just a start. Or if you already have one from previous classes, take this time to revise it and change things as you see fit. Your statement will say many things, but at the heart of it is sharing your vision of how theory is translated into practice. Some important aspects you may want to convey are

- your beliefs about best practices in early childhood education;
    - what you believe are the rights of all children;
    - how teaching looks when children are valued and respected;
    - what qualities make a "great teacher" in your view;
- your vision of the ideal learning environment;
    - how environments look when children are valued and respected;
- your beliefs about children;
    - how children grow, learn, think, and feel;
    - children are active in driving their own learning or building their own knowledge;
- the role teachers play in young children's lives;
    - the ways you hope to affect children's lives;
    - what you believe teachers' responsibilities to children are;
- the role teachers play in families' lives;
- what it means to work collaboratively in planning, teaching, and assessing;
    - whether you view teachers as a team and how you will embody this team approach;
- why you want to be a teacher; and
- the strengths you possess or are honing that will make you a great teacher.

To get started, you can brainstorm a list of key words and phrases that embody your beliefs and ideals about teaching and education and write them on small adhesive notes. Organize these words in categories that make sense, such as teachers, children, learning, teaching, environment, your own skills, your motivations, and so on. After your sections are grouped, you can start writing paragraphs and organizing your material into a logical statement.

Activity 4, Vision of the Child   In small groups, think about all the images of children and teachers you have read about throughout the book. Recall how key theorists described their beliefs about children and teachers. What ideals do you believe in? These may be your own ideas or the ideas of those you have read about in this book or other books. Create a visual representation of your vision of children as well as your vision of early childhood teachers. Use any materials you have available—paper and marker; collage; sculpture; papier mâché; or perhaps even a dance, poem, or skit. Be sure to make your beliefs and ideals clear.

Activity 5, Classroom Visit: Observing Diversity and Inclusion   Based on the classroom visit described below, analyze and describe 10 specific examples of practices that support diversity and inclusion in the classroom.

Classroom Example	Describe How This Supports Diversity and/or Inclusion

On this snowy afternoon in Mr. Washington's mixed-age kindergarten–1st grade classroom, the children are working on a project about the weather. The class decided to produce a weather-reporting station during the course of their science unit. Mr. Washington is one of a team of teachers in the K–3 school who started a pilot program aimed at integrating MI theory and differentiated instruction practices into the classroom. He meets you at the door and welcomes you to the classroom.

"For three weeks, the children have been working on a weather station project each afternoon. This is an integrated project where kids work alone and in groups on different activities and constructions related to gathering and reporting on daily weather. All of their content areas are represented here. We spend time each morning on focused lessons in different content areas to build specific skills. Then in the afternoon we have a long block where the students apply their knowledge and skills in the real-life project. I see how meaningful their learning is by having the balance of short, guided instruction and then the time to apply and use the skills. This weather channel experience will really show you that."

Most of the children are working in groups, although one child is sitting at a table writing in his personal journal with an adult's help. There is a wheeled walker next to them. A small group is working with a student teacher to create a background map for the weather reporter's desk. They are using a large-scale projection of a local map and drawing it on poster paper. The teacher is working with four children on setting up a video camera for the daily weather report recording. Two children are sitting by a window, making notes with pictures about current weather conditions and reading a thermometer and a precipitation gauge on the outside of the window. Four children are sitting at another table, excitedly talking about a script for their report while an adult volunteer takes dictation. One of the children is holding a bumpy rubber ball and squeezing it as she's talking. One girl is compiling the previous week's forecasts into graphs on poster board using picture symbols to track weather. She is working from her observation journal, which is written in Spanish (her home language). Another team is working in a music center, deciding what clips sound seasonally themed for music to accompany their weather reports. A boy in this group is sitting on a large yoga ball and bouncing slightly. They pause the recording periodically to discuss which selection best represents how the cold, gray, snowy weather felt when they were outside this morning. The stack of CDs they are selecting from includes a wide range of music from classical to rap.

Around the room, you notice a series of signs posted on the walls that describe the different ways of thinking in MI theory. They are printed in three different languages. The signs include positive statements that cover all the MI categories along with diverse pictures of people doing activities that embody the different ways of thinking and expressing: word smart (a Korean language teacher), number smart (a street market vendor exchanging money with a customer), picture smart (a coach making a diagram of plays), body smart (a Paralympian), nature smart (a biologist at a microscope), people smart (a pastor), me smart (Buddhist monk meditating), music smart (group of teens breakdancing). As you think about the categories, you start to see them represented in the children's activities. Some children are writing, drawing, taking measurements, building, listening to music, and talking. The classroom is set up with group tables, not rows of desks, and there are learning stations around the room. There is a weather observation station set up at a low window; a music center; a writing and drawing station; a numbers and math area; a computer area; and an open carpet space with boxes, blocks, scarves, textured balls, and other gross-motor materials.

You also notice how many different activities the children are engaged in related to their science unit on the weather. Even though it is a science unit, the children are still working on all their skills and subject areas: mathematics, social studies, language arts, social skills, and creative arts. The student teacher later explains that, as part of their weather station reporting, the children also research weather conditions in other states. In this way, geography standards are covered within the weather project. Both teachers look as excited about the weather station as the children when they explain that the children periodically interview school staff and other classes about their weather experiences. The children also decided to start a weather newspaper with the help of the third-graders, in addition to their video program, which they will distribute daily to the school.

Passionate early childhood teachers find joy in exploring the world, just as children do.

Activity 6, Ideal School   In small groups, create your own ideal school. Pull together the elements from the programs you have read about that appeal to you and align with your own beliefs about best practice and what early childhood should be all about. Create your own personal method and approach to teaching young children. You can use the charts to give you ideas of key elements you want to include. Be sure to identify which program/method/theory (which chapter) your specific elements/ideas come from.

Include the following structural elements:

- A name and logo
- A mission or program philosophy
- Overarching goals: How will your mission be achieved?
- Expectations of teachers: teacher roles, credentials
- Expectations of children: behavior, performance, place in the school community
- Expectations of families: What role will families play in the school?
- Daily schedule
- Basic curriculum plan: What kinds of experiences will be provided for children? What will children learn? How will you promote learning and development?
- Administration: How will your schools' administration be handled? Teacher run, parent run, or administrative professionals?

Now start having some fun! Make a brochure to educate the public about your program. Make an ad campaign to market your new school. Make floor plan designs of your school building(s). Let your imagination run wild.

Activity 7, Partnering with Families   Working in small groups, identify a topic that is important in the lives of children and their families. Consider the topics you've read about, or select one that is interesting to you. Here are some examples:

Understanding behavior

Healthful nutrition

Kindergarten readiness

Toilet training

Promoting literacy at home

Home safety

Accessing community resources

After you have selected your topic, create a workshop that could be presented at a parent evening. Include the following components:

I. Workshop Topic
- What is your workshop topic?
- Make a workshop title that will grab attention.

II. Workshop Goals
- What three things do you hope your workshop attendees will get from the workshop?

III. Methods of Instruction
- What techniques are you going to employ to keep the attendees' attention?

IV. Workshop Content
- How will you guide your participants through the session? What information will you cover?
- Content outline

V. Ending the Workshop
- How are you going to wrap up the workshop?
- How are you going to evaluate the workshop to assess effectiveness? (Consider a participant survey or checklist or a question session.)

To accompany your parent workshop, create an information brochure that briefly presents the highlights from your topic. This should be a pamphlet that educates parents about the topic and provides them with sources for more information. You can hand out your brochure at the parent meeting. Create brochures in English and Spanish or another language spoken in your community. If you are not bilingual yourself, this part of the activity will include researching resources to help you communicate in another language. Check out Internet sources, student language groups at your school, language faculty members, and other community resources. It will be important to know how to find resources to facilitate communications with linguistically diverse families when you become a teacher.

Activity 8, Child Study   You probably have already completed at least one observation of a classroom or child. These one-time visits provide only a glimpse into children's lives and learning and are made truly effective when completed systematically and repeatedly over time and when they are included with other sources of information about the child. Parent interviews or checklists, informal notes about highlights from the child's day, and checklists help round out the picture of who the child is and how development is progressing. For your child study activity, select a child (with parent permission) to observe over a few months. Complete the following for your focus child:

- Biweekly observations where you document as many details as possible about what the child does and says for a 30-minute time period
- Weekly anecdotal records (brief notes capturing a highlight from a day—something the child did or said)
- Formal developmental checklist (covering all developmental domains)
- Parent interview/home visit; write up a one-page summary of the experience and what you learned from the family. (Be sure to remain positive, supportive, and respectful when working with families; even if their home environment is different than what you are used to, be sure to hold back from making judgments!)
- Work samples—drawings, photos of block structures or clay sculptures, writing samples, dictated stories, and so on

Write a summative evaluation statement at the end of your observation period where you tie all your artifacts together and provide a snapshot of your focus child's development and describe your focus child's progress and change over time. Try to keep your reports as objective as possible; meaning that you report what you observe and not your opinions about what you saw. Teachers' analyses can add valuable insight to children's assessments, but at this point in your professional development, focus on making more objective reports.

Activity 9, "Look What's Developing . . ." Wall Charts   Many teachers struggle to share with families the valuable and important learning and development that happens in a classroom that is organized in centers or activity areas and schedules long blocks of time

TABLE 12-1 Look What We're Learning in the Creative Arts Center

Knowledge	Skills
• Colors and shapes	• Fine motor—grasping, pinching, squeezing
• How different tools make different textures and lines	• Drawing, forming shapes
• How shape, color, texture, and line combine to affect composition	• Gross motor—mixing, kneading, molding
• Color mixing	• Turn-taking, sharing
• Physics of how different materials move, are shaped, and their different qualities	• Caring for materials and space
	• Pouring
	• Measuring
	• Stacking, rolling, pounding, stretching

Dispositions	Feelings
• Persistence	• Sense of accomplishment
• Risk-taking	• Validation of unique ideas
• Willingness to try new things	• Joy of making something new
• Wondering	• Caring about own ideas and those of others
• Willingness to express ideas	• Enjoyment—the fun and freedom of creating, getting messy, and experimenting!
• Sharing	
• Validating multiple perspectives	

for center choice time. One way to emphasize the value of learning/activity centers is to post charts on the walls in or near the centers that list the key goals reached by playing or working in that area. Table 12-1 is an example of a poster that can hang in a creative arts center. Using this as an example, create your own series of posters for the following centers: Creative Arts, Language Arts, Manipulatives, Blocks, Sensory, Science, Dramatic Play, and Outdoors. Use your observations, online sources, interviews, and video clips to guide you.

Activity 10, Article Review/Research Summary   Using your school's library system or online professional journal (NAEYC offers select copies of its professional journal, *Young Children,* online at www.naeyc.org/yc/ or find the entire *Early Childhood Research and Practice* journal online at http://ecrp.uiuc.edu), locate a recent article on an issue relating to policies or laws affecting early childhood practice and write an article review paper. Be sure to include a copy of the article and the following components in your two-page report:

1. Reference (author, date, article title, journal/source title, volume/issue, page numbers)
2. Brief summary of article (key points or findings of the article)
3. Your response to article (What did you learn from the article? Do you think the article is useful for early childhood teachers? What new points can you apply in your work with young children?)

Activity 11, Evidence-Based Decision-Making   Evidence-based practice and decisions are made by integrating recommendations and information from three key sources:

1. Family goals, perspectives, and knowledge
2. Knowledge from research on best practices
3. Professional knowledge and experience

Synthesizing information representing these three perspectives as applied to the case studies below, make instructional decisions to support each child's development and learning. Complete the EBP flow charts and write a brief description and rationale statement for your decisions for each child that you would share with the family and include in the child's file.

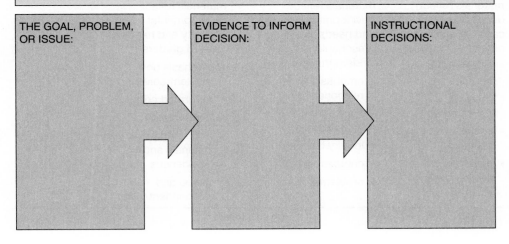

Activity 12, Professional Skills Self-Reflection   Recent research has identified seven key criteria that constitute high-quality instructional practice and are effective in any early childhood setting, including highly diverse and inclusive classrooms (reviewed in Downer et al., 2012). The criteria and examples from practice across the early years are presented in Table 12-2. In the final column, make notes to describe your confidence and professional competence in each area. What skills do you have that will help you achieve these criteria for high-quality practice, and which areas do you need to strengthen?

TABLE 12-2 High Quality ECE Practice

Quality ECE Criteria	Examples from Practice with Infants and Toddlers	Examples from Practice with Preschooler–Kindergarten	Examples from Practice with Early Elementary	Your Skills and Competencies
Clear Goals and Learning Objectives: • Overarching goals are based on developmental theory, individual children, and family culture • Objectives for group and each child are clear and measurable	• Example of goal: Develop relationships with others • Example of objective: Identify emotional expressions (happy, sad, mad) • Integration of state/national early learning standards	• Example of goal: Develop curiosity about the world around them • Example of objective: Generate questions and seek answers through active exploration • Integration of state/national early learning standards • Beginning in Kindergarten: Practice aligned with Common Core State Standards (start with developmentally appropriate practice then make connections to CCSS)	• Example of goal: Develop proficiency in beginning literacy • Example of objective: Write a personal story with a beginning, middle, and end. • Integration of state/national early learning standards • Practice aligned with Common Core State Standards (start with integrated instruction then make connections to CCSS)	

Challenging and Motivating Context:
 	
• Plans for each child's strengths and needs
• Choice and interest-based plans
• Authentic, real-world problem solving
	• Practices, environments, and materials reflect developmental capacity and needs of infants/toddlers
	  • emphasis on relationships
	  • physical development
	  • social relationship building
	  • development of sense of self
		• Practices, environments, and materials reflect developmental capacity and needs of preschoolers/kindergarteners
		  • emphasis on social relationships
		  • hands-on experiences
		  • inquiry learning
		  • choice-making
		  • problem-solving
			• Practices, environments, and materials reflect developmental capacity and needs of 1st–3rd graders
			  • emphasis on problem-solving
			  • integrated content
			  • literature rich
			  • increasingly complex materials and experiences
			  • shared and independent work	

TABLE 12-2 (Continued)

Quality ECE Criteria	Examples from Practice with Infants and Toddlers	Examples from Practice with Preschooler–Kindergarten	Examples from Practice with Early Elementary	Your Skills and Competencies
Well-designed, clearly structured, and appropriately paced instruction: • Differentiated instruction • Spiral curriculum • Responsive to children's learning	• Curriculum focuses on relationships and meaningful interactions • Adult-child interactions are warm and responsive; child-child interactions are supported and facilitated through play • Natural sense of wonder and curiosity is supported through exploration of interesting materials and appropriate environments • Daily routines (feeding, changing, hand-washing) focus on building relationships and learning through warm, gentle, and playful interactions • Routines and activities are individualized based on children's habits, strengths, and interests	• Instruction focuses on facilitating preschoolers' active, hands-on exploration of their world • Individual and small-group instruction allows for individualization • Whole-group activities promote cohesive community-building • Learning experiences integrate visual, verbal, auditory, and physical activities • Observation and authentic assessment drives instructional planning for individuals and groups • Short- and long-term goals and objectives both guide planning and adjust based on assessment evidence • Learning builds on previous experiences • Daily routines organize the day and are used to build relationships among children and with adults	• Content is introduced and revisited at increasingly complex levels • Learning experiences are integrated and connected across content areas • Ongoing formative assessments inform pace of instruction • Evidence of children's learning is used to determine pace and sequence of activities • Children reflect on own learning outcomes and evidence • Balance of whole-group, small-group, and individual activities allows for individualized instruction and assessment • Flexible grouping promotes relationships and individualization for specific learning tasks	

(Continued)

TABLE 12-2 (*Continued*)

Quality ECE Criteria	Examples from Practice with Infants and Toddlers	Examples from Practice with Preschooler–Kindergarten	Examples from Practice with Early Elementary	Your Skills and Competencies
Active Engagement and Participation: • Each child is able to participate in appropriate ways • Materials, activities, or settings are modified to include all children • Activities are appropriate for each child and group	• Environments are designed for safe, active exploration • Steps, hills, and ramps provide accessible experience with levels and motion • Multiple materials available to reduce conflicts • Children's unique interests and developmental capabilities guide curriculum and environmental design • Children given choices	• Environments are varied over time to stimulate interest • Flexible groupings encourage peer-to-peer support and challenge • Ample time throughout day given to social experiences • Environments provide access to quiet and active spaces and activities • Children's unique interests and developmental capabilities guide curriculum and environmental design • Children given choices	• Technologies are used effectively to engage children with diverse abilities • Instruction and environment are accommodated and modified to support diverse abilities and ways of thinking • Children's unique interests and developmental capabilities guide curriculum and environmental design • Children given choices	
Opportunities to practice, apply, and transfer new learning: • Curriculum reflects authentic activities • Play provides platform for meaningful practice of emerging skills	• Flexible and predictable schedule of routines organizes the day • Time and space to practice emerging skills (dressing, toileting, etc.) • Manipulatives echo developing skills such as opening/closing, lacing, latching, zipping	• Open-ended materials and activities align with emerging skills and knowledge • Authentic projects integrate content knowledge and give opportunities to practice emerging skills	• Real-world problems provide opportunity to practice problem-solving and use developing skills and competencies • Balanced instruction (teacher-guided, child-initiated, and problem-based project applications)	

TABLE 12-2 *(Continued)*

Quality ECE Criteria	Examples from Practice with Infants and Toddlers	Examples from Practice with Preschooler–Kindergarten	Examples from Practice with Early Elementary	Your Skills and Competencies
Feedback on Correct and Incorrect Responses: • Adult-child interactions are warm, supportive, and encourage child autonomy • Materials, environment, schedules, and adult guidance all contribute to providing feedback • Portfolios provide robust evidence of children's learning and development	• Adult interactions are warm and responsive to children's moods, activity level, and actions • Adults support children's autonomy with patience and encouragement during trial-and-error • Adults model positive behaviors • Adults responsively scaffold children's efforts with appropriate challenge, verbal cues, suggestions, and modeling • Open-ended and self-correcting materials allow children to learn from hands-on experiences	• Adults use verbal and nonverbal cues to guide behavior and actions • Adults responsively scaffold children's efforts with appropriate challenge, verbal cues, suggestions, and modeling • Open-ended and self-correcting materials allow children to learn from hands-on experiences • Schedules designed to minimize behavior challenges (active/rest routines planned to meet children's needs; transitions organized and timely) • Adults model positive behaviors and encourage self-regulation	• Adults responsively scaffold children's efforts with appropriate challenge, verbal cues, suggestions, and modeling • Children participate in self-reflection and assessment of own learning • Expectations for behavior and task completion are clear (i.e., rubrics, checklists) • Children's self-regulation of behaviors and activities encouraged through positive modeling and feedback	
Opportunities to Interact with Other Students in Various Contexts: • Children engage with others in different settings in class and in outside community • Families meaningfully integrated into classroom and program/school	• Furniture arrangements support alone and group time • Outings and walks bridge community and classroom • Families welcomed to participate in classroom activities	• Mixed ability and age groupings used when possible • Community interactions through walks, trips, and in-class guests promote cohesion between classroom and community • Guests in class provide access to multiple perspectives • Families welcomed to participate in classroom activities	• Interactions between groups, classes, and schools used when possible • Field trips and community-based projects • Families welcomed to participate in classroom activities • Interviews and guest speakers bring authentic perspectives to projects	

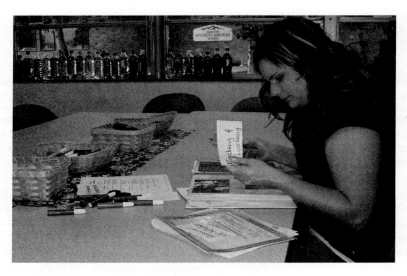

Creating your professional portfolio is a reflective and on-going process.

Activity 13, Sharing Who You Are in Families' Lives   Now we can roll all these activity experiences together. You have read about authentic assessments and portfolios in several chapters. Now it is your time to create your own portfolio. You can use any format to compile your information, but keep in mind that you will want to add and change artifacts throughout your studies and career. Aim for a flexible format such as a three-ring binder, accordion file, or even a Web site.

Start by thinking about who you are as a student, teacher, and person. Your philosophy statement is a good start. Think about what other items you would like to add that create as true, detailed, descriptive, and vivid a picture of yourself as possible. Be reflective, selective, and creative with this. Think about the following items to get you started, and try to come up with others that share who you are and where you are going. Be sure to include a paragraph statement about why each artifact is significant as a cover page for each entry.

Sample Portfolio Outline:

Table of Contents
Autobiography
Goal statement
Résumé
Transcripts
Beliefs statements
Photographs
Artifacts with reflective statements (from activities in this chapter, chapters throughout the text, other classes, or your own work experience)

Figure 12-1 presents a sample professional portfolio instruction and rubric guide from an initial teacher preparation and licensure program using the InTASC standards.

Now go for it! Start gathering, creating, organizing, embellishing, and refining your portfolio. This is your masterpiece; let your personality shine through.

FIGURE 12-1

Sample Professional Portfolio Instructions and Rubric

Instructions on Creating Your Portfolio

Outcomes:

1. The student will demonstrate competency in 10 InTASC professional standards for new teachers.
2. The student will identify and involve himself or herself with the field of early childhood and integrate knowledgeable, reflective, and critical perspectives on early education.

Your portfolio should have three parts

I. Introduction

1. Résumé including professional memberships, volunteer activities, description of fieldwork, etc.
2. Two letters of recommendation
3. Praxis scores
4. BEO self-assessment checklist
5. Transcript

II. Reflective Statement—Philosophy of Education

Your statement coveys your overarching beliefs about teaching, learning, and the educational process and should be one, single-spaced page. Some important aspects you should cover in your well-written statement are the following:

- What it means to be a teacher
- Your beliefs about how to promote learning
- What strengths you possess or are honing that will make you a great teacher
- Your vision of the ideal learning environment
- Your beliefs about children: how they grow, learn, think, feel

- What roles teachers play in children's lives
- What roles teachers play in families' lives

III. Documentation—Artifacts

The early childhood professional portfolio will be organized around the InTASC Standards (see standards summary).

The Learner and Learning

1. Learner development
2. Learning differences
3. Learning environments

Content Knowledge

4. Content knowledge
5. Application of content

Instructional Practice

6. Assessment
7. Planning for instruction
8. Instructional strategies

Professional Responsibility

9. Professional learning and ethical practice
10. Leadership and collaboration

   Each standard needs to contain a one- to two-page essay describing your growth toward the standards and one or two examples of your work that document your competency with the standard. All documentation must be labeled with a brief description of the artifact and your rationale for selection.

The ultimate aim of education is to enable individuals to become the architects of their own education and through that process to continually reinvent themselves.

The important outcomes of schooling include not only the acquisition of new conceptual tools, refined sensibilities, a developed imagination, and new routines and techniques, but also new attitudes and dispositions. The disposition to continue to learn throughout life is perhaps one of the most important contributions that schools can make to an individual's development.

—ELLIOT W. EISNER

Professional Portfolio Rubric

Component	Basic/Unacceptable (0–6 pts)	Developing (6.1–7.5 pts)	Proficient (7.6–8.9 pts)	Distinguished (9–10 pts)
1 Introduction Materials Résumé Letters Praxis transcript	Two or fewer items present Not presented in an organized way Poor résumé No letters	One item not present Organized Résumé adequate though lacks professional polish, clear formatting, or important academic and practical substance Letters missing or poor	All present Organized Good résumé in content and appearance, includes adequate/good coverage of academic and practical preparation and experience Good letters	All present Organized Excellent résumé in content and appearance, includes comprehensive coverage of academic and practical preparation and experience Excellent letters
2 Education Philosophy	Not well developed Lacks insights Poorly written	Some insights into growth and understanding Quality of writing lacks polish, contains inaccuracies of content or grammar	Well developed and contains good insights into growth and understanding Well written with clear flow and few grammatical errors Demonstrates understanding of context of teaching and learning	Very well developed, complete, and includes insights of personal growth and understanding Writing is clear and accurate, cohesive flow, no grammatical errors Demonstrates student knowledge of the context of teaching and learning with strong examples
3 The Learner and Learning Standards 1–3	Missing 2 or more artifacts or standards Rationale statement incomplete, not included, or poorly written All artifacts fail to demonstrate competency	Missing 1 artifact or standard Rationale statement lacks clarity Writing contains few errors 1–2 artifacts fail to demonstrate competency at a passing level or are incomplete	1–2 artifacts for each standard Rationale stated Well-written statements, none or few errors Artifacts demonstrate competency at a good level	1–2 artifacts for each standard Rationale clearly stated Thoughtful selection Very well written Artifacts demonstrate competency at the highest level

Professional Portfolio Rubric (*Continued*)

Component	Basic/Unacceptable (0–6 pts)	Developing (6.1–7.5 pts)	Proficient (7.6–8.9 pts)	Distinguished (9–10 pts)
4 Content Knowledge Standards 4–5	Missing 2 or more artifacts or standards Rationale statement incomplete, not included, or poorly written All artifacts fail to demonstrate competency	Missing 1 artifact or standard Rationale statement lacks clarity Writing contains few errors 1–2 artifacts fail to demonstrate competency at a passing level or are incomplete	1–2 artifacts for each standard Rationale stated Well-written statements, none or few errors Artifacts demonstrate competency at a good level	1–2 artifacts for each standard Rationale clearly stated Thoughtful selection Very well written Artifacts demonstrate competency at the highest level
5 Instructional Practice Standards 6–8	Missing 2 or more artifacts or standards Rationale statement incomplete, not included, or poorly written All artifacts fail to demonstrate competency	Missing 1 artifact or standard Rationale statement lacks clarity Writing contains few errors 1–2 artifacts fail to demonstrate competency at a passing level or are incomplete	1–2 artifacts for each standard Rationale stated Well-written statements, none or few errors Artifacts demonstrate competency at a good level	1–2 artifacts for each standard Rationale clearly stated Thoughtful selection Very well written Artifacts demonstrate competency at the highest level
6 Professional Responsibility Standards 9–10	Missing 2 or more artifacts or standards Rationale statement incomplete, not included, or poorly written All artifacts fail to demonstrate competency	Missing 1 artifact or standard Rationale statement lacks clarity Writing contains few errors 1–2 artifacts fail to demonstrate competency at a passing level or are incomplete	1–2 artifacts for each standard Rationale stated Well-written statements, none or few errors Artifacts demonstrate competency at a good level	1–2 artifacts for each standard Rationale clearly stated Thoughtful selection Very well written Artifacts demonstrate competency at the highest level

(*Continued*)

Professional Portfolio Rubric (*Continued*)

Component	Basic/Unacceptable (0–6 pts)	Developing (6.1–7.5 pts)	Proficient (7.6–8.9 pts)	Distinguished (9–10 pts)
7 Level of Reflection and Application	Not well developed Lacks insights Selections and statements do not include sufficient reflection or connection to practical experiences No demonstration of ability to apply concepts or skills Connections to practice are unclear	Some insights into growth and understanding Selections and statements demonstrate rudimentary self-reflection or application of knowledge Few connections to personal skills and competencies are made; links to practical examples do not align with competencies being described	Well developed and contains good insights into growth and understanding Selections and statements demonstrate good self-reflection and application of knowledge Some personal skills, competencies, and dispositions are clearly conveyed; appropriate practical examples are used to illustrate competencies	Very well developed, complete, and includes insights of personal growth and understanding Selections and statements demonstrate a high degree of self-reflection and application of knowledge Several personal skills, competencies, and dispositions are clearly conveyed; exemplary practical examples are used to illustrate competencies through sophisticated connections
8 Level of Critical Thinking and Creativity	Selections and statements do not demonstrate sufficient critical thinking or creativity	Beginning critical analysis of own teaching is demonstrated through reflections of practical experiences, though more emphasis is on summary of experience; connections across program and to field in general are not clear	Some critical analyses of own teaching in relation to theoretical foundations and relevant practical experiences throughout the preparation program are conveyed through reflective connections between self and practical experiences	Strong critical analyses of own teaching in relation to theoretical foundations and relevant practical experiences throughout the preparation program are clearly conveyed through reflective connections between self, practical experiences, and field in general Creativity in practice is made evident through innovative design of instructional experiences and/or presentation of professional competencies

Professional Portfolio Rubric (*Continued*)

Component	Basic/Unacceptable (0–6 pts)	Developing (6.1–7.5 pts)	Proficient (7.6–8.9 pts)	Distinguished (9–10 pts)
9 Organization and Presentation	Not clearly marked, hard to find, not organized	Marked, easy to locate, well organized	Clearly marked, easy to locate, well organized	Clearly marked, easy to locate, well organized
	Writing quality is not sufficient, many errors, lacks clarity, unreadable	Writing contains some errors, lacks clarity, not well developed	Writing well developed, few errors, clear and concise	Writing highly developed, no errors, clear and concise, flows logically
	Presentation format or design is unclear or contains inappropriate material	Presentation format is unclear or lacks aesthetic polish	Presentation format is aesthetically pleasing	Presentation format is very aesthetically pleasing
10 Timeliness	Portfolio submitted more than 2 weeks late	Portfolio submitted 1 week after due date	Portfolio submitted 1–6 days past due date	Portfolio submitted on or prior to due date
	Basic/Unacceptable: 0–60 pts	**Developing: 61–75 pts**	**Proficient: 76–89 pts**	**Distinguished: 90–100 pts**

RELATED WEB LINKS

Early Childhood and Parenting Collaborative
http://ecap.crc.uiuc.edu

Resource for Portfolios, Lesson Plan Ideas, Homemade Toys, and More
www.teachnet.com

Language-Translation Services
www.babelfish.com

Early Childhood Research & Practice
http://ecrp.uiuc.edu

APPENDIX A

Early Childhood Education Historical Time Line and Notes

Date Period	View of Children	Education Practices	Societal Influences	Key People
1600–1700	–Viewed as small adults	–Harsh punishment	–Emphasis on Bible and morality	–Locke
1700–1800				
1800–1900				
1900–2000				
Current Issues				

APPENDIX B | Key Contributors

Who Was the Theorist?	What Did He or She Do in His or Her Own Time?	Where Was He or She Influential or From?	When Was He or She Active in the Field?	How Has He or She Impacted the Field Now or Then?
Rousseau	–Author of several education books –proposed children be educated in rural, harmonious envi-ronments free from adult dominance	–Influential in Europe and America	–Mid to late 1700s	–Emphasized out-of-home schooling –Viewed children as innately good
Pestalozzi				
Froebel				
Hall				
Dewey				

Who Was the Theorist?	What Did He or She Do in His or Her Own Time?	Where Was He or She Influential or From?	When Was He or She Active in the Field?	How Has He or She Impacted the Field Now or Then?
Mitchell				
Piaget				
Vygotsky				
Montessori				
Steiner				
Gardner				

Guiding Principles: Meshing Approaches

Use the following chart or your own graphic organizer to identify aspects from the chapters that you might use in teaching. For each item you select, create one concrete strategy that you can apply that addresses the item. Identify the origin of the idea (theorist/approach).

Teacher's Role	View of Children	Environmental Design	Philosophy, Mission, Program Goals	Cultural/Individual Responsiveness and Inclusion
–Spark children's thinking, curiosity, desire to know more (constructivism)	–Powerful and capable (Reggio)	–Beautiful, gentle, hands-on (Waldorf)	–Parents are essential, valuable partners (Head Start)	–Validating each child's abilities and potential, not in comparison with others (High/Scope)

Multiple Intelligence Planning Web

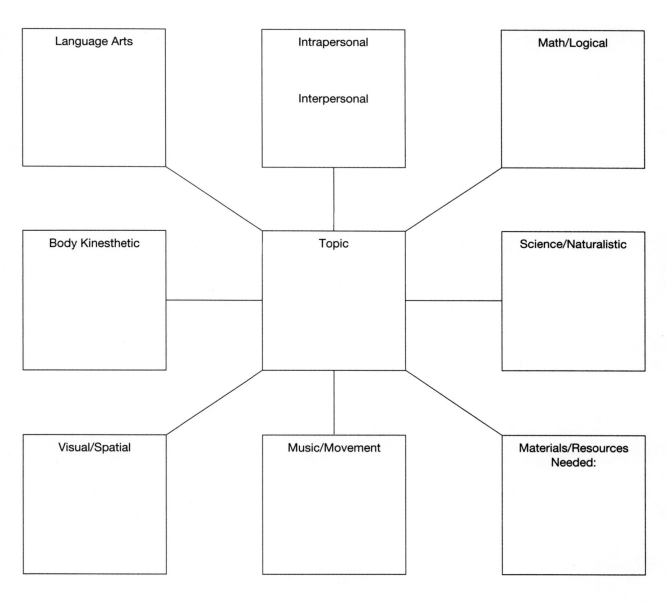

| Language Arts | Intrapersonal

Interpersonal | Math/Logical |

| Body Kinesthetic | Topic | Science/Naturalistic |

| Visual/Spatial | Music/Movement | Materials/Resources Needed: |

Sample Professional Portfolio Rubric
Early Childhood Education Programs— Student Assessment

Based on NAEYC, state, and CDA standards and requirements
Certificate level completes partial portfolio with additional Degree-level portfolio requirements in bold

Component	Courses Artifact Assigned To	Purpose of Artifact	Exceeds Expectations–15	Meets Expectations–10	Does Not Meet Expectations–5
Section I-Intro. Materials - Résumé - Autobiography - **Transcripts** - **2 references**	Intro to ECE Practicum I, II	Self-reflection Professional identity development Credential review	All present Well-written, typed Formatted for easy reading	Two present Few minor writing errors Typed or clearly printed	One or fewer Many writing errors Not Presented in an organized way
Section III-Standards 1. Child Development - Two resources for supporting positive behaviors - One assessment tool to document children's behavior; one copy blank one completed - Weekly learning plan (inclusive) - **Four pamphlets or articles informing families how birth-8 year olds develop and learn**	Child Growth and Development or Developmental Psych Observation, Guidance, and Assessment EC Curriculum Diversity in ECE	Demonstrate knowledge of general and unique attributes of growth Reflect competence in guiding child's development Apply principles of development to learning experiences	Four artifacts Typed and clearly formatted Accurate and up-to-date information (current years) Pamphlets demonstrate foundational knowledge of child development and how theories relate to practice Learning plans are inclusive, tied to appropriate developmental expectations and include appropriate assessment and reflection	Three artifacts Typed or clearly printed Accurate information from within the past 5 years Pamphlets demonstrate foundational knowledge of child development Learning plans are inclusive and tied to appropriate developmental expectations	Two or less artifacts Hard to read (penmanship or copies) Inaccurate and/or out-of-date information Pamphlets demonstrate lack of foundational knowledge of child development Learning plans are not inclusive and tied to appropriate developmental expectations

Component	Courses Artifact Assigned To	Purpose of Artifact	Exceeds Expectations–15	Meets Expectations–10	Does Not Meet Expectations–5
- Poster series documenting development and learning in classroom centers - Developmental theorist review chart - Family literacy brochure	Child Growth and Development or Developmental Psych	Apply knowledge to classroom settings	Seven artifacts Typed and clearly formatted Accurate and up-to-date information Artifacts demonstrate knowledge of developmental theories	Five artifacts Typed or clearly printed Accurate information from within the past 5 years Artifacts demonstrate knowledge of developmental theories	Three or fewer artifacts Hard to read (penmanship or copies) Inaccurate and/or out-of-date information Artifacts demonstrate lack of knowledge of key developmental theories
2. Family and Community - Contact information on family nutrition education agency - Contact information for family counseling referrals - Resource contacts for non-English speaking families - Parent handbook	Diversity in ECE Practicum I, II Administration of EC Programs	Knowledge of community resources Apply knowledge of community resources	Four artifacts Typed and clearly formatted Accurate and up-to-date information (current years) Resources and handbook demonstrate family-centered, supportive, inclusive attitude and practice	Three artifacts Typed or clearly hand-printed Accurate information from within the past 3 years Resources and handbook demonstrate family-centered, supportive, inclusive attitude	One or no artifact Hard to read (penmanship or copies) Inaccurate and/or out-of-date information Resources demonstrate student bias
- NAEYC position statement on Dual Language Learners - Plan for a family workshop	Diversity in ECE Administration of EC Programs	Apply knowledge of family needs and skills in interacting with families	Six artifacts Typed and clearly formatted Accurate and up-to-date information (current years)	Four artifacts Typed or clearly hand-printed Accurate information from within the past 3 years	Two or fewer artifacts Hard to read (penmanship or copies) Inaccurate and/or out-of-date information
3. Observe & Assess - 3 record keeping form samples (accident report, emergency contact form, and one other) - Copies of two developmental checklists (one blank and one completed)	Observation, Guidance, and Assessment	Awareness of assessment tools	Two artifacts Appropriate resources Typed and clearly formatted Developmental checklist demonstrates clear knowledge of assessment purpose and practice	Two artifacts Typed or clearly hand-printed Appropriate resources Developmental checklist completed appropriately	One or no artifact Hard to read (penmanship or copies) Inappropriate resources Developmental checklists not completed/missing

Component	Courses Artifact Assigned To	Purpose of Artifact	Exceeds Expectations–15	Meets Expectations–10	Does Not Meet Expectations–5
- Two sample standardized assessments designed for young children - NAEYC position statement on Kindergarten screening - Photos of documentation panel chronicling children's group project (including analysis)	Intro to ECE EC Curriculum	Demonstrate knowledge of and application of authentic assessment Awareness of professional policies	Five artifacts Accurate and up-to-date information (current years) Appropriate resources Typed and clearly formatted Documentation panel is organized, neat, includes a variety of forms of data, comprehensively chronicles children's learning process	Four artifacts Typed or clearly hand-printed Accurate information from within the past 3 years Appropriate resources Documentation panel is organized, neat, includes some forms of data, chronicles children's learning process but leaves some gaps that require explanation	Two or fewer artifacts Hard to read (penmanship or copies) Inaccurate and/or out-of-date information Inappropriate resources Documentation panel is unorganized, cluttered, does not include variety of data, does not clearly chronicle children's learning process or is missing
4. Using Developmentally Effective Approaches - 4 songs, poems, or fingerplays to promote phonological awareness - Bibliography of 10 books helping children cope with challenging situations	Infant and Toddler Programs Children's Literature	Demonstrate knowledge of DAP	Typed and clearly formatted Accurate and up-to-date information (books within past 5 years) Appropriate resources Book list includes diverse topics	Typed or clearly hand-printed Accurate information within the past 8 years (8 books included) Appropriate resources Book list includes few diverse topics	Hard to read (penmanship or copies) Inaccurate and/or out-of-date information (5 or fewer books included) Inappropriate resources Book list does not include diverse topics
- Project documentation including web, KWHL, doc panel, and notes - Behavior plan for addressing challenging behavior	Intro to ECE EC Curriculum	Apply DAP through project with children	Appropriate resources Typed and clearly formatted Project is clearly and thoroughly documented and clearly demonstrates children's learning process, includes dialogues, photos, teacher reflections, child artifacts Behavior plan integrates 3 positive guidance strategies	Typed or clearly hand-printed Appropriate resources Project is partially documented and demonstrates some of the children's learning process, does not include variety of data sources Behavior plan integrates 1 positive guidance strategy	Hard to read (penmanship or copies) Inappropriate resources Project documentation fails to demonstrate children's process, does not include data Behavior plan incomplete, does not include positive guidance strategies

Component	Courses Artifact Assigned To	Purpose of Artifact	Exceeds Expectations–15	Meets Expectations–10	Does Not Meet Expectations–5
5. Using Content Knowledge - 9 learning plans covering NAEYC content areas (defined in Standards)	Language Arts Birth-8 EC Science, Math, and Social Science	Demonstrate content knowledge	Learning plans demonstrate theoretical knowledge and practical applicability (9 included)	Learning plans demonstrate theoretical knowledge and practical applicability (7 included)	Learning plans fail to demonstrate knowledge of appropriate theory and practice (6 or fewer)
6. Professionalism - Current CPR certification - Summary of child abuse and neglect reporting requirements - Two resources from national ECE association websites (NAEYC and one other) - Child Care licensing agent contacts - Copy of Child Care licensing manual and NAEYC accreditation standards for teacher qualifications - Written statement relating at least two important requirements to your practice - Contact info for 2 agencies serving children with special needs	Basic Emergency Care (or private CPR class) Administration of EC Programs	Demonstrate standard of professional knowledge and credential	Eight artifacts Accurate and up-to-date information (current years) Appropriate resources Typed and clearly written/ formatted statement Statement reflects complex analyses and applications of advocacy and professionalism issues	Six artifacts Typed or clearly hand-printed Accurate information from within the past 3 years Appropriate resources Statement includes 4 or more grammatical errors Statement reflects basic knowledge of central policy and advocacy and professionalism issues	Four or fewer artifacts Hard to read (penmanship or copies) Inaccurate and/ or out-of-date information Inappropriate resources Statement poorly written, not typed Statements demonstrate lack of understanding of central policy issues and advocacy and professionalism issues
- NAEYC/ state (or other professional association) student membership - copy of state early learning guidelines or standards	Administration of EC Programs	Engage in profession	Ten artifacts Accurate and up-to-date information (current years) Appropriate resources	Seven artifacts Typed or clearly hand-printed Accurate information from within the past 3 years Appropriate resources	Five or fewer artifacts Hard to read (penmanship or copies) Inaccurate and/ or out-of-date information Inappropriate resources

Component	Courses Artifact Assigned To	Purpose of Artifact	Exceeds Expectations–15	Meets Expectations–10	Does Not Meet Expectations–5
Level of reflection in entire portfolio			Very well developed, complete, clearly written, and includes insights of personal growth and understanding	Well developed and contains good insights into growth and understanding, most items well-written	Not well developed. Lacks insights and connections to practice, many items contain writing errors
Portfolio organization and presentation			Clearly marked with dividers and tabs, sections easy to locate, well organized. Very aesthetically pleasing (all typed, proper formatting, clear copies)	Marked with dividers, sections easy to locate, most sections organized. Aesthetically pleasing (neat writing, most copies clear)	Not clearly marked or sections hard to find, not organized with tabs or dividers. Poor penmanship, copies marked up, smudged, or unclear, items not typed
Score at certificate level			_____ /	_____ /	_____ /
Score at Degree Completion Level			_____ /	_____ /	_____ /

NAEYC (National Association for the Education of Young Children). (2009). NAEYC Standards for early childhood professional preparation. Washington, DC: NAEYC. Retrieved on February 20, 2014 from www.naeyc.org.

The Child Development Associate/ Assessment System and Competency Standards for Preschool Caregivers. (1999). Washington, D.C.: The Council for Professional Recognition.

Look What We Are Developing in the Creative Arts Center!

Knowledge	Skills
• Colors and Shapes • How different tools make different textures and lines • How shape, color, texture, and line combine to affect composition • Color mixing • Physics of how different materials move, are shaped, and their different qualities	• Fine motor—grasping, pinching, squeezing • Drawing, forming shapes • Gross motor—mixing, kneading, molding • Turn taking, sharing • Caring for materials and space • Pouring • Measuring • Stacking, rolling, pounding, stretching
Dispositions	**Feelings**
• Persistence • Risk-taking • Willingness to try new things • Wondering • Willingness to express ideas • Sharing • Validating multiple perspectives	• Sense of accomplishment • Validation of unique ideas • Joy of making something new • Caring about own ideas and those of others • Enjoyment—the fun and freedom of creating, getting messy, and experimenting!

References

Chapter 1

Allen, K., & Marotz, L. (2003). *Developmental profiles: Prebirth through twelve* (4th ed.). Clifton Park, NY: Delmar Learning.

Baker, A., & Manfredi/Petitt, L. (2004). *Relationships: The heart of quality care.* Washington, DC: National Association for the Education of Young Children.

Barnett, W. S., Jung, K., Yarosz, D. J., Thomas, J., Hornbeck, A., Stechuk, R., & Burns, S. (2008). Educational effects of the tools of the mind curriculum: A randomized trial. *Early Childhood Research Quarterly, 23*(3), 299–313.

Bayat, M., Mindes, G., & Covitt, S. (2010). What does RTI (response to intervention) look like in preschool? *Early Childhood Education Journal, 37,* 493–500.

Bodrova, E., & Leong, D. J. (2007). *Tools of the mind: The Vygotskian approach to early childhood education* (2nd ed.). Upper Saddle River, NJ: Prentice Hall.

Bredekamp, S., & Copple, C. (Eds.). (2009). *Developmentally appropriate practice in early childhood programs* (rev. ed.). Washington, DC: National Association for the Education of Young Children.

Bruder, M. (2010). Early childhood intervention: A promise to children and families for their future. *Exceptional Children, 76*(3), 339–355.

Bullock, A., & Hawk, P. (2001). *Developing a teaching portfolio: A guide for preservice and practicing teachers.* Upper Saddle River, NJ: Merrill/Prentice Hall.

Burchfield, D. W. (1996). Teaching all children: Four developmentally appropriate curricular and instructional strategies in primary-grade classrooms. *Young Children, 52*(1), 4–10.

Buysse, V., Winton, P. J., Rous, B., Epstein, D. J., & Lim, C. (2012). Evidence-based practice. *Zero to Three.* Washington, DC. Retrieved from http://main.zerotothree.org/site/DocServer/32-4_Buysse_linked_copy.pdf.

Cassidy, D., & Buell, M. (1996). Accentuating the positive? An analysis of teacher verbalizations with young children. *Child and Youth Forum, 25*(6), 403–414.

Council of Chief State School Officers. (2011). Interstate Teacher Assessment and Support Consortium (InTASC) model core teaching standards: A resource for state dialogue. Retrieved from http://www.ccsso.org/intasc.

Darragh, J. (2010). *Introduction to early childhood education: Equity and inclusion.* Upper Saddle River, NJ: Pearson.

Doorey, N. A. (2013). Coming soon: A new generation of assessments. *Educational Leadership, 70*(4), 28–34.

Dyson, L. (2005). Kindergarten children's understanding of and attitudes toward people with disabilities. *Topics in Early Childhood Special Education, 25*(2), 95–105.

Eisner, E. (2004). Multiple intelligences: Its tensions and its possibilities. *Teachers College Record, 106*(1), 31–39.

Elkind, D. (2003). Thanks for the memories: The lasting value of true play. *Young Children, 58*(3), 46–50.

Fraser, S. (2007). Play in other languages. *Theory Into Practice, 46*(1), 14–22.

Gainsely, S. (2008). Learning environments that support complex play. *High Scope Extensions, 22*(3), 1–4.

Gargiulo, R. (2006). Homeless and disabled: Rights, responsibilities, and recommendations for serving young children with special needs. *Early Childhood Education Journal, 33*(5), 357–362.

Gelfer, J., Xu, Y., & Perkins, P. (2004). Developing portfolios to evaluate teacher performance in early childhood education. *Early Childhood Education Journal, 32*(2), 127–132.

Girolametto, L., Weitzman, E., & Greenberg, J. (2003). Training day care staff to facilitate children's language. *American Journal of Speech Pathology, 12*(3), 299–311.

Grennon Brooks, J., & Dietz, M. E. (2013). The dangers and opportunities of the common core. *Educational Leadership, 70*(4), 64–67.

Hirsh, R. (2004). *Early childhood curriculum: Incorporating multiple intelligences, developmentally appropriate practice, and play.* Boston: Allyn and Bacon.

Jackson, S., Pretti-Frontczak, K., Harjusola-Webb, S., Grisham-Brown, J., & Mulato, J. (2009). Response to intervention: Implications for early childhood professionals. *Language, Speech, and Hearing Services in Schools, 40,* 424–434.

Jalongo, M. R., Fennimore, B., Pattnaik, J., Laverock, D., Brewster, J., & Mutuku, M. (2004). Blended perspectives: A global vision for high-quality early childhood education. *Early Childhood Education Journal, 32*(3), 143–155.

Jenkinson, S. (2001). *The genius of play.* Gloucestershire, UK: Hawthorn Press.

Landerholm, E., Gehrie, C., & Hao, Y. (2004). Educating early childhood teachers for the global world. *Early Childhood Development and Care, 174*(7–8), 593–606.

National Association for the Education of Young Children. (2011). *2010 NAEYC standards for early childhood professional preparation.* Retrieved from http://www.naeyc.org/ncate/files/ncate/NAEYC%20Initial%20and%20Advanced%20Standards%2010_2012.pdf.

National Association for the Education of Young Children. (2012). The Common Core State Standards: Caution and opportunity for early childhood education. Washington, DC: Author.

National Governors Association Center for Best Practices, Council of Chief State School Officers. (2010). *Common Core State Standards.* Washington DC: Author.

Nikolaraizi, M., Kumar, P., Favazza, P., Sideridis, G., Koulousiou, D., & Riall, A. (2005). A cross-cultural examination of typically developing children's attitudes toward individuals with special needs. *International Journal of Disability, Development and Education, 52*(2), 101–119.

Noddings, N. (1995). Teaching themes of caring. *Education Digest, 61*(3), 24–29.

Noddings, N. (2005). What does it mean to educate the whole child? *Educational Leadership, 63*(1), 8–13.

Pool, C. (1997). Brain-based learning and students. *Education Digest, 63*(3), 10–16.

Ryan, S., & Grieshaber, S. (2004). It's more than child development: Critical theories, research, and teaching young children. *Young Children, 59*(6), 44–52.

Shanahan, T. (2013). The Common Core ate my baby and other urban legends. *Educational Leadership, 70*(4), 11–16.

Spencer, T. D., Detrich, R., & Slocum, T. A. (2012). Evidence-based practice: A framework for making effective decisions. *Education and Treatment of Children, 35*(2), 127–151.

Stanford, P. (2003). Multiple intelligence for every classroom. *Intervention in School and Clinic, 39*(2), 80–85.

The Division for Early Childhood of the Council for Exceptional Children (DEC), National Association for the Education of Young Children (NAEYC), & National Head Start Association (NHSA). 2013. "Frameworks for Response to Intervention in Early Childhood: Description and Implications."

Chapter 2

Adelman, C. (2000). Over two years, what did Froebel say to Pestalozzi? *History of Education, 29*(2), 103–114.

Aldrich, R. (2002). The first 100 years. *Education Journal, 65,* 8.

Antler, J. (1987). *Lucy Sprague Mitchell: The making of a modern woman.* New Haven, CT: Yale University Press.

Archambault, R. (Ed.) (1964). *John Dewey on education: Selected writings.* Chicago: University of Chicago Press.

Beatty, B. (1995). *Preschool education in America: The culture of young children from the colonial era to the present.* New Haven, CT: Yale University Press.

Berk, L., & Winsler, A. (1995). *Scaffolding children's learning: Vygotsky and early childhood education.* Washington, DC: National Association for the Education of Young Children.

Blow, S. E. (1999). Kindergarten education. In K. M. Paciorek & J. H. Munro (Eds.), *Sources: Notable selections in early childhood education* (2nd ed.) (pp. 179–184). Guilford, CT: Dushkin/McGraw-Hill. (Original work published 1900)

Bowers, F., & Gehring, T. (2004). Johann Heinrich Pestalozzi: 18th-century Swiss educator and correctional reformer. *Journal of Correctional Education, 55*(4), 306–319.

Bredekamp, S. (1997). NAEYC issues revised position statement on developmentally appropriate practice in early childhood programs. *Young Children, 52*(2), 34–40.

Bredekamp, S., & Copple, C. (Eds.). (2009). *Developmentally appropriate practice in early childhood programs* (3rd. ed.). Washington, DC: National Association for the Education of Young Children.

Bronfenbrenner, U. (1986). Ecology of the family as a context for human development: Research perspectives. *Developmental Psychology, 22*(6), 723–742.

Bruner, J. (1991). The narrative construction of reality. *Critical Inquiry, 18*(1), 1–21.

Castro, D. C., Paez, M. M., Dickinson, D. K., & Frede, E. (2011). Promoting language and literacy in young dual-language learners: Research, practice, and policy. *Child Development Perspectives, 5*(1), 15–21.

Desimone, L. (2013). Reform before NCLB. *Kappan, 94*(8), 59–61.

Dewey, J. (1938). *Experience and education.* New York: Touchstone.

Dewey, J. (1999). Three years of the university elementary school. In K. M. Paciorek & J. H. Munro (Eds.), *Sources: Notable selections in early childhood education* (2nd ed.) (pp. 158–163). Guilford, CT: Dushkin/McGraw-Hill. (Original work published 1899)

Dombrowski, K. (2002). Kindergarten teacher training in England and the United States 1850–1918. *History of Education, 31*(5), 475–489.

Geist, E., & Baum, A. (2005). Yeah, but that keeps teachers from embracing an active curriculum: Overcoming the resistance. *Young Children, 60*(1), 28–36.

Gesell, A. (1999). Early mental growth. In K. M. Paciorek & J. H. Munro (Eds.), *Sources: Notable selections in early childhood education* (2nd ed.) (pp. 209–217). Guilford, CT: Dushkin/McGraw-Hill. (Original work published 1940)

Goswami, U. (2001). Cognitive development: No stages please—we're British. *British Journal of Psychology, 92*(1), 257–278.

Gregory, M. R. (2002). Constructivism, standards, and the classroom community of inquiry. *Educational Theory, 52*(4), 43–51.

Grinberg, J. (2002). "I had never been exposed to teaching like that": Progressive teacher education at Bank Street during the 1930s. *Teachers College Record, 104*(7), 1422–1460.

Hacsi, T. (1995). From indenture to family foster care: A brief history of child placing. *Child Welfare, 74*(1), 162–181.

Hall, G. S. (1999). The contents of children's minds on entering school. In K. M. Paciorek & J. H. Munro (Eds.), *Sources: Notable selections in early childhood education* (2nd ed.) (pp. 324–334). Guilford, CT: Dushkin/McGraw-Hill. (Original work published 1907)

Hall, J. (2000). Psychology and schooling: The impact of Susan Issacs and Jean Piaget on 1960s science education reform. *History of Education, 29*(2), 153–170.

Henson, K. (2003). Foundations for learner-centered education: A knowledge base. *Education, 124,* 5–16.

Hill, P. S. (1999). Kindergarten. In K. M. Paciorek & J. H. Munro (Eds.), *Sources: Notable selections in early childhood education* (2nd ed.) (pp. 81–90). Guilford, CT: Dushkin/McGraw-Hill. (Original work published 1941)

Horn, D. M., Caruso, D. A., & Golas, J. (2003). Head Start teaching center: Differential training effects for Head Start personnel. *Child & Youth Care Forum, 32*(1), 23–40.

Hoxie, F. (1984). *A final promise: The campaign to assimilate Indians.* Lincoln: University of Nebraska Press.

Hulbert, A. (1999). The century of the child. *Wilson Quarterly, 23*(1), 14–30.

Hyun, E., & Marshall, J. (2003). Teachable-moment-oriented curriculum practice in early childhood education. *Journal of Curriculum Studies, 35*(1), 111–127.

Isaacs, S. (1999). Childhood and after: Some essays and clinical studies. In K. M. Paciorek & J. H. Munro (Eds.), *Sources: Notable selections in early childhood education* (2nd ed.) (pp. 64–69). Guilford, CT: Dushkin/McGraw-Hill. (Original work published 1966)

James, W. (2008). Jerome Bruner, born 1915. *Times Educational Supplement. Issue 4816,* special section 3, 24.

Jones, J. (2004). Framing the assessment debate. *Young Children, 59*(1), 14–18.

Kelleher, M. (2011). States face challenges in early-education race to the top scramble. *Education Week, 30*(36), 26–37.

Kontio, K. (2003). The idea of autarchy in Rousseau's natural education: Recovering the natural harmony? *Scandinavian Journal of Educational Research, 47*(1), 3–19.

Lascarides, V., & Hinitz, B. (2000). *History of early childhood education.* New York: Falmer Press.

Lindqvist, G. (1995). *The aesthetics of play: A didactic study of play and culture in preschools.* (Report no. ISSN-0347-1314). Uppsala, Sweden: Uppsala University. (ERIC Document Reproduction Service no. ED396824).

Margolis, E., & Rowe, J. (2004). Images of assimilation: Photographs of Indian schools in Arizona. *History of Education, 33*(2), 199–230.

Matthews, W. (2003). Constructivism in the classroom: Epistemology, history, and empirical evidence. *Teacher Education Quarterly, 30*(3), 51–64.

Maxwell, L. A. (2012). RTT early-learning winners have work cut out for them. *Education Week, 31*(15), 22.

McMillan, M. (1999). The nursery school. In K. M. Paciorek & J. H. Munro (Eds.), *Sources: Notable selections in early childhood education* (2nd ed.) (pp. 185–189). Guilford, CT: Dushkin/McGraw-Hill. (Original work published 1919)

Montessori, M. (1966). *The secret of childhood.* New York: Ballantine Books.

Moran, R. F. (2005). Undone by law: The uncertain legacy of *Lau v. Nichols. Berkeley La Raza Law Journal, 16*(1), 1–10.

National Association for the Education of Young Children. (1995). *Responding to linguistic and cultural diversity: Recommendations for effective early childhood practice.* Washington, DC: Author.

Null, J. W. (2004). Is constructivism traditional? Historical and practical perspectives on a popular advocacy. *Educational Forum, 68,* 180–188.

O'Connor, S. M. (1995). Mothering in public: The division of organized child care in the kindergarten and day nursery, St. Louis, 1886–1920. *Early Childhood Research Quarterly, 10*(1), 63–80.

Owen, R. (1999). The life of Robert Owen. In K. M. Paciorek & J. H. Munro (Eds.), *Sources: Notable selections in early childhood education* (2nd ed.) (pp. 273–276). Guilford, CT: Dushkin/ McGraw-Hill. (Original work published 1857)

Peabody, E. P. (1999). Guide to the kindergarten and intermediate class. In K. M. Paciorek & J. H. Munro (Eds.), *Sources: Notable selections in early childhood education* (2nd ed.) (pp. 77–80). Guilford, CT: Dushkin/ McGraw-Hill. (Original work published 1877)

Piaget, J. (1929). *The child's conception of the world.* London: Rutledge & Kegan Paul.

Piaget, J. (1954). *The construction of reality in the child.* New York: Basic Books.

Piaget, J. (1969). *The psychology of the child.* New York: Basic Books.

Piaget, J. (1975). *The development of thought.* New York: Viking Press.

Piaget, J. (1999). The stages of the intellectual development of the child. In K. M. Paciorek & J. H. Munro (Eds.), *Sources: Notable selections in early childhood education* (2nd ed.) (pp. 3–10). Guilford, CT: Dushkin/ McGraw-Hill. (Original work published 1961)

Powell, M. (2000). Can Montessorians and constructivists really be friends? *Montessori Life, 21*(1), 44–51.

Procher, L. (1998). Missing pieces: A review of history chapters in introductory early childhood education textbooks. *Journal of Early Childhood Teacher Education, 19*(1), 31–42.

Read, J. (2003). Froebelian women: Networking to promote professional status and educational change in the nineteenth century. *History of Education, 32*(1), 17–33.

Reynolds, A. J., Miedel, W. T., & Mann, E. A. (2000). Innovation in early intervention for children in families with low incomes: Lessons from the Chicago Child-Parent Centers. *Young Children, 55*(2), 84–88.

Sameroff, A., & McDonough, S. C. (1994). Educational implications of developmental transitions: Revisiting the 5- to 7-year shift. *Phi Delta Kappan, 76*(3), 188–193.

Sandsmark, S. (2002). A Lutheran perspective on education. *Journal of Education and Christian Belief, 6*(2), 97–106.

Saracho, O. N., & Spodek, B. (1995). Children's play and early childhood education: Insights from history and theory. *Journal of Education, 117*(3), 129–148.

Schickedanz, J. (1995). Early education and care: Beginnings. *Journal of Education, 177*(3), 1–7.

Spodek, B. (1985). Early childhood education's past as prologue: Roots of contemporary concerns. *Young Children, 40*(5), 3–7.

Sullivan, K. (1996). Progressive education: Where are you now that we need you? *Oxford Review of Education, 22*(3), 349–356.

Swiniarski, D. (2005). Elizabeth P. Peabody's bicentennial birthday: A celebration of a past legacy and a future vision for kindergarten. *Early Childhood Education Journal, 34*(4), 219–220.

Takanishi, R. (1981). Early childhood education and research: The changing relationship. *Theory Into Practice, 10*(2), 86–92.

Trotter, A., Keller, B., Zehr, M., Manzo, K., & Bradley, A. (1999). Lessons of a century: Faces of a century. *Education Week, 19*(16), 27–38.

Turnbull, R., & Cilley, M. (1999). *Explanations and implications of the 1997 amendments to IDEA.* Upper Saddle River, NJ: Merrill/Prentice Hall.

U.S. Department of Education (2004a). *A guide to No Child Left Behind.* Washington, DC: U.S. Department of Education, Office of the Secretary, Office of Public Affairs.

U.S. Department of Education (2004b). *Overview: Four pillars of NCLB.* Washington, DC: U.S. Department of Education, Office of the Secretary, Office of Public Affairs. Retrieved from www.ed.gov/nclb/overview/intro/4pillars.html.

U.S. Department of Education. (2009). Race to the Top program executive summary. Washington, DC: Author.

Vander Zanden, J. (2003). *Human development.* Boston: McGraw-Hill.

Verbruggen, R. (2012). No Child Left Behind, left behind. *National Review, 64*(19), 53–54.

Vygotsky, L. S. (1978). *Mind in society: The development of higher psychological processes.* Cambridge, MA: Harvard University Press.

Vygotsky, L. S. (1999). From thought and language. In K. M. Paciorek & J. H. Munro (Eds.), *Sources: Notable selections in early childhood education* (2nd ed.) (pp. 11–18). Guilford, CT: Dushkin/McGraw-Hill. (Original work published 1962)

Chapter 3

Association for Childhood Education International. (n.d.). *The ACEI experience.* Retrieved from www.acei.org/history.htm.

Baptiste, N., & Reyes, L. (2002). *Ethics in early care and education.* Upper Saddle River, NJ: Merrill/Prentice Hall.

Barnett, W. S. (2004). Better teachers, better preschools: Student achievement linked to teacher qualifications.

Preschool Policy Matters (2). New Brunswick, NJ: National Institute for Early Education Research.

Bredekamp, S. (1997). NAEYC issues revised position statement on developmentally appropriate practice in early childhood programs. *Young Children, 52*(2), 34–40.

Bredekamp, S., & Copple, C. (Eds.). (1997). *Developmentally appropriate practice in early childhood programs* (rev. ed.). Washington, DC: National Association for the Education of Young Children.

Bredekamp, S., & Copple, C. (Eds.). (2009). *Developmentally appropriate practice in early childhood programs* (3rd. ed.). Washington, DC: National Association for the Education of Young Children.

Cassidy, D. J., Hestenes, L. L., Hegde, A., Hestenes, S., & Mims, S. (2005). Measurement of quality in preschool child care classrooms: An exploratory and confirmatory factor analysis of the early childhood environment rating scale—revised. *Early Childhood Research Quarterly, 20*(3), 345–360.

Caulfield, R. (1997). Professionalism in early care and education. *Early Childhood Education Journal, 24*(4), 261–263.

Dickinson, D. (2002). Shifting images of developmentally appropriate practice as seen through different lenses. *Educational Researcher, 31*(1), 26–32.

Downer, J. T., Lopez, M. L., Grimm, K. J., Hamagami, A., Pianta, R. C., Howes, C. (2012). Observations of teacher-child interactions in classrooms serving Latinos and dual-language learners: Applicability of the Classroom Assessment Scoring System in diverse settings. *Early Childhood Research Quarterly, 27*, 21–32.

Dunn, L., & Kontos, S. (1997). What have we learned about developmentally appropriate practice? *Young Children, 52*(5), 4–13.

Feeney, S., & Freeman, N. K. (1999). *Ethics and the early childhood educator: Using the NAEYC code.* Washington, DC: National Association for the Education of Young Children.

Freeman, N. K. (2000). Professional ethics: A cornerstone of teachers' preservice curriculum. *Action in Teacher Education, 22*(3), 12–18.

Hamre, B. K., Goffin, S. G., & Kraft Sayre, M. (2009a). *CLASS Implementation Guide.* Retrieved from http://www.classobservation.com/wp-content/uploads/2010/06/CLASSImplementationGuide.pdf

Hamre, B. K., Goffin, S. G., & Kraft-Sayre, M. (2009b). *Classroom Assessment Scoring System: Implementation Guide.* Charlotte, VA: Center for Advanced Study of Teaching and Learning.

Katz, L., & Ward, E. (1978). *Ethical behavior in early childhood education.* Washington, DC: National Association for the Education of Young Children.

Martin, S., Meyer, J., Jones, R. C., Nelson, L., & Ting, L. (2010). Perceptions of professionalism among individuals in the child care field. *Child Youth Care Forum, 39*(5), 341–349.

Moore, K. (2000). Assessing children's learning and development. *Scholastic Early Childhood Today, 14*(4), 14–15.

Moyles, J. (2001). Passion, paradox, and professionalism in early years education. *Early years, 21*(2), 81–95.

National Association for the Education of Young Children. (2004). About NAEYC. Retrieved from www.naeyc.org/content/about-naeyc.

National Association for the Education of Young Children. (2011). Code of ethical conduct and statement of commitment. Retrieved from http://www.naeyc.org/files/naeyc/file/positions/Ethics%20Position%20Statement2011.pdf.

Owocki, G. 2001. Make way for literacy: Teaching the way young children learn. Portsmouth, NH: Heinemann

Sandell, E. J., Hardin, B. J., & Wortham, S. (2010). Using ACEI's global guidelines assessment for improving early education. *Childhood Education, 86*(3), 157–160.

U.S. Department of Education, National Center for Educational Statistics. (2009a). Common Core of Data, "Public Elementary/Secondary School Universe Survey," 2007–08. Retrieved from http://nces.ed.gov/pubs2010/2010015/figures/figure_7_1.asp.

U.S. Department of Education, National Center for Educational Statistics. (2009b). Status and trends in the education of ethnic and racial minorities. Common Core of Data, "Public Elementary/Secondary School Universe Survey," 2000–01, 2003–04, and 2007–08. Retrieved from http://nces.ed.gov/pubs2010/2010015/tables/table_7_1a.asp.

Warash, B. G., Ward, C., & Rotilie, S. (2008). An exploratory study of the application of early childhood environemt rating scale criteria. *Education, 128*(4), 645–658.

Chapter 4

Anderson, R. (1998). Why talk about different ways to grade? The shift from traditional assessment to alternative assessment. *New Directions for Teaching and Learning, 74*, 5–16.

Arcaro-McPhee, R., Doppler, E. E., & Harkins, D. A. (2002). Conflict resolution in a preschool constructivist classroom: A case study in negotiation. *Journal of Research in Childhood Education, 17*(1), 19–25.

Berk, L., & Winsler, A. (1995). *Scaffolding children's learning: Vygotsky and early childhood education*. Washington, DC: National Association for the Education of Young Children.

Bredekamp, S., & Copple, C. (2009). *Developmentally appropriate practice in early childhood programs* (3rd ed.). Washington, DC: National Association for the Education of Young Children.

Bronfenbrenner, U. (1994). Ecological models of human development. In *International Encyclopedia of Education, 3*, (2nd ed.). Oxford: Elsevier. Reprinted in M. Gauvain & M. Cole (Eds.). *Readings on the development of children* (2nd ed.). (1993, pp. 37–43). New York: Freeman.

Bronfenbrenner, U. (2005a). The bioecological theory of human development. In Bronfenbrenner, U. (Ed.). *Making human beings human* (pp. 3–15). White Plains, NY: Longman.

Bronfenbrenner, U. (2005b). The future of childhood. In Bronfenbrenner, U. (Ed.), *Making human beings human* (pp. 246–259). Thousand Oaks, CA: SAGE Publications.

Castle, K. (1997). Constructing knowledge of constructivism. *Journal of Early Childhood Education, 18*(1), 55–67.

Darragh, J. (2007). Universal design for early childhood education: Ensuring access and equity for all. *Early Childhood Education Journal, 33*(2), 167–171.

Davis, B., & Sumara, D. (2002). Constructivist discourses and the field of education: Problems and possibilities. *Educational Theory, 52*, 409–428.

DeVries, R., & Zan, B. (1995). Creating a constructivist classroom atmosphere. *Young Children, 51*(1), 4–13.

DeVries, R., & Zan, B. (2003). When children make rules. *Educational Leadership, 61*(1), 64–67.

Dewey, J. (1938). *Experience and Education*. New York: Touchstone.

Dixon-Krauss, L. (1996). *Vygotsky in the classroom: Mediated literacy instruction and assessment*. White Plains, NY: Longman.

Ediger, M. (2000). Purposes in learner assessment. *Journal of Instructional Psychology, 27*(4), 244–250.

Gregory, M. R. (2002). Constructivism, standards, and the classroom community of inquiry. *Educational Theory, 52*(4), 43–51.

Izumi-Taylor, S. (2013). Scaffolding in group-oriented Japanese preschools. *Young Children, 68*(1), 70–75.

Knight, C. C., & Sutton, R. E. (2004). Neo-Piagetian theory and research: Enhancing pedagogical practice for educators of adults. *London Review of Education, 2*(1), 47–60.

Low, J. M., & Shironaka, W. (1995). Letting go: Allowing first graders to become autonomous learners. *Young Children, 51*(1), 21–25.

Marcon, R. (2002). Moving up the grades: Relationship between preschool model and later school success. *Early Childhood Research and Practice, 4*(1). Retrieved from ecrp.uiuc.edu/v4nl/marcon.html.

Matthews, W. (2003). Constructivism in the classroom: Epistemology, history, and empirical evidence. *Teacher Education Quarterly, 30*(3), 51–64.

McAfee, O., Leong, D. J., & Bodrova, E. (2004). *Primer on early childhood assessment: What every teacher should know*. Washington, DC: National Association for the Education of Young Children.

Piaget, J. (1929). *The child's conception of the world*. London: Routledge & Kegan Paul.

Piaget, J. (1969). *The psychology of the child*. New York: Basic Books.

Piaget, J. (1975). *The development of thought*. New York: Viking Press.

Powell, M. (2000). Can Montessorians and constructivists really be friends? *Montessori Life, 21*(1), 44–51.

Ray, J. (2002). Constructivism and classroom teachers: What can early childhood teacher educators do to support the constructivist journey? *Journal of Early Childhood Teacher Education, 23*, 319–325.

Richardson, V. (2003). Constructivist pedagogy. *Teachers College Record, 105*, 1623–1640.

Schuh, K. (2003). Knowledge construction in the learner-centered classroom. *Journal of Educational Psychology, 95*, 426–442.

Schweinhart, L. J., Barnes, H., & Weikart, D. P. (1993). Significant benefits: The High/Scope Perry Preschool study through age 27. (Monographs of the High/Scope Educational Research Foundation, 10). Ypsilanti, MI: High/Scope Press.

Simpson, T. (2002). Dare I oppose constructivism? *The Educational Forum, 66*, 347–354.

Suizzo, M. (2000). The socioemotional and cultural contexts of cognitive development: Neo-Piagetian perspectives. *Child Development, 71*(4), 846–849.

Vygotsky, L. S. (1978). *Mind in society: The development of higher psychological processes*. Cambridge, MA: Harvard University Press.

Chapter 5

Addy, S., Wright, V. (2012). Basic facts about low-income children. National Center for Children in Poverty. Retrieved from http://www.nccp.org/publications/pub_1049.html

American Psychological Association. (2005). Lesbian and gay parenting. Washington, DC: American Psychological Association Lesbian, Gay, and Bisexual Concerns Office.

Armstrong, T. (1994). *Multiple intelligences in the classroom.* Alexandria, VA: Association for Supervision and Curriculum Development.

Banks, J. A. (2006). *Cultural diversity and education: Foundations, curriculums, and teaching* (5th ed.). Boston, MA: Pearson Education, Inc.

Batalova, J., & McHugh, M. (2010). Top languages spoken by English-language learners nationally and by state. Washington, DC: Migration Policy Institute.

Bredekamp, S., & Copple, C. (Eds.). (2009). *Developmentally appropriate practice in early childhood programs.* Washington, DC: National Association for the Education of Young Children.

Bucher, R. D. (2010). *Diversity consciousness: Opening our minds to people, cultures and opportunities* (3rd ed.). Upper Saddle River, NJ: Pearson Education, Inc.

Campbell, L., Campbell, B., & Dickinson, D. (2004). *Teaching and learning through multiple intelligences.* Boston: Allyn and Bacon.

Carlisle, A. (2001). Using multiple intelligences theory to assess early childhood curricula. *Young Children, 56*(6), 77–83.

Division for Early Childhood. 2007. Promoting positive outcomes for children with disabilities: Recommendations for curriculum, assessment, and program evaluation. Missoula, MT: Author.

Division for Early Childhood/National Association for the Education of Young Children. (2009). Early childhood inclusion: A joint position statement of the Division for Early Childhood (DEC) and the National Association for the Education of Young Children (NAEYC). Chapel Hill: The University of North Carolina, FPG Child Development Institute.

Ennis, S. R., Rios-Vargas, M., & Albert, N. G. (2011). The Hispanic population: 2010. (Census Briefs C2010BR-04). Washington, DC: U.S. Census Bureau.

Follari, L.. (2015). Valuing Diversity in Early Childhood. Upper Saddle River, NJ: Pearson.

Gardner, H. (1993). *Multiple intelligences: The theory in practice.* New York: Basic Books.

Gardner, H. (1995). Reflections on multiple intelligences: Myths and messages. *Phi Delta Kappan, 77,* 200–203.

Gardner, H. (1997). Multiple intelligences as a partner in school reform. *Educational Leadership, 55,* 20–21.

Gardner, H. (2006). *Multiple Intelligences.* New York: Basic Books.

Gartrell, N., & Bos, H. (2010). U.S. national longitudinal lesbian family study: Psychological adjustment of 17-year-old adolescents. *Pediatrics, 126*(1), 1–9.

Gollnick, D. M., & Chinn, P. C. (2009). *Multicultural education in a pluralistic society* (8th ed.). Upper Saddle River, NJ: Pearson Education, Inc.

Government Printing Office. (2012). Title 34: Education. Part 300: Assistance to states for the education of children with disabilities. 71 FR 46753, Aug. 14, 2006, as amended at 72 FR 61307, Oct. 30, 2007. Retrieved from http://www.ecfr.gov/cgi-bin/text-idx?c=ecfr&sid=96025ad40230ae0f4a530ec51d0519ca&rgn=div5&view=text&node=34:2.1.1.1.1&idno=34#34:2.1.1.1.1.36.7.

Greeff, A., & Du Toit, C. (2009). Resilience in remarried families. *The American Journal of Family Therapy, 37*(2), 114–126.

Houston, D., & Kramer, L. (2008). Meeting the long-term needs of families who adopt children out of foster care: A three-year follow-up study. *Child Welfare, 87*(4), 145–170.

Humes, K. R., Jones, N. A., & Ramirez, R. R. (2011). *Overview of race and Hispanic origin: 2010* (2010 Census Briefs #C2010BR-02). Washington, DC: U.S. Census Bureau. Retrieved from http://www.census.gov/prod/cen2010/briefs/c2010br-02.pdf

Kids Count. (2012). *2012 Kids Count Data Book.* Annie E. Casey Foundation. Retrieved from http://www.aecf.org/KnowledgeCenter/Publications.aspx?pubguid=%7B68E8B294-EDCD-444D-85E4-D1C1576830FF%7D.

Kreider, R., & Ellis, R. (2011). Living arrangements of children: 2009. *Current Population Reports, 70–126.* Washington, DC: U.S. Census Bureau.

Nuzzi, R. (1997). A multiple intelligence approach. *Momentum, 28,* 16–19.

Office for Civil Rights. (2011). Protecting students with disabilities: Frequently asked questions about Section 504 and the education of children with disabilities. Retrieved from http://www2.ed.gov/about/offices/list/ocr/504faq.html.

Office of Special Education Programs, U.S. Department of Education. (2012). *Infants and toddlers receiving early intervention services in accordance with Part C, 2011.* USDOE OSEP Data Analysis System (DANS). Data updated as of July 15, 2012. OMB #1820-0557

Reiff, J. (1996). Multiple intelligences: Different ways of learning. Association for Childhood Education International. Retrieved from www.udel.edu/bateman/acei/multint9.htm.

Schonfeld, D. J. (2011). An interview with David Schonfeld: The educator's role in helping children with grief. *North American Journal of Psychology, 13*(2), 275-280.

Snyder, T. D., & Dillow, S. A. (2012). *Digest of Education Statistics, 2011* (NCES 2012-001). Washington, DC: National Center for Education Statistics, Institute of Education Sciences, U.S. Department of Education.

Stanford, P. (2003). Multiple intelligence for every classroom. *Intervention in School and Clinic, 39*(2), 80–85.

U.S. Census Bureau. (2012). Current Population Survey: 2012. Retrieved from http://www.census.gov/popest/data/.

U.S. Census Bureau. (2013). *America's children: Key national indicators of well-being, 2013.* Washington, DC: Author. Retreived from http://www.childstats.gov/americaschildren/famsoc1.asp.

U.S. Department of Health and Human Services. (2013). Annual update of the HHS poverty guidelines. 2013-01422. Retrieved from https://www.federal-register.gov/articles/2013/01/24/2013-01422/annual-update-of-the-hhs-poverty-guidelines.

Wood, D. (2003). Effect of child and family poverty on child health in the United States. *Pediatrics, 112*(3 Part 2), 707–711.

York, S. (2003). *Roots & Wings*. St. Paul, MN: Red Leaf Press.

Chapter 6

Aber, L., & Palmer, J. (1999). Poverty and brain development in early childhood. National Center for Children in Poverty, Mailman School of Public Health, Columbia University. Retrieved from www.nccp.org/pub_pbd99.html.

Addy, S., Engelhardt, W., & Skinner, C. (2013). Basic facts about low-income children: Children under 6 years, 2011. National Center for Children Living in Poverty. New York, NY: Mailman School of Public Health, Columbia University.

Blair, C., Peters, R., & Lawrence, F. (2003). Family dynamics and child outcomes in early intervention: The role of developmental theory in the specification of effects. *Early Childhood Research Quarterly, 18*, 446–467.

Bloom, B. (1964). *Stability and change in human characteristics*. New York: Wiley.

Bredekamp, S., & Copple, C. (2009). *Developmentally appropriate practice in early childhood programs* (3rd ed.).

Washington, DC: National Association for the Education of Young Children.

Caputo, R. (2003). Head Start, other preschool programs, and life success in a youth cohort. *Journal of Sociology and Social Welfare, 30*(2), 105–126.

Champion, T., Hyter, Y., McCabe, A., & Bland-Stewart, L. (2003). "A matter of vocabulary": Performances of low-income African-American Head Start children on the Peabody Picture Vocabulary Test-III. *Communication Disorders, 23*(3), 121–127.

Children's Defense Fund. (2003). *Head Start reauthorization: Questions and answers*. Washington, DC: Author.

Diamond, M., & Hopson, J. (1998). *Magic trees of the mind: How to nurture your child's intelligence, creativity, and healthy emotions from birth through adolescence*. New York: Plume Books.

Elliot, J., Prior, M., Merrigan, C., & Ballinger, K. (2002). Evaluation of a community intervention programme for preschool behaviour problems. *Journal of Pediatric Child Health, 38*, 41–50.

Gershoff, E. (2003). Living at the Edge Research Brief No. 4: Low income and the development of America's kindergarteners. National Center for Children in Poverty, Mailman School of Public Health, Columbia University. Retrieved from www.nccp.org/publications/pub_533.html.

Hall, J., Sylva, K., Melhuish, E., Sammons, P., Siraj-Blatchford, I., & Taggart, B. (2009). The role of pre-school quality in promoting resilience in the cognitive development of young children. *Oxford Review of Education, 35*(3), 331–352.

Halle, T., Forry, N., Hair, E., Perper, K., Wandner, L., Wessel, J., & Vick, J. (2009). Disparities in early learning and development: Lessons from the early childhood longitudinal study—birth cohort. Washington, DC: Child Trends.

Hanson, M. (2003). Twenty-five years after early intervention: A follow-up of children with Down syndrome and their families. *Infants and Young Children, 16*(4), 354–365.

Head Start Bureau. (1997). Head Start program performance standards and other regulations (Health and Developmental Services). Washington, DC: Head Start Bureau, Administration on Children, Youth, and Families, U.S. Department of Health and Human Services. Retrieved from www.acf.hhs.gov/programs/hsb/pdf/1304_ALL.pdf.

Hume, K., Bellini, S., & Pratt, C. (2005). The usage and perceived outcomes of early intervention and early childhood programs for young children with Autism

Spectrum Disorder. *Topics in Early Childhood Special Education, 24*(4), 195–207.

IDEA. (2004). Individuals with Disabilities Education Improvement Act of 2004, Pub. L. No. 108–446, §2, 118 Stat. 2647 (2004).

Jacobson, L. (2003). Head Start reauthorization goals detailed. *Education Week, 23*(9), 23–25.

Jacobson, L. (2004). Criticism over new Head Start testing program mounts. *Education Week, 23*(4), 10–12.

Kagan, J. (2002). Empowerment and education: Civil rights, expert-advocates, and parent politics in Head Start, 1964–1980. *Teachers College Record, 104*(3), 516–562.

Knitzer, J., & Lefkowitz, J. (2006). Helping the most vulnerable infants, toddlers, and their families. National Center for Children in Poverty, Mailman School of Public Health, Columbia University. Retrieved from www.nccp.org/publications/pub_669.html#1.

Lascarides, V., & Hinitz, B. (2000). *History of early childhood education*. New York: Falmer Press.

Lee, V., Brooks-Gunn, J., Schnur, E., & Liaw, F. (1990). Are Head Start effects sustained? A longitudinal follow-up comparison of disadvantaged children attending Head Start, no preschool, and other preschool programs. *Child Development, 61*(2), 495–507.

Marcon, R. (2002). Moving up the grades: Relationship between preschool model and later school success. *Early Childhood Research and Practice, 4*(1). Retrieved from ecrp.uiuc.edu/v4nl/marcon.html.

Muennig, P., Schweinhart, L., Montie, J., & Neidell, M. (2009). Effects of a prekindergarten educational intervention on adult health: 37-year follow-up results of a randomized controlled trial. *Research and Practice, 99*(8), 1431–1437.

Nord, C., & Rhoads, A. (1992). *The survey of income and program participation as a source of data on children: A statistical profile of at-risk children in the United States.* Washington, DC: U.S. Department of Education. ED415992.

Parke, B., & Agness, P. (2002). Hand in hand: A journey toward readiness for profoundly at-risk preschoolers. *Early Childhood Education Journal, 30*(1), 33–37.

Peth-Pierce, R. (2000). *A good beginning: Sending America's children to school with the social and emotional competence they need to succeed.* Bethesda, MD: Child Mental Health Foundations and Agencies Network, National Institute of Mental Health.

Powell, M. (2000). Can Montessorians and constructivists really be friends? *Montessori Life, 21*(1), 44–51.

Rappaport, M., McWilliam, R., & Smith, B. (2004). Practices across disciplines in early intervention: The research base. *Infants and Young Children, 17*(1), 32–44.

Rauh, V., Parker, F., Garfinkel, R., Perry, J., & Andrews, H. (2003). Biological, social, and community influences on third-grade reading levels in minority children: A multi-level approach. *Journal of Community Psychology, 31*(3), 255–278.

Robbins, T., Stagman, S., & Smith, S. (2012). Young children at risk. *Oct 2012 Fact Sheet.* National Center for Children Living in Poverty. Mailman School of Public Health, Columbia University.

Samuels, C. (2013). New scrutiny as Head Start centers recomplete for aid. *Education Week, 32*(19), 6.

Schmit, S., & Ewen, D. (2012a). *Putting children and families first: Head Start in 2010. Brief number 10.* Washington, DC: Center for Law and Social Policy.

Schmit, S., & Ewen, D. (2012b). *Supporting our youngest children: Early Head Start programs in 2010. Brief Number 11.* Center for Law and Social Policy: Washington, DC. Retrieved from http://www.clasp.org/admin/site/publications/files/EHS-Trend-Analysis-Final.pdf.

Schweinhart, L. J., Barnes, H. V., & Weikart, D. P. (1993). *Significant benefits: The High/Scope Perry preschool study through age 27.* (Monographs of the High/Scope Educational Research Foundation, 10). Ypsilanti, MI: High/Scope Press. PS 021 998.

Smith, B. J. (1988). Does early intervention help? *ERIC Digest* No. 455. ED295399.

U.S. Department of Health and Human Services. (2002a). Head Start history. Washington, DC: U.S. Government Printing Office. Retrieved from www.acf.hhs.gov/programs/opre/hs/ch_trans/reports/transition_study/trans_study_pt1.html.

U.S. Department of Health and Human Services. (2002b). Making a difference in the lives of infants and toddlers and their families: The impacts of Early Head Start. Washington, DC: U.S. Government Printing Office. Retrieved from www.acf.hhs.gov/programs/opre/ehs/ehs_resrch/reports/impacts_exesum/impacts_exesum.html.

U.S. Department of Health and Human Services. (2003). Head Start FACES 2000: A whole-child perspective on program performance. Washington, DC: U.S. Government Printing Office. Retrieved from www.acf.hhs.gov/programs/opre/hs/faces/.

U.S. Department of Health and Human Services. (2006). FACES findings: New research on Head Start outcomes and program quality. Retrieved from www. acf.hhs.gov/programs/opre/hs/faces/reports/faces_findings_06/faces_findings.pdf.

U.S. Department of Health and Human Services. (2008). Head Start reauthorization: P.L. 110–134. Retrieved from http://www.gpo.gov/fdsys/pkg/PLAW-110publ134/pdf/PLAW-110publ134.pdf

U.S. Department of Health and Human Services. (2010). *Head Start impact study. Final report.* Washington, DC: Administration for Children and Families.

U.S. Department of Health and Human Services. (2011). *Head Start development and early learning framework.* Washington, DC: Administration for Children and Families.

U.S. Department of Health and Human Services. (2012a). Head Start program facts fiscal year 2012. Retrieved from http://eclkc.ohs.acf.hhs.gov/hslc/mr/factsheets/docs/hs-program-fact-sheet-2012.pdf.

U.S. Department of Health and Human Services. (2012b). *Third grade follow-up to the Head Start impact study. Final report.* Washington, DC: Administration for Children and Families.

U.S. Department of Health and Human Services. (2013). 2013 poverty guidelines. *Federal Register, 78*(16), 5182–5183. Retrieved from http://aspe.hhs.gov/poverty/13poverty.cfm.

Vander Zanden, J. (2003). *Human development.* Boston: McGraw-Hill.

Chapter 7

Bracey, G. W. (2003). Investing in preschool. *American School Board Journal, 190*(1), 32–35.

Child Care Information Exchange. (2002). Celebrating a life for children: An interview with David Weikart. *Child Care Information Exchange, 144,* 30–31.

Epstein, A. S. (2003). How planning and reflection develop young children's thinking skills. *Young Children, 58*(5), 28–36.

Epstein, A. S. (2005). *All about High/Scope.* Ypsilanti, MI: High/Scope Educational Research Foundation. Retrieved from www.highscope.org/about/allabout.htm.

Epstein, A. S., Schweinhart, L. J., & McAdoo, L. (1996). *Models of early childhood education.* Ypsilanti, MI: High/Scope Press.

File, N., & Kontos, S. (1993). The relationship of program quality to children's play in integrated early intervention settings. *Topics in Early Childhood Special Education, 13,* 1.

Girolametto, L., Weitzman, E., van Lieshout, R., & Duff, D. (2000). Directiveness in teacher's language input to toddlers and preschoolers in day care. *Journal of Speech, Language, and Hearing Research, 43*(4), 1101–1104.

High/Scope Educational Research Foundation. (2003). *Preschool program quality assessment* (2nd ed.). Ypsilanti, MI: High/Scope Press.

High/Scope Educational Research Foundation. (2005). *Child observation record information for decision makers.* Ypsilanti, MI: High/Scope Press. Retrieved from www.highscope.org/file/Assessment/cor_decision_maker.pdf.

High/Scope Educational Research Foundation. (2009a). *Infant and toddler key experiences.* Ypsilanti, MI: High/Scope Press. Retrieved from www.highscope.org/Content.asp?ContentId=94.

High/Scope Educational Research Foundation. (2009b). *Key developmental indicators.* Ypsilanti, MI: High/Scope Press. Retrieved from www.highscope.org/Content.asp?ContentId=275.

Maehr, J. (2003). High/Scope preschool key experiences: Language and literacy [videotape]. Ypsilanti, MI: High/Scope Educational Research Foundation.

Marcon, R. A. (1992). Differential effects of three preschool models on inner-city 4-year-olds. *Early Childhood Research Quarterly, 7,* 517–530.

Muennig, P., Schweinhart, L., Montie, J., & Neidell, M. (2009). Effects of a prekindergarten educational intervention on adult health: 37-year follow-up results of a randomized controlled trial. *Research and Practice, 99*(8), 1431–1437.

National Association for the Education of Young Children. (1995). *Responding to linguistic and cultural diversity: Recommendations for effective early childhood practice.* Washington, DC: Author.

Quindlen, A. (2001). Building blocks for every kid. *Newsweek, 137*(7), 68–69.

Schweinhart, L. J. (2003). *Validity of the High/Scope preschool education model.* Ypsilanti, MI: High/Scope Educational Research Foundation.

Schweinhart, L. J., Montie, J., Xiang, Z., Barnett, W. S., Belfield, C. R., & Nores, M. (2005). *Lifetime effects: The High/Scope Perry Preschool Study through age 40.* (Monographs of the High/Scope Educational Research Foundation, 14). Ypsilanti, MI: High/Scope Press.

Shouse, A. C. (1995). *High/Scope preschool curriculum: Educational programs that work.* Ypsilanti, MI: High/Scope Educational Research Foundation.

Sylva, K., & Evans, E. (1999). Preventing failure at school. *Children and Society, 13,* 278–286.

Trawick-Smith, J. (1994). Authentic dialogue with children: A sociolinguistic perspective on language learning. *Dimensions of Early Childhood, 22*(4), 9–16.

Chapter 8

Beneke, S. (2000). Implementing the project approach in part-time early childhood education programs. *Early Childhood Research Quarterly, 2*(1). Retrieved from http://ecrp.uiuc.edu/v2n1/beneke.html.

Chard, S. (1998a). *The project approach: Book 1.* New York, NY: Scholastic Inc.

Chard, S. (1998b). *The project approach: Book 2.* New York, NY: Scholastic Inc.

Edwards, C., & Springate, K. (1993). Inviting children into project work. *Dimensions of Early Childhood, 22*(1), 9–12, 40.

Gallick, B. (2000). The hairy head project. *Early Childhood Research Quarterly, 2*(2). Retrieved from ecrp.uiuc.edu/v2n2/gallick.html.

Gregory, M. R. (2002). Constructivism, standards, and the classroom community of inquiry. *Educational Theory, 52*(4), 43–51.

Helm, J., & Katz, L. (2001). *Young investigators: The project approach in the early years.* New York: Teachers College Press.

Hertzog, N. B. (2007). Transforming pedagogy: Implementing the Project Approach in two first-grade classrooms. *Journal of Advanced Academics, 18*(4), 530–564.

Katz, L. (1998). Issues in selecting topics for projects. *ERIC* digest no. ED424031 1998-10-00. Retrieved from www.eric.ed.gov/ERICDocs/data/ericdocs2sql/content_stoage_01/0000019b/80/16/f2/ed.pdf.

Katz, L., & Chard, S. (2000). *Engaging children's minds: The project approach.* Stamford, CT: Ablex Publishing.

Mitchell, S., Foulger, T. S., Wetzel, K., & Rathkey, C. (2009). The negotiated Project Approach: Project-based learning without leaving standards behind. *Early Childhood Education Journal, 36,* 339–346.

Trepanier-Street, M. (1993). What's so new about the Project Approach? *Childhood Education, 20,* 25–28.

Vygotsky, L. S. (1978). *Mind in society: The development of higher psychological processes.* Cambridge, MA: Harvard University Press.

Chapter 9

Bredekamp, S. (1993). Reflections on Reggio Emilia. *Young Children, 49*(1), 13–17.

Bredekamp, S., & Rosengrant, T. (Eds.). (1992). *Reaching potentials: Appropriate curriculum and assessment for young children* (Vol. 1). Washington, DC: National Association for the Education of Young Children.

Caldwell, L. B. (1997). *Bringing Reggio Emilia home.* New York: Teachers College Press.

Danko-McGhee, K., & Slutsky, R. (2003). Preparing teachers to use art in the classroom: Inspirations from Reggio Emilia. *Art Education, 56*(4), 12–18.

Day, C. B. (2001). Loris Malaguzzi, founder: The Reggio Emilia approach, believing in the power of the child. *Scholastic Early Childhood Today, 15*(8), 46.

Edwards, C. P. (2003). "Fine designs" from Italy: Montessori education and the Reggio Emilia approach. *Montessori Life, 15*(1), 34–39.

Edwards, C. P., Gandini, L., & Forman, G. (Eds.). (1996). *The hundred languages of children: The Reggio Emilia approach to early childhood education.* Norwood, NJ: Ablex.

Gandini, L. (1997). The Reggio Emilia story: History and organization. In J. Hendrick (Ed.), *First steps toward teaching the Reggio way* (pp. 2–13). Upper Saddle River, NJ: Merrill/ Prentice Hall.

Gandini, L. (2002). The story and foundations of the Reggio Emilia approach. In V. Fu, A. Stremmel, & L. Hill (Eds.), *Teaching and learning: Collaborative exploration of the Reggio Emilia approach* (pp. 13–21). Upper Saddle River, NJ: Merrill/ Prentice Hall.

Gilman, S. (2007). Including the child with special needs: Learning from Reggio Emilia. *Theory into Practice 46*(1), 23–31.

Goffin, S. G. (2000). The role of curriculum models in early childhood education. Washington, DC: Office of Educational Research and Improvement. (ERIC Document Reproduction Service no. ED 443597). Retrieved from www.eric.ed.gov/ERICDocs/data/ericdocs2sql/content_storage_01/0000019b/80/16/57/e9.pdf.

Grieshaber, S., & Hatch, A. (2003). Pedagogical documentation as an effect of globalization. *Journal of Curriculum Theorizing, 19*(1), 89–102.

Hewett, V. M. (2001). Examining the Reggio Emilia approach to early childhood education. *Early Childhood Education Journal, 29*(2), 95–100.

Hughes, E. (2007). Linking past to present to create an image of the child. *Theory Into Practice, 46*(1), 48–56.

Krechevsky, M., & Stork, J. (2000). Challenging educational assumptions: Lessons from an Italian-American collaboration. *Cambridge Journal of Education, 30*(1), 57–75.

Linn, M. I. (2001). An American educator reflects on the meaning of the Reggio experience. *Phi Delta Kappan, 83,* 332–335.

Massey, A., & Burnard, S. (2006). "Here's one I made earlier!" A qualitative report on creativity in a residential primary school for children with social, emotional and behavioral difficulties. *Emotional and Behavioural Difficulties, 11*(2), 121–133.

McClow, C. S., & Gillespie, C. W. (1998). Parental reactions to the introduction of the Reggio Emilia approach in Head Start classrooms. *Early Childhood Education Journal, 26*(2), 131–136.

New, R. S. (2003). Reggio Emilia: New ways to think about schooling. *Educational Leadership, 60*(7), 34–38.

Reggio Children (Producer). (1980). *To make a portrait of a lion* [Film]. Reggio Emilia, Italy: Author.

Reggio Children (Producer). (1994). *A message from Loris Malaguzzi* [Film]. Reggio Emilia, Italy: Author.

Rinaldi, C. (2001). Documentation and assessment: What is the relationship? In Project Zero & Reggio Children (Eds.), *Making learning visible: Children as individual and group learners* (pp. 78–93). Reggio Emilia, Italy: Reggio Children.

Seefeldt, C. (1995). Art—serious work. *Young Children, 50*(3), 39–45.

Strozzi, P. (2001). Daily life at school: Seeing the extraordinary in the ordinary. In Project Zero & Reggio Children (Eds.), *Making learning visible: Children as individual and group learners* (pp. 58–77). Reggio Emilia, Italy: Reggio Children.

Tarr, P. (2003). Reflections on the image of the child: Reproducer or creator of culture. *Art Education, 56*(4), 6–11.

Turner, T., & Krechevsky, M. (2003). Who are the teachers? Who are the learners? *Educational Leadership, 60*(7), 40–44.

U.S. Department of Health and Human Services. (2005). Head Start program performance standards *(45-CFR 1304)*. Washington, DC: Author. Retrieved from www.acf.hhs.gov/programs/hsb/performance/index.htm.

Warash, B., Curtis, R., Hursh, D., & Tucci, V. (2008). Skinner meets Piaget on the Reggio playground: Practical synthesis of applied behaviour analysis and developmentally appropriate practice orientations. *Journal of Research in Childhood Education 22*, 441–454.

Zhang, J., Fallon, M., & Kim, E. (2009). The Reggio Emilia curricular approach for enhancing play development of young children. *Curriculum and Teaching Dialogue, 12*(1,2), 85–89.

Chapter 10

American Montessori Society. (n.d.). Essential elements of public Montessori schools. Retrieved from www.amshq.org/schools_public.htm.

Cossentino, J. (2006). Big work: Goodness, vocation, and engagement in the Montessori method. *Curriculum Inquiry, 36*(1), 63–92.

Edwards, C. P. (2002). Three approaches from Europe: Waldorf, Montessori, and Reggio Emilia. *Early Childhood Research and Practice, 4*(1). Retrieved from http://ecrp.uiuc.edu/v4n1/edwards.html.

Elkind, D. (2003). Montessori and constructivism. *Montessori Life, 15*(1), 26–29.

Gartner, A., Lipsky, D. K., & Dohrmann, K. R. (2003). *Outcomes for students in a Montessori program: A longitudinal study of the experience in the Milwaukee public schools.* Rochester, NY: Association Montessori Internationale.

Gettman, D. (1987). *Basic Montessori: Learning activities for under-fives.* New York: St. Martin's Press.

Goffin, S. (1994). *Curriculum models and early childhood education.* Upper Saddle River, NJ: Merrill/Prentice Hall.

Henry-Montessori, M. (n.d.). Portrait of Mario Montessori. Association Montessori Internationale. Retrieved from www.montessori-ami.org.

Lascarides, V., & Hinitz, B. (2000). *History of early childhood education.* New York: Falmer Press.

Lillard, A., & Else-Quest, N. (2006). Evaluating Montessori education. *Science, 313*, 1893–1894.

Montessori, M. (1965). *Dr. Montessori's own handbook: A short guide to her ideas and materials.* New York: Schocken Books.

Montessori, M. (1966). *The secret of childhood.* New York: Ballantine Books.

Montessori, M. (1967). *The discovery of the child.* New York: Ballantine.

Montessori, M. (1999). The Montessori method: Scientific pedagogy as applied to child education in the Children's Houses. In M. Paciorek & J. Munro (Eds.), *Sources: Notable selections in early childhood education.* Guilford, CT: McGraw-Hill. (Original work published 1965)

Mooney, C. G. (2000). *Theories of childhood: An introduction to Dewey, Montessori, Erikson, Piaget and Vygotsky.* St. Paul, MN: Redleaf Press.

North American Montessori Teachers' Association. (2013). About NAMTA. Retrieved from http://www.montessori-namta.org/About-Montessori

Rambusch, N. (1992). Montessori's "method": Stewardship of the spirit. *ReVision, 15*(2), 79–81.

Rathunde, K. (2003). A comparison of Montessori and traditional middle schools: Motivation, quality of experience, and social context. *NAMTA Journal, 28*(3), 12–52.

Shute, N. (2002). Madam Montessori. *Smithsonian Magazine,* September, 70–74.

Sobe, N. W. (2004). Challenging the gaze: The subject of attention and a 1915 Montessori demonstration classroom. *Educational Theory, 54*(3), 281–297.

Soundy, C. (2003). Portraits of exemplary Montessori practice for all literacy teachers. *Early Childhood Education Journal, 31*(2), 127–131.

Swan, D. (1987). Foreword. In D. Gettman, *Basic Montessori: Learning activities for under-fives* (pp. ix–xii). New York: St. Martin's Press.

Williams, N., & Keith, R. (2000). Democracy and Montessori education. *Peace Review, 12*(3), 217–222.

Chapter 11

Almon, J. (1992). Educating for creative thinking: The Waldorf approach. *ReVision, 15*(2), 71–79.

Astley, K., & Jackson, P. (2000). Doubts on spirituality: Interpreting Waldorf ritual. *International Journal of Children's Spirituality, 5*(2), 221–227.

Association of Waldorf Schools of North America. (n.d.). About AWSNA. Retrieved from www.awsna.org.

Association of Waldorf Schools of North America. (Producer). (1996). *Waldorf education: A vision of wholeness* [Film]. Available from Association of Waldorf Schools of North America, 3911 Bannister Road, Fair Oaks, CA 95628, 916-961-0927.

Bureau of Labor Statistics. (2008). College enrollment and work activity of 2007 high school graduates. Retrieved from www.bls.gov/news.release/hsgec.nr0.htm.

Byers, P., Dillard, C., Easton, F., Henry, M., McDermott, R., Oberman, I., & Uhrmacher, B. (1996). *Waldorf education in an inner city public school: The Urban Waldorf School of Milwaukee.* Spring Valley, NY: Parker Courtney Press.

Cicala Filmworks, Inc. (Producer). (n.d.). *Taking a risk in education: Waldorf-inspired public schools* [Film]. Available from Cicala Filmworks, Inc., 115W. 29th Street, Suite 1101, New York, NY 10001.

Clouder, C. (2003). The push for early academic instruction: A view from Europe. *Encounter, 17*(1), 10–16.

Dancy, R. B. (2004). The wisdom of Waldorf. *Mothering, 123,* 62–73.

Easton, F. (1997). Educating the whole child, "head, heart, and hands": Learning from the Waldorf experience. *Theory Into Practice, 36*(2), 87–95.

Edwards, C. P. (2002). Three approaches from Europe: Waldorf, Montessori, and Reggio Emilia. *Early Childhood Research and Practice, 4*(1). Retrieved from http://ecrp.uiuc.edu/v4n1/edwards.html.

Enten, A. (2005). Life after Waldorf High School. *Renewal Magazine.* Retrieved from www.awsna.org/renlifeafter.html.

European Council for Steiner Waldorf Education. (2007). Waldorf schools against discrimination: Stuttgart declaration. Retrieved from http://www.ecswe.org/downloads/statements/ecswe_discriminationstatement.pdf.

Fenner, P. J., & Rivers, K. (1995). *Waldorf education: A family guide.* Amesbury, MA: Michaelmas Press.

Hegde, A., & Cassidy, D. (2004). Teacher and parent perspectives on looping. *Early Childhood Education Journal, 32*(2), 133–138.

Iannone, R., & Obenauf, P. (1999). Toward spirituality in curriculum and teaching. *Education, 119*(4), 737–743.

Miller, R. (2006). Reflecting on spirituality in education. *Encounter, 19*(2), 6–9.

Mitchell, D., & Gerwin, D. (2007). Survey of Waldorf graduates, Phase II. Research Institute for Waldorf Education. Retrieved from www.waldorfresearchinstitute.org/pdf/WEPhaseII0307.pdf.

Mitchell, R. (2007). Seeking the archetype of the teacher. *Encounter, 20*(2), 27–35.

Mollet, D. (1991). How the Waldorf approach changed a difficult class. *Educational Leadership, 49,* 55–56.

Nicholson, D. (2000). Layers of experience: Forms of representation in a Waldorf school classroom. *Journal of Curriculum Studies, 32*(4), 575–587.

Oberman, I. (1997). *Waldorf history: Case study of institutional memory.* Paper presented at the annual meeting of the American Education Research Association, Chicago, IL. (ERIC Document Reproduction Service No. ED409108).

Oberman, I. (2008). Waldorf education and its spread into the public sector. *Encounter, 21*(2), 11–14.

Oberski, I., Pugh, A., MacLean, A., & Cope, P. (2007). Validating a Steiner-Waldorf teacher education programme. *Teaching in Higher Education, 12*(1), 135–139.

Ogletree, E. (1975). Geometric form drawing: A perceptual-motor approach to preventive remediation (the Steiner approach). *Journal of Special Education, 3,* 237–243.

Oppenheimer, T. (1999). Schooling the imagination. *Atlantic Monthly, 282*(3), 71–83.

Ruenzel, D. (2001). The spirit of Waldorf education. *Education Week, 20*(41), 38–46.

Schmitt-Stegmann, A. (1997). *Child development and curriculum in Waldorf education* (ERIC document no. ED 415 990).

Steiner, R. (1997). *Education as a force for social change.* Hudson, NY: Anthroposophic Press.

Steiner, R. (2005). *Encyclopedia britannica.* Retrieved from Encyclopedia Britannica Premium Service www.britannica.com/eb/article-9069553.

Waldorf Kindergarten Association. (1993). *An overview of the Waldorf kindergarten.* Silver Spring, MD: Author.

Waldorf Kindergarten Association. (1994). *Understanding young children: Excerpts from lecture by Rudolf Steiner.* Silver Spring, MD: Author.

Ward, W. (2005). Is Waldorf education Christian? *Renewal Magazine.* Retrieved from www.awsna.org/renchristian.html.

Chapter 12

Bredekamp, S., & Copple, C. (Eds.). (2009). *Developmentally appropriate practice in early childhood programs* (3rd. ed.). Washington, DC: National Association for the Education of Young Children.

Downer, J. T., Lopez, M. L., Grimm, K. J., Hamagami, A., Pianta, R. C., & Howes, C. (2012). Observations of teacher-child interactions in classrooms serving Latinos and dual-language learners: Applicability of the Classroom Assessment Scoring System in diverse settings. *Early Childhood Research Quarterly, 27,* 21–32.

Index